Professional
Visual Basic 6
Distributed Objects

Rockford Lhotka

Wrox Press Ltd. ®

Professional Visual Basic 6
Business Objects

wrox

Published by Wrox Press Ltd. Arden House, 1102 Warwick Road,
Acocks Green, Birmingham, B27 6BH
Printed in Canada
ISBN 1-861002-07-6

Trademark Acknowledgements

Wrox has endeavored to provide trademark information about all the companies and products mentioned in this book by the appropriate use of capitals. However, Wrox cannot guarantee the accuracy of this information.

Credits

Author
Rockford Lhotka

Managing Editor
Dominic Shakeshaft

Project Manager
Tony Berry

Editors
Jon Duckett
Karli Watson

Index
Catherine Alexander

Technical Reviewers
Richard Bonneau
Reed Call
Henri Cesbron
Michael Erickson
John Harris
Boyd Nolan
Dan Stern
Dorai Thodla
Donald Xie

Design/Layout
John McNulty

Cover
Andrew Guillaume
Concept by Third Wave

About the Author

Rockford Lhotka is the author of *Visual Basic 6 Business Objects*.

He has over 12 years experience in software development, starting out in Pascal, then moving to FORTRAN and Basic on VAX/VMS computers for a number of years until Windows NT and Visual Basic 1.0 first became available. Rockford has worked on many projects in various roles, including software development and design, network administration, help desk management and project management.

With the release of Visual Basic 4.0, Rockford began designing and developing n-tier client/server systems using component-based technology and has been doing so ever since. Rockford has been involved in the design and development of a number of successful, enterprise-level, applications based on the techniques discussed in this book.

In addition to designing and writing software, Rockford is an avid proponent of distributed object design and development using Visual Basic and COM. He regularly speaks on these topics, as well as evangelizing the concepts to friends, coworkers and clients.

Rockford currently works for BORN Information Services, an IT consulting company headquartered in Minneapolis, Minnesota. He the Microsoft National Technology Leader for BORN, and is responsible for coordinating the company's strategic direction regarding Microsoft technologies.

Dedication

To my wife, Teresa, and our sons, Timothy and Marcus.

Acknowledgments

Writing this book has been a lot of fun, and a lot of work. My family has been very supportive, and it is only with their love and patience that I was able to complete this work.

Thanks go to the BORN Microsoft Architecture Group for putting up with all my crazy ideas and helping to keep me honest. Thank you to Kevin Ford, who has always made himself available to bounce ideas off from, and always has ideas of his own in return. Thanks also to Robert Macdonald, the author of an article on OLE DB providers who was very helpful as I tried to figure out the details of Chapter 5.

My deepest thanks to the excellent team of reviewers and editors from Wrox Press. Their feedback and support have been outstanding and I appreciate them greatly!

Finally, thank YOU for purchasing this book. I sincerely hope that you find it as enjoyable and useful to read as it has been to write!

Windows programming, and more specifically Visual Basic programming has an incredibly bright future in the object-oriented, client/server and Internet environments. I am firmly convinced that, by using object-oriented design along with COM, MTS, MSMQ and other Win32 services, we'll see Visual Basic become the pre-eminent development tool for enterprise-level solutions.

Thanks, code well and have fun!

Table of Contents

Table of Contents

Table of Contents

Table of Contents

Table of Contents

Table of Contents

Introduction

Increasingly, Visual Basic developers are building client/server applications. Additionally, more and more applications are being developed based on object-oriented designs. When we combine object-oriented and client/server technologies we are able to implement *distributed objects*. This book is intended to provide a practical and pragmatic approach to developing applications based on distributed objects and written with Visual Basic in the Microsoft COM environment.

We'll start by discussing some basic concepts, providing at least one definition of the term **distributed objects**. Then we'll develop a simple application to illustrate an architecture based on distributed objects. To illustrate the concepts and technologies in the book, we'll develop an application that tracks projects and tasks for various clients. It will not be terribly complex, but it will serve as a good example for the topics that we'll cover. The application will be used throughout the book as we explore a number of very interesting and important concepts – developing solutions for each in turn.

This book is a sequel to *Visual Basic 6 Business Objects*. Throughout this book I'll be building on the concepts and techniques introduced in that book, though it's certainly not a requirement that you have read it. *Professional Visual Basic 6 Distributed Objects* covers all the key concepts that are required to build a distributed object application.

What's Covered in This Book

This is a book about distributed *objects*. It is also a book about developing business applications, so the objects we'll be discussing are business objects. Business objects provide a very good basis for developing applications, allowing our software to model the real-world entities and concepts within our business.

Of course it is also a book about *distributing* objects. To do this, we'll be employing client/server technologies. These technologies will allow our applications to be highly scalable, providing good performance to many users.

Introduction

Merging object-oriented design and development with client/server technologies brings us up against a whole new set of issues. In this book I will cover a number of the most common issues we encounter when creating applications where our business objects are distributed across a network, including:

- ❑ Component-based Scalable Logical Architecture
- ❑ Complex object state rollback (n-level state stacking)
- ❑ Implementing n-level has-a relationships
- ❑ Data binding with business objects
- ❑ Asynchronous messages via MSMQ
- ❑ Merging browser-based technologies with distributed objects
- ❑ Load balancing across MTS servers

Each of these is an issue or technology that can apply to many common types of application. In this book we'll examine each one and see how we can adapt or leverage the concepts and techniques from *Visual Basic 6 Business Objects* along with these new concepts and technologies to implement applications based on distributed objects.

The underlying concept we'll be using throughout this book is that of *distributed objects*. We'll really dig in and explore this concept and what it means in Chapter 1, but for now we can think of distributed objects as an architecture or design that combines the concepts of client/server and object-oriented technologies – allowing us to develop an object-based application where our objects are distributed across two or more machines on a network.

COM and DCOM

The primary technology we'll be using to implement distributed objects is Microsoft's Component Object Model – or COM. COM is a powerful base on which to build applications, since it provides a standard mechanism by which objects in various components or applications can communicate with each other.

Distributed COM is a ubiquitous extension to COM that allows objects to communicate across the network – allowing us to build distributed object applications by using the same syntax and programming model we'd use with COM on a single machine.

COM is both a standard and a Windows-based implementation of an infrastructure for inter-object communication. Other implementations of the COM standard also exist on non-Windows platforms such as some flavors of Unix, OpenVMS, etc.

COM provides the 'plumbing' that enables objects in different components to communicate. To make this work, COM also dictates how components must be constructed at a binary level – ensuring that the underlying plumbing can communicate effectively with these components.

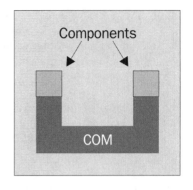

The diagram opposite illustrates how COM connects components together. The two components can interact with each other through COM as long as both components follow the standards defined by COM for components.

Note that COM is a *binary standard*. This means that COM components can be constructed in any language or tool – as long as they conform to the standard once they are compiled. When we write a program to interact with a COM component, we don't need to know or care what language was used to create it – all we need to know is that it supports COM.

Method calls to objects in COM components are *synchronous*. This means that the calling code is suspended until the code in the method is complete. Such a model is familiar to most programmers, since most calls to functions in any program are synchronous. The nice thing about COM is that it makes calls synchronous even if the object being called is running in another process or is part of another application.

Distributed COM has often been called 'COM with a longer wire'. Effectively, DCOM allows us to do exactly the same things that COM does – build objects in components that can communicate with each other – except that this communication can happen over the network.

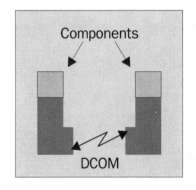

The diagram opposite is virtually identical to the previous one describing COM – except here the two components are running on different computers, connected by a network. For each component there is no difference between this scenario (communicating via DCOM) and a scenario where they communicate via COM itself.

Of course it isn't really this simple behind the scenes, since DCOM does quite a lot of work to create the illusion that there is no network between the two components. We won't go into the details of how DCOM actually pulls this off – it is enough to realize that there's no real difference between COM and DCOM in terms of the code used to create or interact with components. At least, this is true from a Visual Basic developer's perspective.

COM and DCOM together provide a powerful feature called **location transparency**. This means that if we can write code to interact with a COM object running within our application, we can then move that object into another component, another application or even another machine on the network *without changing the code that uses the object*. The location of the object – in our process, local or remote across the network – is immaterial to our code.

> *Obviously, location transparency doesn't eliminate design ramifications caused by objects running across the network. It does, however, eliminate coding and syntax differences – making the implementation of distributed systems much easier than many other environments.*

Another important characteristic of DCOM is that it is **connection based**. When an object on one computer gains a reference to an object on another computer via DCOM, a connection between those two objects is established. This connection is maintained as long as the object reference exists.

Typically this connection based approach is beneficial, as it increases performance if the objects communicate frequently. There is always some overhead involved in the creation of a connection, so keeping the connection alive avoids a recurrence of this overhead each time the objects communicate.

On the other hand, holding a connection open consumes resources on the computers involved. It is this cost that often drives an application design to be connectionless. This type of environment can be provided in a DCOM setting by only holding object references while they are being actively used – releasing the references when there is no immediate need for inter-object communication.

Component-based Scalable Logical Architecture

The concepts and techniques we'll be using throughout this book are based on an application architecture that blends many of the best features of object-oriented and client/server technologies. This architecture is the Component-based Scalable Logical Architecture, or CSLA.

> *For ease, I pronounce this 'cuz-la' – but you can make up any pronunciation that works for you.*

The CSLA is a form of distributed object architecture – something we explored in *Visual Basic 6 Business Objects* as we extended the Component-based Scalable Logical Architecture in the chapters covering DCOM and MTS. With this book we'll go further, looking at some of the more complex issues and technologies common in this type of architecture.

First though, it is important to take a moment to get a basic understanding of the CSLA itself. We'll cover it in quite a lot of detail in Chapter 2, but let's take a quick look now as well.

CSLA is a logical architecture. This means that it defines the parts, or tiers, of an application without specifying on which machines they'll physically be run. The logical tiers are:

- ❑ User interface
- ❑ UI-centric business logic
- ❑ Data-centric business logic
- ❑ Data services

Each tier has an important role to play in the function of an application.

The user interface provides the user with a display and accepts user input – allowing the user to interact with the application. No business logic resides in the user interface – just code to handle display and interaction.

The UI-centric business logic tier contains one half of the business logic for the application. In order to create a rich, robust user experience it is important to provide validation and other business logic in a physical location as close to the user interface as possible. By including a logical tier to contain this type of business logic, we gain the flexibility of physically placing it where it can do the most good.

The data-centric business logic tier contains the other half of the business logic. Often, business rules are enforced through interaction with a database or other data store. To get reasonable performance, these business rules must be run in close proximity to the data store. Additionally, most applications need to store and retrieve data from a database – the data-centric business logic manages this as well.

Almost all interaction with a data store revolves around basic create, read, update and delete functionality. In most cases, we also are provided with transactional support and other data services such as backup, journaling, etc. These are all part of the data services tier.

The CSLA is component-based. It relies on the Microsoft Component Object Model (COM) to provide a structure within which we can construct our objects. In this context, a **component** is a black box – a precompiled binary entity that exposes a defined set of interfaces.

Finally, the CSLA is scalable. Its scalability is primarily gained by enabling us to distribute an application's processing across all the available processors in a given physical environment. By logically dividing an application into four well-defined tiers, we gain a lot of flexibility in terms of choosing what code is best run on various machines in our network.

Additionally, the data-centric tier is designed specifically to take advantage of Microsoft Transaction Server, with objects that are stateless and have atomic methods. This type of design maximizes our use of an MTS application server, supporting large numbers of users with good performance.

While the CSLA (as developed in *Visual Basic 6 Business Objects*) is a good architecture for application development, I was unable to cover some of the more advanced – and yet common – issues that we face when developing a distributed object application. That is the focus of this book – to address those issues.

n-level Object State Rollback

One of the first things many people run into when implementing applications based on the CSLA is the complexity involved in implementing *n*-level rollback for our objects.

n-level rollback is the concept that the user can cancel changes they may have made to one of our objects, and our object will reset to its last saved state. With the CSLA we implement each object with 3 methods to support this functionality on a basic level: `BeginEdit` to be called when editing begins, `CancelEdit` so that the changes made since `BeginEdit` was called can be discarded, and `ApplyEdit` to commit the changes made to an object since the `BeginEdit` method was called.

Introduction

Things get more complex when we have objects with related child objects. For instance, we may have an `Invoice` object with `LineItem` child objects as shown in the following diagram.

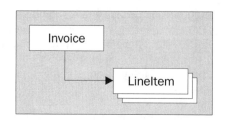

If we implement `BeginEdit`, `CancelEdit` and `ApplyEdit` on each of these objects, then we can individually start editing and then cancel the editing on each object. However, since the `LineItem` objects are subordinate to the `Invoice` object, we really don't want to allow editing of the `LineItem` objects if the `Invoice` object itself isn't editable.

This is where things get even more complex. Imagine the user making changes to a `LineItem` object's data, on an existing parent `Invoice` object. Once they have altered the `LineItem` objects, they go back to the parent `Invoice` object and decide to cancel the changes when editing the `Invoice`. In such a situation we really need to reset not only the `Invoice` object to its previous state, but we also need to restore all the changed child objects to their previous states as well. Otherwise a change to a child object's properties could inadvertently and permanently change the parent object. Take this one stage further and changing the `Amount` property on a `LineItem` object would probably affect the `Total` property on the `Invoice` – so calling `CancelEdit` on the `Invoice` object needs to reset the `LineItem` object's `Amount` property in order to correct the Invoice object's `Total` property.

In *Visual Basic 6 Business Objects* we implemented a new set of methods on each child object, `ChildBeginEdit`, `ChildCancelEdit` and `ChildApplyEdit` – thus providing a mechanism by which the parent object, `Invoice`, could control whether the subordinate child objects, `LineItem`, could be edited. This technique also allowed us to cascade the `CancelEdit` call from the parent object down to its child objects.

The problem with this approach is that it only easily supports one level of child objects. While we could implement methods such as `GrandChildBeginEdit` and `GreatGrandChildBeginEdit` for each deeper level, making it possible to extend this technique to grandchild and great-grandchild objects, things obviously get very difficult very fast.

In Chapter 3 we'll explore this issue in some detail. We'll look at the exact problems encountered when using the `ChildBeginEdit`, `ChildCancelEdit` and `ChildApplyEdit` technique and we'll develop a solution that easily provides Cancel and Apply functionality to child objects that are *n*-levels deep.

Implementing n-level has-a Relationships

The parent object, child object relationship we were just discussing has a more formal name. The parent object *has a* child object – a phrase implying a level of control or ownership of the child by the parent. Another term used in this setting is **containment** – because the parent object *contains* the child objects.

> *Many people coming from an object-oriented background are used to using terms such as parent and child in the context of inheritance. In this book we'll be using these terms to describe a containment relationship – where one object (the parent) contains, or owns, another object (the child).*

Going back to our `Invoice` and `LineItem` example, we can see how this makes sense. The `Invoice` object owns the `LineItem` objects – we can't have a `LineItem` object without an `Invoice`, for instance. Moreover, if we save the `Invoice` object to a database, we must also save its related `LineItem` objects – failure to do so is guaranteed to leave us with some pretty invalid data in the database.

In *Visual Basic 6 Business Objects* we altered our objects so that the parent object collected the state data of its child objects, then passed the collected state data across the network as a set of parameters to a `Save` method call. We then used the capabilities of Microsoft Transaction Server (MTS) to implement transactional support as we saved all these objects – ensuring that we'd either save all of them or none of them and thus preserving the integrity of our data.

As with implementing *n*-level rollbacks via `ChildCancelEdit`, this approach can be made to work with any level of child, grandchild and greatgrandchild objects. However, the implementation of the code gets more complex as we add each level of child objects to our object family. By the time our `Invoice` has a `LineItem` that has a `Payment` that has a `PaymentType` we'll find our code gets pretty messy.

In Chapter 4 we'll develop the concept of a **superstate**, which comprises the state of all the objects in an entire family. Where we've been serializing each individual object and then working with the resulting state data, the new superstate is the combined, serialized, data from *all* the related objects.

We'll explore different technologies that we can use to store and serialize the state data for our objects. As with serializing a single object in *Visual Basic 6 Business Objects*, we have a number of different options at our disposal for serializing an entire family of related objects.

With a superstate we have a practical, easy way to transport entire groups of objects across the network from one computer to another. It is this underlying concept that makes the entire distributed objects architecture a realistic option for our applications.

Data Binding With Business Objects

One of Visual Basic's primary strengths is its rapid application development (RAD) capabilities. Much of this power is tied into the concept of data binding – where we can bind UI components, such as a `TextBox`, to a field in a `Recordset` object. This capability has been with us for many years now, and it has allowed developers to create powerful data-oriented programs with minimal code.

> *Of course, data binding has historically required the use of the infamous data control. For all its RAD power, data binding has been largely avoided by most serious programmers. With the advent of Visual Basic 6.0 and its new data binding capabilities this is changing. Visual Basic 6.0 has a whole new, and much more powerful, approach to data binding. Most of the performance and flexibility issues that have plagued developers since Visual Basic 3.0 have been minimized or eliminated in Visual Basic 6.0.*

Introduction

With Visual Basic 6.0 we gained the ability to create objects that look and act like a `Recordset`. This powerful capability allows us to leverage all of Visual Basic's data binding and manipulation capabilities without limiting us to traditional data sources. For instance, we can create a data source object to read and write to a simple text file, a data stream off the Internet or virtually anything else.

This capability is most visible in the `DataSourceBehavior` property that has been added to class modules in Visual Basic 6.0.

At first glance it appears that we can simply change this property on our business objects and have them become data sources to which we can bind UI components. Unfortunately it is not anywhere near that easy to provide data binding capabilities to our business objects.

In Chapter 5 we'll explore Visual Basic's new capability to create data source objects. Then we'll develop a data source object that does allow us to leverage the capabilities of data binding against our UI-centric business objects from the CSLA.

Asynchronous Messages Via MSMQ

The CSLA is designed around COM – a technology that allows us to make synchronous calls to our objects. This means that the code that makes a method call to an object is stopped until that method completes. It also means that a connection exists between the calling code and the object being called – and that connection is there from before the method is called until after the method is complete.

While synchronous calls are perfectly useful in most situations, they aren't always the ideal. We may need to distribute our objects between two machines that aren't always connected to each other. Or worse still, perhaps the network connection between the machines goes down or is unreliable.

Using COM, if the network is down or unavailable we can't make method calls from one object to another across the network. To solve this we really need some way for an object to make a method call, but have that call stored up, or queued, until the network does become available and the call can be completed. Obviously, in this scenario we don't want our calling code to have to wait until the call is complete – since for all we know that could take hours or even days.

Microsoft Message Queue (MSMQ) is a technology available from Microsoft that provides asynchronous, store-and-forward messaging across a network. With MSMQ we can guarantee that our messages will be delivered to the destination machine, even if the network is down. In which case the messages are queued up for delivery when the network becomes available.

Asynchronous operations require us to think differently about the way we structure applications. It is possible to have an application work in a mixture of synchronous and asynchronous communication modes simultaneously.

In Chapter 6 we'll see how we can use MSMQ's asynchronous messaging capabilities to extend the CSLA. We'll discuss where asynchronous messaging makes the most sense and how we can easily use it to facilitate communication between our various business objects.

RDS: Object State Passing Via HTTP

Distributed COM (DCOM) is the most ubiquitous technology available for distributing our objects across a network. However, DCOM has some drawbacks in some circumstances that may make it less than ideal.

In particular, DCOM requires a persistent connection between the machines running our objects, thus potentially consuming resources we might use elsewhere. If we choose to continually drop and recreate our connections we swiftly find that DCOM connections are relatively expensive to create and so we have potential performance problems unless we do keep the connection open.

Additionally, DCOM requires us to set up and use the Windows NT security model. While this is frequently a good thing, it can often add extra complexity to our overall solution. This can become a serious roadblock if our client workstations are deployed outside a firewall or other security gateway, as many network administrators are reluctant to open their firewalls enough to allow DCOM traffic to come and go freely.

On the other hand, virtually every firewall allows HTTP traffic to pass without restriction.

HTTP is the Internet protocol that supports interaction between web browsers and web servers. However, it is not limited to that role – it is just used by those particular types of application. HTTP, in a more general sense, is a simple protocol that allows one application to send data to, or request it from, an application on another machine.

HTTP is designed to be lightweight and connectionless. This means that HTTP connections are relatively inexpensive to create, and the protocol doesn't maintain a connection once the requested communication is complete.

HTTP has become largely ubiquitous due to the Internet. Combining its wide availability with the fact that it is allowed through most firewalls and provides a scalable protocol for communication, it is a good choice for communication across the network.

It would certainly be nice if we could call methods on objects across the network using HTTP – thus avoiding the worries about firewalls, and potentially even dodging some of the complexities of the Windows NT security model.

Fortunately Microsoft has developed RDS – Remote Data Services – a technology that does allow a client workstation to create an object on the server and make method calls to it over HTTP. This technology was originally developed to allow Internet Explorer based applications to retrieve ADO `Recordset` objects from the server back to the client, but we can make use of it as well, using it to pass our object state between the client and server over HTTP.

Using RDS we can take advantage of distributed object design and the CSLA, as well as leveraging the power of Internet protocols and technologies – very useful for remote client workstations. We'll see how to do this in Chapter 7.

Load balancing across MTS servers

The final topic we'll cover in the book is one that addresses scalability and reliability for our applications. So far, the CSLA has relied on UI-centric business objects communicating with data-centric objects on a server. However, we've basically assumed a single server in every case.

A single server can do a lot, but if we're dealing with hundreds of concurrent connections we'll need to distribute the activity across multiple servers. By spreading the load we can support many more clients than we could with a single server. This is one of the key benefits of distributed object architecture – the ability to easily scale up by adding servers.

Another consideration is reliability. If we rely on a single server and that server becomes unavailable, then our application stops. However, if we have multiple servers we can reduce that impact since other servers can pick up the load of the server that is unavailable.

Of course, Microsoft has indicated that Windows 2000 will provide us with load balancing capabilities. If the need for scalability is not immediate, we may choose to wait for that solution.

For those who need this increased scalability and reliability now, we'll take a look at how we can implement our own basic load balancing capability for our servers. In Chapter 8 we'll develop a COM based load balancing mechanism for use with MTS 2.0 servers.

Who Is This Book For?

The book is intended for use by computer professionals who have:

❑ a solid knowledge of programming with Visual Basic 6
❑ an understanding of object-oriented programming concepts
❑ an understanding of Microsoft SQL Server and SQL queries
❑ familiarity with MTS, DCOM and MSMQ

What You'll Need To Use This Book

This book requires the following tools and technologies:

❑ Visual Basic 6.0 Enterprise Edition
❑ Microsoft SQL Server (preferably 7.0)
❑ A Windows NT 4.0 (or Windows 2000) Server to host DCOM servers
❑ A Win32 workstation to act as a client (Win9x or Windows NT)
❑ MTS 2.0
❑ MSMQ
❑ IIS 4.0 with ASP 2.0

Conventions Used

We use a number of different styles of text and layout in the book to help differentiate between different kinds of information. Here are some examples of the styles we use and an explanation of what they mean:

> **These boxes hold important, not-to-be forgotten, mission critical details that are directly relevant to the surrounding text.**

Background information, asides and references to information located elsewhere appear in text like this.

❑ **Important Words** are in a bold font
❑ Words that appear on the screen, such as menu options, are in a similar font to the one used on the screen – the File menu, for example
❑ All filenames are in this style: getRenderer.asp
❑ Functions and methods look like this: Render()

Code that's new, important or relevant to the current discussion will be presented like this:

```
' Create a Profile and Logon
' This will create the CDO session object
Set objOMSession = Server.CreateObject("MAPI.Session")
bstrProfileInfo = bstrExchServer + vbLF + bstrMailbox
objOMSession.Logon "", bstrPassword, False, True, 0, False, bstrProfileInfo
```

However, code that you've seen before, or which has little to do with the matter at hand, looks like this:

```
' Create a Profile and Logon
' This will create the CDO session object
Set objOMSession = Server.CreateObject("MAPI.Session")
bstrProfileInfo = bstrExchServer + vbLF + bstrMailbox
objOMSession.Logon "", bstrPassword, False, True, 0, False, bstrProfileInfo
```

Tell Us What You Think

We've tried to make this book as accurate and enjoyable as possible, but what really matters is what the book actually does for you. Please let us know your views, either by returning the reply card in the back of the book, or by contacting us via e-mail at feedback@wrox.com

Source Code

All the source code from the examples in this book is available for download from the Wrox Press web site:

```
http://www.wrox.com
```

Support

We've made every effort to make sure there are no errors in the text or the code. However, to err is human and as such we recognize the need to keep you, the reader, informed of any mistakes as they're spotted and corrected. The web site acts as a focus for providing the following information and support:

- ❑ Errata sheets
- ❑ Information about current and forthcoming titles
- ❑ Sample chapters
- ❑ Source code downloads
- ❑ An e-mail newsletter
- ❑ Articles and opinion on related topics

Errata sheets are available for all our books – please download them, or take part in the continuous improvement of our products and upload a 'fix' or a pointer to the solution.

1

Distributed Objects

Overview

This is a book about *distributed objects*, or more specifically it is a book where we'll discuss some concepts and technologies that allow us to develop applications based on distributed objects. This book is also a sequel to *Visual Basic 6 Business Objects* (ISBN 1-861001-07-X, from Wrox Press), which lays out a great many concepts that are important for distributed object design and development.

Before we launch into discussing *how* to implement applications based on distributed objects, it seems appropriate to spend some time discussing what distributed objects really are – at least as I will be using the term in this book. In this chapter we'll do the following:

- ❑ Define what I mean by distributed objects
- ❑ Review the key concepts from Visual Basic 6 Business Objects
- ❑ Design an example application for use through the rest of the book

In the first section of this chapter we'll cover distributed objects. Then we'll review the **Component-based Scalable Logical Architecture** (or **CSLA**) developed in Visual Basic Business Objects (VBBO). Following on from this review we'll look at designing a simple task tracking application based on the CSLA.

Distributed Objects

The phrase **distributed objects** is fairly self-descriptive. We are essentially talking about applications that are designed following object-oriented principles, but where the objects are distributed across a network in some manner. In essence our application will be a cross between client/server and object-oriented technologies.

The architecture used in this book is structured first around ensuring that we end up with a workable, high-performance client/server application. Object-oriented design principles are used as much as possible within this context, but there are certainly cases where strict OO design is compromised in order to build a better client/server application.

Client/Server

The term *client/server* has many meanings. In the context of distributed objects, we'll want to limit the meaning of client/server to narrow it down. Client/server typically covers a number of scenarios:

- ❑ A client workstation running lots of code with the data stored in a database on a server
- ❑ A client workstation running very little code, with the data and program logic in a database on a server
- ❑ A thin client (or terminal) with an application server running lots of code and the data in a database on another server
- ❑ A client workstation running some code, an application server running some code and the data in a database on another server

Of course, there are many other possible variations. There are, however, a couple of key underlying themes here:

- ❑ More than one computer is involved
- ❑ At least some meaningful processing occurs on two or more computers

When we describe client/server in these terms, it seems practical to generalize what's going on by describing it as **distributed processing**. After all, what we're doing is taking the processing required by our application and distributing across two or more networked computers.

At this point it may be helpful to quickly think through the types of processing that we'd expect an application to be doing. Most applications can, at least, do the following:

- ❑ Calculations or other business processing
- ❑ Enforcement of business rules or business-related data validation
- ❑ Data manipulation and enforcement of relational data rules
- ❑ Interact with external applications or services
- ❑ Interact with the user

Typically, when discussing client/server applications, we generalize these activities into three groups (or tiers): the user interface (presentation tier), business processing (business tier) and data processing (data services tier) .

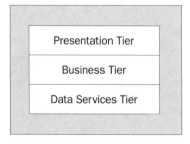

It is important to remember that these are *logical* tiers, and don't necessarily reflect any physical choices about computers, terminals or other hardware. We can develop a client/server application based on these three tiers and have the entire application run on one single computer. Alternately we may spread these tiers across a great number of different computers on a network. Either way, we've developed a logical 3-tier client/server application. Let's take a look at each of these in turn.

Presentation Tier

The presentation tier provides our application with a User Interface (UI). This is where our application is allowed to present information to the user and to accept input or responses from the user for use by our program.

The fact that the UI is considered a tier can be an interesting topic of discussion. Ideally, the UI itself doesn't perform any sort of business processing or business rule validation. Instead, the UI should rely on the business tier to handle those issues. This is important, especially today, because it is very common for an application to have multiple UI's, or for our customers to request that we discard one UI and replace it with another. For instance, we may develop an application with a traditional GUI, and then be required to replace it with a browser-based UI, perhaps using Active Server Pages (ASP).

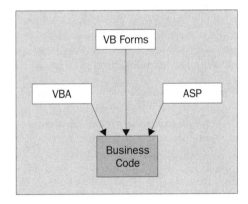

Where this gets interesting is when we consider all the possible types of UI we might encounter. For instance, consider these:

- ❏ VT100 terminals
- ❏ 3270 terminals
- ❏ Web browsers
- ❏ X-windows
- ❏ Windows form-based interfaces
- ❏ Microsoft Office
- ❏ Any COM-compliant application

Few people would consider VT100 or 3270 terminals to be a tier in an application. At the same time, there are those who would argue that a web browser using simple HTML *is* a tier.

The VT-series and 3270-style terminals are essentially dumb data displays, where a central server handles all the application's processing and the terminal merely displays data and retrieves the user's input. At best, these terminals understand the concept of an entry field and whether it is numeric or can accept any text.

The real trick here is to remember that we are discussing *logical* tiers of our application. Regardless of the hardware sitting in front of the user, the fact of the matter is that our application has code to create the display the user sees and to accept any input provided by the user through the UI.

Thus, even an application with a UI based on VT100 hardware has the logical concept of a presentation layer. After all, we'll have code that sends the appropriate text to the terminal for display, presumably formatting everything to be consistent and pleasing for the user. There'll also be code to accept the keystrokes entered by the user, rendering that input into some form that can be used by our business tier.

Regardless of the hardware being used, one of the most difficult and important factors when building a client/server application is to retain complete separation between the presentation logic and the business logic. It is incredibly tempting for developers to mix these two tiers, putting some field validation or other business processing into the presentation tier rather than the business tier.

For instance, were we to add code into our user interface to ensure a numeric entry was between 1 and 100, we would have written field validation into the UI. The problem with *only* having it in the UI is that we may end up using the same data in some other part of our UI. Hopefully, the developer building that part of the UI will remember to add the same validation code – otherwise we'll end up with a mess on our hands.

To avoid this, such validation logic should always reside in our business objects. In this way we'll know that it is available to any and all UI components that may use our objects.

This is not to say that the logic shouldn't also be in the UI. In a conventional client/server application where the business logic is all contained on a central server we are left with a choice – either provide the user with a batch oriented UI, so all the rules are processed when a screen is complete, or implement the rules on the client, so the user has a rich experience with responsive feedback to their data entry.

Business Tier

Every application has code to implement business rules, business-related processing or calculations, and other business-related activities. Collectively this code is considered to make up the business tier.

One of the primary tenants of logical client/server design is that the business logic should remain separate from both the presentation logic and the data services. This doesn't necessarily mean that the business logic is physically somewhere else; rather our concern is that it is separate in a *logical* sense.

There are many ways to logically separate our business logic. If we're following a modular or procedural programming model, we'll probably just ensure that our business logic is in procedures that contain no UI or data services code. If our programming model is more object-oriented then it is more common to encapsulate the business logic in a set of objects that don't contain presentation or data services code.

Having logically separated our business logic from both the presentation and data services tiers, we gain significant flexibility in terms of where we *physically* place the business logic. For instance, we may choose to place the business logic on each client workstation, or perhaps we'll opt to run the business logic on an application server, allowing all clients to access it as a centralized resource.

Data Services Tier

Most applications interact with data, and store that data in some form of database. There are some basic functions that are common to all data processing: creating data, reading data, updating data and deleting data. Additionally, we typically have more advanced services available, including searching, sorting, filtering and so forth.

Of course, the definition of a 'database' is changing. With the advent of ADO and OLE DB we are seeing a growth in the use of data stores that don't follow the conventional relational-data model. By keeping data services separated into a tier we dramatically enhance our ability to maintain our application as the nature of our data sources change over time.

Data services can include more than basic database functions. In many cases we might also include our application's code that interacts with the database itself. If we're working with a relational database for instance, our application will have code that either calls stored procedures or generates SQL statements that are sent to the database server. All of this code can be considered part of the data services tier.

Many applications make no distinction between business logic and the data services logic that interacts with the database. However, there are substantial benefits to be gained by keeping this code separate, including:

- We can more easily accommodate changes to the underlying database structures
- It is easier to switch to a new type of database
- It becomes practical to physically move the data-related code closer to the database
- Such data-related code is often transactional in nature, keeping it separate makes it easier to take advantage of facilitating software such as Microsoft Transaction Server

Designing for Scalability

One final characteristic of client/server design that is important to note is that of scalability. Client/server systems are harder to develop than more monolithic systems in many cases – so there must be a reason why we create them. The primary reason is that by distributing our application's processing across multiple computers we are able to leverage much more computing power than we could otherwise.

The issue of scalability and related design not only involves the logical concept of a 3-tier application, but also the physical deployment of those tiers across our computers.

The oldest and most time tested physical client/server design is to have intelligent clients using a centralized database server. As shown in the diagram, the presentation and business tiers reside on the client workstation, while the data services are hosted on the database server machine.

Client Workstation	Presentation Tier
	Business Tier
Database Server	Data Services Tier

In this model we are utilizing each individual client workstation's processing capabilities, and minimizing the work performed by any centralized resource. This is particularly useful if our environment is comprised of powerful computers on our user's desktops with limited server resources.

Alternately we may be in a physical 3-tier setting, with the processing largely centralized on an application server. In this scenario the presentation tier resides on the client workstation, with the business tier running on an application server and the data services hosted on a database server.

Client Workstation	Presentation Tier
Application Server	Business Tier
Database Server	Data Services Tier

The scalability benefit here is that we can support large numbers of low-end client workstations or terminals by installing high-end servers to run our business logic.

A third option, and possibly the most scalable, is to distribute the processing between client workstations and a centralized application server. In this case the presentation tier *and part of the business tier* run on the client workstation, with the remainder of the business tier running on a centralized application server and the data services remaining on a database server machine.

Client Workstation	Presentation Tier
Application Server	Business Tier
Database Server	Data Services Tier

In this way we can tap into the power of large numbers of client workstations, leveraging substantial processing power. At the same time, we can perform some processing in a centralized location, allowing us to leverage the power of high-end servers or very high-speed network connections between that server and our database server.

Object-Oriented Development

Object-oriented design is a design philosophy revolving around the use of objects to model our business concepts and entities. By implementing these objects in software we can then create an application that models our business processes. Object-oriented development provides us with a very powerful way to encapsulate our business logic and processing, and has the added benefit of making our application reusable and easier to maintain.

Overview of Objects

To understand business objects, we first need to understand the concept of an **object**:

> **An object is a code-based abstraction of a real world entity or relationship**

In the computer, an object consists of some data (state information) and behavior (a set of routines).Our programs use an **interface** to get access to an object's data and behavior. We can represent the object as something like the following diagram:

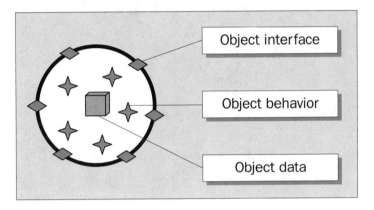

Objects and Classes

All objects are defined by a **class**:

> **A class is essentially a template from which the object is created, which means that we can create many objects based on a single class.**

Each such created object is referred to as an **instance** of the class.

The word 'class' is pretty descriptive, since we're basically classifying our objects. For instance, if we have a couple of objects, *Squirrel* and *Rabbit*, they could be instances of a *Mammal* class.

To use a more business-like example, we may have a *Customer* class. From this class we could create instances to represent each of our customers, such as *Fred Smith* and *Mary Jones*. Each actual customer would have its own object, but all the objects would be created from the same template, the Customer class.

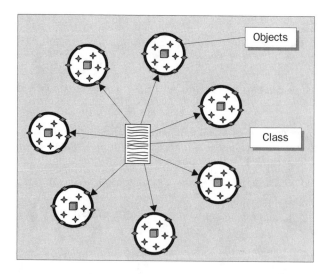

This concept is called **abstraction**, since the *Customer* is an abstract representation of both *Fred* and *Mary*.

In Visual Basic, we define classes using **class modules**. We can then create objects based on the class module, with each object being an instance of the class.

Class modules are like form or standard modules, in that they have a declaration section followed by a series of `Sub`, `Function` and `Property` subroutines.

> *The difference between standard modules and class modules is that is that class modules facilitate encapsulation of variables and methods, while standard modules merely provide a repository for code – with no encapsulation.*

Anatomy of an Object

An object is an instance of a class. The class is a template, providing the code which implement's the object's behaviors and defines the data contained by the object. Each object will have three primary attributes:

- ❑ Interface
- ❑ Implementation
- ❑ State

Let's discuss each of these attributes in turn.

Object Interface

It is through an object's interface that any client code from a program or another object interacts with our object. Code outside our object can only make calls to methods or properties that are part of our object's interface.

Visual Basic objects are essentially also COM objects. This means that our object's interface not only provides a way for other code within our application to interact with the object, but it may also be accessible by COM clients outside our application.

Any method (`Sub` or `Function`) or property (`Property Get/Let/Set`) that is declared in our class module using the `Public` keyword is part of our object's interface.

Additionally, methods and properties can accept parameters – values passed into the method by the calling code. Though it may not be entirely obvious, the parameters for each method are also considered to be part of the object's interface.

Once we've written client code to interact with our object's interface, we obviously can't easily make any changes to that interface. If we were to make a change, say removing a parameter or even worse removing a method, any code written to call that method would fail.

> Due to this, each object's interface can be viewed as a contract. Once we've begun writing code to interact with our object, that code should be able to rely on the object's interface remaining consistent – with no changes to any existing methods, properties or parameters.

To make things even more interesting, Visual Basic objects can have **multiple interfaces**. This is a result of Visual Basic's close relationship with COM, since multiple interfaces are an integral part of COM.

If we create an object from a class we built in Visual Basic, that object will have at least the one interface we defined in our class module. In this simple case, it appears as though our program has direct access to the object, although in reality we're getting at the object through an interface defined by the class:

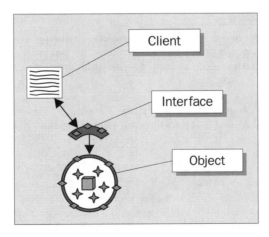

> With Visual Basic 6.0, a client program never has direct access to an object, only to one of the object's interfaces.

Sometimes, one interface isn't enough. Our object may represent more than one real world entity, and we need to be able to model this in Visual Basic. For instance, a *Customer* object is great, but a real customer is also a person. To model this in our application, we might need our Customer object to also act like a *Person* object from time to time.

To accomplish this, we can just add the Person interface to our object, which already implements the customer interface. Therefore, a client program can use our object through the original Customer interface with its set of properties and methods, while it may also use the object through the Person interface, with its own separate set of properties and methods. This way, the client can use the same object in whichever way is appropriate at any given time:

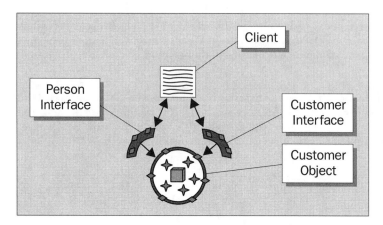

As we've discussed, when we create a class in Visual Basic, its `Public` members comprise the interface for our object. However, we can also use the `Implements` statement to add another interface to our object. The `Implements` keyword requires that we supply a class name with which it will work. We'll see how to use the `Implements` keyword as we get into code later in this chapter.

Object Behavior or Implementation

While an object's interface provides a mechanism by which client code can interact with the object, the interface does not actually perform any work. Within each class module we need to write code to implement any behaviors or perform any actions that should happen as a result of some code making a call to our interface.

This code is called the object's **implementation**. Typically we'll place the implementation code in the class module within the various `Public` procedures or properties that make up our interface. For instance:

```
Public Function Calculate() As Single
   Calculate = msngValue1 + msngValue2
End Function
```

Alternately, we may choose to put the implementation code in `Private` procedures that are called from our `Public` routines:

```
Private Function Calc() As Single
   Calc = msngValue1 + msngValue2
End Function

Public Function Calculate() As Single
   Calculate = Calc
End Function
```

This second approach is most useful if we have multiple interfaces for our object, since we can easily reuse the code.

This next code snippet uses the `Implements` keyword to add a second interface to our object. This new interface is called `Interface2`, and would be declared in a separate class module named `Interface2` with the following code:

```
Option Explicit

Public Function Calculate() As Single

End Function
```

Notice that there is no actual code in the `Interface2` module – it is just there to define the interface. We can them implement that interface in our object by using the `Implements` keyword.

```
Implements Interface2

Private Function Calc() As Single
   Calc = msngValue1 + msngValue2
End Function

Public Function Calculate() As Single
   Calculate = Calc
End Function

Private Function Interface2_Calculate() As Single
   Interface2_Calculate = Calc
End Function
```

Notice that the `Calculate` method from `Interface2` is included here as a `Private` method and the name is not just `Calculate`, but `Interface2_Calculate`. This is just due to the way Visual Basic handles implementation of multiple interfaces. Were this method `Public`, it would be part of our primary interface – which is not what we're after. Instead, it needs to be `Private` and have a special name, so that Visual Basic can find it when the calling code goes to use the `Interface2` interface.

Of course, most of the code that we write will tend to interact with data of some sort, which leads us to our next topic: object state.

Object State

Most objects contain some data that is manipulated by the object's implementation code to do useful work. This data is called the object's **state**. Another way to think about this is that the object's state is only the data that we'd need to store in a database so that we could recreate the object later.

In general terms, we might consider any module level variables declared within our class module to be part of the object's state. After all, any of those module level variables will contain values that are available to all the implementation code within the object, and are valid as long as the object remains in existence. However, this definition is really somewhat broad.

We can narrow the definition of object state to only include those values that – were we to remove them from the object, blank all values in the object and then restore the original values – would leave the object in exactly the same condition as when we started.

It is very practical that some objects may have module level variables with values that can be recreated from the object's state data. For instance, an object may have a `mlngCount` variable to keep track of the number of child objects owned by the object. Or perhaps we have a `mdblTotal` variable that is the sum of several other values contained within the object. These values could easily be module level variables that are *not* part of the object's state.

As an example, consider an object that adds together a couple numbers. Admittedly this is a contrived example, but it should illustrate the point:

```
Option Explicit

Private mlngA As Long
Private mlngB As Long
Private mlngTotal As Long

Public Property Let A(Value As Long)
  mlngA = Value
  mlngTotal = mlngA + mlngB
End Property

Public Property Get A() As Long
  A = mlngA
End Property

Public Property Let B(Value As Long)
  mlngB = Value
  mlngTotal = mlngA + mlngB
End Property

Public Property Get B() As Long
  B = mlngB
End Property

Public Property Get Total() As Long
  Total = mlngTotal
End Property
```

In this case our object's state includes the values for A and B. However, the value for Total can be regenerated at any time given A and B – thus it is not state even though it is stored in a module-level variable.

Business Objects

There are many different ways to categorize objects. As Visual Basic developers, we often work with ActiveX controls. These controls are most often based on a type of visual object, or GUI object. We also frequently interact with data objects such as `Recordset` objects, `Connection` objects and the like. These could be categorized as utility, or environmental, objects.

When designing a business application, we'll usually be building and working with **business objects**. Since this term means different things to different people, we need to make sure that we're all talking about the same thing before proceeding any further.

Just looking at the words, you might decide that these are *objects* that reflect or represent your *business*. And you'd pretty much be right – at a high level it really is that simple. The programs we write can be viewed as models of the real world. We create programs to simulate parts of the world around us – to record what's happening or to make predictions about what might happen.

The world around us is made up of both physical objects and abstract concepts. To effectively model or simulate the real world and human processes in our code, it would be good if our software could be made up of representations of these real-world objects. As we have seen in the previous section, object-oriented programs attempt to do just that.

Business objects are designed to represent real 'objects' and concepts in our business. Here are some examples of these real 'objects':

- ❏ An employee
- ❏ A purchased part
- ❏ A manufactured part
- ❏ A work order
- ❏ A customer

All of these are objects in the physical world, and the whole idea behind using software business objects is to create representations of these same objects inside our applications. Then our application can make these objects interact with each other just as they would in the physical world. For instance, an *employee* might create a *work order* to build a *manufactured part* from one or more *purchased parts* that are then sold to the *customer*.

Following this logic, we can create a *work order* business object that contains all the code it needs to manage itself – so we never need to replicate code to create work orders, we just use the object.

Similarly, a *customer* object contains and manages its own data. A well-designed customer object can contain all the data and routines needed to represent a customer throughout an entire business and this can be used across all the applications for that business. We may use our customer object when taking an order. We might later use it when sending out a bulk mailing, or to analyze sales patterns – without affecting any of the code that uses the object to take an order. Of course, over time, the customer object may evolve: it may gain new properties or new methods to support more functionality; the point is that the previous properties and methods can and should remain the same, so that existing applications that use the object need not be changed.

Distributed Objects: Combining C/S and OO

Now that we've had a quick review of the characteristics of client/server and object-oriented design, let's see how we can merge the two concepts into the concept of distributed objects.

The client/server model provides us with a way to distribute our application across multiple machines on a network, leveraging the processing power of many computers to increase the scalability of our application. The particular model we'll be exploring in this book is a 3-tier or *n*-tier model, including client workstations, application servers and database servers. This model will allow us to distribute the application across all three types of computer, taking advantage of the capabilities of each.

The object-oriented model gives us a powerful tool for analyzing our business concepts (such as a travel itinerary or other intangible idea), entities (such as a customer, product, etc.) and their relationships. Using OO techniques, we can translate our real-world 'objects' into a set of class modules that allow us to create software objects to simulate, or model, our real-world 'objects'. This approach helps us develop applications that are easily maintained and modified over time.

It can be a challenge to leverage the advantages of both client/server and object-oriented models. A 3-tier client/server model puts some of the processing on a centralized application server, yet there are design constraints on that middle-tier which are antithetical to traditional object-oriented design principles. In particular, middle-tier 'objects' virtually never maintain state. Instead they are designed more as a repository of related functions – less like an object and more like a function library, unlike traditional OO designed objects. Also, while object-oriented development is inherently 'client/server' in nature, OO designs rarely take into account the high cost of sending messages over a network from one object to another.

The distributed object model attempts to merge these two models, taking the best of both the client/server and OO worlds and putting them together to achieve an architecture we can use to build applications which are highly scalable, maintainable and easily modified over time.

Component-based Scalable Logical Architecture

In *Visual Basic 6 Business Objects* I introduced a **logical architecture** we can use when developing applications based on business objects: the Component-based Scalable Logical Architecture (CSLA), which we shall look at in a moment.

The CSLA not only provides us with a solid architecture for building applications based on business objects, but it also provides a solid foundation for building applications based on *distributed objects*. We saw this in *Visual Basic 6 Business Objects* as we modified our sample application to be distributed across a network using DCOM, MTS and web technologies.

> *The CSLA is far from the only architecture that utilizes the concept of distributed objects. We might also employ an architecture where each class exists on every machine that we want to perform processing on, and the object's state is moved from machine to machine as needed. Other variations exist as well. However, the CSLA is a very powerful model – essentially distributing processing between two logical halves of the same business object: UI-centric and data-centric.*

Throughout this book, I'll continue to use the CSLA as the foundation for our application development. We'll see how to leverage the architecture and how to modify it to make developing complex distributed applications easier and faster.

Before we get into the new material however, let's quickly review the CSLA.

Overview of the CSLA

The primary goals for the CSLA are to:

❑ Allow for flexible physical implementations with the same logical model
❑ Enable reuse of code through the use of a component-oriented design model
❑ Provide a scalable architecture, supporting applications on one machine or hundreds on a network

The following sections will cover the CSLA, showing how it meets these goals.

First we'll discuss the architecture from a logical perspective – independently of how it might be physically deployed across machines on a network. An understanding of the logical concepts behind the architecture is critical to its effective use.

Once we have a good grasp of the logical concepts, we'll explore various physical architectures where the CSLA can be deployed. There are many different ways to apply a logical model to a physical architecture – we'll explore the most common and useful ones in this chapter.

Finally, we'll go through the specifics of object implementation following the CSLA. This will include some in-depth exploration of the standard methods and properties for all business objects – providing a framework on which we can build any business objects within the architecture.

Logical Architecture

It is very important to remember that the CSLA is a *logical* architecture. The CSLA itself doesn't dictate how many machines will be running portions of the application, nor does it dictate exactly how much processing will be performed on any given machine.

At the same time, as a logical model the CSLA does provide a general guide we can use when determining the optimal physical architecture we might use. We'll get into more detail on various physical architectures later in this chapter.

Earlier in this chapter we discussed a logical client/server architecture, where an application is logically divided into three tiers.

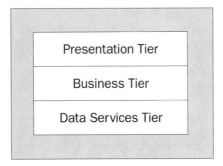

While this is a powerful model, it isn't as flexible as we might like. In particular, with this model we're stuck physically placing the business tier either on a client workstation or on a server machine.

This can be less than optimal in many cases, primarily because not all business logic is the same. Some business logic is very data-intensive, requiring fast and efficient access to the database. Other business logic doesn't require frequent data access, but is often used by a robust user interface for entry field validation or other user interaction.

If we want a robust, rich user experience we'll need field level validation, screen level validation and perhaps some real-time calculations or other business logic. We can consider this type of business logic to be UI-centric, since it is mostly used by the user interface. With traditional client/server models we are given the choice of placing this logic physically on the client workstation, or placing it on a centralized server and then replicating the code in the UI, to provide the high quality UI.

Neither choice is terribly attractive. Placing all the business logic on a client workstation can make the application's data access slow – reducing performance. Placing the business logic on a server, and replicating the logic in the UI itself creates a maintenance nightmare. We end up writing the business logic both in the UI and on the server, providing many openings for inconsistency and effectively increasing our development effort overall.

What the CSLA does, from a logical perspective, is build on the client/server model, incorporating the concept of UI-centric and data-centric business logic. By splitting the broad concept of a 'business tier' into two tiers, we provide much more flexibility in our application's design.

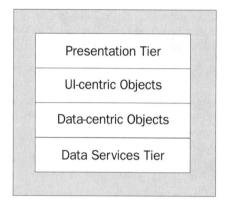

As we'll see later in the chapter, we can physically place the UI-centric and data-centric business logic on various computers to optimize performance and to achieve the richest possible user experience through the UI.

Component-based

The term **component** tends to be overloaded in the IT industry, meaning different things to different groups. We don't need to engage in the debate over the meaning of the term here, but it is important that I define the term as we'll use it through the remainder of the book.

A component is a binary (pre-compiled) group of reusable code. Components always expose an interface in a standard fashion so client programs can access the code they contain. The code within a component may or may not be created using object-oriented technologies and concepts, though most components can be viewed as a collection of pre-compiled objects.

> *For the purposes of this book, we'll be using components created to follow Microsoft's Component Object Model (COM). COM-based components meet the definition we set out for components. Not coincidentally, they are also trivial to create using Visual Basic.*

The CSLA is based on this binary component concept. We assume that an application designed to follow the CSLA will be composed of various components that work together to provide the desired functionality. Since it is component-based, our application can interact with components we author or components provided by other sources.

In a sense, we're assuming that each of the four logical tiers of our application is composed of one or more components. This means that we'll treat the UI, the UI-centric and data-centric business logic and the data processing as a set of components that interact with each other.

This is a powerful model. For instance, by considering the UI as a collection of components, we can easily replace those components with another complete set – thus replacing the UI – often with little impact to the other three tiers of our application.

Or perhaps we'll need to swap out the database. By treating the data processing as a set of components, we can relatively easily replace the database, with minimal changes to any other tier in the application.

Scalable

This architecture is inherently scalable – primarily due to its flexibility.

Scalability comes not only from a logical model, but also by virtue of how we apply the logical model to a physical architecture. Since the CSLA is quite flexible, we have many options when applying the various logical tiers of our application to a physical environment – thus providing us with the power to create highly scalable designs.

For instance, if our client workstations are very powerful and our network bandwidth high, we may choose to put quite a lot of processing on those workstations – thus taking full advantage of all that distributed processing power.

The reason that high bandwidth is important in this case is that the client would most likely be retrieving large amounts of data to process. Much of that data may not be required, but we wouldn't find that out until the processing on the client was completed. This scenario is not unlike what we might find with applications built using Microsoft Access or similar tools.

In a more typical scenario, our client workstations may be powerful, but our network bandwidth somewhat limited. The CSLA allows us to place the UI and some processing on the clients to take advantage of that distributed computing power, but also place the data-related logic and processing on centralized servers to minimize the network traffic.

In this case we can minimize what is sent across the network by applying some business logic on the server to isolate meaningful data. Once the server has reduced the data to only what is essential, we can send it across the network to the client – minimizing the network load.

Alternatively, we may have very limited client workstations – or we may want to minimize the components deployed to the clients. In such a case we can place only the UI on the client, with all the processing and business logic on centralized servers. With this scenario we give up a robust user interface, but we retain high performance and scalability.

It is worth noting that this last scenario may require more network bandwidth than an intelligent client environment. With an intelligent client we only need to send the required data back and forth. However, with a 'thin client' approach we need to not only send data, but also all the information required to render the interface for the user. This can amount to a lot of data sent across the network.

Physical Model

Since scalability and performance are closely tied not only to the logical CSLA, but also to physical deployment, let's go through some common physical architectures and see how the CSLA fits into them.

Of the possible physical architectures, three of them are perhaps most important:

- ❑ *n*-tier
- ❑ Single computer
- ❑ Browser-based (intelligent client)

In Visual Basic 6 Business Objects *we discussed these architectures along with various other possible architectures. I only revisit these here because they are scenarios that we'll be covering in some detail later in the book. The n-tier architecture will be our baseline as we explore distributed objects in Chapters 3-5. We'll see how to use MSMQ in a detached single tier in Chapter 6, and we'll see how to use RDS for object state passing in Chapter 7.*

The *n*-tier physical architecture is the most common one we'll encounter when creating any enterprise-wide application. Such applications demand very high scalability and reliability and are typically designed such that they are distributed across client workstations, application servers and database servers. In many cases the servers are fault tolerant, multi-processor machines with substantial amounts of memory and other resources available.

The single computer scenario is important because it not only represents a standalone workstation running our application, but also provides us with the basis for a disconnected workstation such as a sales force automation application.

Examples of such disconnected devices include laptop computers and handheld Windows CE devices. Of course, even in a disconnected scenario the device will be periodically connected to the central servers to exchange data – updating both the server and the device as appropriate.

Some industry analysts predict that disconnected computers will become more and more prevalent as the hardware for handheld PCs, automobile PCs and other devices become more common. These devices are typically connected by very low bandwidth connections, or by being periodically connected to the server to exchange data.

Either way, applications written for such a scenario must operate under the assumption that network connections may or may not be available and that any network communications must be performed as quickly, efficiently and as fault tolerant as possible.

Browser-based architectures have become quite prevalent over the past few years with the rise of the World Wide Web. There are two general categories of browser-based application:

- ❑ Where the browser is a colorful terminal displaying HTML
- ❑ Where the browser is a container for an application running on the client workstation.

The science and techniques involved in building terminal-based applications (even colorful ones) is far from new. People have been developing such applications for over two decades. However, the technology and techniques involved in building browser-based applications that use the browser to contain a full-blown client application are quite new, and quite powerful.

By leveraging the browser as a deployment vehicle, we are able to easily deploy program components to the client workstation. Once we've done that, we can utilize the client workstation's processing capabilities much like we would in an *n*-tier architecture.

It is my personal belief that this is the type of Internet application we'll see more and more often. Not to say that this is a trivial thing to consider, but I find it hard to believe that users are going to willingly return to batch-oriented user interfaces for the long term, and yet few IT managers want to deal with the deployment issues of a client/server application. By creating an intelligent client that is browser-based, we can provide the user with a robust interface and still dodge most of the deployment issues dreaded by IT managers. The demand for more robust user interaction will drive the industry to develop solutions to today's technical limitations.

Let's examine these three physical architectures in detail.

n-tier

Most large, enterprise systems physically distribute their processing across a number of machines. Most often this includes the client workstation, one or more application servers and one or more database servers. This configuration provides optimal flexibility and scalability, although it is at the cost of increased complexity.

Client Workstation	Presentation Tier
	UI-centric Objects
Application Server	Data-centric Objects
Database Server	Data Services Tier

This diagram illustrates how we can map the logical tiers from the CSLA into such a physical environment.

We continue to keep the UI itself, along with the UI-centric objects, on the client workstation. This allows us to provide the richest possible interface to the user, and also lets us take advantage of the processing power of the client workstation.

The data-centric objects are placed on a centralized application server. These objects are characterized by their interaction with the database, and in many cases the application server will have a high-bandwidth connection to the database servers to increase overall performance. Additionally, such an application server can frequently employ resource-conserving features such as database connection pooling, object pooling and so forth.

In many cases our application will need to interact with multiple data sources as well. For instance, we may have most of our data in an Oracle database, but we may also need to interact with other databases such as a DB2 or SQL Server database. The data-centric objects running on an application server can almost entirely shield the UI-centric objects and the UI itself from all the complexity of working with these disparate data sources.

Single Computer

The simplest case is where we have an application that needs to run on a single workstation, unattached to any network resources. This might be a standalone point of sale system, or a sales force automation system where the database is replicated to each individual client. Either way, our application needs to run entirely on a single machine.

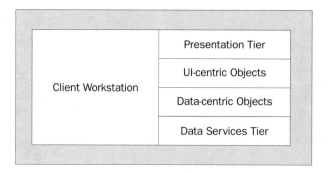

This is basically the model that we examined in Chapter 8 of *Visual Basic 6 Business Objects*, as it can be as easily applied to the 2-tier, intelligent client variety of client/server.

Client Workstation	Presentation Tier
	UI-centric Objects
	Data-centric Objects
Database Server	Data Services Tier

Regardless, all the user interface and business logic for the application resides on the client workstation. Other than basic data services, all the processing for the application occurs on the client, typically with SQL statements and result sets being the only data moving back and forth over the network.

> *In most cases, we won't physically implement separate data-centric objects for a single tier or 2-tier scenario. It is much less complex (and higher performance) if we simply implement the data-centric behaviors as a set of private methods within each UI-centric business object. This is the approach followed in* Visual Basic 6 Business Objects, *and is something to keep solidly in mind when designing this type of system.*

> *It is important to remember, however, that most systems 'grow up' and become larger than originally anticipated. Be sure to take this into account before designing the system to follow this type of physical architecture.*

This has the advantage of fully exploiting the processing power of each client workstation – thus providing a high degree of scalability. Unfortunately we have the logistic drawback of needing to install the bulk of the application on each individual client machine.

In its simplest form, as shown in these diagrams, we also have no distributed objects. Thus one could ask why I'm even discussing this model in a distributed object book. The reason is that we can use distributed object technologies even if the machines we're having do our distributed processing aren't connected full-time by a network.

Most large corporate systems that are running on standalone client workstations still do periodic data exchanges between the client and some centralized server. Sometimes data from the central server is sent to the client to update information there, other times data or transactions entered on the client are sent to the central server for storage or further processing.

While this can often be handled by database replication or similar technologies, we can also leverage the concept of distributed objects in many cases. This can be particularly powerful if we don't merely want to move data between machines, but we also want to perform some processing when the data arrives. With distributed objects we can contain the code to handle this processing in a set of objects that communicate between the client and server machines.

In Chapter 6 we'll take a look at Microsoft Message Queue (MSMQ). This product can allow us to post messages to be transferred to the server, or allow the server to post messages that are to be transferred back to the client. Using this technology, we can move an object's state from client to server or vice versa, ensuring that it will arrive at its destination where it can be managed by one of our objects.

We'll see how MSMQ fits into the CSLA, allowing UI-centric and data-centric objects to communicate, even if the object state data being sent back and forth moves through an asynchronous queue rather than a synchronous DCOM method call.

Browser-based (intelligent client)

Browser-based applications, for the most part, have been designed to have a very thin client running in the browser, with all business logic and processing handled by the web server or other servers invoked by the web server.

This has the advantage of virtually eliminating any logistic concerns about deployment or updates to the client workstations. However, logistic simplicity comes at the expense of a robust user interface. With such thin clients, the only way to provide validation, calculations or processing is to request it from the server – we basically treat the client workstation as a graphical terminal.

However, technologies are rapidly advancing on this front, allowing us to more easily take advantage of the client workstation's processing power, while retaining most of the deployment benefits from the browser environment. Such an application model is very attractive, since we may be able to achieve the logistic benefits, and still provide a user experience that is as robust as that which we might create with a VB form-based interface.

The Visual Basic related technologies available to us include:

- ❑ DHTML Applications
- ❑ VB ActiveX components (controls or DLLs) invoked by HTML or DHTML
- ❑ ActiveX Documents

> **These technologies require (or at least work best with) Internet Explorer.**

Note that I didn't mention WebClass-based applications (IIS Applications) here. This is because WebClass applications are entirely server-side, just like Active Server Pages (ASP) or other related technologies. Such technologies don't directly do anything to facilitate the creation of an intelligent client in the browser.

The physical architecture of an intelligent, browser-based application includes a client workstation or device, a web server, possibly application servers and, of course, database servers. We can map the CSLA into this environment as shown in the following diagram:

Client Workstation	Presentation Tier
	UI-centric Objects
Web Server	Data-centric Objects
Database Server	Data Services Tier

This approach may add substantial load to our web server, since the data-centric objects are running physically on that server. This can limit overall scalability of the system, so we may opt to run the data-centric objects on an application server instead, using the web server merely as a conduit for communications between the client and the application server.

Client Workstation	Presentation Tier
	UI-centric Objects
Web Server	↕
Application Server	Data Services Tier
Database Server	Data Services Tier

In either case, we are relying on the browser technologies to handle all the downloading and installation of our UI components and the UI-centric business object components. Using the new DHTML Applications in Visual Basic 6, ActiveX controls or DLLs invoked from DHTML or ActiveX Documents, Internet Explorer will automatically handle these deployment issues for us.

Once the components are on the client workstation, the browser can host the user interface, making full use of our UI-centric business objects to provide a robust user experience – much like in our previous two physical architectures.

As with the *n*-tier architecture, our data-centric objects will be running on a centralized server (presumably with a high-speed connection to the database server). In a browser-based setting this may be either our web server or a separate application server.

We are left with two major issues to resolve. First off, browser-based technologies are page based. This means that each time a new page is displayed in the browser, all associated components and their data are lost and must be recreated. Secondly, the UI-centric business objects need some way to communicate with the data-centric objects – presumably without using DCOM, since DCOM isn't the obvious choice for Internet-based communications, as we'll see later.

Page-based State Management

State management is one of the biggest, if not the single biggest, technical issue faced by Internet developers. This holds true for us as we implement Internet applications using distributed objects as well.

The challenge is that each page of information displayed to the user in a browser contains data. It may contain data from our objects or a database that is displayed for the user, and it may contain data entered by the user. The problem is, that when the user moves from this page to the next page within the browser, the browser looses any data from the page.

For a single page this isn't usually a problem since the data can be sent back to the server and processed. However, things get dicey if we have subsequent pages that also need the data – such as a multi-page wizard for data entry or a series of pages that allow display or entry of related data. In such a case we need some way to relay data from one page to the next.

There are a number of common solutions to this problem in the Internet development arena, each with its own drawbacks. Here are some of the possible solutions:

Solution	Consequences
When a page is accepted by the user the data is sent to the server. The server generates the next page to be displayed – storing the previous page's data in hidden fields within the new page.	This approach requires that all the data be transferred to and from the client multiple times – at least one time for each page displayed to the user.
When a page is accepted by the user the data is sent to the server. The data is stored in memory (such as the ASP `Session` object), a temporary database or file on the server and is given a unique key value. The unique key value is sent back to the browser and stored in a cookie. The server can use this cookie value over time to keep all the related data together.	This approach avoids sending the data back and forth to the client each time. However, if the user simply abandons our web site the temporary data is left on the server – leaving us to periodically run jobs to clean up old data. If we've opted to retain the temporary data in memory there's a more pressing need to clean up the data, since memory is typically a limited server resource.
When a page is accepted by the user the data is stored in a cookie on the client. This may be done through script code in the browser or by sending the data to the server and having the server create the cookie on the client.	This approach may avoid sending data back and forth from the client – or at least minimize the data transfers. It also avoids tying up server-side resources, since temporary data is stored on the client. Of course many users turn off cookies for privacy or security reasons. Additionally, client-side cookies often have size limitations that preclude storing any substantial amount of data there.

When creating browser-based applications based on business objects we face the same challenges – and in many cases we have the same options for managing our state data.

As I noted earlier, we have three main options that allow us to support objects on a client workstation with a browser-based user interface: DHTML Applications, ActiveX controls invoked by DHTML or ActiveX Documents. The common theme across all these technologies is that they store no data as they transition from page to page within the browser.

Unfortunately for us, this includes references to objects that may be running on the client workstation. This typically means that our objects will be destroyed – no references means no object in the COM world. To put it simply, we are left with no easy way to retain a business object from one page to the next.

This is quite a different environment than the one we have with a traditional forms-based application, where we can retain a reference to a given business object even if the user moves from form to form within our program.

So how does this tie back to the various state management techniques used by web developers? Well, our business objects have state. If we can't come up with some way to keep the objects around from page to page, we'll need to come up with a way to pass the *state* from page to page so each page can recreate the objects.

And this brings us back to the techniques available to web developers for state management. To retain state from page to page (whether from objects or not) we need to figure out a way to temporarily store it on the client, on the web server or elsewhere.

We do have an advantage that the traditional web developer doesn't have – we are writing the objects in Visual Basic and thus we have full access to the capabilities of our development tool. This adds a couple of new scenarios for state management that we might consider, though neither of these is terribly attractive either:

Solution	Consequences
Using frameset technology within the browser, we can use our UI-centric business objects within the browser just as we do within a conventional Visual Basic user interface.	In this scenario our objects would *not* be destroyed as the user moves from page to page since they'll be 'owned' by the frameset rather than any specific page displayed to the user.
	There are some issues to deal with however. First off, we're requiring that all pages in our application be displayed within a frame.
	We're also dictating that the frameset page contain an object tag to create our objects.
	Of course this also means we'll be installing ActiveX DLL's on the client workstations. While the browser will do this for us (via the `codebase` tag), it may be a significant drawback in many settings.

Solution	Consequences
Before moving off the current page, the object can be notified, allowing it to save its state into a temporary file on the client workstation's hard drive.	This approach avoids sending data back and forth from the client. It also avoids tying up server-side resources, since temporary data is stored on the client.
This is similar to the client-side cookie mentioned earlier, but is more powerful since we aren't subject to the rules that govern cookies.	We are still left with the issue that the user may leave our site entirely – leaving the temporary files on their hard drive with no mechanism to remove them.

Many web developers may feel uncomfortable with this approach, as storing data on the client workstation is generally frowned upon. |

In the end, the best options are those used most often by web developers, either passing the state back to the web server for storage, or shuttling the state back and forth from client to server and back to the client with each page transition.

> *I really wish there were a better solution. Perhaps something like ASP's* Session *object, but within the browser on the client. However, at least today it appears that the browser-based development environment still has some maturing to do relative to other client alternatives.*

In Chapter 7 we'll explore some of these options, including a form of Session object within the browser. Though the technologies at our disposal today are limited, at least we'll have some techniques available for our use.

Object Communication over HTTP

OK, so state management across page transitions is the first major obstacle we face when creating intelligent, browser-based client applications. The other major obstacle mentioned earlier is that the UI-centric business objects on the client need some way to communicate with the data-centric objects on the server.

Typically this is done with DCOM, and in some cases we can continue to use DCOM with a browser-based client. However, in many cases DCOM may be less than ideal. For instance, if a firewall exists between the client workstation and our server it is most likely that only HTTP will be allowed through. Also, the overhead in creating a DCOM connection can be high, especially if the Internet connections between the client and server are under load or there are many network hops between the machines.

> *DCOM does have the ability to run over HTTP. This capability was provided with a later service pack of Windows NT 4.0. Utilization of this requires installation of the supporting software on each computer which will use it, and Windows NT on both the client and server machines. While this is an interesting alternative, we'll see that Remote Data Services provide a much more ubiquitous solution to the problem.*

Microsoft recognized this as a problem some time ago, as they started to develop technologies to allow scripted applications in a browser to request data from the server. To meet this need, Remote Data Services (RDS) was developed.

We'll cover RDS in some detail in Chapter 7. For now I'll provide a quick summary.

RDS is a technology that allows code on a client to create an object on the web server and then call methods on that object. So far this sounds like something we'd do with DCOM right? With RDS though, all the communications are handled through the HTTP protocol – thus flowing right through most firewalls and also leveraging the speed of connecting via HTTP (typically faster than DCOM).

While there are some definite limitations on what we can do with objects using RDS, it is a very powerful technology. This is particularly true when developing applications following the CSLA, since RDS provides us with all the capabilities for server-side objects that the CSLA requires. This means we can essentially develop applications based on CSLA, regardless of whether we'll be using DCOM or RDS between the client and server machines.

So, in the end we don't have an elegant solution to handle the problem of losing state data during page transitions within the browser. But we do have a nice solution for client to server communication through the use of RDS – which we'll explore in more detail in Chapter 7.

Implementing Applications with CSLA

Having reviewed the CSLA itself and also examined how it can be applied to some key physical architectures, let's dive down into some more detail. The CSLA is more than simply a high-level model for our application, it also provides us with a specific design we can use when creating the UI-centric and data-centric business objects. From there we can also derive some key characteristics of a robust user interface that might be built on top of the UI-centric objects.

Business Objects

The fundamental architecture of the CSLA is based on business objects – for example a *Customer* object. These objects represent real-world entities or concepts within our application and provide an abstract model of our business on which we can build computer systems.

Overview

In their simplest form, business objects are composed of a public interface, an implementation of that interface and state (or data) on which the implementation acts.

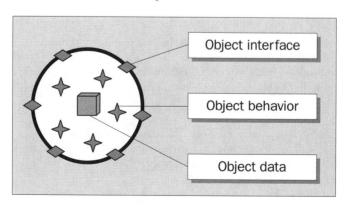

However, the CSLA is not only concerned with objects, it is also a client/server architecture. To this end, we don't simply implement a business object as a single entity. Instead, we separate the behaviors that support a robust user interface from those that primarily interact with data sources. Conceptually we still have a single object, but in reality that 'single object' is represented by two different objects within our architecture:

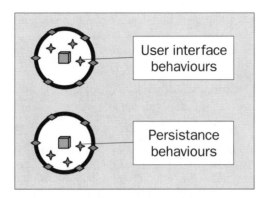

To use the example of a *Customer* object, we will in fact have a concept of a *Customer* object within our application. However, that object will be represented by a UI-centric *Customer* object and a data-centric *Customer* object – each of which relies on the other in order to provide the appropriate types of behaviors.

The UI-centric half of our *Customer* object will provide properties and methods for use by the user interface developer. Examples may include properties for ID, Name, Address, etc. and methods to create an invoice, file a complaint or other actions appropriate to a customer.

The data-centric half of our *Customer* object will provide behaviors that interact with the database. Some obvious ones include retrieving and storing the customer data. However, the data-centric behaviors may be substantially more complex – possibly involving interaction with other data sources. For instance, we may also retrieve a map to the customer's location and tap into a specialized system to determine the optimal route for driving there.

We'll get into the specifics of both UI-centric and data-centric object implementations shortly. First though, let's discuss an important type of relationship which may occur between objects – the parent-child relationship.

Child Objects

There are a number of relationships that can occur between objects in an object-oriented setting. Of these, one of the most common is the 'has-a' relationship. In this relationship, one object *has a* child object – implying a form of ownership or containment.

For example, an *Invoice* object will have child *LineItem* objects. These *LineItem* objects can't stand alone – and neither can the *Invoice*. The child objects are required by, and are part of, the parent *Invoice* object. Neither can exist without the other.

Virtually every business application has some type of parent-child relationship between its objects. In fact, it is hard to imagine a system of any complexity that doesn't have such a situation. Because of this, the CSLA is designed to handle the issues that come up with dealing with parent-child relationships.

Of course, child objects may have child objects of their own. An *Order* may have *LineItems* and those *LineItems* may have *DetailLines*. Chapters 3 and 4 will cover the issues that come into play when we have this type of arrangement.

For the rest of this chapter however, we'll remain focused on simple parent-child relationships.

This relationship is important because parent objects are implemented in a slightly different way to child objects. Primarily this comes into play with the editing process and the storing and retrieving of object data from the database.

When the user interacts with our objects, the object data will be changed. One of the features provided by the CSLA is to allow the objects to reset their data to an original point before any changes were made – a form of undo capability. Child objects not only need to be able to undo changes if they are told to, but they may need to reset their state if their *parent* object is told to reset.

Additionally, since parent and child objects can't exist without each other, we can't store a child object into the database without its parent being stored (and visa versa). This impacts how the objects are designed, as we want to ensure that anytime a parent object is stored or retrieved that its child objects are also stored or retrieved as appropriate.

Given all this, let's see how UI-centric and then data-centric objects are implemented.

Implementation of UI-centric Business Objects

UI-centric business objects provide behaviors which are typically used by the user interface, but which don't interact directly with data sources.

If we are creating a simple *Customer* object, for instance, our UI-centric object will likely provide properties for `CustomerNumber`, `Name`, `Address`, `Phone` and so forth. It might also provide methods that may be called from the UI, such as `CreateInvoice`, `AddContact`, etc.

These are all properties and methods that support a robust UI, but they are also specific to this particular object. Other objects (such as an *Invoice*, *Product*, etc.) will have entirely different properties and methods as appropriate to model the real-world entity or concept they represent.

Common Behaviors

At the same time, there are certain behaviors common to all UI-centric business objects created following the CSLA. These behaviors provide basic functionality to control how the object's data is edited, with support for the concept of 'undo' to restore the original object data if required. Other common behaviors are also supported, including tracking whether the object is new, dirty or deleted and more.

Here is a comprehensive list of the methods and properties common to all CSLA designed UI-centric objects:

Method	Description
BeginEdit	This method must be called by the UI prior to attempting to call any `Property Let` procedures or any methods that change the state of the object.
CancelEdit	This method may be called by the UI after `BeginEdit` has been called and changes to the object's state have been made. Calling this method will cause the object to reset to the state it was in when the `BeginEdit` method was called. It is often called when the user clicks a Cancel button within the UI. Once this method has been called, `BeginEdit` must be called before any object state can be changed.
ApplyEdit	This method may be called by the UI after `BeginEdit` has been called and changes to the object's state have been made. Calling this method will cause the object to commit any changes to its state since the call to `BeginEdit`. It is often called when the user clicks an OK or Apply button within the UI. Once this method has been called, `BeginEdit` must be called before any object state can be changed. For a child object, this method simply updates the object's internal state so it knows the changes are committed. For a parent object, this method causes the object and all its child objects to be stored into a database – typically by calling methods on its corresponding data-centric business object.
Load	This method causes the object to retrieve its state from a database. It must be called before `BeginEdit` is called. Once this method has been called, the object will assume the state that was previously stored in the database. The state data is typically retrieved by calling a method on a corresponding data-centric business object which interacts with the actual data store to retrieve the data.
Delete	This method causes the object to be *marked* for deletion. The object is not immediately deleted, but will be deleted when the object's state is updated into the database with a call to `ApplyEdit`.

Property	Description
IsValid	This property is a `Boolean` that indicates whether the object is currently in a valid, or savable, condition. Essentially, this property returns `True` if no business rules are currently broken based on the state of the object.
Valid *(event)*	This event is raised any time that the object changes from being valid to being invalid, or from being invalid to being valid. The UI can receive this event, allowing the UI developer to make any required changes to the user's display – such as enabling and disabling the OK button, etc.

Continued on following page

Property	Description
IsNew	This property is a Boolean that indicates whether the object is new. A new object is defined such that the object's state is not currently stored in the database. Once the object's state data has been stored in the database it is no longer new.
IsDirty	This property is a Boolean that indicates whether the object is dirty. An object is dirty once any of its state data has been changed through a Property Let or a method call that changed the state.
IsDeleted	This property is a Boolean that indicates whether the object is marked for deletion. An object is marked for deletion once its Delete method has been called. Calling the CancelEdit method will restore the object such that it is no longer marked for deletion.

Child Objects

Child objects have some extra methods as well. Here are the methods and a description:

Method	Description
ChildBeginEdit	This method is called by the parent object when its BeginEdit method is called. When this method is called, the object stores a copy of its current state so it can roll back to this point if need be. The child object's BeginEdit method is still called by the UI like normal, ChildBeginEdit is an extra method called only by the parent object.
ChildCancelEdit	This method is called by the parent object when its CancelEdit method is called. When this method is called, the object restores its state to the point it was at when ChildBeginEdit was called. The child object's CancelEdit method is still called by the UI like normal, ChildCancelEdit is an extra method called only by the parent object.
ChildApplyEdit	This method is called by the parent object when its ApplyEdit method is called. When this method is called, the object commits any changes to its state since the ChildBeginEdit method was called. The child object's ApplyEdit method is still called by the UI like normal, ChildApplyEdit is an extra method called only by the parent object.

Collectively, these methods allow a parent object to control its child objects. The UI may allow the user to directly edit a child object, but the parent object retains the ability to undo those changes – even if the UI calls ApplyEdit on the child object.

In reality the parent object doesn't directly undo the changes to child objects – each object maintains control over its own internal state. However, the Child*Edit methods provide a mechanism by which the parent object can ask its child objects to reset their states to a previous point.

This makes sense. Consider an *Order* object with *LineItem* objects representing the specific items being ordered. Even if the user makes a change to a specific *LineItem* object – if they then cancel any changes to the *Order* object we'd expect that all changes to the *Order* object's children would be canceled as well.

As we'll see later in this chapter, this approach works very well for objects that have child objects. However, it doesn't work well if those child objects have children in turn. In Chapter 3 we'll see why this is, and explore some more powerful ways of handling the behaviors implemented by these child objects – in such a way that we can have child, grandchild and greatgrandchild objects. In fact, the solution in Chapter 3 will allow us to easily support any number of levels of child objects.

Implementing Property Get Procedures

In addition to the set of properties and methods we've discussed so far, all business objects designed following the CSLA implement their other properties and methods with some specific design elements.

Property Get procedures do not typically change any state data within an object – instead they simply provide values for use by the UI or other client code. The CSLA adds no specific requirements to these procedures.

A typical Property Get procedure might appear as follows:

```
Public Property Get Name() As String
  Name = Trim$(mudtProps.Name)
End Property
```

Were a Property Get to change state data for some reason, we'd need to code it as shown in the section on Property Let procedures.

Implementing Property Let Procedures

Property Let procedures almost always change state data within an object. The UI or other client code provides a new value to the object, which is stored as part of the object's state.

Any time we write code that changes our object's state, we need to make sure that the object is being edited – meaning that the BeginEdit method has been called. As we'll see later in the chapter when we implement an application following the CSLA, each object has a variable, mflgEditing, which indicates whether the BeginEdit method has been called.

In each Property Let procedure we'll simply add code to check the mflgEditing variable. If the object is not currently editable, our procedure will raise an error indicating that the property is not available.

```
Public Property Let Name(Value As String)
  If Not mflgEditing Then Err.Raise 383

  mudtProps.Name = Value
End Property
```

The error value here, 383, corresponds to the Visual Basic error message 'Set not supported (read-only property)', thus indicating that the object is currently in a read-only state until the `BeginEdit` method is called.

Implementing Methods that Don't Change State

As with `Property Get` procedures, we may also have methods that just return values or perform other work that doesn't change the object's state. In such a case the CSLA doesn't add any constraints to the method. A method of this type may appear as follows, to simply calculate and return a value:

```
Public Function CalculateAverage() As Double
   Dim dblValue As Double
   Dim dblSum As Double

   For Each dblValue In mcolData
     dblSum = dblSum + dblValue
   Next
   CalculateAverage = dblSum / mcolData.Count
End Function
```

Since this procedure doesn't change any of the object's state values, it doesn't matter if it is called before or after a `BeginEdit` method has been called.

Implementing Methods that Change State

Many methods *do* change the state of an object however. As with the `Property Let` procedures, any time we change the state of our object we need to ensure that the `BeginEdit` method has been called. We can easily do this by checking the value of the `mflgEditing` variable implemented within all CSLA business objects.

We may have a method to add values to our internal collection (following the theme of the `CalculateAverage` method we just looked at):

```
Public Sub AddValue(Value As Double)
   If Not mflgEditing Then Err.Raise 445

   mcolData.Add Value
End Sub
```

If `BeginEdit` has not been called then the `mflgEditing` flag will be `False` and we can simply raise an error to indicate that this method is not accessible. To do this, we raise error 445, which translates to the Visual Basic error 'Object doesn't support this action'.

Once we've implemented the properties and methods common to all CSLA objects, and ensured that our property and method procedures follow the rules we just discussed, our object will fit seamlessly into any application designed to follow the CSLA.

What we've discussed so far are UI-centric business objects, which exist primarily to support a robust user interface. Now let's move on and discuss the design parameters for data-centric business objects.

Implementation of Data-centric Business Objects

Data-centric business objects exist primarily to implement behaviors that require direct access to our data sources.

Going back to our conceptual *Customer* business object, we've already seen the common behaviors and implementation rules for the UI-centric portion, now we can explore the common behaviors for the data-centric portion of that same object.

> **Even though we're discussing two different physical objects (UI-centric and data-centric) it is important to remember that they are really two halves of the same conceptual object.**

Unlike the UI-centric business objects, the data-centric objects have very few specific requirements in terms of properties or methods. However, the requirements that do exist are very important to ensure high performance and scalability.

Most data-centric business objects exist to provide CRUD (create, read, update and delete) services for their UI-centric counterparts. To this end, they often implement just three methods:

Method	Description
Fetch	This method is called by the UI-centric object when its Load method is called. The Fetch method retrieves the appropriate data from the database and returns it to the UI-centric business object.
Save	This method is called by the UI-centric object when its ApplyEdit method is called. The Save method determines whether the object is new, in which case it adds it to the database, or whether it is an existing object, in which case it updates the associated data in the database.
DeleteObject	This method is called by the UI-centric object when its ApplyEdit method is called and the UI-centric object has been marked for deletion. The DeleteObject method removes the object's data from the database.

Some data-centric objects may implement other methods as needed by the design of the application. In all cases, these methods follow a set of rules to ensure they operate as efficiently as possible.

Atomic Methods

First of all, we are assuming that our data-centric objects will be located on a central application server, so they will be used by many different clients. In many cases these objects may be running within the context of Microsoft Transaction Server (MTS).

It is important that the time a client is interacting with a server-side object be as short as possible. This allows more clients to use the server, since the load on the server is kept to a minimum.

Additionally, when working with MTS and using it to provide 2-phase commit transactional support, each individual method should indicate to MTS whether or not it was successful. This is the easiest and best performing way to work with MTS.

Both of these issues are discussed in detail in Visual Basic 6 Business Objects.

2-phase commit is a powerful technique for processing transactions. Essentially, what happens is that a series of database changes (transactions) occur. These changes may be to one database or even spread across multiple databases on different servers. If any one of them fails for any reason, the 2-phase commit infrastructure (provided for us by the Distributed Transaction Coordinator or DTC) will roll back all the changes to all the databases.

If this sounds complex – it is. Fortunately, MTS and the DTC hide all the complexity. Our components merely need to interact with the database as required – calling `SetComplete` if they are successful or `SetAbort` if they fail for any reason.

If we design our data-centric objects to have **atomic methods** we will meet these requirements. An atomic method is one that does not require any property or method to be called ahead of time, nor does it care if any other property or method may be called later.

Atomic methods accept all data they require as parameters, do their work, return their result and then wait for the next time they are called. Nothing is remembered or retained from one method call to the next.

This design allows our UI-centric object to quickly and simply interact with our data-centric objects. The UI-centric object simply creates a reference to the data-centric object, calls the method and releases the reference. Very clean, very fast, and with minimal impact on the shared server, since each client only interacts with the server for a brief time when needed.

Our data-centric object is also ready to work with MTS. Since each method is atomic, it is not dependant on any previous or subsequent method calls. Thus, by the time our method is complete it knows whether or not it was successful in completing its work. It can then call the `SetComplete` or `SetAbort` method to indicate to MTS whether it was successful.

Use of the ByVal Keyword

Having our methods be atomic means that each individual method call will be completed as rapidly and efficiently as possible. However, the process of actually *making* the method call is important as well.

Our method calls are handled by DCOM. The UI-centric object creates a reference to the data-centric object using DCOM, then makes a method call (which is handled by DCOM) and finally drops the reference to the object – allowing DCOM to release the server-side object.

When we make a method call using DCOM, all the parameters on our method need to be packaged up to be sent efficiently across the network. This process is called **marshaling**, and is a service provided by DCOM.

One of the things that DCOM looks at when it marshals our method's parameters is whether the parameter is being passed by **reference** or whether it is being passed by **value**.

A parameter passed by reference is not only sent *to* the server, but it is also sent back to the client! This is because a parameter that is passed to a method by reference can be changed within that method and the calling code will expect to see those changes.

A parameter passed by value is merely sent to the server. The value is not also sent back to the client. A parameter passed to a method by value can be changed within the method, but the calling code expects that those changes *will not* affect its own data. In other words, a parameter passed by value is a write-only parameter – not read-write. The data goes in, but doesn't come out.

Obviously we can minimize the amount of data going back and forth across the network by passing our parameters by value whenever possible. If we do this, our parameter values will only go from the client to the server – they won't also be returned from the server back to the client.

> *None of this has any impact on values returned from a* Function. *The results of a* Function *type method are always returned – but like parameters passed by value, they only go across the network once, from the server back to the client.*

To pass parameters by value, we use the ByVal keyword in Visual Basic. For instance, we might declare our Fetch method as follows:

```
Public Function Fetch(ByVal CustomerID As Long) As String
```

With this declaration, the CustomerID parameter will be sent from the client to the server, but won't be returned from the server back to the client – thus minimizing traffic on the network.

As we implement data-centric business objects, it is important to make the methods atomic and use the ByVal keyword to declare parameters whenever possible. By doing this, we help ensure that our server-side objects will be as scalable, efficient and high-performance as possible.

Characteristics of a User Interface

Having reviewed how a conceptual business object can be implemented as a pair of UI-centric and data-centric objects, it seems appropriate to quickly review the general characteristics of the user interface.

The CSLA allows us to create user interfaces that are quite robust – assuming our UI development tool also allows this level of interaction with the user. Visual Basic form-based and DHTML script-based interfaces can be very interactive and responsive, while a basic HTML interface based on Active Server Pages (ASP) can't be nearly so interactive. Still, the CSLA business object model allows us to create both types of UI with ease.

The CSLA is designed to provide a specific set of capabilities to UI developers for their use. Individual developers may or may not choose to use these capabilities, or specific UI development tools may preclude their use. Let's take a look at the capabilities provided by the CSLA.

OK, Cancel and Apply

One of the fundamental design goals of the CSLA is to make it easy for a UI developer to implement OK, Cancel and Apply buttons on their forms. Not all interfaces may provide all these buttons, but the basic behaviors of editing data and then being able to cancel or accept those changes are fundamental to almost all applications.

Our UI-centric business objects provide support for these behaviors through the BeginEdit, CancelEdit and ApplyEdit methods. Before any editing of the object's data is allowed, the UI must call the BeginEdit method – thus allowing the object to know that it is about to be changed so it can store its current state.

If the user later clicks the Cancel button or otherwise indicates to the UI that they want to undo their changes, the UI can simply call the CancelEdit method on a UI-centric object – causing the object to reset its state to where it was when BeginEdit was called.

If the user clicks the OK or Apply buttons, or otherwise indicates to the UI that they want to commit their changes, the UI can simply call the `ApplyEdit` method on a UI-centric object. This tells the object that it can commit any changes – requiring that `BeginEdit` be called before any further editing is allowed.

Essentially, this type of behavior means that our UI developers can count on a single level of undo to be provided by all business objects. Regardless of the type of UI developed, changes to the object can always be undone by calling `CancelEdit`.

At the same time, we haven't precluded more batch-oriented operations such as we might find with a browser-based interface. Code in the web server can instantiate our object, use its data to create a display for the user and then discard the object – all without ever even calling the `BeginEdit` method.

If the user changes values in their browser and posts the changes back to the web server, code in the web server can again instantiate our object, call `BeginEdit` and update the values within the object itself. Then it can immediately call `ApplyEdit` on the object to commit the changes.

By supporting the concept of OK, Cancel and Apply buttons we enable a very rich user interface, but don't stop a UI developer from creating a more basic type of interface if desired.

Checking Business Rules

Much of the reason for basing our applications on a set of business objects is to centralize the business logic and business validation code within the objects. This helps us avoid writing the same business code over and over again each time that we use it. Instead, we can write various user interfaces or other client code to use our business objects – thus reusing our business logic over and over.

One implication of this approach is that the UI must rely on the business object to handle validation of data entry and enforcement of business rules. Business objects designed following the CSLA indicate that business rules are broken in one of two ways: either by raising the `Valid` event when the object becomes invalid, or by raising a Visual Basic error.

For rules or validations that are immediate and severe, an error is often raised. For instance, if an object's `Name` field is limited to 20 characters the object is likely to raise an error if the UI attempts to put a 21 character value into the object. The UI can trap this error and immediately notify the user that the value is too long.

Many rules don't require such strong feedback, or may even be expected. Consider a date property that requires a past date. While the business object may require a valid date in the field, it may not be appropriate to raise an error if a current or future date value is provided. Instead the object may choose to raise the `Valid` event with a `False` parameter to inform the UI that the object contains one or more values that break business rules. Once a date in the past has been provided to the object, it can raise the `Valid` event with a `True` parameter so the UI knows the object has valid data.

The common theme is that the UI is relying on the business object to validate all business rules. It is entirely up to the UI developer to decide how to respond when the object either raises an error or the `Valid` event – thus providing centralized rule processing with a great deal of UI flexibility. For the most flexibility we often want to do both (raise an error and provide events). This allows the UI developer to have the most freedom in choosing how to handle the problems that arise.

Summary

In this chapter we have defined what we mean by distributed objects. Distributed objects take advantage of the best of both client/server and object-oriented design approaches, merging them to provide highly scalable distributed applications that are based on an object-oriented logical model of our business entities and concepts.

This is done by designing our application using object-oriented design principles, and then distributing those objects across two or more machines on our network. Of course there are some compromises that must be made from both the object-oriented design and the client/server design to merge the two design approaches effectively.

The Component-based Scalable Logical Architecture (CSLA) from *Visual Basic 6 Business Objects* provides us with an architecture we can use for distributed objects. There are many other architectures for distributed objects, but the CSLA is designed to leverage Microsoft technologies such as Visual Basic and MTS.

The CSLA provides a mechanism by which we can create an object-oriented design for our application, and then split each conceptual business object into a UI-centric and a data-centric object. This allows us to distribute the UI-centric behaviors so they are physically close to the user interface and the data-centric behaviors so they are physically close to the database.

Applications based on the CSLA are designed with object-oriented principles, but take advantage of client/server technologies to achieve high performance and scalability.

In the next chapter we'll build a simple Task Manager application based on the CSLA. Then, through the rest of the book, we will explore various ways to improve this application by adding important capabilities such as:

- n-level undo of object state changes
- Efficiently passing the state of complex object hierarchies across the network
- Using Visual Basic's data binding capabilities against business objects
- Passing object state asynchronously via MSMQ
- Passing object state over the Internet using RDS
- Implementing load balancing to distribute server-side load across multiple machines

Task Manager Application

2

Overview

In the first chapter we defined distributed objects and reviewed the CSLA. The CSLA provides a good architecture for developing applications based on distributed objects.

The CSLA can be used equally well when building applications that will run entirely on a single machine, or those that are distributed across multiple computers on a network. There are, however, a number of concepts and topics that only apply in a distributed setting – and those are the focus of this book.

Before we get into discussing these issues however, let's create an application that we can use through the rest of the book as an illustration. We'll build this application following the CSLA, thus providing a solid starting point if you are a new reader, or a consistent transition if you've already read *Visual Basic 6 Business Objects*.

The application will be quite straightforward. Rather than focusing on building a complex application, I want this book to focus on applying some new and powerful techniques.

In this chapter we'll build a fully functioning application based on the CSLA. First off we'll build a set of UI-centric business objects, which will provide a logical model of our business entities and concepts.

We'll then build the data-centric counterparts to these UI-centric objects, providing data access to a relational data model through an object-oriented link.

With our objects built, we'll move on to add a database and tables to store our objects' data within Microsoft SQL Server. On top of the objects and database we'll finish up by building a simple Visual Basic form-based user interface.

Task Manager Application

This application will allow us to track projects for our clients or customers. Each client may have a number of projects.

> *In Chapter 3 we'll extend the model so each project can have multiple specific tasks as well. If we view a* Project *object as a child of a* Client, *then a* Task *object will be a grandchild. Unfortunately the CSLA, as it stands, makes it very difficult to deal with grandchild objects. Thus, in this chapter we'll stick with implementing the* Client *and* Project *objects and we'll add* Task *objects in Chapter 3 to demonstrate how the CSLA can be enhanced to manage any number of child objects.*

Logical Object Diagram

Based on that simple description we can infer that there will be a Client object and a Project object as part of our application. They have a parent-child relationship, where a Client object has or owns a number of Project objects. We can represent this logical object design in UML as follows:

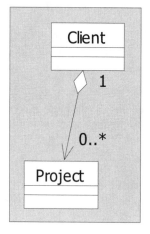

> *This diagram was created using Microsoft Visual Modeler, which is provided free with Visual Basic Enterprise Edition.*

Now let's think through the business-specific properties and methods these objects are likely to have.

The Client object represents the concept of a client that we might find in real life. In many cases we may want to store quite a lot of information about our clients, including their name, addresses, phone numbers, who to contact at the client and so forth. For this example, however, we'll restrict the list to very basic data:

- ❑ ID number
- ❑ Name
- ❑ Contact name
- ❑ Phone number
- ❑ Projects

Likewise, the `Project` object represents a project that is being done for or by the client. There's a lot of information that can be stored about a project as well, including the project's name, who is assigned to it, its expected duration and cost, etc. Again we'll restrict our list to the very basics:

❑   ID number
❑   Name

With this information, we can enhance our UML diagram as follows:

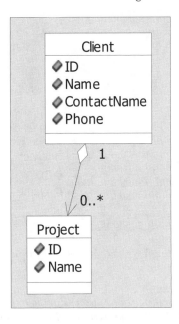

It is worth noting that this diagram is a departure from strict usage of UML in terms of how I portray Property elements in the object's interface. UML would have us indicate the Property Get and Property Let routines as separate methods in the diagram. I am choosing to portray them as data elements for the object as a form of shorthand (and because I think this is easier to read).

Physical Object Diagram

The logical diagram gives us a great overview of the objects that will make up our system and their relationships. However, this is not enough detail for us to actually *implement* the system. Thus, we need to derive a more detailed, physical object diagram from the logical diagram.

In a typical parent-child relationship, such as the one we have here, the child objects are managed by another object based on the `Collection` class. Rather than diluting the `Client` object with all the code required to manage a group of child objects, we'll move these behaviors into a separate `Projects` object, and then make that object available to any calling code by adding a `Projects` property to the `Client` object.

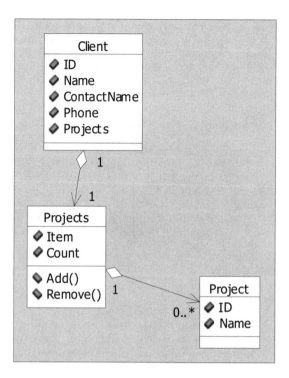

With this new diagram we have all the detail we should need to implement our objects – or at least our UI-centric objects.

> *I haven't included the common CSLA properties and methods in these objects for clarity. In a truly accurate diagram we'd also include all the properties and methods that we discussed in Chapter 1, since we will be adding them to these objects.*

Our physical diagram should also include our data-centric objects and their relationships. This addition (see below) gives us a clear and complete picture of our application and how it works. Since our focus is on distributed objects, we'll design this application to minimize network traffic and maximize scalability by having the data-centric objects invoked only from the parent object – in this case `Client`.

The `Client` object will call a limited number of methods on the `ClientPersist` object – sending and retrieving data in as efficient a format as possible. This will provide us with the ability to distribute our objects across the network while still providing good performance for the user.

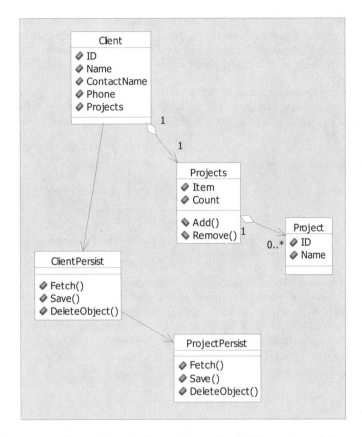

With this final diagram we have defined all the objects, both UI-centric and data-centric. Now let's dive in and implement them.

UI-centric Objects

Our UI-centric objects include `Client`, `Projects` and `Project`. These objects will not only include the properties and methods shown in the physical object diagram from above, but will also include those from the CSLA as discussed in Chapter 1.

As the standard CSLA properties and methods were discussed in Chapter 1 and were covered in detail in *Visual Basic 6 Business Objects*, I won't discuss them in detail here. There are, however, some minor improvements in how these objects are implemented as compared to *Visual Basic 6 Business Objects*, and I'll point them out as we go along.

The UI-centric business objects will be contained within an ActiveX DLL component. To start off, open Visual Basic and create a new ActiveX DLL project.

Using the Project | Properties dialog, change the project's name to `TaskObjects`.

BrokenRules Object

Objects need some way to keep track of business rules that are broken. In many cases, a rule may be enforced across more than one property in our object.

For instance, in an *Attendee* object for a conference registration program we may have fields for both date of birth and whether the person requested a drinking badge. One rule we may implement is a minimum drinking age, under which a person can't request a drinking badge. These two fields are interrelated – a change to either one could break or un-break the rule.

To keep track of which rules are broken at any given time, we can use a specialized object that contains a collection of the rules that are broken. In Visual Basic 6 Business Objects we implemented such an object – named `BrokenRules`. We'll make use of this same object in this book.

The code for `BrokenRules` is in Appendix A, so you can enter it from there or download the code from our web site at `http://www.wrox.com/`

Add the `BrokenRules` class module to the project and then proceed to build the `Client` object.

Client Object

The `Client` object is the parent object for our `Project` objects. We can consider it a **top level** object, since it isn't owned by any other object.

If you are using the business object template from *Visual Basic 6 Business Objects*, remove the Class1 module and add a new class using that template. Otherwise keep the Class1 module in the project and use it for the `Client` object. If you are not using the template, you will need to enter *all* the code shown below regardless of whether it is highlighted, and if you are using the template just enter or change the highlighted code. Remember, you can always download this template, along with the rest of the source code for this book from our web site at `http://www.wrox.com/`.

Change the module's name to Client.

Defining the Object's State

Add a BAS module to the project. Change its name to TOtypes and add the following code.

```
Option Explicit

Public Type ClientProps
   IsNew As Boolean
   IsDirty As Boolean
   IsDeleted As Boolean
   ID As Long
   Name As String * 50
   ContactName As String * 50
   Phone As String * 25
End Type

Public Type ClientData
   Buffer As String * 131
End Type
```

In Visual Basic 6.0 it is now possible to declare a UDT in a class module and make it Public so that it's available to an entire application, or even other applications. While the end result is similar to placing the definitions in a BAS module (in that we can use the UDT throughout a program), the underlying mechanism is quite different. By placing the UDT in a class module it would become part of a COM interface – thus hard to change or redeploy (at least in a relative sense). Additionally, it requires a newer version of COM than is currently installed on most computers – thus causing a deployment issue as the COM DLLs themselves may have to be installed.

The `ClientProps` data type contains all the elements needed to store our object's state data. Since we're operating in a distributed setting the data type also includes variables to record whether the object is new, dirty or deleted as well as the values specific to this object.

The `ClientData` data type is composed of a single string that is as long as the total length (in bytes) of the `ClientProps` type. The length of the String value here is 131 characters. The process of deriving the length of this buffer is the trickiest part of the process, so let's go through it briefly.

Calculating the Size of the UDT

First, we need to count the number of *bytes* consumed by our detailed UDT. Each `Boolean` is of length 2, the `Long` is of length 4 and each `String` is *twice* the length indicated in the UDT. This is because strings in Visual Basic are all Unicode – so each character is two bytes in length.

Adding all that together and we'll get 260 bytes. However, this isn't the correct value due to something called **longword alignment**. Certain data types *must* start on a longword boundary (every 4 bytes), even if it means there's a gap between the previous element in the UDT and the next one.

This is the case with the `Long` data type. It always must start on a longword boundary – or byte 0, 4, 8, 12, etc. Adding up the three `Boolean` elements, we see that they end on byte 5 – meaning that the next element in the UDT could start on byte 6. The `Long` *can't* start on byte 6 for the reasons we've just seen, so two bytes are automatically inserted as a filler and the `Long` starts on byte 8.

We need to add these two bytes of filler to our total length – thus bringing the length of the data to 262 bytes total.

Of course the `String` buffer is not 262 in length. This is because each Unicode character is two bytes – meaning the `String` variable will be exactly *half* the number of bytes – or 131 characters.

We'll use this and the `LSet` method within Visual Basic to efficiently convert our object's state to and from a single, basic data type – in this case a `String`.

CSLA Properties and Methods

Return to the `Client` class module.

It is worth noting that the template uses the `mflgNew`, `mflgDirty` and `mflgDeleted` variables. These variables are best considered part of the object's state. In a distributed setting we can view the object's state as being any values that are required by both UI-centric and data-centric objects, and that includes these values. In *Visual Basic 6 Business Objects* we copied these values in and out of `mudtProps`, but in this case I've simply used the values directly out of `mudtProps` and dropped the separate variables to simplify the code in our objects.

If you are using the class template make the following changes, otherwise enter all the following code, which we will discuss next:

```
Option Explicit

Event Valid(IsValid As Boolean)

Private mudtProps As ClientProps
Private mudtSave As ClientData
Private mcolProjects As Projects
```

```vb
Private mflgEditing As Boolean
Private WithEvents mobjValid As BrokenRules

Public Sub BeginEdit()
  If mflgEditing Then Err.Raise 445

  ' save object state
  LSet mudtSave = mudtProps
  mflgEditing = True
  mcolProjects.BeginEdit
End Sub

Public Sub CancelEdit()
  If Not mflgEditing Then Err.Raise 445

  mflgEditing = False
  mudtProps.IsDeleted = False
  ' restore object state
  LSet mudtProps = mudtSave
  mcolProjects.CancelEdit
End Sub

Public Sub ApplyEdit()
  Dim objPersist As ClientPersist
  Dim strProjects As String

  If Not mflgEditing Then Err.Raise 445

  Set objPersist = New ClientPersist
  If mudtProps.IsDeleted Then
    ' code to delete the object's data goes here
    objPersist.DeleteObject mudtProps.ID
    mudtProps.IsNew = True
    mudtProps.IsDeleted = False
  ElseIf IsDirty Or mudtProps.IsNew Then
    If Not IsValid Then Err.Raise 445
    ' save object to database if appropriate
    ' save object state
    LSet mudtSave = mudtProps
    strProjects = mcolProjects.GetState
    SetState objPersist.Save(GetState, strProjects)
    mcolProjects.SetState strProjects
    mudtProps.IsNew = False
  End If
  mudtProps.IsDirty = False
  mflgEditing = False
  mcolProjects.ApplyEdit
End Sub

Private Sub Class_Initialize()
  Set mobjValid = New BrokenRules
  Set mcolProjects = New Projects

  mudtProps.IsNew = True
  ' if we know any rules are broken on startup
  ' then add code here to initialize the list
  ' of broken rules
  '
  ' mobjValid.RuleBroken "RuleName", True
End Sub
```

```vb
Private Sub Class_Terminate()
  Set mobjValid = Nothing
  Set mcolProjects = Nothing
End Sub

Public Property Get IsValid() As Boolean
  IsValid = (mobjValid.Count = 0)
End Property

Private Sub mobjValid_BrokenRule()
  RaiseEvent Valid(False)
End Sub

Private Sub mobjValid_NoBrokenRules()
  RaiseEvent Valid(True)
End Sub

Public Sub Load(ID As Long)
  Dim objPersist As ClientPersist
  Dim strProjects As String

  If mflgEditing Then Err.Raise 445
  If Not mudtProps.IsNew Then Err.Raise 445

  mudtProps.IsNew = False

  ' code to load the object goes here
  Set objPersist = New ClientPersist
  SetState objPersist.Fetch(ID, strProjects)
  Set objPersist = Nothing
  Set mcolProjects = New Projects
  mcolProjects.SetState strProjects
End Sub

Public Sub Delete()
  If Not mflgEditing Then Err.Raise 445

  mudtProps.IsDeleted = True
  mudtProps.IsDirty = True
End Sub

Public Property Get IsDeleted() As Boolean
  IsDeleted = mudtProps.IsDeleted
End Property

Public Property Get IsNew() As Boolean
  IsNew = mudtProps.IsNew
End Property

Public Property Get IsDirty() As Boolean
  IsDirty = mudtProps.IsDirty Or mcolProjects.IsDirty
End Property

Private Function GetState() As String
  Dim udtData As ClientData

  LSet udtData = mudtProps
  GetState = udtData.Buffer
End Function
```

```
Private Sub SetState(Buffer As String)
   Dim udtData As ClientData

   udtData.Buffer = Buffer
   LSet mudtProps = udtData
End Sub
```

The changes to the template code customize it for this particular object. The `ApplyEdit` and `Load` methods are perhaps the most changed, since they need to have code that interacts with the data-centric object that we'll create later.

The `GetState` and `SetState` methods are also new, and are required to serialize and deserialize the object's state data into and out of a simple `String` variable.

> **These two methods are part of the primary message of this book – which is to come up with an effective way to transport object state from one place to another. It is this underlying concept through which we are able to distribute our objects across the network.**

Serialization of the data is key to performance, as it allows us to send all the object's data across the network in a single stream.

Client Object Properties

Now that we have the standard CSLA code in our object, let's add the code to implement the properties specific to this particular business object. Enter the following code.

```
Public Property Get ID() As Long
   ID = mudtProps.ID
End Property

Public Property Get Name() As String
   Name = Trim$(mudtProps.Name)
End Property

Public Property Let Name(Value As String)
   If Not mflgEditing Then Err.Raise 383

   mudtProps.Name = Value
   mudtProps.IsDirty = True
End Property

Public Property Get ContactName() As String
   ContactName = Trim$(mudtProps.ContactName)
End Property

Public Property Let ContactName(Value As String)
   If Not mflgEditing Then Err.Raise 383

   mudtProps.ContactName = Value
   mudtProps.IsDirty = True
End Property

Public Property Get Phone() As String
   Phone = Trim$(mudtProps.Phone)
End Property
```

```
Public Property Let Phone(Value As String)
  If Not mflgEditing Then Err.Raise 383

  mudtProps.Phone = Value
  mudtProps.IsDirty = True
End Property

Public Property Get Projects() As Projects
  Set Projects = mcolProjects
End Property
```

The `ID` property is read-only. This is because we'll allow the database itself to generate unique values for the ID of each client, so we can't allow the UI to set or alter that value.

Notice how each of the `Property Let` routines not only stores the value from the UI, but also sets the `mudtProps.IsDirty` variable to `True`. This is important, since the object's state has been changed and so the object has become 'dirty'.

The `Property Get Projects` procedure simply returns a reference to the `Projects` object contained within the `Client` object. We'll be creating this object shortly.

Now is a good time to save the project, since our `Client` class is ready to go. We can move on to the other major UI-centric object in our application – the `Project`.

Project Object

The `Project` object is a child object, meaning that it is owned by another object – in this case the `Client` object.

Child objects require some extra code, as we discussed in Chapter 1. We need to implement the `ChildBeginEdit`, `ChildCancelEdit` and `ChildApplyEdit` methods in addition to the other standard CSLA properties and methods. It also means that our `Project` object won't have a `Load` method.

Add a new class module to the `TaskObjects` project and change its name to `Project`. Also change its **Instancing** property to **2-PublicNotCreatable**. The only way to create this type of object is through the parent object, `Client`.

Defining the Object's State

Open the `TOtypes` BAS module and add the following code.

```
Public Type ProjectProps
  IsNew As Boolean
  IsDirty As Boolean
  IsDeleted As Boolean
  ID As Long
  Name As String * 50
End Type

Public Type ProjectData
  Buffer As String * 56
End Type
```

As with the `Client` object we've added two types, `ProjectProps` to store the detailed state data and `ProjectData` with a single `String` variable that is the same length. The `LSet` statement can be used to translate data between these two types. With the object's data in a single byte stream we can easily and efficiently send it across the network.

The length of the `Buffer` variable is derived by adding together the total number of bytes in `ProjectProps`. 6 bytes for the `Booleans`, 2 filler bytes before the `ID` (since it is a `Long` and must be longword aligned), 4 for the `Long` itself and 100 for the `Name` variable. This totals to 112 bytes.

We then divide that by 2 to get the number of characters for the `Buffer` variable – 56. Remember that each *character* is really two bytes since Visual Basic `String` variables are all Unicode.

By using these two UDTs and the `LSet` statement we can very efficiently convert our object's data into a simple byte stream so we can send it across the network.

CSLA Properties and Methods

Return to the new `Project` class module. If you used the business object template to create this class make the following changes that are highlighted, otherwise enter all of the following code.

```
Option Explicit

Event Valid(IsValid As Boolean)

Private mudtProps As ProjectProps
Private mudtSave As ProjectData
Private mudtChildSave As ProjectData
Private mobjParent As Projects

Private mflgEditing As Boolean
Private mflgChildEditing As Boolean
Private WithEvents mobjValid As BrokenRules

Public Sub BeginEdit()
  If Not mflgChildEditing Then Err.Raise 445
  If mflgEditing Then Err.Raise 445

  ' save object state
  LSet mudtSave = mudtProps
  mflgEditing = True
End Sub

Public Sub CancelEdit()
  If Not mflgChildEditing Then Err.Raise 445
  If Not mflgEditing Then Err.Raise 445

  mflgEditing = False
  mudtProps.IsDeleted = False
  ' restore object state
  LSet mudtProps = mudtSave
End Sub

Public Sub ApplyEdit()
  If Not mflgChildEditing Then Err.Raise 445
  If Not mflgEditing Then Err.Raise 445
```

```
    If Not mobjParent Is Nothing Then
      mobjParent.AddProject Me
      Set mobjParent = Nothing
    End If
  mflgEditing = False
End Sub

Friend Sub Initialize(Parent As Projects)
    If mudtProps.IsNew Then Set mobjParent = Parent
End Sub

Friend Sub ChildBeginEdit()
    If mflgChildEditing Then Err.Raise 445

    LSet mudtChildSave = mudtProps
    mflgChildEditing = True
End Sub

Friend Sub ChildCancelEdit()
    If Not mflgChildEditing Then Err.Raise 445

    LSet mudtProps = mudtChildSave
    mflgChildEditing = False
End Sub

Friend Sub ChildApplyEdit()
    If Not mflgChildEditing Then Err.Raise 445

    LSet mudtChildSave = mudtProps
    mflgChildEditing = False
End Sub

Private Sub Class_Initialize()
  Set mobjValid = New BrokenRules

  mudtProps.IsNew = True
  ' if we know any rules are broken on startup
  ' then add code here to initialize the list
  ' of broken rules
  '
  ' mobjValid.RuleBroken "RuleName", True
End Sub

Private Sub Class_Terminate()
  Set mobjValid = Nothing
End Sub

Public Property Get IsValid() As Boolean
  IsValid = (mobjValid.Count = 0)
End Property

Private Sub mobjValid_BrokenRule()
  RaiseEvent Valid(False)
End Sub

Private Sub mobjValid_NoBrokenRules()
  RaiseEvent Valid(True)
End Sub

Public Sub Delete()
  If Not mflgEditing Then Err.Raise 445
```

```
    mudtProps.IsDeleted = True
    mudtProps.IsDirty = True
  End Sub

  Public Property Get IsDeleted() As Boolean
    IsDeleted = mudtProps.IsDeleted
  End Property

  Public Property Get IsNew() As Boolean
    IsNew = mudtProps.IsNew
  End Property

  Public Property Get IsDirty() As Boolean
    IsDirty = mudtProps.IsDirty
  End Property

  Friend Function GetState() As String
    Dim udtData As ProjectData

    LSet udtData = mudtProps
    GetState = udtData.Buffer
  End Function

  Friend Sub SetState(Buffer As String)
    Dim udtData As ProjectData

    udtData.Buffer = Buffer
    LSet mudtProps = udtData
  End Sub
```

The changes here are a bit more extensive since this is a child object.

The `ApplyEdit` method is substantially simpler than it is for a parent object. Since the parent object handles the work of actually saving the child object's data, the child object's `ApplyEdit` method doesn't have much left to do.

However, what the `ApplyEdit` does do is critical. When the child object is first created, its immediate parent (the `Projects` collection object) calls its `Initialize` method so the `Project` object has a reference to its parent. When the `ApplyEdit` method is called, and if the child object is new, it calls back into the `Projects` object to get itself added to the collection of child objects.

This code takes care of the case where the user may start to add a child object – then simply cancel out without ever adding the new object. We only want to add the child object to the `Projects` collection object when the user accepts the new object and the `ApplyEdit` method is run.

We've also added the `ChildBeginEdit`, `ChildCancelEdit` and `ChildApplyEdit` methods. This means we also needed a variable, `mflgChildEditing`, to track whether the `ChildBeginEdit` method has been called. This variable is checked at the top of key methods to ensure they are only called once the `ChildBeginEdit` method has been called.

As with the `Client` object, we have also added `GetState` and `SetState` methods so we can easily serialize and deserialize the object's state.

Project Object Properties

With the standard CSLA properties and methods in place, add the following code to the module.

```
Public Property Get ID() As Long
   ID = mudtProps.ID
End Property

Public Property Get Name() As String
   Name = Trim$(mudtProps.Name)
End Property

Public Property Let Name(Value As String)
   If Not mflgEditing Then Err.Raise 383

   mudtProps.Name = Value
   mudtProps.IsDirty = True
End Property
```

As with the Client object, the ID field is read-only. We'll let the database generate a unique value for this field the first time the object is saved.

The only other property in this object is the Name property, which is a simple read-write property.

Save the project and let's move on to our final UI-centric object.

Projects Object

While each Project object is conceptually owned by a Client object, in reality we'll implement an intermediate object to manage all those child Project objects.

This is done to keep the Client object's code focused on modeling a client. There's a fair amount of code involved in managing a collection of child objects and it is better to keep this code self-contained rather than diluting the Client object with it.

Also, we may want to add a different kind of child object to our Client object at some later point. If we directly expose the Project objects from the Client object it can be very difficult to add yet another type of child object later. By keeping the code to manage the child objects separate from the parent, it becomes very easy to add new types of child object later – all we need to do is add another object similar to the Projects object we're about to create.

Add a new, standard, class module to the TaskObjects project. Change the name to Projects, and the Instancing property to 2-PublicNotCreatable. This object should never be created directly by the UI, rather it should be accessed from its associated Client object.

Implementing a Custom Collection

This object will be a custom Collection object, so it is a bit different than the Client and Project objects. To get started, let's create the basic procedures required by a Collection object. Enter the following code.

```
Option Explicit

Private mcolItems As Collection
```

```
Private mflgEditing As Boolean

Private Sub Class_Initialize()
   Set mcolItems = New Collection
End Sub

Private Sub Class_Terminate()
   Set mcolItems = Nothing
End Sub

Public Function Count() As Long
   Count = mcolItems.Count
End Function

Public Function NewEnum() As IUnknown
   Set NewEnum = mcolItems.[_NewEnum]
End Function

Public Function Item(ByVal Index As Variant) As Project
   Set Item = mcolItems.Item(Index)
End Function
```

A custom collection is based on an underlying Visual Basic Collection object, in this case we're basing our object on the mcolItems object. It is a Private variable within our class, and in the Class_Initialize procedure we create an instance of the object.

Collection objects typically have a Count method so code using the object can determine how many items are contained in the object. They also have an Item method that is used to retrieve specific items from the Collection object.

We've also implemented a NewEnum method, which is a special method required to support the use of the For...Each loop.

Once this code has been entered we need to set some special attributes to make the object operate as a Collection. Choose the Tools | Procedure Attributes... menu option to bring up the Procedure Attributes dialog. Click on the Advanced button.

Using this dialog, set the Procedure ID for the Item procedure to (default). Also, set the Procedure ID for the NewEnum procedure to the magic number of −4 and click the Hide this member option for NewEnum as well.

The Procedure ID setting indicates the type of procedure, enabling various specialized behaviors as appropriate. Setting this field to (default) causes the method to become the default – like the Item method on a Collection – so it is optional in code that uses our object. Setting the Procedure ID to −4 indicates that the method is to be used by the For...Each logic to loop through the object's elements.

The Hide this member option simply sets a flag on the method so it is hidden from object browsers – at least by default. If you right-click in the Visual Basic object browser you can choose to see hidden methods on the objects shown in the browser.

At this point our object will have basic Collection-like behaviors.

Adding Project Objects

Now let's add the code that allows the UI to add new `Project` objects to a `Client`. This requires two methods, an `Add` method and an `AddProject` method.

```
Public Function Add() As Project
  Dim objProject As Project

  If Not mflgEditing Then Err.Raise 445

  Set objProject = New Project
  objProject.Initialize Me
  objProject.ChildBeginEdit
  Set Add = objProject
  Set objProject = Nothing
End Function

Friend Sub AddProject(Child As Project)
  mcolItems.Add Child
End Sub
```

The `Add` method is `Public` and is used by the UI to add a new `Project` object. However, it doesn't actually add the new child object to the `Collection`. Instead, it provides the new child object with a reference back to our `Projects` object by calling the `Initialize` method.

This is done because the user could always choose to cancel the process of adding the new child object. If we'd already added it to the list at that point, we'd end up with a blank or at least invalid child object in our list.

With this implementation, the new child object will use its reference to our `Projects` object to call the `AddProject` method once it knows for a fact that the user has accepted it. In this case, the `ApplyEdit` method of the `Project` object contains the call to `AddProject`.

Removing Project Objects

Now that we can add `Project` objects, we should add the ability to remove them as well. Each `Project` object has its own `Delete` method that marks the object for deletion. However, most `Collection` objects also have a `Remove` method that can be used to delete items, so we'll add one of those.

Additionally, it may be nice to provide the UI with an easy way to delete all the child `Project` objects, so we'll implement a `Delete` method to handle that.

```
Public Sub Remove(ByVal Index As Variant)
  If Not mflgEditing Then Err.Raise 445

  With mcolItems(Index)
    .BeginEdit
    .Delete
    .ApplyEdit
  End With
End Sub

Public Sub Delete()
  Dim objProject As Project
```

```
    If Not mflgEditing Then Err.Raise 445

    For Each objProject In mcolItems
      With objProject
        .BeginEdit
        .Delete
        .ApplyEdit
      End With
    Next
  End Sub
```

Of course neither of these methods actually deletes the Project objects. The child objects are simply marked for deletion – they'll be actually deleted if the ApplyEdit method of the Client object is called.

Save the project before continuing, to protect our work so far.

Serializing and Deserializing

In a distributed environment such as ours, it is very important that we are able to transfer our objects across the network very efficiently. With child objects this is a bit of a challenge, since we may have a lot of them.

Each individual Project object has GetState and SetState methods, so we can easily serialize and deserialize them object by object. What we need is some way to combine all those separate object states into a single stream. This can be accomplished through the use of a Buffer object.

Buffer is an object that can combine any number of elements of the same length and efficiently convert them into a single stream. Once such a stream of data is sent across the network it can then recreate the individual elements so we can use them to reconstitute the individual Project objects.

The code for the Buffer object can be found in Appendix A. Enter that code into a new class module in the project and make sure that module's name is set to Buffer.

The following code implements GetState and SetState methods for the Projects object by using Buffer.

```
Friend Sub SetState(Buffer As String)
  Dim objBuffer As Buffer
  Dim lngIndex As Long
  Dim objProject As Project

  Set objBuffer = New Buffer
  Set mcolItems = Nothing
  Set mcolItems = New Collection
  With objBuffer
    .SetState Buffer
    For lngIndex = 1 To .Count
      Set objProject = New Project
      objProject.SetState .Item(lngIndex)
      If mflgEditing Then objProject.ChildBeginEdit
      mcolItems.Add objProject
      Set objProject = Nothing
    Next
  End With
End Sub
```

```
Friend Function GetState() As String
  Dim objBuffer As Buffer
  Dim objProject As Project
  Dim udtData As ProjectData

  Set objBuffer = New Buffer
  With objBuffer
    .Initialize Len(udtData.Buffer), 10
    For Each objProject In mcolItems
      .Add objProject.GetState
    Next
    GetState = .GetState
  End With
  Set objBuffer = Nothing
End Function
```

Cascading BeginEdit, CancelEdit and ApplyEdit

The remaining methods allow the Client object to cascade any calls to its BeginEdit, CancelEdit and ApplyEdit methods down to its child Project objects.

When BeginEdit is called on the Client object, it calls BeginEdit in this object. This object then runs through all the individual child objects, calling ChildBeginEdit on each one in a chain-like fashion.

The same thing is done for CancelEdit and ApplyEdit. This was discussed in more detail in Chapter 1. Make the following changes to the Projects class module:

```
Public Sub BeginEdit()
  Dim objProject As Project

  If mflgEditing Then Err.Raise 445

  For Each objProject In mcolItems
    objProject.ChildBeginEdit
  Next

  mflgEditing = True
End Sub

Public Sub ApplyEdit()
  Dim objProject As Project

  If Not mflgEditing Then Err.Raise 445

  For Each objProject In mcolItems
    objProject.ChildApplyEdit
  Next

  mflgEditing = False
End Sub

Public Sub CancelEdit()
  Dim lngIndex As Long
  Dim objProject As Project

  If Not mflgEditing Then Err.Raise 445
```

```
     For lngIndex = 1 To mcolItems.Count
       Set objProject = mcolItems(lngIndex)
       With objProject
         If Not .IsNew Then
            .ChildCancelEdit
         Else
            mcolItems.Remove lngIndex
         End If
       End With
       Set objProject = Nothing
     Next

     mflgEditing = False
   End Sub

   Public Function IsDirty() As Boolean
     Dim objProject As Project

     For Each objProject In mcolItems
       If objProject.IsDirty Or objProject.IsNew Then
         IsDirty = True
         Exit For
       End If
     Next
   End Function
```

That completes our UI-centric objects. Other than their dependence on the data-centric objects, these objects are ready for use. Even as they are, they provide a solid foundation that a UI developer could use to begin building a user interface.

Make sure you save the project before continuing.

Data-centric Objects

In many ways, the UI-centric objects we've just created are the heart and soul of our application. They provide the highest level, most object-oriented view of the business entities and concepts within the program.

At the same time, they are virtually useless without their counterparts – the data-centric objects. The data-centric objects retrieve, update and remove data from the database. In a very real sense, they map the relational data in a database into our object-oriented model and then map the object-oriented data back into a relational database upon request.

For the Task Manager application there are just two data-centric objects, one for the Client object and one for the Project object.

While the UI-centric objects will probably be physically running on each individual client workstation so they are close to the user interface, the data-centric objects will be running on an application server so they have high-speed access to the database server. This means we can't put them directly in the same DLL with the UI-centric objects.

Setting up the Project

Open up a new ActiveX DLL project in Visual Basic. Change the project's name to `TaskServer` by using the Project | Properties menu option.

Use the Project | Add File... menu option to add the `TOtypes.BAS` file to this project. `TOtypes` is the module where we placed the user defined types (UDTs) for the state data of the `Client` and `Project` objects. We'll need those same UDTs in this project for the data-centric objects.

> *If you are using Visual SourceSafe (VSS) you can ensure that these files stay in sync. VSS will allow you to link a file between multiple projects. Once that's done, if the file is changed in any one project, it will automatically be updated in the other projects the next time the development machine's local copy is updated from VSS.*

Also add the `Buffer.cls` file to this project. We used `Buffer` in the `Projects` object to serialize all the child `Project` objects and we'll need it in our server-side project in order to decode that data. The code for `Buffer` can be found in Appendix A.

Only one bit of setup remains. Throughout our data-centric code we'll be creating ADO `Recordset` and `Connection` objects. These require a connection string so that ADO knows how to reach our database.

Add a new BAS module to the project and name it `TSmain`. Add the following code.

```
Option Explicit

Public Const DB_CONN = _
    "Provider=SQLOLEDB.1;Persist Security Info=False;User ID=sa;" _
    & "Initial Catalog=TaskMgr;Data Source=MYSERVER"
```

This text is the connection string for the database we'll be using throughout the project. I generated this string by adding an ADO data control to a form and using its ability to build a connection string through a graphical dialog. Simply click the [...] button next to the `DataSource` property of the control.

The resulting string indicates the driver, `SQLOLEDB.1`, the `User ID`, database (`TaskMgr`) and database server (`MYSERVER`).

In the case that you don't have access to a SQL Server database, you may choose to generate a connection string to almost any database of your choosing. Anything from an Access database to Oracle to DB2 will work just fine.

> **You will need to change MYSERVER to match your server name, and you may need to change the User ID and Catalog values as well depending on your environment. We'll go through the specific tables for the database later in this chapter.**

With that setup work done we are ready to create the data-centric business objects for the application.

ClientPersist Object

In our application design, the `Client` object is the only UI-centric object that interacts with the data-centric objects. The only data-centric object it calls is the `ClientPersist` object.

This means that the `ClientPersist` object either directly or indirectly provides all the data-centric behaviors for the `Client` object and all its child objects.

When the `Client` object wants to save its data (and that of its child objects), it collects all the state data from itself and its child objects, then calls the `ClientPersist` object's `Save` method to save all the data.

Likewise, the `ClientPersist` object's `Fetch` method not only retrieves the `Client` object's data, but also all the child `Project` objects' data. All of the collected data is returned to the `Client` object in a single method call so the `Client` can set its own state and also create any appropriate child objects.

The `ClientPersist` object will rely on the `ProjectPersist` object to handle the data for the `Project` objects, but the UI-centric objects will never talk directly to the `ProjectPersist` object, as shown in the UML diagram we saw earlier:

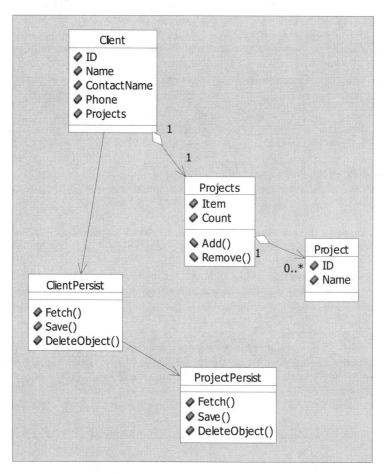

Overall, the `ClientPersist` object will implement a `Fetch` method, a `Save` method and a `DeleteObject` method. Each of these methods will directly retrieve, update or delete the appropriate `Client` object data, but they will also make use of the `ProjectPersist` object to provide data-centric services for the child `Project` objects.

In the `TaskServer` project, select the `Class1` module and change its name to `ClientPersist`.

Using Microsoft Transaction Server

Microsoft Transaction Server (MTS) is a powerful tool for use in developing distributed applications. While it provides us with a number of benefits, two stand out as being primary motivations for using MTS:

❑ Transactional support
❑ Management of the middle-tier (scalability)

Any time an application has to store data into tables with foreign keys or parent-child type relationships we have a transactional requirement. It is invalid to save a parent record without the child records, and it is invalid to store a child record without a parent. Likewise, it is invalid to write a foreign key value without the target record existing.

While we can certainly implement our own transactional code – starting a transaction, writing all the data, then committing the transaction – it can become a lot of work. MTS hides all the complexity of managing transactions from us – allowing us to write simple, modular code to interact with the database and allowing MTS to ensure that the data is written with integrity.

Even better, MTS will take care of transactions that span multiple database server machines. This is virtually impossible to do by hand as it is so complex. MTS makes use of the Distributed Transaction Coordinator (DTC) to provide this support behind the scenes – giving us an incredibly powerful environment in which to work.

MTS should be seriously considered for every application with transactional requirements, which means virtually every application you can think of. Without MTS we must write all our data access code with transactions in mind – but with MTS we can just write code and let MTS worry about the details.

The other primary reason for using MTS is scalability. A primary reason for implementing an *n*-tier application is to support large numbers of concurrent users. While MTS is not required in this context, it does simplify things dramatically. Without MTS we'll need to come up with some way to manage the threads used by our application, monitor the usage of our application's objects, shut down server components and so on.

MTS provides a good management console for our middle tier, providing all these services for monitoring and controlling our components. Additionally, building our applications to make use of MTS today will also strategically position them for an easy transition to COM+ when it becomes available.

If you will be running this object within MTS, change the MTSTransactionMode property to 2-RequiresTransaction. Since this is a top-level parent object that has child objects, the entire operation of saving the `Client` and any associated `Project` objects needs to be wrapped within a transaction. This will ensure that they are all saved or that none of them are saved – so the database won't be left in an indeterminate state.

The available options for the MTSTransactionMode property are:

Value	Description
0-NotAnMTSObject	(default) This object is totally unaware of MTS and may not play by its rules.
1-NoTransactions	This object is aware of MTS but will not participate in any transactions.
2-RequiresTransaction	This object must run within the context of an MTS transaction. If one is already started it will join in, otherwise it will start a new transaction.
3-UsesTransaction	This object will join into a transaction if one is already started – otherwise it will run outside the context of a transaction.
4-RequiresNewTransaction	This object not only requires a transaction, but it will *always* start a new transaction – even if one is already started.

By setting our ClientPersist object to **2-RequiresTransaction** we've indicated that it will either join into a transaction if one is started, or it will start one if one isn't already going. In most cases, this will mean that a new transaction will be started any time we go to save our Client object's data.

We'll also set the ProjectPersist object to **2-RequiresTransaction** so it will join into the transaction started by the ClientPersist object – thus telling MTS to transactionally protect both the ClientPersist and ProjectPersist objects within the same transaction.

> **The code shown here detects whether it is being run in MTS, so it can be run in or out of MTS. However, to properly run this code without MTS you would need to rewrite the code to provide your own transactional support, since this code lets MTS deal with those details.**

To use MTS within our project, we must first add a reference to the Microsoft Transaction Server Type Library. This is done using the Project | References menu option and then selecting the item as shown in the diagram:

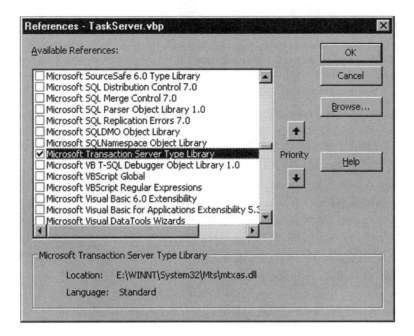

Adding this library makes the features of MTS available for use by our application.

While we're adding references, add a reference to the Microsoft ActiveX Data Objects 2.1 Library. As we'll be using ADO for data access, this reference will be required.

> *Note that I didn't indicate the library version here. I'm using version 2.1, but you could use version 2.1 or higher with no problem. Visual Basic Service Pack 3 provides this new version of ADO.*

Getting ObjectContext

There are two important factors to deal with when coding for MTS.

First, we need a reference to the `ObjectContext` object for our data-centric business object. The `ObjectContext` is what allows us to interact with MTS, which we need to do in order to tell MTS whether each individual method succeeds or fails.

Second, we can implement the `ObjectControl` interface so MTS can tell our object when it is about to be used and when it is done being used via the `ObjectControl_Activate` and `ObjectControl_Deactivate` events. These events are particularly useful for retrieving and destroying a reference to the `ObjectContext` object.

We'll also add some code to make debugging easier. We may want to run our code outside of MTS in order to test it more easily – for instance stepping through the code in the Visual Basic IDE to use the debugger. This is easily done by adding a Boolean variable (`mflgInMTS`) to indicate whether we are running within MTS or not. If we are not running in MTS we can use this variable to skip past MTS-specific code in our program.

In the declarations section of the `ClientPersist` class module add the following code.

```
Option Explicit

Implements ObjectControl

Private mobjContext As ObjectContext
Private mflgInMTS As Boolean
```

Then add the following code to implement the `ObjectControl` interface and to create and destroy a reference to our `ObjectContext` object.

> Note that we also set the **mflgInMTS** variable to **True** in the **ObjectControl_Activate** event. The variable will of course default to the **False** value. Since **ObjectControl_Activate** will *only* be run if we are in MTS, it will only be set to **True** in the case that we are in an MTS environment. Thus we can use this variable to determine whether MTS-specific code should be run throughout the rest of the module.

```
Private Sub ObjectControl_Activate()
   Set mobjContext = GetObjectContext
   mflgInMTS = True
End Sub

Private Function ObjectControl_CanBePooled() As Boolean
   ObjectControl_CanBePooled = False
End Function

Private Sub ObjectControl_Deactivate()
   Set mobjContext = Nothing
End Sub
```

It is important to note that the `ObjectControl_CanBePooled` function is set to return `False`. At this time, MTS doesn't provide any form of object pooling, so the return value is ignored. However, in the future object pooling will be supported. At this time we do not know whether Visual Basic objects will support object pooling appropriately or not. So far Microsoft has indicated that Visual Basic 6.0 objects won't support pooling properly. By returning `False` from this function we are hedging our bets – hopefully ensuring that our application will continue to run even after object pooling is introduced in COM+.

As we implement the `Fetch`, `Save` and `DeleteObject` methods, we can now use the `mobjContext` variable to interact with MTS. Within each method we'll call the `SetComplete` and `SetAbort` methods on this object to inform MTS whether the method completes successfully or whether it fails.

Fetch Method

The `Fetch` method is called by the `Client` object to retrieve data for a specific client – and to retrieve any associated project data. Enter the following code:

```
Public Function Fetch(ByVal ID As Long, Projects As String) As String
  Dim rsClient As Recordset
  Dim strSQL As String
  Dim udtProps As ClientProps
  Dim udtData As ClientData
  Dim objPersist As ProjectPersist

  Set rsClient = New Recordset
  strSQL = "SELECT * FROM CLIENTS WHERE ID=" & CStr(ID)
  rsClient.Open strSQL, DB_CONN, _
    adOpenForwardOnly, adLockReadOnly
  On Error GoTo ERRH
  If Not rsClient.EOF Then
    With udtProps
      .ID = rsClient("ID")
      .Name = rsClient("Name")
      .ContactName = rsClient("ContactName")
      .Phone = rsClient("Phone")
      .IsNew = False
      .IsDirty = False
      .IsDeleted = False
    End With
    rsClient.Close
    Set rsClient = Nothing
    LSet udtData = udtProps
    Fetch = udtData.Buffer

    If mflgInMTS = True Then
      Set objPersist = mobjContext.CreateInstance("TaskServer.ProjectPersist")
    Else
      Set objPersist = CreateObject("TaskServer.ProjectPersist")
    End If

    Projects = objPersist.Fetch(ID)
    Set objPersist = Nothing
  Else
    ' force an error
    rsClient.MoveNext
  End If
  If mflgInMTS = True Then mobjContext.SetComplete
  Exit Function

ERRH:
  If Not rsClient Is Nothing Then
    rsClient.Close
    Set rsClient = Nothing
  End If
  If mflgInMTS = True Then mobjContext.SetAbort
  Err.Raise Err.Number
End Function
```

The bulk of this code creates a `Recordset` object to retrieve the appropriate client data from the database, stores it in the `ClientProps` UDT, converts it to a `String` by using the `LSet` statement and then returns that as the result of the function.

The remaining code creates an instance of the `ProjectPersist` object and uses its `Fetch` method to retrieve a `String` variable that contains the state data for all child objects associated with this client.

If we are in MTS we must use the `CreateInstance` method to create the `ProjectPersist` object to ensure that it will participate in the same transaction as the current `ClientPersist` object. However, if we are not running in MTS we should use the standard `CreateObject` method. To determine whether we are in MTS or not the code checks the `mflgInMTS` flag that we set earlier in the module.

The `mflgInMTS` flag is also checked prior to the calls to `SetComplete` and `SetAbort`. In this way the code will only attempt to call these methods if our component is running within MTS.

Notice that the `Projects` parameter on this `Fetch` method is *not* declared using the `ByVal` keyword. This is important, since this parameter is used to return the child objects' state data back to the client workstation.

Save Method

As with the `Fetch` method, the `Save` method is responsible for not only saving the client data, but also all the data for the associated projects. Enter the following code.

```
Public Function Save(ByVal Buffer As String, Projects As String) As String
    Dim rsClient As Recordset
    Dim strSQL As String
    Dim udtProps As ClientProps
    Dim udtData As ClientData
    Dim objPersist As ProjectPersist

    udtData.Buffer = Buffer
    LSet udtProps = udtData

    strSQL = "SELECT * FROM CLIENTS WHERE ID=" & CStr(udtProps.ID)
    Set rsClient = New Recordset
    rsClient.Open strSQL, DB_CONN, adOpenKeyset, adLockOptimistic
    On Error GoTo ERRH
    If udtProps.IsNew Then rsClient.AddNew

    With udtProps
        rsClient("Name") = .Name
        rsClient("ContactName") = .ContactName
        rsClient("Phone") = .Phone
        rsClient.Update
        If .IsNew Then
            rsClient.Bookmark = rsClient.Bookmark
            .ID = rsClient("ID")
        End If
        .IsNew = False
        .IsDirty = False
    End With
    rsClient.Close
    Set rsClient = Nothing

    If mflgInMTS = True Then
        Set objPersist = mobjContext.CreateInstance("TaskServer.ProjectPersist")
    Else
        Set objPersist = CreateObject("TaskServer.ProjectPersist")
    End If

    Projects = objPersist.Save(Projects, udtProps.ID)
    Set objPersist = Nothing
```

```
    LSet udtData = udtProps
    Save = udtData.Buffer
    If mflgInMTS = True Then mobjContext.SetComplete
    Exit Function

ERRH:
  If Not rsClient Is Nothing Then
    rsClient.Close
    Set rsClient = Nothing
  End If
  If mflgInMTS = True Then mobjContext.SetAbort
  Err.Raise Err.Number
End Function
```

Most of this code handles the `Client` object's data – creating an ADO `Recordset` object and then using it to either update or add the data to the database.

A `ProjectPersist` object is also created and the `Project` parameter (containing all the state data for the child objects) is passed to its `Save` method for processing (we'll come back to the `ProjectPersist` object shortly).

Again we have the code to check `mflgInMTS` to determine whether to call the `CreateInstance` method of the context object or to just use `CreateObject`. It is also checked before the calls to `SetComplete` and `SetAbort` to ensure that they aren't called unless we're running inside MTS.

Notice that both the `Client` object's state and the child objects' state data is returned back to the client workstation once the update is complete. This is because the data may have been changed while it was being saved to the database.

An obvious example is where we are allowing the database to generate unique ID values for both `Client` and `Project` objects. These new ID values need to be returned to the UI-centric objects to keep them fully in sync with the data in the database.

DeleteObjectMethod

The final method on our `ClientPersist` object is the `DeleteObject` method. This method is not terribly complex, since it simply removes the appropriate client record from the database, along with any associated project records. Enter the following code:

```
Public Sub DeleteObject(ByVal ID As Long)
  Dim cnClient As Connection
  Dim strSQL As String
  Dim objPersist As ProjectPersist

  Set cnClient = New Connection
  On Error GoTo ERRH
  With cnClient
    .Open DB_CONN
    strSQL = "DELETE FROM CLIENTS WHERE ID=" & CStr(ID)
    .Execute strSQL
    .Close
  End With
  Set cnClient = Nothing

  If mflgInMTS = True Then
    Set objPersist = mobjContext.CreateInstance("TaskServer.ProjectPersist")
  Else
```

```
    Set objPersist = CreateObject("TaskServer.ProjectPersist")
  End If

  objPersist.DeleteObject ID
  Set objPersist = Nothing
  If mflgInMTS = True Then mobjContext.SetComplete
  Exit Sub

ERRH:
  Set cnClient = Nothing
  If mflgInMTS = True Then mobjContext.SetAbort
  Err.Raise Err.Number
End Sub
```

As with `Fetch` and `Save`, we first delete the client data and then use the `ProjectPersist` object to take care of the associated project data.

`mflgInMTS` is used to make sure that MTS-specific code isn't called unless the component is running within MTS.

With this method complete we've finished the `ClientPersist` object. Now would be a good time to save the project before we move on to create the last object in our application.

ProjectPersist Object

As we've already discussed, the `ProjectPersist` object is never called directly from the UI-centric objects. It is always called from the `ClientPersist` object as part of retrieving or saving data for a client.

This object will have three methods – `Fetch`, `Save` and `DeleteObject` – to handle all the data related to our `Project` objects.

Add a new standard class module to the `TaskServer` project. Change its name to `ProjectPersist`. If you will be running this object within MTS, change its **MTSTransactionMode** property to **2-RequiresTransaction**. Since `ProjectPersist` is managing child objects, we know that it must always be running within the context of a transaction to ensure that all the child objects are saved along with the parent object.

> *It would be nice if we could set the object's Instancing property to PublicNotCreatable. Unfortunately, this setting is incompatible with MTS. All objects running within MTS are actually created by MTS. This means that they are created by something external to our component itself, and so they must be marked as publically creatable.*

> **Again, the code shown here detects whether it is being run in MTS, so it can be run in or out of MTS. However, to properly run this code without MTS you would need to rewrite the code to provide your own transactional support, since this code lets MTS deal with those details.**

As with the `ClientPersist` object, this object will contain code to avoid calling MTS-specific methods if the component is not running within MTS. This facilitates debugging of the application by allowing us to run the code within the Visual Basic IDE or where MTS is unavailable for debugging purposes.

Getting ObjectContext

As in the `ClientPersist` object, we'll need to add code so we can interact effectively with MTS.

In the declarations section of the `ProjectPersist` class module add the following code.

```
Option Explicit
```

```
Implements ObjectControl

Private mobjContext As ObjectContext
Private mflgInMTS As Boolean
```

As with the `ClientPersist` object, we've declared the `mflgInMTS` variable for use throughout the module in determining whether the component is being run within MTS. The `ObjectControl_Activate` method is only called if we're running within MTS, so this variable will remain set to `False` unless that method is called.

Then add the following code to implement the `ObjectControl` interface and to create and destroy a reference to our `ObjectContext` object.

```
Private Sub ObjectControl_Activate()
  Set mobjContext = GetObjectContext
  mflgInMTS = True
End Sub

Private Function ObjectControl_CanBePooled() As Boolean
  ObjectControl_CanBePooled = False
End Function

Private Sub ObjectControl_Deactivate()
  Set mobjContext = Nothing
End Sub
```

As we implement the `Fetch`, `Save` and `DeleteObject` methods, we can now use the `mobjContext` variable to interact with MTS. Within each method we'll call the `SetComplete` and `SetAbort` methods on this object to inform MTS whether the method completes successfully or whether it fails.

Fetch Method

The `Fetch` method is called from the `ClientPersist` object to retrieve all the project data for a given client. `Fetch` accepts just one parameter – the `ID` value for the client being retrieved. This value is a foreign key for the project data, and is used to find all the appropriate project data for that client.

Enter the following code.

```
Public Function Fetch(ByVal Client As Long) As String
  Dim rsProject As Recordset
  Dim strSQL As String
  Dim udtProps As ProjectProps
  Dim udtData As ProjectData
  Dim objBuffer As Buffer

Set rsProject = New Recordset
  strSQL = "SELECT * FROM PROJECTS WHERE Client=" & CStr(Client)
  rsProject.Open strSQL, DB_CONN, _
    adOpenForwardOnly, adLockReadOnly
  Set objBuffer = New Buffer
  objBuffer.Initialize Len(udtData.Buffer), 10
  On Error GoTo ERRH
  Do While Not rsProject.EOF
    With udtProps
      .ID = rsProject("ID")
      .Name = rsProject("Name")
      .IsNew = False
      .IsDirty = False
      .IsDeleted = False
    End With
    LSet udtData = udtProps
    objBuffer.Add udtData.Buffer
    rsProject.MoveNext
  Loop
  rsProject.Close
  Set rsProject = Nothing
  Fetch = objBuffer.GetState
  If mflgInMTS = True Then mobjContext.SetComplete
  Exit Function

ERRH:
  If Not rsProject Is Nothing Then
    rsProject.Close
    Set rsProject = Nothing
  End If
  If mflgInMTS = True Then mobjContext.SetAbort
  Err.Raise Err.Number
End Function
```

Notice that the `Client` parameter is declared using the `ByVal` keyword for performance reasons.

As we retrieve each row of project data from the database it is stored in the `ProjectProps` UDT, converted to `ProjectData` with the `LSet` command and then stored in a `Buffer` object. The final result is a single `String` variable that contains all the data for our `Project` objects.

Before calling either `SetComplete` or `SetAbort`, the `mflgInMTS` flag is checked. The code is only run if the component is running within MTS.

Save Method

The `Save` method is called from the `ClientPersist` object to save all the project data for a given client. `Save` accepts two parameters, the combined state data for all the `Project` objects, and the `ClientID` value that will act as a foreign key to link all the project data back to the appropriate client.

Enter the following code.

```
Public Function Save(ByVal Buffer As String, ByVal ClientID As Long) As String
   Dim rsProject As Recordset
   Dim strSQL As String
   Dim udtProps As ProjectProps
   Dim udtData As ProjectData
   Dim objBuffer As Buffer
   Dim objNewBuffer As Buffer
Dim lngIndex As Long

   Set objBuffer = New Buffer
   With objBuffer
     .SetState Buffer

     Set objNewBuffer = New Buffer
     objNewBuffer.Initialize .Length, .Count
   End With

   Set rsProject = New Recordset

   On Error GoTo ERRH
   For lngIndex = 1 To objBuffer.Count
     udtData.Buffer = objBuffer.Item(lngIndex)
     LSet udtProps = udtData

     If Not udtProps.IsDeleted Then
       strSQL = "SELECT * FROM PROJECTS WHERE ID=" & CStr(udtProps.ID)
       rsProject.Open strSQL, DB_CONN, adOpenKeyset, adLockOptimistic
       If udtProps.IsNew Then rsProject.AddNew

       With udtProps
         rsProject("Name") = .Name
         rsProject("Client") = ClientID
         rsProject.Update
         If .IsNew Then
           rsProject.Bookmark = rsProject.Bookmark
           .ID = rsProject("ID")
         End If
         .IsNew = False
         .IsDirty = False
       End With
       LSet udtData = udtProps
       objNewBuffer.Add udtData.Buffer
       rsProject.Close
     Else
       DeleteObject udtProps.ID
     End If
   Next

   Set objBuffer = Nothing
   Set rsProject = Nothing

   Save = objNewBuffer.GetState
   Set objNewBuffer = Nothing
   If mflgInMTS = True Then mobjContext.SetComplete
   Exit Function

ERRH:
```

```
      Set objBuffer = Nothing
      Set objNewBuffer = Nothing
      Set rsProject = Nothing
      If mflgInMTS = True Then mobjContext.SetAbort
      Err.Raise Err.Number
   End Function
```

Both parameters are declared using the `ByVal` keyword to ensure that they are not passed back to the calling code unnecessarily.

This routine unpacks the state data parameter using a `Buffer` object. It then loops through all the elements in the `Buffer` object, copying each one into a `ProjectProps` UDT variable to get at the detailed state information.

Each object is deleted, added or updated into the database as appropriate.

Before calling either `SetComplete` or `SetAbort`, the `mflgInMTS` flag is checked. The code is only run if the component is running within MTS.

Since we're potentially deleting or changing the state data of various objects within this procedure, we create a *new* `Buffer` object to contain the resulting data. Deleted `Project` objects are not copied into the new `Buffer`, while new and updated state data is copied into the new `Buffer` after the database operations are complete.

This resulting data in the new `Buffer` object is returned as a result of the method. It will be returned to the UI-centric objects by the `ClientPersist` object – allowing the UI-centric `Client` object to refresh the data for all its child objects so they are in sync with the data in the database.

DeleteObject Method

The last method we need to add is the `DeleteObject` method. `DeleteObject` is called from the `ClientPersist` object's `DeleteObject` method to remove all the project data for the client that was just deleted. The `ClientID` value is passed as a parameter that we can use as a foreign key to delete the appropriate records.

Enter the following code.

```
Public Sub DeleteObject(ByVal ClientID As Long)
   Dim cnProject As Connection
   Dim strSQL As String

   Set cnProject = New Connection
   On Error GoTo ERRH
   With cnProject
     .Open DB_CONN
     strSQL = "DELETE FROM PROJECTS WHERE CLIENT=" & CStr(ClientID)
     .Execute strSQL
     .Close
   End With
   Set cnProject = Nothing
   If mflgInMTS = True Then mobjContext.SetComplete
   Exit Sub

ERRH:
   Set cnProject = Nothing
   If mflgInMTS = True Then mobjContext.SetAbort
   Err.Raise Err.Number
End Sub
```

This routine simply opens a connection to the database and then executes a SQL statement to delete all the project data associated with the client in question.

Before calling either `SetComplete` or `SetAbort`, the `mflgInMTS` flag is checked. The code is only run if the component is running within MTS.

Save the project – and now it is complete. We've developed both the UI-centric and data-centric objects for our application. Once we've built the database our objects will be fully operational.

> *In Chapter 3 we'll enhance the application so it tracks specific tasks for each project. Just at the moment though, the CSLA techniques we've been using to handle child objects make it very difficult to implement such objects.*

Compiling the Project

In order to use our objects within MTS we need to compile our DLL. This is done by choosing the File | Make TaskServer.dll menu option.

> **Once we've compiled the DLL the first time, it is of critical importance that we make a copy of our DLL and change the compatibility setting of the project to Binary Compatibility, ensuring that it remains compatible with this copy.**

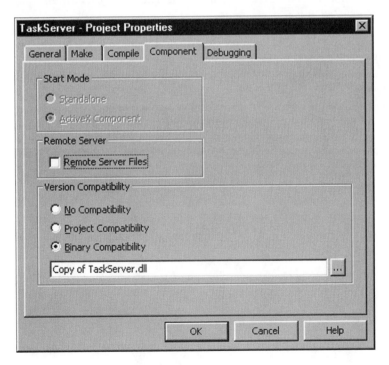

The reasoning behind this is explained in detail in Visual Basic 6 Business Objects.

In summary, the default setting for Version Compatibility doesn't ensure that the unique GUID (global unique identifier) values for our COM component or the classes within it will remain constant. By default, we may get new values assigned each time we compile the component – making it very difficult for MTS or our client applications to consistently interact with our objects.

Binary Compatibility helps ensure that the GUID values associated with our COM server and its classes remain consistent (based on certain rules). By changing this setting our component will play nicely in the COM world by retaining its identifying ID values each time it is compiled.

Microsoft recommends setting binary compatibility to a *copy* of the server rather than to the DLL we compile each time. This is done to provide long-term consistency of the component. If we are always compatible with the previous compile it can be far too easy to change the component – breaking compatibility with all client programs.

Using MTS

Now that we have a compiled DLL, we need to add it to MTS so it can run in that environment. This is easily done – in fact it is just a drag and drop operation.

Before we can drag our DLL into MTS, however, we need to add an MTS package to hold the component. Packages are important in MTS, as they contain components. Many components (DLLs) can be installed into a single MTS package.

Each package provides a single process within which objects can run. All the objects within a given package will run inside the same process. This means that the objects within a package can communicate quite efficiently.

It also means they share the same memory space. Thus, if one crashes, all the other objects running in that package may crash along with it.

Creating a Package

Creating a package is done by using the **Microsoft Transaction Server Explorer**. The option for this tool is typically found under the Start | Programs | Windows Option Pack menu.

Bring up the explorer and open the Computers\My Computer\Packages Installed entries in the left-hand pane.

Then right-click on Packages Installed and choose the New | Package entry.

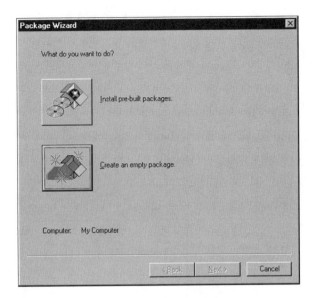

This simple wizard will help us create a package. Since our package is new, choose the Create an empty package option.

The next page prompts for the name of the package. Enter TaskServer as the name and click the Next button.

This last tab is the most complex. Here we choose the user under which the component will be run. The default is to run the component under the currently logged in user – however this is almost never the correct setting since it is hard to predict who, if anyone, will be logged into our server machine.

The better choice is to pick a specific user under which the components in the package will be run.

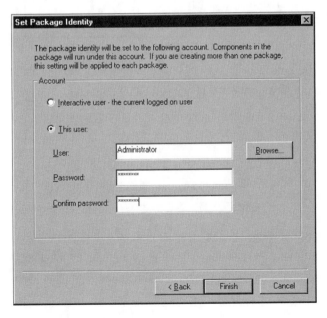

In this diagram I've chosen to run the package under the Administrator user.

Once done click Finish to add the package to MTS.

Installing TaskServer into MTS

Installing the DLL into the package is a drag and drop operation. Click the + to expand the tree for the TaskServer package. You'll see the Components and Roles entries.

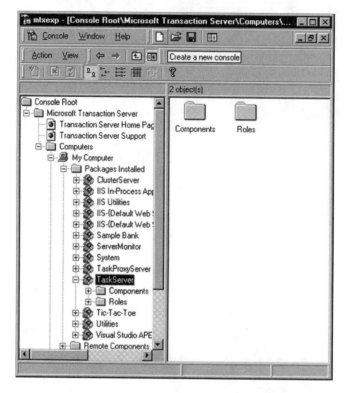

Now open up a regular explorer window to the directory where the TaskServer.dll file is located.

Simply drag the DLL into the Components folder in the MTS Explorer.

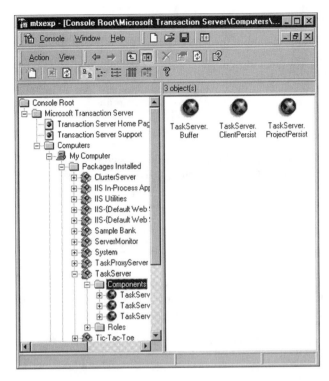

And that's it. Now, any time one of our objects is accessed it will be run inside the context of MTS.

Adding a Reference from TaskObjects

With our data-centric objects created and compiled and installed into MTS, we need to briefly return to the `TaskObjects` project and give it a reference to our data-centric objects.

Open the `TaskObjects` project in Visual Basic and choose the Project | References menu option. In the resulting dialog, find and select the entry for TaskServer from the list and click OK.

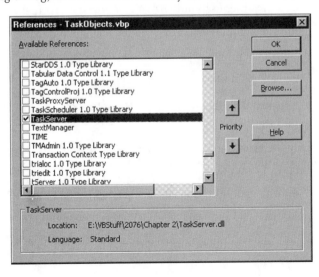

Now our UI-centric objects are aware of, and can interact with, our data-centric objects.

With this done we can create any number of different UIs to interact with these objects. Since they are COM objects, other applications can incorporate our UI-centric objects into their processing, providing unparalleled flexibility and reuse of code.

At this point we should compile the `TaskObjects` project to create its DLL for use by our user interface.

> As with the `TaskServer` project, the `TaskObjects` project should also be set for **Binary Compatibility**. Otherwise the GUID values are subject to change – which could break the user interface programs built to use those objects.

Data Tables

The Task Manager application's business logic and basic processing is complete now that we've created all the business objects. However, our data-centric objects are built to interact with a database, so we need to create that database with the appropriate tables.

The SQL used in the data-centric business objects is not complex. Virtually any relational database can handle those statements – which is a powerful benefit of this type of application model.

The only real constraint we have on the database is that it is expected to automatically generate unique ID values for any new client or project we add. Most databases provide this type of capability. SQL Server provides it via the `Identity` flag on a column, while Access provides it via the `Autonumber` data type.

I will be using Microsoft SQL Server 7.0 throughout this book. While other databases can certainly be used in its place, the examples will be for SQL Server and can be translated for use with any other database as desired.

As mentioned earlier, the connection string used in the `TaskServer` project is specific to this database. If you are using a different type of database you'll need to change the provider and database server name as appropriate.

Creating the Database

Visual Basic 6.0 provides us with some powerful capabilities for dealing with database tables through the Data View window. One key capability *not* provided by the Data View window is that of creating a database to start with.

To create a database we can use the Microsoft SQL Server Enterprise Manager application. This application allows us to manage virtually all aspects of the SQL Server itself and the databases it contains. Through this application we can create the database, as well as any tables or other objects we might need. In this case however, we'll create the database using the Enterprise Manager and then use Visual Basic's Data View window to add our tables.

Open the Enterprise Manager and select the SQL Server with which we'll be working. In the left-hand pane of the application you should see a list of the entities within this server, including an entry for Databases.

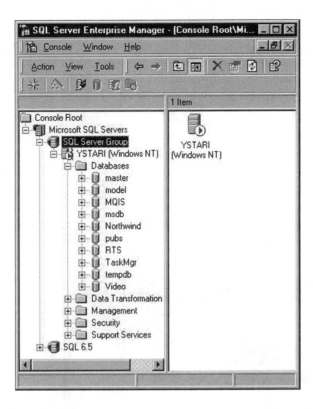

Right-click on the Databases entry and choose the New Database menu item to bring up a
Database Properties dialog. Enter TaskMgr into the Name field of this dialog. Click the Initial size
(MB) entry in the table and change the starting size of our database to 10 megabytes.

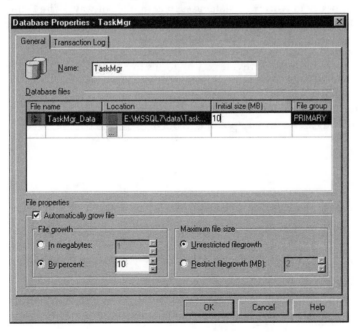

Once that's done, click the OK button to create the database.

That's it. SQL Server 7.0 makes this process substantially easier than previous versions of the product!

Now close the Enterprise Manager application. We'll add our tables to the database using Visual Basic's new Data View window.

Adding the Tables

Our database isn't very complex. We'll have a table for our Client objects' information and a table for our Project objects' information and that's it. In Chapter 3 we'll add a table to store information about the Task objects that we'll add, but we won't worry about that for now.

Open Visual Basic and bring up the TaskServer project. Choose the View | Data View Window menu option to bring up the Data View window.

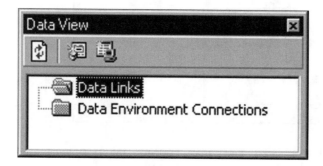

The Data View window allows us to work with databases in a number of ways. The Data Environment Connections entry provides a way for us to interact with DataEnvironment objects in our project, although we won't be using this capability in this book.

The Data Links entry, on the other hand, provides a way for us to create a link directly to a data source and work with that data source in a number of ways. This is the entry we'll be using here.

Right-click on Data Links and choose the Add a Data Link... menu option. This will bring up a Data Link Properties dialog that we can use to set up a link to our TaskMgr database.

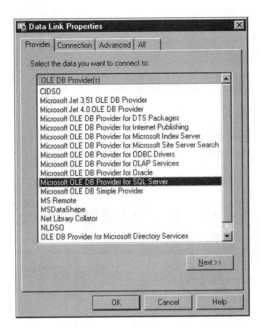

Choose the Microsoft OLE DB Provider for SQL Server entry (or an entry appropriate for your database if that is different) and click the Next button. This will switch the display to allow us to enter specific connection information for our data source.

If no OLE DB provider exists for your database, you can select the Microsoft OLE DB Provider for ODBC Drivers and use an existing ODBC DSN to gain access to your database.

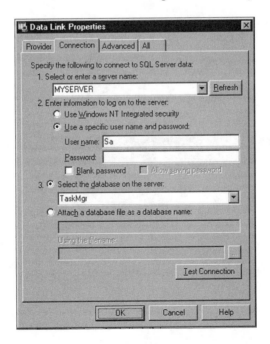

Fill in the entries as shown (substituting the MYSERVER entry for the name of your server).

Typical entries that must be filled in include the database server name, a user name and password for logging into the server and the name of the database within the server – in this case TaskMgr.

Note that this tab may appear differently for other data providers.

Once that's done click the OK button and we're on our way. Back in the Data View window, change the name of this new data link to TaskMgr. To do this, right-click on the entry and choose the Rename menu option, then type in the new name.

Click on the + symbol to the left of the entry to expand the tree.

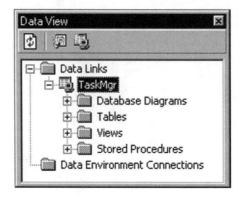

Clients Table

While there are a number of activities we can perform at this point, our interest is in adding tables to our database. To do this, right-click on the Tables entry and choose the New Table... menu option.

When prompted for the table name, enter Clients and click OK.

We'll be presented with a form where we can set up all the fields within our table. Make the entries as shown in the diagram.

Column Name	Datatype	Length	Precision	Scale	Allow Nulls	Default Value	Identity	Identity Seed	Identity Increment
ID	int	4	10	0			✓	1	1
Name	varchar	50	0	0					
ContactName	varchar	50	0	0	✓				
Phone	varchar	25	0	0	✓				

To set the primary key on the table, right-click just to the left of the Column Name column for the ID field and choose the Set Primary Key menu option.

Also notice that the ID column has the Identity entry checked. This is used to indicate that the database itself should generate unique values for this column. The Identity Seed indicates the starting value for the field, and the Identity Increment column tells the database how to increment that value for each new row in the table.

Close this window. You will be prompted for whether you want to save changes to the table, so choose Yes. The table will be added to the SQL Server database and is ready for our use.

Projects Table

We'll add the Projects table the same way. Just right-click on the Tables item in the Data View window and choose the New Table... menu option.

Name the new table Projects and fill in the form so it appears as shown in the diagram.

Column Name	Datatype	Length	Precision	Scale	Allow Nulls	Default Value	Identity	Identity Seed	Identity Increment
ID	int	4	10	0			✓	1	1
Name	varchar	50	0	0					
Client	int	4	10	0					

To set the primary key on the table, right-click just to the left of the Column Name column for the ID field and choose the Set Primary Key menu option.

Close this window. You will be prompted for whether you want to save changes to the table, so choose Yes.

Now both our business objects have tables in which to store their data. At this point our business objects should be fully functional and ready for use by any UI or COM-compliant client program.

A Simple User Interface

So far in this chapter we've created UI-centric business objects to provide a logical model of our business entities and concepts. We then moved on to create their counterparts, the data-centric objects that retrieve and store data, providing a mapping function between the object-oriented UI-centric objects and the relational database. Most recently we added a database and tables within Microsoft SQL Server so our objects have somewhere to store their data.

All that remains for a fully functional application is to create a user interface. The CSLA supports many different types of user interface, including:

- Visual Basic form-based interface
- Microsoft Office (VBA) interface
- Simple HTML browser-based interface using IIS Applications, ASP or similar technologies
- Intelligent browser-based interface using DHTML Applications, ActiveX components or similar technologies
- Any COM-compliant development tool

To keep our application as simple as possible, and so I can illustrate all the concepts covered throughout the book, we'll create a simple Visual Basic form-based user interface. In keeping with the theme of creating a simple application that doesn't distract us from examining the concepts we'll be covering through the book, this UI will be quite simplistic – providing merely the basic functionality that we might expect from a UI.

The two main forms in the UI will be a `ClientEdit` form that we can use to add and edit `Client` objects, and a `ProjectEdit` form that allows the user to add or edit `Project` objects.

In a regular application we'd probably also have a screen that allows us to browse for specific `Client` objects. This would require us to create a couple of new UI-centric business objects – `Clients` and `ClientDisplay`.

Objects of this type are covered in *Visual Basic 6 Business Objects* and would easily fit into the application we've developed so far. These objects would provide the capability to retrieve a set of client data from the database for display to the user. Once the user chooses a client from the list the appropriate `Client` object can be loaded for use by the user.

To keep our UI as simple as possible, we'll just create a simple form that just prompts for the `Client` object's ID value and loads a `Client` object based on that value.

Setting up the Project

Open up a new Standard EXE project in Visual Basic. Change the project's name to `TaskManager` using the Project | Properties menu option.

Since this project will make heavy use of our UI-centric business objects, we'll need to add a reference to the `TaskObjects` DLL. To do this, use the Project | References menu option to bring up the appropriate dialog. Find and select the entry for TaskObjects and click OK.

There are a couple of utility routines that we'll be using across our forms. These were discussed in Visual Basic 6 Business objects, and provide a very nice way to standardize the handling of the `Change` and `LostFocus` events for all `TextBox` controls on our forms. The routines are based on the new `CallByName` command available in Visual Basic 6.0.

Add a new BAS module to the project and name it `TUImain`. Enter the following code into the module.

```
Option Explicit
```

```
Public Sub TextChange(Ctl As TextBox, Obj As Object, Prop As String)
  Dim lngPos As Long

  On Error GoTo INPUTERR
  CallByName Obj, Prop, VbLet, Ctl.Text
  Exit Sub

INPUTERR:
  Beep
  lngPos = Ctl.SelStart
  Ctl = CallByName(Obj, Prop, VbGet)
  If LmgPos > 0 Then Ctl.SelStart = lngPos - 1
End Sub

Public Function TextLostFocus(Obj As Object, Prop As String) As String
  TextLostFocus = CallByName(Obj, Prop, VbGet)
End Function
```

We will call the TextChange routine from within the Change event handler for each TextBox on our forms. It places the current value from the TextBox control into the appropriate property on the business object.

Likewise, the TextLostFocus routine will be called from the LostFocus event handler for each TextBox control. This routine retrieves the current value from the business object and updates the display in the TextBox control so they are kept in sync.

Now that our project's properties are set up and we've added our common utility routines, we can move on to add our forms.

The Startup Form

The first form we'll create is the simplest. In a full-blown UI we'd probably provide some browsing capability to allow the user to select a client and then edit it. To keep this application as simple as possible, we'll replace that capability with a much simpler screen – one that prompts the user for the ID number of a client and brings up that client for editing.

Select the Form1 that was automatically added to the new project and change its name to StartForm.

Add controls to the form as shown in the diagram.

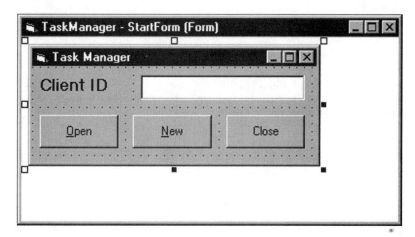

Control	Type	Value
Label1	Label	Client ID
txtID	TextBox	
cmdOpen	CommandButton	&Open
cmdNew	CommandButton	&New
cmdClose	CommandButton	Close

There's no code behind either the Label or TextBox controls on this form, so we can move on and examine the code that goes behind each button.

Close Button

The button `cmdClose` has the simplest code. All it needs to do is close down our application by unloading the current form. Enter the following code.

```
Private Sub cmdClose_Click()
   Unload Me
End Sub
```

When the user clicks Close, the form will be unloaded and the application will end.

New Button

The New button is designed to allow the user to add a new client to the system. Enter the following code.

```
Private Sub cmdNew_Click()
   Dim objClient As Client
   Dim frmClient As ClientEdit

   Set objClient = New Client
   Set frmClient = New ClientEdit

   frmClient.Component objClient
   frmClient.Show vbModal

   Set frmClient = Nothing
   Set objClient = Nothing
End Sub
```

This code creates a new `Client` object and an instance of the `ClientEdit` form that we'll create next. The form is provided a reference to the new `Client` object by using a `Component` method and then it is shown modally to the user.

By showing the form modally we are keeping our UI as simple as possible. Since the `ClientEdit` form is modal, there is no way for the user to return to the `StartForm` without closing the `ClientEdit` form by clicking OK or Cancel.

The code we've implemented here does not guarantee that a new `Client` object will be added to the database. That depends entirely on the user clicking OK or Apply on the `ClientEdit` form to save the object. If the user uses the Cancel button to leave the `ClientEdit` form then the `Client` object we've created here will be discarded and never saved to the database.

Open Button

The Open button allows the user to bring up an existing `Client` object for editing. It first needs to ensure that the user has entered a value into the `txtID` field on the screen.

We also need to take into account that the ID value entered by the user might not be valid. We can trap this by adding error handling code when we call the `Load` method of our `Client` object.

Enter the following code.

```
Private Sub cmdOpen_Click()
  Dim objClient As Client
  Dim frmClient As ClientEdit

  If Val(txtID) > 0 Then
    Set objClient = New Client
    On Error Resume Next
    objClient.Load Val(txtID)
    If Err Then
      MsgBox "Client ID not on file", vbExclamation
      Exit Sub
    End If
    On Error GoTo 0
    Set frmClient = New ClientEdit
    frmClient.Component objClient
    frmClient.Show vbModal
  Else
    MsgBox "You must supply a value", vbInformation
  End If
  Set frmClient = Nothing
  Set objClient = Nothing
End Sub
```

Notice how the code creates an instance of the ClientEdit *form, sets a property on it and then explicitly calls the* Show *method. An interesting thing to note about forms in Visual Basic is that they are essentially a specialized form of class – thus we can manipulate and work with them just like any other object without ever making the form visible to the user.*

Assuming that the user has entered a number into the txtID field and that the Load method succeeds, we simply create an instance of the ClientEdit form and give it a reference to our fully populated Client object by calling its Component method.

The form is then shown modally, just as with the **New** button's code. Whether any changes are actually made to the Client object is up to the user and is handled by the Client object and the ClientEdit form.

Now is a good time to save the project. Our first form is complete and we're ready to move on and create the ClientEdit form.

The ClientEdit Form

The ClientEdit form is quite a bit more complex than the StartForm we just created. This form needs to not only allow the user to edit the Client object itself, but it also needs to allow the user to add, edit and remove Project objects that are owned by the Client.

Add a new form module to the project and change its name to ClientEdit. You may choose to use the business form template from *Visual Basic 6 Business Objects* to minimize the amount of code to be entered. If you are using the template, make the code changes as highlighted – otherwise enter all the code shown in this section.

Add controls as shown in the diagram.

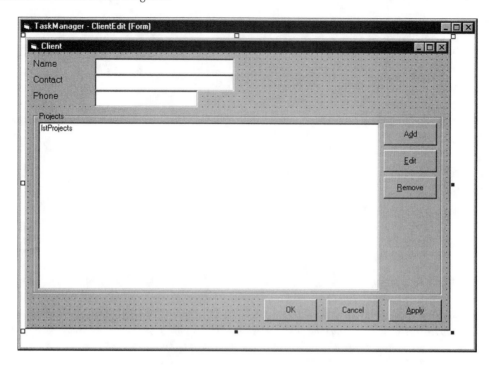

Control	Type	Value
Label1	Label	Name
Label2	Label	Contact
Label3	Label	Phone
txtName	TextBox	
txtContactName	TextBox	
txtPhone	TextBox	
cmdOK	CommandButton	OK
cmdCancel	CommandButton	Cancel
cmdApply	CommandButton	&Apply
Frame1	Frame	Projects
lstProjects	ListBox	
cmdAdd	CommandButton	A&dd
cmdEdit	CommandButton	&Edit
cmdRemove	CommandButton	&Remove

Business Form Common Code

There is quite a bit of code that is common to all CSLA forms that edit business objects. This code is part of the business form template we created in *Visual Basic 6 Business Objects*, and is customized slightly for each form as shown here.

```
Option Explicit

Private mflgLoading As Boolean

Private WithEvents mobjClient As Client

Public Sub Component(ClientObject As Client)
   Set mobjClient = ClientObject
End Sub

Private Sub Form_Load()
   mflgLoading = True
   With mobjClient
      EnableOK .IsValid
      ' load object values into form controls
      txtName = .Name
      txtContactName = .ContactName
      txtPhone = .Phone
      ListProjects
      .BeginEdit
   End With
   mflgLoading = False
End Sub

Private Sub cmdOK_Click()
   mobjClient.ApplyEdit
   Unload Me
End Sub

Private Sub cmdCancel_Click()
   mobjClient.CancelEdit
   Unload Me
End Sub

Private Sub cmdApply_Click()
   mobjClient.ApplyEdit
   ListProjects
   mobjClient.BeginEdit
End Sub

Private Sub EnableOK(flgValid As Boolean)
   cmdOK.Enabled = flgValid
   cmdApply.Enabled = flgValid
End Sub

Private Sub mobjClient_Valid(IsValid As Boolean)
   EnableOK IsValid
End Sub
```

If using the template, most of these changes can be accomplished by doing a mass replace of the word 'Business' with the word 'Client' throughout the module.

This code lays the groundwork for our form, allowing the StartForm to provide a reference to our business object through the Component method and providing basic OK, Cancel and Apply functionality for our form.

103

TextBox Event Handling

Our form contains three TextBox controls to allow the user to edit the basic Client property values. We've already added two utility routines to our project to make working with TextBox controls easy – TextChange and TextLostFocus.

For each TextBox control's Change and LostFocus events, we'll simply add code to call these routines. Enter the following.

```
Private Sub txtContactName_Change()
  If mflgLoading Then Exit Sub

  TextChange txtContactName, mobjClient, "ContactName"
End Sub

Private Sub txtContactName_LostFocus()
  txtContactName = TextLostFocus(mobjClient, "ContactName")
End Sub

Private Sub txtName_Change()
  If mflgLoading Then Exit Sub

  TextChange txtName, mobjClient, "Name"
End Sub

Private Sub txtName_LostFocus()
  txtName = TextLostFocus(mobjClient, "Name")
End Sub

Private Sub txtPhone_Change()
  If mflgLoading Then Exit Sub

  TextChange txtPhone, mobjClient, "Phone"
End Sub

Private Sub txtPhone_LostFocus()
  txtPhone = TextLostFocus(mobjClient, "Phone")
End Sub
```

Each Change event also checks the mflgLoading variable. This is set to True while the form is loading, and during the process of initially setting all the form's values. We don't need to do any processing in the Change events. After all, during the load process we are copying values out of the object and into the form – there's no need to turn right around and copy those same values back into the object.

All that remains now is to add code to handle the child Project objects.

ListProjects Method

The Form_Load and cmdApply procedures each make calls to a ListProjects method. It is this method that loads the lstProjects ListBox control with the names of the child Project objects.

The code in this routine simply loops through the collection of Project objects associated with the Client object. Enter the following code:

```
Private Sub ListProjects()
  Dim objProject As Project
  Dim lngIndex As Long
```

```
      lstProjects.Clear
      For lngIndex = 1 To mobjClient.Projects.Count
        Set objProject = mobjClient.Projects(lngIndex)
        With objProject
          If .IsDeleted Then
            lstProjects.AddItem .Name & " (d)"
          ElseIf .IsNew Then
            lstProjects.AddItem .Name & " (new)"
          Else
            lstProjects.AddItem .Name
          End If
          lstProjects.ItemData(lstProjects.NewIndex) = lngIndex
        End With
      Next
    End Sub
```

Each `Project` is checked to see if it is new or has been marked for deletion. In these cases the display is altered to visually inform the user of the item's status. Additionally, the `ItemData` field for each element is set to the index value from the `Projects` collection – making it easy to return to that item when selected by the user.

Now that the child objects will be displayed, we can implement code behind the Add, Edit and Remove buttons to allow the user to manipulate the objects.

Add, Edit and Remove for Projects

All that remains is to allow the user to manipulate the child `Project` objects. The code to do this is very similar to that we used in the `StartForm` for the `Client` object.

To add a new `Project` object all we need to do is create an instance of the `ProjectEdit` form and pass it a reference to a new `Project` object. A new `Project` object can be created by calling the `Add` method on the `Projects` object. Enter the following:

```
    Private Sub cmdAdd_Click()
      Dim frmProject As ProjectEdit

      Set frmProject = New ProjectEdit
      frmProject.Component mobjClient.Projects.Add
      frmProject.Show vbModal
      ListProjects
      Set frmProject = Nothing
    End Sub
```

Editing a `Project` object is very similar, though instead of passing a reference to a new `Project` object, we'll provide a reference to the object selected on the form by the user. Remember that we stored the index value for each item in the list into the `ItemData` field of the `ListBox`, so we can simply use that value to retrieve the appropriate object from the `Projects` collection.

```
    Private Sub cmdEdit_Click()
      Dim frmProject As ProjectEdit

      Set frmProject = New ProjectEdit
      frmProject.Component _
        mobjClient.Projects(lstProjects.ItemData(lstProjects.ListIndex))
      frmProject.Show vbModal
      ListProjects
    End Sub
```

The final button requiring code is the Remove button. In some ways this is the easiest, since it doesn't even need to invoke the ProjectEdit form. Instead, we can simply call BeginEdit, Delete and ApplyEdit on the appropriate Project object; a sequence of calls which is carried out by the Remove method of the Projects object.

```
Private Sub cmdRemove_Click()
   mobjClient.Projects.Remove lstProjects.ItemData(lstProjects.ListIndex)
   ListProjects
End Sub
```

At the end of each routine we call the ListProjects method to ensure that the ListBox control contains a correct display of the child Project objects. This is important, since the user may have added, edited or deleted objects by the time each of these methods has completed.

That completes our ClientEdit form. All that remains is to add the ProjectEdit form and our application will be complete.

Now is a good time to save the project and protect the work we've done so far.

The ProjectEdit Form

Add a new form to the project and change its name to ProjectEdit. If you have the business form template from *Visual Basic 6 Business Objects*, use it to create this form and make the highlighted code changes. Otherwise add a standard form and enter all the code in this section.

Add controls to the form as shown in the diagram.

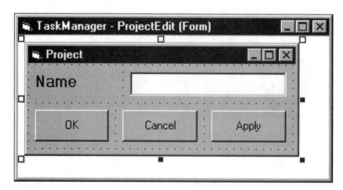

Control	Type	Value
Label1	Label	Name
txtName	TextBox	
cmdOK	CommandButton	OK
cmdClose	CommandButton	Cancel
cmdApply	CommandButton	&Apply

At this point the ProjectEdit form is very simplistic. In Chapter 3, when we add Task objects, this form will become more complex.

Business Form Common Code

As with the `ClientEdit` form, there is a fair amount of code that is quite standard for any form that interacts with a CSLA-based business object. Make the appropriate changes to the code as shown.

```
Option Explicit

Private mflgLoading As Boolean

Private WithEvents mobjProject As Project

Public Sub Component(ProjectObject As Project)
   Set mobjProject = ProjectObject
End Sub

Private Sub Form_Load()
  mflgLoading = True
  With mobjProject
    EnableOK .IsValid
    ' load object values into form controls
    txtName = .Name
    .BeginEdit
  End With
  mflgLoading = False
End Sub

Private Sub cmdOK_Click()
  mobjProject.ApplyEdit
  Unload Me
End Sub

Private Sub cmdCancel_Click()
  mobjProject.CancelEdit
  Unload Me
End Sub

Private Sub cmdApply_Click()
  mobjProject.ApplyEdit
  mobjProject.BeginEdit
End Sub

Private Sub EnableOK(flgValid As Boolean)
  cmdOK.Enabled = flgValid
  cmdApply.Enabled = flgValid
End Sub

Private Sub mobjProject_Valid(IsValid As Boolean)
  EnableOK IsValid
End Sub
```

If you are using the template, most of these changes can be accomplished by doing a mass replace of the word 'Business' with the word 'Project' throughout the module.

Given that our form is so simple in this case, there's not much left to do.

TextBox Event Handling

The only editable field on the form at this point is the TextBox that allows the user to edit the `Project` object's `Name` property. As with the TextBox controls on the `ClientEdit` form, we can use the `TextChange` and `TextLostFocus` utility procedures to make handling this control trivial.

107

```
Private Sub txtName_Change()
  If mflgLoading Then Exit Sub

  TextChange txtName, mobjProject, "Name"
End Sub

Private Sub txtName_LostFocus()
  txtName = TextLostFocus(mobjProject, "Name")
End Sub
```

Now we can save the project and we are all done.

At this point we should be able to run the program, adding and editing Client objects and their associated Project objects.

Summary

The CSLA provides a good foundation for creating distributed object applications in the Microsoft Windows environment. In this chapter we've created a basic application that allows a user to enter and edit information about their clients and to list the projects being done for each client.

While this is not a complex application, we have demonstrated how easy it is to create a basic distributed object application. It would be relatively easy to add new business objects to the application at this point – following the same structure and format as the existing objects.

In very short order we could easily have a complex set of UI-centric business objects on which we can build various UIs. At the same time, we'd have a corresponding set of data-centric objects handling data-oriented behaviors.

This type of application is very scalable since it distributes the processing between the client, application server and database server. It is also very flexible, since all our objects are COM objects and can be used by many different COM-compliant development tools and applications.

However, as was discussed in Chapter 1, there are some limitations to this architecture that can make it difficult to implement truly complex applications. Throughout the rest of the book we'll enhance the Task Manager application, using it to illustrate how we can overcome many of the most common problems faced by distributed object developers.

3

Complex Object State Rollback

Overview

In the first chapter of this book we defined distributed objects and reviewed the CSLA. The CSLA provides a good architecture for developing applications based on distributed objects.

In Chapter 2 we developed a basic application using the CSLA. The Task Manager system is an example of a distributed object application, since its objects are distributed between the client workstation and an application server running MTS. The design of the UI-centric objects follows object-oriented principles, but at the same time, the application's processing is distributed across several machines.

The Task Manager application, as it stands, has a parent Client object with a number of Project objects as children. The Client object owns the Project objects, and they are retrieved, stored and deleted along with the Client object itself. In this chapter we'll add Task objects, which are children of a Project object. Thus, they will effectively be grandchildren of the Client object.

In this chapter we'll cover the following topics:

- ❏ The concept of state stacking to allow *n*-level rollback
- ❏ A proof of concept example
- ❏ Adding tasks as grandchild objects to the Task Manager application
- ❏ Modifying the classes built in Chapter 2 to support state stacking
- ❏ Improving the handling of deleted child objects
- ❏ Updating the user interface to reflect these changes

N-level Rollback

The CSLA handles child objects just fine. However, the technique used to manage state for the child objects (ChildBeginEdit, ChildCancelEdit and ChildApplyEdit) doesn't work well for grandchild objects, great-grandchild objects and so forth.

Single-level Rollback

The BeginEdit, CancelEdit and ApplyEdit methods on each CSLA object provide a single level of rollback or undo. Once BeginEdit is called, any number of properties or methods can be called to change that object's state. To restore the object to the state it was in when BeginEdit was called, we implemented the CancelEdit method.

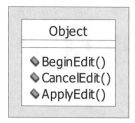

This is good for individual business objects, as it allows a UI developer to easily implement OK, Cancel and Apply buttons (or similar functionality) for any business object. Unfortunately, this technique doesn't help us with child objects.

For example, a user may begin editing a parent object, like a SalesOrder object. They may then choose to edit one or more of the child objects, perhaps LineItem objects.

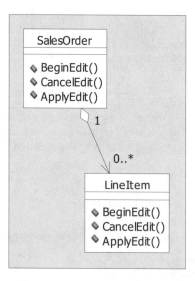

If the user clicks the OK button on a LineItem they expect that any changes to that object will be kept, and if they bring that object up in a form again, the changes should be reflected there. This much we can do with simple BeginEdit, CancelEdit and ApplyEdit functionality.

However, if the user cancels the `SalesOrder` object itself, they would naturally expect that the `SalesOrder` *and its child objects* would revert to the state they were in before any editing took place. This is easy enough for the `SalesOrder` object, since it can simply restore the state it recorded when `BeginEdit` was called, but let's have a look at how we would deal with the `LineItem` objects.

2-level Rollback

For the `LineItem` objects, things are not so simple. Their changes were committed when the user clicked OK on whatever form was used to edit those objects. Without some extra work, they have no way of recording their state as of the time the `SalesOrder` object's `BeginEdit` was called.

The CSLA solves this problem by implementing `ChildBeginEdit`, `ChildCancelEdit` and `ChildApplyEdit` methods on all child objects. We saw this in Chapter 2 as we implemented the Task Manager application. Let's review the code that handles the editing of both the parent `Client` and child `Project` objects.

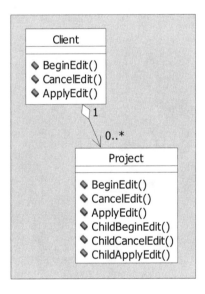

Consider what happens when we call `BeginEdit` on a parent object such as the `Client` object.

```
Public Sub BeginEdit()
  If mflgEditing Then Err.Raise 445

  ' save object state
  LSet mudtSave = mudtProps
  mflgEditing = True
  mcolProjects.BeginEdit
End Sub
```

The important line here is where we cascade the `BeginEdit` down to our child objects. This is done by calling a `BeginEdit` method on the `Collection` object that manages our child objects.

```
    mcolProjects.BeginEdit
```

If we trace this down to the `Projects` object's `BeginEdit` method, we'll find that it calls `ChildBeginEdit` for each child `Project` object.

```
Public Sub BeginEdit()
  Dim objProject As Project

  If mflgEditing Then Err.Raise 445

  For Each objProject In mcolItems
    objProject.ChildBeginEdit
  Next

  mflgEditing = True
End Sub
```

The `ChildBeginEdit` method in the `Project` object simply saves a copy of the current object state and sets a flag to indicate that it is editable.

```
Friend Sub ChildBeginEdit()
  If mflgChildEditing Then Err.Raise 445

  LSet mudtChildSave = mudtProps
mflgChildEditing = True
End Sub
```

So far so good.

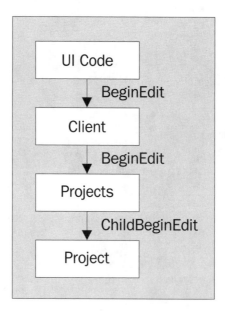

With this code we've accomplished that, when editing is started for the `Client` object – with a `BeginEdit` call – we trap all the state data for any child `Project` objects. This means that we have the ability to restore that object state should `CancelEdit` be called on the `Client` object.

Each individual `Project` object still manages its own state using `BeginEdit`, `CancelEdit` and `ApplyEdit` methods. It also has a second level of rollback capability via the `Child*Edit` methods (which are only called by the object's parent – they aren't even available to the UI developer).

N-level Rollback

Things get more difficult if we try to add another level of child object, such as `Task` objects below our `Project` objects.

Introducing GrandChild Objects

If we introduced a `Task` object we would need to be able to edit it directly using `BeginEdit` and `CancelEdit`. We also need to be able to cancel changes when its parent object, `Project`, is canceled – perhaps through the use of `ChildBeginEdit` and `ChildCancelEdit`. However, we also need to be able to cancel changes when the top level parent, `Client`, is canceled.

How do we do this?

One approach would be to add yet another level of methods – `GrandChildBeginEdit`, `GrandChildCancelEdit` and `GrandChildAppyEdit` to the `Task` object. This will certainly work, but it doesn't seem very elegant.

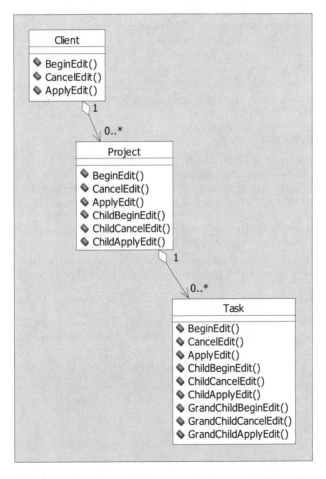

And consider what happens if the `Task` objects get their own children. Do we then implement `GreatGrandChildBeginEdit` and so forth? Obviously we need a better solution!

State Stacking

The solution lies in a concept we'll call **state stacking**. This is the idea that a given object can keep a stack of states. Rather than maintaining a finite set of states for use in rolling back, the object can keep any number of such states, allowing *n*-levels of rollback.

The term stack in this context is the classical concept of a stack in computer science. It is a first-in-last-out list of elements. This means we can push elements on top of the stack, or pop elements off the top of the stack, but we can't manipulate any elements that are not on top of the stack.

State stacking is a specific application of the Memento design pattern as described in *Design Patterns: Elements of Reusable Object-Oriented Software* (Gamma, Helm, et al). The state stacking technique we'll develop in this chapter varies from the Memento pattern in that it avoids externalizing the object's state in any way – instead keeping a stack of states within each specific object.

> **It is important to keep in mind that one object never directly interacts with the internal state of another object; otherwise it would break the encapsulation. Fortunately state stacking provides powerful undo capabilities without breaking encapsulation at all.**

This technique will not only allow us to handle grand and greatgrandchild objects, it also eliminates the need for the `Child*Edit` methods on regular child objects. So, we not only gain *n*-level rollback, but we'll simplify the code for single child objects as well. Before taking a look at implementing state stacking, let's quickly re-cap on how we would have handled grandchildren.

Recap of the old CSLA Approach

In the CSLA we implemented `BeginEdit` to store a copy of the object's state, before alterations were made. Then, later, we had the capability of restoring the object to that stored state if `CancelEdit` was called. If `ApplyEdit` was called we basically discarded the stored state, since `ApplyEdit` indicates that the object's new state is to be considered permanent.

This worked great for a single object, but not if the object had a parent. In that case, the object's state needed to be stored both when the parent's `BeginEdit` is called *and* when the actual object's `BeginEdit` is called. We did this by declaring two different variables, one to store the state when the parent's `BeginEdit` is called, `mudtChildSave`, and one for the object's `BeginEdit` itself, `mudtSave`.

> *To implement this technique for grandchild objects would require* three *different variables. Obviously this technique isn't ideal as we get more and more levels of child object.*

The parent object's `BeginEdit` method not only stored its own state, but also called the `ChildBeginEdit` of each child object (via the intermediate `Collection` object). I prefer to describe this process as *cascading* the `BeginEdit` call down to all the child objects.

Introducing State Stacking

With state stacking, we'll continue to follow the basic concept used in the CSLA, but in a more powerful fashion. The parent object will still cascade all calls to `BeginEdit`, `CancelEdit` and `ApplyEdit` down to all its child objects. However, those cascading calls *will not* result in a call to `ChildBeginEdit`, `ChildCancelEdit` and `ChildApplyEdit`. Instead, a call to the parent's `BeginEdit` will result in a cascaded call to the child object's `BeginEdit`.

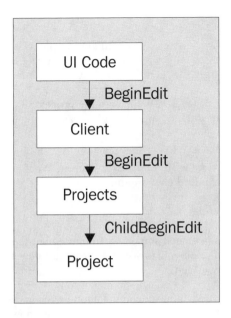

To make this work, we will enhance the BeginEdit method so it is capable of being called multiple times. After all, a child object can expect that its BeginEdit method will be called once when its parent object's BeginEdit method is called – and then again when the UI wants to edit the child object itself.

That's where the stack comes into play. A call to BeginEdit will cause each object to actually add a copy of its current state on top of the its internal stack – accomplishing the same thing as copying the object's current state into another variable such as mudtSave.

Each call to CancelEdit can then restore the object's state to match the state most recently stored by BeginEdit by taking that entry back off the stack and copying it back into the object. Correspondingly, a call to ApplyEdit can commit the object's current state by simply taking the most recent entry off the stack and discarding it.

So, within each object there will be a stack of that object's states. Each object will implement BeginEdit, CancelEdit and ApplyEdit methods with the following behaviors:

Method	Behavior
BeginEdit	Push the current state onto the stack
CancelEdit	Pop the top state off the stack and restore the object's current state using those values
ApplyEdit	Pop the top state off the stack and discard it

Since each object totally manages its own state, this technique can be extended to any number of levels of child objects.

State Stacking Class

Let's take a look at how this will work by creating a single, simple, class that can be easily modified to act as a parent, child, grandchild, etc. This will work well to illustrate the basic technique involved in state stacking, and then we can apply the technique to CSLA-style business objects.

Once we have the basic class down, we'll walk through the process of creating grandchild, child and parent objects to see how the state stacking mechanism works.

Setting up the Project

Bring up Visual Basic and create a new **Standard EXE** project. We'll use the form that's created by default later, but for now add a standard class module to the project.

Change the name of the class module to `Stacker`.

If we are going to stack our states, we need some way to implement the stack itself. A stack is a simple construct, basically a list of elements to which we can add new elements, then access and remove the element most recently added.

A stack can be implemented in many different ways. The most common approach may be the use of an array. Visual Basic provides the `Collection` object, which is an even easier technology for managing a list of elements – especially when we don't know up front how many elements we'll have.

Add the following declaration to the class module, along with the code to create and destroy the object.

```
Option Explicit

Private mcolStack As Collection

Private Sub Class_Initialize()
  Set mcolStack = New Collection
End Sub

Private Sub Class_Terminate()
  Set mcolStack = Nothing
End Sub
```

In order to see how we will stack state within our class, we'll need some state to stack. While the CSLA typically would have us store state in a UDT, in this case the state can be a simple variable so things aren't complicated. Let's make our state a numeric value that can be stored in a `Long`. Add the following declaration.

```
Option Explicit

Private mcolStack As Collection
Private mlngNumber As Long
```

Since the object has state, we should add a property so any calling code can set and retrieve the value. Add the following code.

```
Public Property Let Value(Value As Long)
  mlngNumber = Value
End Property

Public Property Get Value() As Long
  Value = mlngNumber
End Property
```

At this point we have a `Collection` object to act as our stack, and we have a `Long` to hold a numeric value for our object's state.

Implementing BeginEdit

The `BeginEdit` method is called prior to an object's state being altered by any calling code. The whole reason for calling `BeginEdit` is to give the object the opportunity to take a snapshot of its current state so it can be restored in the case that the `CancelEdit` method is called.

In the CSLA our `BeginEdit` method typically copies the object's current state, stored in `mudtProps`, into another UDT-based variable, `mudtSave`. Somewhat along this line:

```
Public Sub BeginEdit()
  LSet mudtSave = mudtProps
End Sub
```

State stacking will accomplish the same goal, but we'll do it by pushing the current state onto our stack rather than storing it in a single variable.

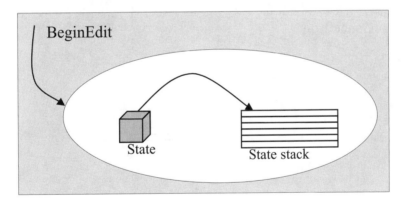

Enter the following code:

```
Public Sub BeginEdit()
  mcolStack.Add mlngNumber
End Sub
```

With this approach we've not only stored the current state data for the object, but we've done it in such a way that we can store more than just one set of state data. In fact, each time `BeginEdit` is called this routine will store another copy of the current state to the stack since the `Add` method is being called.

Remember that, each time a `BeginEdit` is called, the call is cascaded down to all child objects. If we have a parent object, a child object and a grandchild object, and we call begin edit on that parent object, the `BeginEdit` call will cascade to its child object, which in turn cascades down to *its* child object – the grandchild.

Then the BeginEdit may be called again on the child object so that it can be editied. This will add another copy of its current state to the child object's stack – which now holds two levels of state. It will also call `BeginEdit` on its child object – the grandchild.

Should we then call `BeginEdit` on the grandchild, a third copy of the grandchild's state will be added to the stack. So, you can see how it builds up, with each object holding its own state information.

As we discussed earlier, we're now able to implement `CancelEdit` to restore the object to the most recently stored state, and `ApplyEdit` to discard it, thus effectively committing to the object's current state.

Implementing CancelEdit

The `CancelEdit` method in CSLA simply restores the object's state by copying the state that was saved in `BeginEdit` back into the object's live set of variables.

```
Public Sub CancelEdit()
   LSet mudtProps = mudtSave
End Sub
```

A state stacking implementation of `CancelEdit` will do the same thing – conceptually. However, instead of restoring the state from a single variable, we'll restore the state by using the value on top of the stack of states.

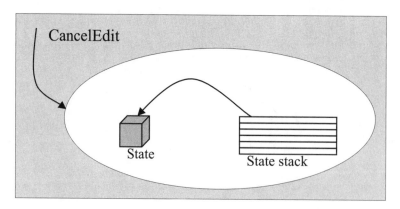

Of course, the only way to get at the top value on a stack is to *pop* that value off the stack – thus removing it from the stack itself – and then using it. In our case we're implementing the stack by using a `Collection` object. As Visual Basic developers, we know that we don't need to remove a value from a `Collection` to use it. But we need to simulate that behavior since this whole approach relies on the fact that values are popped off the stack to be used.

Enter the following code.

```
Public Sub CancelEdit()
   If mcolStack.Count = 0 Then Err.Raise 445

   mlngNumber = mcolStack.Item(mcolStack.Count)
   mcolStack.Remove mcolStack.Count
End Sub
```

Each call to `BeginEdit` adds a copy of the object's current state to the top of the stack, or `Collection` object. With this new code, `CancelEdit` now takes the topmost value from the stack and uses it to restore the object's current state to that value. The topmost value is then removed from the `Collection` (using the `Remove` method) – emulating the concept of popping the value off the stack.

Note that the first thing we do in this new `CancelEdit` routine is ensure that there is at least one value on the stack already. This is basically the same as in the CSLA model, where we check the `mflgEditing` flag to ensure that the object is being edited prior to allowing the `CancelEdit` method to be called.

With this code, we now have an object which will store its state any number of times through the `BeginEdit` call. After each `BeginEdit` call the object's state can be altered at will – and then we can call the `CancelEdit` method to undo any of those changes by restoring the object to the state it was at when `BeginEdit` was most recently called.

Were this object to have child objects, this code would also need to call the `CancelEdit` method of each of those children. Each child object would implement its own `CancelEdit` method to restore its state and pop the top item from its own internal stack.

Implementing ApplyEdit

The last `Public` method we need to implement is the `ApplyEdit` method. `BeginEdit` is used to tell the object that it is about to be edited, and `CancelEdit` is used to tell the object that any changes are to be undone. `ApplyEdit`, then, is used to tell the object that any changes made since the last `BeginEdit` method call are to be kept or made permanent.

In the CSLA, `ApplyEdit` doesn't do anything with the `mudtProps` variable or the `mudtSave` variable. Basically it just resets the `mflgEditing` variable to indicate that the object is no longer editable. Essentially what happens is that the object's current state is committed – it can no longer be undone with a call to `CancelEdit`.

With state stacking, the `ApplyEdit` method acts a bit differently. We still want to ensure that the object's state is committed and can't be undone with a call to `CancelEdit`, after `ApplyEdit` has been called. However, we also need to manage our stack of state data.

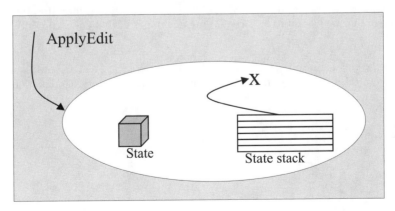

Enter the following code.

```
Public Sub ApplyEdit()
   If mcolStack.Count = 0 Then Err.Raise 445

   mcolStack.Remove mcolStack.Count
End Sub
```

This implementation of ApplyEdit doesn't make any changes to the object's current state – a call to ApplyEdit is supposed to indicate that the current state is to be kept.

It does, however, pop the topmost value off our stack, or Collection. After all, part of the reason for calling ApplyEdit is to indicate that we can't roll back to the state stored by the most recent call to BeginEdit – therefore there's no reason to keep that state on the stack.

Were this object to have child objects, this code would also need to call the ApplyEdit method of each of those children. Each child object would implement its own ApplyEdit method to pop the top item from its own internal stack.

This almost completes our basic state stacking object. Each call to BeginEdit stores the object's state, and we can then restore that state with CancelEdit or keep the current state with ApplyEdit.

Ensuring Symmetric Method Calls

The last code we need to write is primarily a debugging aid. It is very important that all calls to BeginEdit be matched by a call to either CancelEdit or ApplyEdit. Each call to CancelEdit or ApplyEdit indicates that the state stored with each BeginEdit call is to be restored into the object then discarded or simply that it is discarded. Regardless, the stack (or Collection in our case) should be empty by the time we're done.

> Each call to **BeginEdit** requires a symmetric call to either **CancelEdit** or **ApplyEdit**.

By the time our object is destroyed, its stack should be empty. If it is not, then the code written to use our object is in error and we'll want to ensure that the developer of that code knows they did something wrong.

The last routine to be run as our object is destroyed will be Class_Terminate. It is in this routine that we'll add code to raise an error in the case that our stack is not empty. Update that method as shown.

```
Private Sub Class_Terminate()
   If mcolStack.Count > 0 Then _
     Err.Raise vbObjectError + 1001, , "State stack is not empty"

   Set mcolStack = Nothing
End Sub
```

By adding this code, we provide a powerful tool for any developer writing code to use our object, since they'll quickly know that they've made a call to BeginEdit that has no matching call to either CancelEdit or ApplyEdit.

With that, our basic state stacking object is complete. Now is a good time to save the project – keep it open though, as we're not done working with it.

Using the Stacker Class

The `Stacker` class that we just implemented provides a basic outline of how any object based on state stacking will be constructed. The important thing to understand is the behaviors of `BeginEdit`, `CancelEdit` and `ApplyEdit` and how each method affects both the object's state and the stack.

To see how it all works, let's walk through the process of creating grandchild, child and parent objects. Once they've been created, we can build some very simple test code to see how the state stacking mechanism provides *n*-level rollback capabilities to all the objects.

Since the easiest class to build is the grandchild, we'll start from the bottom and work our way to the top.

Creating a Grandchild Object

Add a new class module to the project and change its name to `GrandChild`. Copy all the code from the `Stacker` class module into this new class module – we'll basically treat `Stacker` as a template.

Since `GrandChild` is the lowest level of our family – it has no child objects – we don't need to make any changes to the code. We've already implemented all the state stacking code and so we're all set.

Creating a Child Object

The `Child` object will be a bit more interesting, since it does have a child object. Again, add a new class to the project – change its name to `Child`. Copy all the code from the `Stacker` module into this class module.

Although all the state stacking code is in place, we still need to enhance the code in this class so it manages its child object – `GrandChild`. Fortunately these changes are quite minor. Add the following declaration.

```
Option Explicit

Private mcolStack As Collection
Private mlngNumber As Long
Private mobjChild As GrandChild
```

Now that we've got a variable to hold a reference to our child, let's add code to create and destroy the child. Make the following changes.

```
Private Sub Class_Initialize()
  Set mcolStack = New Collection
  Set mobjChild = New GrandChild
End Sub

Private Sub Class_Terminate()
  If mcolStack.Count > 0 Then _
    Err.Raise vbObjectError + 1001, , "State stack is not empty"

  Set mobjChild = Nothing
  Set mcolStack = Nothing
End Sub
```

If we have a child object, we should allow any calling code to get at that object so it is of use. We'll do this by adding a `Property Get` method. Enter the following.

```
Public Property Get Child() As GrandChild
   Set Child = mobjChild
End Property
```

Now things get interesting. We have code to create and destroy our child, and we have provided a `Property Get` so any client code can use the child object. However, we still need to add the code to cascade any calls to our `BeginEdit`, `CancelEdit` and `ApplyEdit` methods down to our child.

With the CSLA this would have meant implementing `Child*Edit` methods in the `GrandChild` object. However, with state stacking things are much easier. The `BeginEdit`, `CancelEdit` and `ApplyEdit` methods in the `GrandChild` object can not only be called when the `GrandChild` object itself is to be edited, but they can also be called when the parent object (the object we're working on now) is about to be edited.

This means that all we need to do is directly cascade each call down to the `GrandChild` object. Make the following changes.

```
Public Sub BeginEdit()
   mobjChild.BeginEdit
   mcolStack.Add mlngNumber
End Sub

Public Sub CancelEdit()
   If mcolStack.Count = 0 Then Err.Raise 445

   mobjChild.CancelEdit
   mlngNumber = mcolStack.Item(mcolStack.Count)
   mcolStack.Remove mcolStack.Count
End Sub

Public Sub ApplyEdit()
   If mcolStack.Count = 0 Then Err.Raise 445

   mobjChild.ApplyEdit
   mcolStack.Remove mcolStack.Count
End Sub
```

In each method we are simply making the exact same method call down to the child object. This means that each time our `BeginEdit` method is called, the `GrandChild` object's `BeginEdit` method will be called as well. The same is true for the other methods.

Notice how the method call to the child object is now made before we make any changes to our own object state or state stack. This is intentional – we want to make sure that there's no error raised from the child object before we go changing our own state.

Since we aren't dictating how each object serializes its data, there could be errors in that process. I am establishing one approach in this book – but there are others, some of which are more or less prone to error. Better to be safe than sorry when it comes to error trapping.

Creating a Parent Object

The last object we need to implement is the `Parent` object itself. Implementing this object will be kind of fun, since we'll get to see just how easy state stacking makes management of an entire tree of parent-child relationships.

Add a new class module to the project and name it `Parent`. Then copy all the code from the `Child` class (not `Stacker`) into this new module. It should be obvious pretty quickly why we're using the `Child` class' code as a template here.

The `Parent` object, like the `Child` object, has children. In this case the `Parent` object is the parent of the `Child` object itself. We've already altered the `Child` class to be a parent for the `GrandChild` object. The really nice thing here, is that the modifications we made to the `Child` object are *the same changes* we need to make for the `Parent` object!

In other words, we need to make no actual coding changes to the `Parent` object. All we need to do is change all references to `GrandChild` so they refer instead to `Child`. This can easily be done by using Visual Basic's capability to do a mass search and replace for the text 'GrandChild' so that all instances become 'Child' throughout this module.

> **The really cool thing is that this is true any time we want to add a new level of child objects. Each given object only knows about itself and its immediate child objects – it has *no explicit knowledge* of how many child objects its children may have – nor does it have any idea if it has a parent object of its own.**

The result is that our `Parent` object will now create, destroy and manage a `Child` object. That `Child` object will, in turn, create, destroy and manage a `GrandChild` object, and so on.

We are now ready to see how *n*-level rollback works with state stacking.

Testing State Stacking

To prove to ourselves that state stacking does what we need, let's create some simple test code. We can use `Form1`, the form that was automatically created along with the project. Return to that form and add a `CommandButton` control to it. Don't bother to change the name or anything, this will be very simple test code. Bring up the code window for the form and make the following declaration.

```
Option Explicit

Private mobjParent As Parent
```

To see how the values change over time, we'll print them into the Immediate window using the `Debug.Print` method. Enter the following routine to make this easy.

```
Private Sub PrintValues()
  Debug.Print "Values:"
  Debug.Print " Parent:     " & mobjParent.Value
  Debug.Print " Child:      " & mobjParent.Child.Value
  Debug.Print " GrandChild: " & mobjParent.Child.Child.Value
  Debug.Print ""
End Sub
```

Now we can write some code behind the `Command1` button to do our testing. First off, let's add code to create an instance of the `Parent` class, set some initial values and display those values – thus providing a nice starting point.

```
Private Sub Command1_Click()
   Set mobjParent = New Parent

   With mobjParent
     .Value = 10
     .Child.Value = 20
     .Child.Child.Value = 30
     PrintValues
   End With
End Sub
```

If the program is run at this point, the **Immediate** window should display the following:

```
Values:
 Parent:    10
 Child:     20
 GrandChild: 30
```

Now let's add some code to simulate a UI that might interact with our objects. Make the following changes.

```
Private Sub Command1_Click()
   Set mobjParent = New Parent

   With mobjParent
     .Value = 10
     .Child.Value = 20
     .Child.Child.Value = 30
     PrintValues
   End With

   ' main screen edits the Parent object
   With mobjParent
     .BeginEdit
     .Value = 11

     ' next screen edits the Child object
     With mobjParent.Child
       .BeginEdit
       .Value = 21

       ' next screen edits the GrandChild
       With mobjParent.Child.Child
         .BeginEdit
         .Value = 31

         ' apply changes to GrandChild
         .ApplyEdit
       End With

       ' apply changes to Child (and GrandChild)
       .ApplyEdit
     End With
```

```
        ' apply changes to Parent (and Child/GrandChild)
      .ApplyEdit
      PrintValues
    End With
  End Sub
```

The comments in the code indicate which 'screen' we're simulating at each point. Notice how each section of code calls `BeginEdit` on an object, then changes the value. Then the next simulated 'screen' works with the child object. The corresponding `ApplyEdit` is called once the child object is done being edited.

This is exactly how our forms work in the Task Manager application – they call `BeginEdit` on the current object and allow the user to manipulate it. The user may also manipulate any child objects. The `ApplyEdit` method isn't called until the user is all done with both the current and any child objects. They then click the OK button and `ApplyEdit` is called.

If we run the program now, the Immediate window will display the following:

```
Values:
  Parent:    10
  Child:     20
  GrandChild: 30

Values:
  Parent:    11
  Child:     21
  GrandChild: 31
```

Of course, this is the simple case – where all changes are committed. Let's change the `Parent` object's `ApplyEdit` call to a `CancelEdit` instead.

```
        ' cancel changes to Parent (and Child/GrandChild)
      .CancelEdit
      PrintValues
    End With
  End Sub
```

Now when the program is run the following is displayed:

```
Values:
  Parent:    10
  Child:     20
  GrandChild: 30

Values:
  Parent:    10
  Child:     20
  GrandChild: 30
```

None of the changes were kept! Because the topmost object in our tree, the `Parent`, had its `CancelEdit` method called, both the `Child` and `GrandChild` objects had their changes rolled back as well.

This is exactly what we set out to accomplish. You can try other combinations of `ApplyEdit` and `CancelEdit` calls to experiment. You'll find that a `CancelEdit` call to an object always restores its own state and the state of all the objects it owns – down to *n* levels deep.

This program is a simple example of the state stacking concept. Now let's apply it to the CSLA and see how easily it fits into that architecture by updating the Task Manager application to use state stacking.

Updating the Task Manager Application

The Task Manager application, as built in Chapter 2, doesn't actually deal with tasks at all – just clients and projects. That was because we had no easy way to provide OK, Cancel and Apply functionality down to a grandchild object. As we've just seen, state stacking provides us with a technique to easily take care of this problem.

In this section we'll do two things. First off, we'll add the `Task` object to the Task Manager application, along with a `Tasks` object to manage the child `Task` objects. Secondly, we'll also update the existing class modules for `Client`, `Projects` and `Project` so they use the state stacking technique.

The `Task` object will be a child of the existing `Project` object. This means that each project may have zero or more tasks involved in completing the project. For each task we'll keep track of a few pieces of information, including the task name, how many days it is projected to take and the percent complete.

The following diagram illustrates the `Task` object, the `Tasks Collection` object and their relationship to the already existing `Project` object.

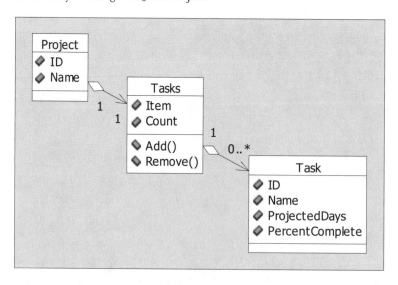

Now that we know how the new `Task` object will fit into the picture, let's get to work. The first thing to do is open up Visual Basic and bring up the `TaskObjects` project.

Adding the Task Class

Add a new class module to the project. Change the class module's name to `Task`. You can either use the business template and make the highlighted changes, or enter all the code in this section.

Setting up the UDTs

Before we get into the class module's code, we need to set up the appropriate UDTs. Open the `TOtypes` module and add the following code.

```
Public Type TaskProps
   IsNew As Boolean
   IsDirty As Boolean
   IsDeleted As Boolean
   ID As Long
   Name As String * 50
   ProjectedDays As Long
   PercentComplete As Single
End Type

Public Type TaskData
   Buffer As String * 60
End Type
```

Again, the length of the `Buffer` variable is calculated by totaling up the number of bytes in the `TaskProps` UDT and dividing by 2.

The length of `TaskProps` is 6 for the `Boolean` variables, plus 2 for the filler before the `Long`. Then 4 for the `Long`, 100 for the `String`, 4 for the `Long` and 4 for the `Single` – totaling to 120.

Divide this by 2 (since each character in a `String` variable is 2 bytes due to Unicode) and we get 60.

Updating the Template Code

With that done, return to the new `Task` class module and we'll make the appropriate changes. These changes are not quite the same as those we've made in the past, since this class will be based on state stacking rather than the normal CSLA techniques.

Declarations

The declarations section will be updated to appear as follows.

```
Option Explicit

Event Valid(IsValid As Boolean)

Private mudtProps As TaskProps
Private mcolStack As Collection
Private mobjParent As Tasks

Private WithEvents mobjValid As BrokenRules
```

Note that the declarations for `mudtSave` and `mflgEditing` have been removed and replaced by the declaration for `mcolStack`.

We've also added a declaration for `mobjParent`, since `Task` is a child object and will need to use the same technique as the `Project` object for adding itself into its immediate parent object, `Tasks`.

As you will see, state stacking will allow us to simplify our code quite a lot – as is already evidenced by the reduction of module-level variables.

Creating and Destroying the mcolStack Object

The `Class_Initialize` routine will need to be updated to create the `Collection` object for `mcolStack`.

```
Private Sub Class_Initialize()
    Set mcolStack = New Collection
    Set mobjValid = New BrokenRules
    mudtProps.IsNew = True
    ' if we know any rules are broken on startup
    ' then add code here to initialize the list
    ' of broken rules
    '
    ' mobjValid.RuleBroken "RuleName", True
End Sub
```

Additionally, a `Class_Terminate` routine needs to be added to destroy the object, and we add the code to check the `Count` property of the `Collection` to raise an error if any elements remain in the stack.

```
Private Sub Class_Terminate()
    If mcolStack.Count > 0 Then _
      Err.Raise vbObjectError + 1001, , "State stack is not empty"

    Set mcolStack = Nothing
    Set mobjValid = Nothing
End Sub
```

Raising an error if any elements remain in the `Collection` is an important debugging tool. It will be invaluable to a UI developer in ensuring that; for each call to `BeginEdit` they've made, a call to either `CancelEdit` or `ApplyEdit` is also made.

Adding GetState and SetState

As with the `Client` and `Project` objects, we need to implement `GetState` to serialize the object's state and `SetState` to deserialize it. These methods will be used as we implement the data-centric `TaskPersist` object (in Chapter 4), but will also be used as part of the state stacking code.

Add the following code to implement these methods.

```
Friend Function GetState() As String
    Dim udtData As TaskData

    LSet udtData = mudtProps
    GetState = udtData.Buffer
End Function

Friend Sub SetState(Buffer As String)
    Dim udtData As TaskData

    udtData.Buffer = Buffer
    LSet mudtProps = udtData
End Sub
```

By now the code in these methods should be old hat.

However, we'll be using these methods in a new way as we change the `BeginEdit` and `CancelEdit` methods.

Updating BeginEdit, CancelEdit and ApplyEdit

Earlier in this chapter we explored state stacking in some detail. Here we'll implement that technique, along with making a few other minor changes to the template code.

Edit the `BeginEdit` method to appear as shown.

```
Public Sub BeginEdit()
  ' save object state
  mcolStack.Add GetState
End Sub
```

We no longer need to check the `mflgEditing` flag, since we actually allow the `BeginEdit` method to be called any number of times. Additionally, instead of using the `LSet` technique to store the object's state into `mudtSave`, this code uses the `GetState` method to retrieve the object's state and add it to our stack of states.

> In Visual Basic 6.0 it is possible to add a UDT directly to a `Collection` object using the `Add` method. However, to do this, the UDT must be declared as `Public` in a class module. Unfortunately, this new feature also requires an upgrade to COM, which can be a logistic problem in many settings. Moreover, as we'll see in Chapter 4, this technique doesn't actually serialize the object's data – precluding implementation of some important capabilities.

`CancelEdit` is also a bit different. Make the following changes.

```
Public Sub CancelEdit()
  If mcolStack.Count = 0 Then Err.Raise 445

  mudtProps.IsDeleted = False
  ' restore object state
  With mcolStack
    SetState .Item(.Count)
    .Remove .Count
  End With
End Sub
```

Again we remove the `mflgEditing` check, in this case replacing it with a check of the `Count` property of our stack, `mcolStack`. This is the same check we implemented earlier, when we explored state stacking.

Also, where we would have used the `LSet` technique to restore the object's state from the `mudtSave` variable, we'll restore state using the `SetState` method taking values from the top of the `mcolStack` state collection. The topmost entry on the stack is also removed – after all, we just popped the value off our 'stack'.

The `ApplyEdit` needs quite a lot of changing. We not only need to update it to handle state stacking, but we also need to make changes similar to those in the `Project` object so the that `Task` object adds itself into the `Tasks` object's `Collection`. As with the `Project` object, we don't want a new `Task` included in the list of tasks until the user has decided that they wish to accept the new object.

Make the following changes:

```
Public Sub ApplyEdit()
  If mcolStack.Count = 0 Then Err.Raise 445

  If Not mobjParent Is Nothing Then
    mobjParent.AddTask Me
    Set mobjParent = Nothing
  End If
  mcolStack.Remove mcolStack.Count
End Sub
```

The `mflgEditing` check is replaced by checking the `Count` property of `mcolStack`. Next, the `mobjParent` variable is used as in the `Project` object to call an `AddTask` method in the `Tasks` object (which we'll implement next).

Finally, the topmost element on our state stack is removed. Each call to `ApplyEdit` needs to pop the top item off the stack, thus effectively committing the object's current state.

The `Project` object also has an `Initialize` method, which is used by its parent `Projects` object. Likewise, the `Task` object will need an `Initialize` method for use by the `Tasks` object. Add the following code.

```
Friend Sub Initialize(Parent As Tasks)
  If mudtProps.IsNew Then Set mobjParent = Parent
End Sub
```

This method will be used by the `Tasks` object as it adds a new `Task` to a `Project`. It sets the `mobjParent` variable that we just used in the `ApplyEdit` method. The exact use of this routine will become clear when we implement the `Add` method of the `Tasks` object later in this chapter.

Replacing mflgEditing Code

Throughout the rest of the code we need to replace each check of the `mflgEditing` flag with a corresponding check of `mcolStack.Count`.

```
Public Property Get IsValid() As Boolean
  IsValid = (objValid.Count = 0)
End Property

Private Sub objValid_BrokenRule()
  RaiseEvent Valid(False)
End Sub

Private Sub objValid_NoBrokenRules()
  RaiseEvent Valid(True)
End Sub

Public Sub Load()
  If mcolStack.Count > 0 Then Err.Raise 445
  If Not mudtProps.IsNew Then Err.Raise 445

  mudtProps.IsNew = False

  ' code to load the object goes here
End Sub
```

```
Public Sub Delete()
  If mcolStack.Count = 0 Then Err.Raise 445

  mudtProps.IsDeleted = True
  mudtProps.IsDirty = True
End Sub

Public Property Get IsDeleted() As Boolean
  IsDeleted = mudtProps.IsDeleted
End Property

Public Property Get IsNew() As Boolean
  IsNew = mudtProps.IsNew
End Property

Public Property Get IsDirty() As Boolean
  IsDirty = mudtProps.IsDirty
End Property
```

With these few changes, the template code has been enhanced to support state stacking, and to make this object work as a child object within the CSLA.

Adding Properties

All that remains to implement the `Task` object is to add the specific `Property Get` and `Property Let` routines appropriate to modeling a task.

```
Public Property Get ID() As Long
  ID = mudtProps.ID
End Property

Public Property Get Name() As String
  Name = Trim$(mudtProps.Name)
End Property

Public Property Let Name(Value As String)
  If mcolStack.Count = 0 Then Err.Raise 383

  mudtProps.Name = Value
  mudtProps.IsDirty = True
End Property

Public Property Get ProjectedDays() As Long
  ProjectedDays = mudtProps.ProjectedDays
End Property

Public Property Let ProjectedDays(Value As Long)
  If mcolStack.Count = 0 Then Err.Raise 383
  If Not mudtProps.IsNew Then Err.Raise 383

  mudtProps.ProjectedDays = Value
  mudtProps.IsDirty = True
End Property

Public Property Get PercentComplete() As Single
  PercentComplete = mudtProps.PercentComplete
End Property
```

```
Public Property Let PercentComplete(Value As Single)
  If mcolStack.Count = 0 Then Err.Raise 383

  mudtProps.PercentComplete = Value
  mudtProps.IsDirty = True
End Property
```

The ID value is read-only, as we'll allow the database to assign a unique ID value for the task. All the other properties are pretty typical.

The one thing of interest in this code is that there are no checks of the `mflgEditing` flag. Instead, we are checking the `mcolStack.Count` value. If it is zero, then `BeginEdit` has never been called and we cannot allow any of the object's state data to be altered.

At this point the `Task` object is ready to roll, so save the project and we'll move on to implement its parent object – `Tasks`.

Adding the Tasks Class

Add a new class module to the project and change its name to `Tasks`. Since we've already got a good `Collection` object in our project, namely the `Projects` class, we can reuse that code. Copy all the code from the `Projects` class module into this new class module.

To make the `Collection` object support the default `Item` method and the `For...Each` functionality, use the **Tools | Procedure Attributes** dialog, and make sure to set the **Procedure ID** for the `Item` property to (default). Also set the **Procedure ID** to –4 and check the **Hide this member** option for the `NewEnum` method.

Then we can move on to update the code in the module.

Obviously we'll need to change all references to the `Project` object so they refer to the `Task` object throughout the module. Use the **Edit | Replace** option to replace all the references.

However, there are some other changes that are key to implementing state stacking that we'll be making in the code.

Changing mflgEditing to mlngEditing

As it stands, the code utilizes the `mflgEditing` variable to determine whether `BeginEdit` has been called. The thing with state stacking is that `BeginEdit` may be called more than once.

A simple `Boolean` is no longer sufficient. In the `Task` object we replaced the `mflgEditing` variable with code to check the `Count` property of the state stack itself. Since the `Tasks` object is a `Collection` object, it has no real state of its own, so there's no reason for a state stack.

However, we can simulate the `Count` property by changing our simple `Boolean` to a number – say a `Long`. In this case, we can just treat the variable as a counter – adding one each time `BeginEdit` is called, and decrementing the count each time `CancelEdit` or `ApplyEdit` are called. This basically simulates what happens to the `Count` property of the `Collection` object in the `Tasks` object.

Change the declaration of `mflgEditing` as follows.

```
Option Explicit

Private mcolItems As Collection

Private mlngEditing As Long
```

Throughout the module we'll need to change any code referencing `mflgEditing`. We'll cover most of these routines as we change the `Project` references to the `Task` object. The `Remove` method can be updated now:

```
Public Sub Remove(ByVal Index As Variant)
  If mlngEditing = 0 Then Err.Raise 445

  With mcolItems(Index)
    .BeginEdit
    .Delete
    .ApplyEdit
  End With
End Sub
```

Let's walk through the remaining changes to the module.

Adding Task Objects

The `Add` and `AddTask` methods are designed to allow the `Projects` class to add new `Project` objects. We need to go through these two routines and change all references to a `Project` object to our new `Task` object as shown here.

```
Public Function Add() As Task
  Dim lngCount As Long
  Dim objTask As Task

  If mlngEditing = 0 Then Err.Raise 445

  Set objTask = New Task
  objTask.Initialize Me
  For lngCount = 1 To mlngEditing
    objTask.BeginEdit
  Next
  Set Add = objTask
  Set objTask = Nothing
End Function

Friend Sub AddTask(Child As Task)

  mcolItems.Add Child

End Sub
```

This doesn't involve any real changes to code, just changes to the class name we're working with. This code corresponds to the code we just implemented in the `Task` object's `ApplyEdit` and `Initialize` methods.

BeginEdit, CancelEdit and ApplyEdit

The changes to the *Edit routines are a bit more interesting. Each of these routines cascades the corresponding method call down to all the child objects. However, the way the code in Projects is written, the calls are made to ChildBeginEdit, ChildCancelEdit and ChildApplyEdit.

With the changes we just made to the Task object, we'll need to alter these routines so they no longer call the Child*Edit methods. Instead, we can simplify the overall process and directly cascade the calls to the methods of the same name.

```
Public Sub BeginEdit()
    Dim objTask As Task

    For Each objTask In mcolItems
        objTask.BeginEdit
    Next

    mlngEditing = mlngEditing + 1
End Sub
```

Note too that we've removed the code that checks mflgEditing and added a line to increment the new mlngEditing variable by one. Thus each time BeginEdit is called our edit counter will go up by one. We can add code to decrement the value in both CancelEdit and ApplyEdit.

```
Public Sub CancelEdit()
    Dim objTask As Task

    If mflgEditing = 0 Then Err.Raise 445

    For Each objTask In mcolItems
        objTask.CancelEdit
    Next

    mlngEditing = mlngEditing - 1
End Sub

Public Sub ApplyEdit()
    Dim objTask As Task

    If mflgEditing = 0 Then Err.Raise 445

    For Each objTask In mcolItems
        objTask.ApplyEdit
    Next

    mlngEditing = mlngEditing - 1
End Sub
```

Of course, we also need to update all references to Project so they are referencing the new Task object as shown above.

The nice thing about these changes though, is that the code is more clear and straightforward. Instead of a call to BeginEdit resulting in a call to ChildBeginEdit on each child object, it simply results in cascading the BeginEdit call to all the child objects.

Updating GetState and SetState

The `GetState` and `SetState` methods can stay pretty much intact. We just need to change the references to `Project` so they refer to `Task`.

Additionally, the `SetState` method calls `BeginEdit` on each child object if an editing session is underway. However, now we need to change this code to call `BeginEdit` on each child object multiple times – in fact, `BeginEdit` needs to be called once for each time that the `Tasks` object's own `BeginEdit` has been called. We have this value in `mlngEditing`, so all we need to do is implement a simple loop.

```
Friend Sub SetState(Buffer As String)
  Dim objBuffer As Buffer
  Dim lngIndex As Long
  Dim lngEdit As Long
  Dim objTask As Task

  Set objBuffer = New Buffer
  Set mcolItems = Nothing
  Set mcolItems = New Collection
  With objBuffer
    .SetState Buffer
    For lngIndex = 1 To .Count
      Set objTask = New Task
      objTask.SetState.Item(lngIndex)
      For lngEdit = 1 To mlngEditing
        objTask.BeginEdit
      Next
      mcolItems.Add objTask
      Set objTask = Nothing
    Next
  End With
End Sub
```

The only other change is in the `GetState` method. Where there is the call to `ChildBeginEdit` it needs to be changed to `BeginEdit`.

```
Friend Function GetState() As String
  Dim objBuffer As Buffer
  Dim objTask As Task
  Dim udtData As TaskData

  Set objBuffer = New Buffer
  With objBuffer
    .Initialize Len(udtData.Buffer), 10
    For Each objTask In mcolItems
      .Add objTask.GetState
    Next
    GetState = .GetState
  End With
  Set objBuffer = Nothing
End Function
```

In Chapter 4 we'll actually *implement* the data-centric `TaskPersist` object, so these methods won't be used until then. However, with these changes in place they are ready to go when we need them.

Updating Delete

The last method in the module is the `Delete` method. This code merely needs to be changed so it references the `Task` object instead of the `Project` object and to use `mlngEditing` instead of `mflgEditing`.

```
Public Sub Delete()
    Dim objTask As Task

    If mlngEditing = 0 Then Err.Raise 445

    For Each objTask In mcolItems
        With objTask
            .BeginEdit
            .Remove
            .ApplyEdit
        End With
    Next
End Sub
```

And that's it – our `Tasks` object is now complete and should interact with our `Task` object as needed. Next we'll return to the `Project` object and make it aware of its new child objects.

Updating the Project Class

Not only do we need to make the `Project` object aware of the child `Task` objects, but we also need to update it to use the new state stacking technique, thus eliminating the `Child*Edit` methods and simplifying the class overall.

Declarations

To start, replace the declarations of `mudtSave` and `mudtChildSave` with a declaration of `mcolStack` as shown.

```
Option Explicit

Event Valid(IsValid As Boolean)

Private mudtProps As ProjectProps
Private mcolStack As Collection
Private mobjParent As Projects

Private WithEvents mobjValid As BrokenRules
```

Also remove the declarations of `mflgEditing`, `mflgChildEditing`, `mudtSave` and `mudtChildSave` as none of these variables will be used when we're done.

Create and Destroy mcolStack

Now that we've got a declaration for our stack, `mcolStack`, let's add code to the `Class_Initialize` routine to create the object. Also add a `Class_Terminate` event as we did with the `Task` object.

```
Private Sub Class_Initialize()
  Set mcolStack = New Collection
  Set mobjValid = New BrokenRules

  mudtProps.IsNew = True
  ' if we know any rules are broken on startup
  ' then add code here to initialize the list
  ' of broken rules
  '
  ' mobjValid.RuleBroken "RuleName", True
End Sub
```

```
Private Sub Class_Terminate()
  If mcolStack.Count > 0 Then _
    Err.Raise vbObjectError + 1001, , "State stack is not empty"

  Set mcolStack = Nothing
  Set mobjValid = Nothing
End Sub
```

Again the `Class_Terminate` not only destroys the `Collection` object, but also makes sure it is empty first, providing a powerful debugging tool.

Referencing the Tasks Object

Since the `Project` object is now going to be a parent object, it will need code to handle the `Task` child objects. This isn't terribly complex, since the `Tasks` object takes care of the details. As with the `Client` object and its `Projects` object, we just need to add a `Private` variable and a `Property Get` routine.

Add the following declaration.

```
Private mobjParent As Projects
Private mobjTasks As Tasks

Private WithEvents mobjValid As BrokenRules
```

The `Class_Initialize` routine will need to create an instance of the `Tasks` object as follows.

```
Private Sub Class_Initialize()
  Set mcolStack = New Collection
  Set mobjTasks = New Tasks
  Set mobjValid = New BrokenRules
```

Also add a `Class_Terminate` routine to clean up our objects.

```
Private Sub Class_Terminate()
  Set mcolStack = Nothing
  Set mobjTasks = Nothing
  Set mobjValid = Nothing
End Sub
```

And finally we'll want to add a `Property Get` routine so the UI developer can utilize the `Task` objects.

```
Public Property Get Tasks() As Tasks
  Set Tasks = mobjTasks
End Property
```

With that done, we can go through the remainder of the code and update it for state stacking and to handle the child `Task` objects.

BeginEdit, CancelEdit and ApplyEdit

We'll need to update the `*Edit` routines. They'll end up looking almost exactly like the ones we created for the `Task` object once we replace the `LSet` technique with state stacking and remove all the `mflgEditing` variable checks. Of course, they'll also need to cascade the method calls down to the child `Task` objects.

```
Public Sub BeginEdit()
  mobjTasks.BeginEdit
  ' save object state
  mcolStack.Add GetState
End Sub

Public Sub CancelEdit()
  If mcolStack.Count = 0 Then Err.Raise 445

  mobjTasks.CancelEdit
  mudtProps.IsDeleted = False
  ' restore object state
  With mcolStack
    SetState .Item(.Count)
    .Remove .Count
  End With
End Sub

Public Sub ApplyEdit()
  If mcolStack.Count = 0 Then Err.Raise 445

  mobjTasks.ApplyEdit
  If Not mobjParent Is Nothing Then
    mobjParent.AddProject Me
    Set mobjParent = Nothing
  End If
  mcolStack.Remove mcolStack.Count
End Sub
```

Also, remove the `ChildBeginEdit`, `ChildCancelEdit` and `ChildApplyEdit` methods from the module. As we've seen, they aren't needed once state stacking is in place.

With these changes our `Project` object is now using state stacking just like the `Task` object.

Updating mflgEditing Checks

All that remains to implement state stacking is to update the `Delete` method and the `Name` property so they no longer reference the `mflgEditing` variable. Instead, they need to check the `mcolStack.Count` property and make sure it is greater than zero. Make the changes as shown.

```
Public Sub Delete()
  If mcolStack.Count = 0 Then Err.Raise 445

  mudtProps.IsDeleted = True
  mudtProps.IsDirty = True
End Sub
```

```
Public Property Let Name(Value As String)
   If mcolStack.Count = 0 Then Err.Raise 383

   mudtProps.Name = Value
   mudtProps.IsDirty = True
End Property
```

As long as `mcolStack.Count` is greater than zero then we know that the `BeginEdit` method has been called at least once and the object is being edited.

That does it for the `Project` object, so let's move on to the `Projects` object. It is calling `Child*Edit` methods that no longer exist in the `Project` object.

Updating the Projects Class

In building the `Tasks` object we've already walked through the changes that we'll need to make here. This object is the direct parent of the `Project` objects and is basically already doing everything it needs. However, as it stands, the `Projects` object is making calls to methods that we've now removed from the `Project` object.

We need to change all references to `ChildBeginEdit`, `ChildCancelEdit` and `ChildApplyEdit` so they call `BeginEdit`, `CancelEdit` and `ApplyEdit`. These changes need to be made in the following methods:

- ❏ Add
- ❏ SetState
- ❏ BeginEdit
- ❏ CancelEdit
- ❏ ApplyEdit

Additionally, we need to change the Boolean variable `mflgEditing` to a `Long` as we did in the `Tasks` object. The `BeginEdit` method needs to increment this value, while the `CancelEdit` and `ApplyEdit` methods need to decrement it. This simulates the behavior of the `Collection` object's `Count` property in the `Task` and `Project` objects.

Only the changed code is listed below – make the changes as shown.

First, the declaration needs to be changed:

```
Option Explicit

Private mcolItems As Collection
Private mlngEditing As Long
```

Then change the following routines as shown.

```
Public Function Add() As Project
   Dim lngCount As Long
   Dim objProject As Project

   If mlngEditing = 0 Then Err.Raise 445
```

```
      Set objProject = New Project
      objProject.Initialize Me
      For lngCount = 1 To mlngEditing
        objProject.BeginEdit
      Next
      Set Add = objProject
      Set objProject = Nothing
  End Function


  Public Sub Remove(ByVal Index As Variant)
      If mlngEditing = 0 Then Err.Raise 445

      With mcolItems(Index)
        .BeginEdit
        .Delete
        .ApplyEdit
      End With
  End Sub
```

The `SetState` has some more substantial changes. We need to change the single call to `BeginEdit` for each child object so there are multiple `BeginEdit` calls – one for each time `BeginEdit` has been called on the `Projects` object itself.

```
  Friend Sub SetState(Buffer As String)
      Dim objBuffer As Buffer
      Dim lngIndex As Long
      Dim lngEdit As Long
      Dim objProject As Project

      Set objBuffer = New Buffer
      Set mcolItems = Nothing
      Set mcolItems = New Collection
      With objBuffer
        .SetState Buffer
        For lngIndex = 1 To .Count
          Set objProject = New Project
          objProject.SetState .Item(lngIndex)
          For lngEdit = 1 To mlngEditing
            objProject.BeginEdit
          Next
          mcolItems.Add objProject
          Set objProject = Nothing
        Next
      End With
  End Sub
```

The `BeginEdit` method needs to increment the value.

```
  Public Sub BeginEdit()
      Dim objProject As Project

      For Each objProject In mcolItems
        objProject.BeginEdit
      Next

      mlngEditing = mlngEditing + 1
  End Sub
```

And the `CancelEdit` and `ApplyEdit` methods need to decrement the value – just as though we were popping an element off the stack like in the `Task` and `Project` objects.

```
Public Sub CancelEdit()
  Dim lngIndex As Long
  Dim objProject As Project

  If mlngEditing = 0 Then Err.Raise 445

  For lngIndex = 1 To mcolItems.Count
    Set objProject = mcolItems(lngIndex)
    With objProject
      If Not .IsNew Then
        .CancelEdit
      Else
        mcolItems.Remove lngIndex
      End If
    End With
    Set objProject = Nothing
  Next

  mlngEditing = mlngEditing - 1
End Sub

Public Sub ApplyEdit()
  Dim objProject As Project

  If mlngEditing = 0 Then Err.Raise 445

  For Each objProject In mcolItems
    objProject.ApplyEdit
  Next

  mlngEditing = mlngEditing - 1
End Sub
```

Finally, update the `Delete` method.

```
Public Sub Delete()
  Dim objProject As Project

  If mlngEditing = 0 Then Err.Raise 445

  For Each objProject In mcolItems
    With objProject
      .BeginEdit
      .Remove
      .ApplyEdit
    End With
  Next
End Sub
```

The only object left at this point is the parent `Client` object.

Updating the Client Class

The changes to the `Client` object center around implementing state stacking. This object is already set up to act as a parent object, so there aren't any changes to be done in that regard.

Declarations

In the declarations section remove the declaration of the `mudtSave` and `mflgEditing` variables and add a declaration for `mcolStack`.

```
Option Explicit

Event Valid(IsValid As Boolean)

Private mudtProps As ClientProps
Private mcolStack As Collection
Private mcolProjects As Projects

Private WithEvents mobjValid As BrokenRules
```

With this declaration set up we can move on to create the object itself.

Create and Destroy mcolStack

In the `Class_Initialize` routine add a line to create the new `Collection` object. Also add a `Class_Terminate` event routine as shown.

```
Private Sub Class_Initialize()
  Set mcolStack = New Collection
  Set mobjValid = New BrokenRules
  Set mcolProjects = New Projects

  mudtProps.IsNew = True
  ' if we know any rules are broken on startup
  ' then add code here to initialize the list
  ' of broken rules
  '
  ' mobjValid.RuleBroken "RuleName", True
End Sub

Private Sub Class_Terminate()
  If mcolStack.Count > 0 Then _
    Err.Raise vbObjectError + 1001, , "State stack is not empty"

  Set mcolStack = Nothing
  Set mobjValid = Nothing
  Set mcolProjects = Nothing
End Sub
```

As with the `Task` and `Project` objects, the `Class_Terminate` destroys the `Collection` object we've created, but also checks to ensure that it is empty first.

BeginEdit, CancelEdit and ApplyEdit

The `BeginEdit` and `CancelEdit` methods need to be changed just as we did with the `Project` object. The `LSet` code will be replaced with code to manage the new stack of states. Also the cascading calls to the `Projects` object will be moved to the top of each routine, ensuring that all the child objects are notified successfully before tampering with the `Client` object's state data.

```
    Public Sub BeginEdit()
      mcolProjects.BeginEdit
      ' save object state
      mcolStack.Add GetState
    End Sub

    Public Sub CancelEdit()
      If mcolStack.Count = 0 Then Err.Raise 445

      mcolProjects.CancelEdit
      mudtProps.IsDeleted = False
      ' restore object state
      With mcolStack
        SetState .Item(.Count)
        .Remove .Count
      End With
    End Sub
```

The `ApplyEdit` method is a bit different from either the `Task` or `Project` objects. Since this is a top-level parent object, it is responsible for interacting with the data-centric `ClientPersist` object to save not only its data, but also that of its child objects.

At this point we'll just update the code to handle state stacking instead of using the UDT `LSet` technique. Make the changes as shown.

```
    Public Sub ApplyEdit()
      Dim objPersist As ClientPersist
      Dim strProjects As String

      If mcolStack.Count = 0 Then Err.Raise 445

      mcolProjects.ApplyEdit
      Set objPersist = New ClientPersist
      If mudtProps.IsDeleted Then
        ' code to delete the object's data goes here
        objPersist.DeleteObject mudtProps.ID
        mcolStack.Remove mcolStack.Count
        mudtProps.IsNew = True
        mudtProps.IsDeleted = False
      ElseIf IsDirty Or mudtProps.IsNew Then
        If Not IsValid Then Err.Raise 445
        ' save object to database if appropriate
        ' save object state
        mcolStack.Remove mcolStack.Count
        strProjects = mcolProjects.GetState
        SetState objPersist.Save(GetState, strProjects)
        mcolProjects.SetState strProjects
        mudtProps.IsNew = False
      Else
        mcolStack.Remove mcolStack.Count
      End If
      Set objPersist = Nothing
      mudtProps.IsDirty = False
    End Sub
```

Notice that an `Else` block has been added to the code. This is because we need to ensure that the topmost element in our stack is removed regardless of whether the object is being deleted or saved. The UDT `LSet` technique doesn't require this step, but state stacking certainly does.

Altering this routine to save not only the client and its child objects, but also its *grandchild* objects is beyond the scope of this chapter. While it might at first glance appear to be an easy problem to solve, it turns out to be quite complex.

Where each `Project` object's state has been a clearly definable byte stream thus far, it will all of a sudden also need to include all the states of its child `Task` objects. Because of this, the length and exact nature of each `Project` object's state becomes hard to predict. Thus we'll cover it in Chapter 4, leaving the `Client` object's `ApplyEdit` as it is – storing only the `Client` and `Project` objects.

Updating mflgEditing Checks

The `Load` method can only be called if the object is not currently being edited. This has been done with a check of the `mflgEditing` flag to date, but now we'll change it to use a check of the `mcolStack.Count` property.

```
Public Sub Load(ID As Long)
   Dim objPersist As ClientPersist
   Dim strProjects As String

   If mcolStack.Count > 0 Then Err.Raise 445
   If Not mudtProps.IsNew Then Err.Raise 445

   mudtProps.IsNew = False

   ' code to load the object goes here
   Set objPersist = New ClientPersist
   SetState objPersist.Fetch(ID, strProjects)
   Set objPersist = Nothing
   Set mcolProjects = New Projects
   mcolProjects.SetState strProjects
End Sub
```

There are four other routines in the class that check the `mflgEditing` flag. In each case, change that check to one which ensures that the `mcolStack.Count` property equals zero.

- ❑ `Delete`
- ❑ `Name` (Property Let)
- ❑ `ContactName` (Property Let)
- ❑ `Phone` (Property Let)

Now that our objects are all set (other than being able to retrieve or save `Task` objects), we need to enhance the ability to delete child objects.

Handling Deletion of Child Objects

The way this is handled currently does not work well overall, since the `Collection` objects continue to display information about child objects even when marked for deletion. Once a child object has been marked for deletion, it really shouldn't appear in the list of valid child objects any longer.

As they are coded, the `Projects` and `Tasks` objects simply call the `Delete` method on a child object when required. It remains up to the user interface to show the user whether a given item is marked for deletion or not. Both the `ClientEdit` and `ProjectEdit` forms currently add a '(d)' behind the child name to indicate that it has been marked for deletion. This is not the ideal solution.

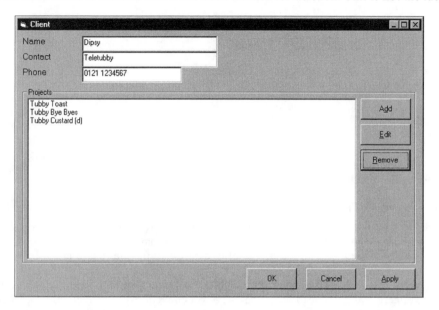

Instead, it would be better if the `Projects` and `Tasks` objects could remove the deleted child objects from their list of children. At the same time, we can't *totally* remove them, since the user could always choose to cancel their changes – meaning that those child objects may no longer be flagged for deletion.

Fortunately, it is relatively easy to enhance a `Collection` object to handle deletion of child objects in a more powerful manner. In particular, we can enhance the `Projects` and `Tasks` objects to hide all child objects that are marked for deletion so they appear to have been removed from the collection – when in fact they are still merely marked for deletion.

To do this, we'll add a second `Collection` object within the `Projects` and `Tasks` objects. This second collection will hold references to those child objects that have been marked for deletion. The `mcolItems` object then, will only hold references to 'valid' child objects that haven't been marked for deletion.

Updating the Projects Object

We'll walk through the changes to the `Projects` object in detail, and then skim through the changes in the `Tasks` object, since they're essentially the same.

Declarations

As noted above, we'll need a `Collection` object to store references to all the objects marked for deletion. We need to retain references to them, since the user could always change their mind and click Cancel – forcing us to restore the child objects to a `valid` status rather than actually deleting them.

However, while an object is marked for deletion, we can't have it stored in the `mcolItems` object since everything in that `Collection` is visible to any client code and we're trying to hide those objects.

```
Option Explicit

Private mcolItems As Collection
Private mcolDeleted As Collection

Private mlngEditing As Long

Private Sub Class_Initialize()
   Set mcolItems = New Collection
   Set mcolDeleted = New Collection
End Sub
```

Thus, this code declares a new object, `mcolDeleted`, and then creates an instance of a `Collection` object when the class is initialized.

Updating the Remove Method

Of all the changes we'll make, the `Remove` method probably best illustrates the technique involved with having a second collection to store references to objects marked for deletion. This method calls the child object's `Delete` method to mark the object for deletion, and that doesn't change.

However, now we not only need to mark the object for deletion, but we need to remove it from the `mcolItems` collection and add it to the `mcolDeleted` collection – effectively hiding it from any client code, since only the `mcolItems` object's members are exposed via the our `Item` method.

```
Public Sub Remove(ByVal Index As Variant)
   If mlngEditing = 0 Then Err.Raise 445

   With mcolItems(Index)
     .BeginEdit
     .Delete
     .ApplyEdit
   End With
   mcolDeleted.Add mcolItems(Index)
   mcolItems.Remove Index
End Sub
```

Now, as each child object is marked for deletion, it is also hidden from the outside world – making it appear as though the object really was removed from the `Projects` object itself.

Updating IsDirty

The `IsDirty` property needs to be updated as well. In fact, it can potentially become more efficient, since we now have a very fast way to determine if any child objects have been deleted – if anything is in the `mcolDeleted` collection then at least one child object is marked for deletion.

```
Public Function IsDirty() As Boolean
   Dim objProject As Project

   If mcolDeleted.Count > 0 Then
     IsDirty = True
   Else
```

```
          For Each objProject In mcolItems
            If objProject.IsDirty Or objProject.IsNew Then
              IsDirty = True
              Exit For
            End If
          Next
        End If
    End Function
```

Updating BeginEdit

The `BeginEdit` method cascades the call down to each child object. Just because an object is marked for deletion doesn't mean it is deleted, so we still need to cascade the call.

```
    Public Sub BeginEdit()
      Dim objProject As Project

      For Each objProject In mcolItems
        objProject.BeginEdit
      Next
      For Each objProject In mcolDeleted
        objProject.BeginEdit
      Next

      mlngEditing = mlngEditing + 1
    End Sub
```

This is done by just looping through the `mcolDeleted` object's members and making the call.

Updating CancelEdit

The `CancelEdit` method is a bit more interesting. Not only does it need to cascade the call down to each child object, but also the result of a `CancelEdit` may be that an object, which was marked for deletion, may become valid once again.

This means that after each object marked for deletion has had its `CancelEdit` method called, we need to check and see if it is *still* marked for deletion. If not, then it must be removed from the `mcolDeleted` collection and restored to the `mcolItems` collection so it appears in the `Projects` object again.

```
    Public Sub CancelEdit()
      Dim lngindex As Long
      Dim objProject As Project

      If mlngEditing = 0 Then Err.Raise 445

      For lngindex = 1 To mcolItems.Count
        Set objProject = mcolItems(lngindex)
        With objProject
          If Not .IsNew Then
            .CancelEdit
          Else
            mcolItems.Remove lngindex
          End If
        End With
        Set objProject = Nothing
      Next
```

```
       For lngindex = mcolDeleted.Count To 1 Step -1
         Set objProject = mcolDeleted(lngindex)
         With objProject
           If Not .IsNew Then
             .CancelEdit
             If Not .IsDeleted Then
               mcolItems.Add objProject
               mcolDeleted.Remove lngindex
             End If
           Else
             mcolDeleted.Remove lngindex
           End If
         End With
         Set objProject = Nothing
       Next

     mlngEditing = mlngEditing - 1
   End Sub
```

Since we may be removing elements from the `mcolDeleted` collection, we need to walk through it from bottom to top. Each element we remove would make the list shorter, so we can't walk from top to bottom without things getting complex.

Basically this new loop is the same as the one which runs through the `mcolItems` object, with the addition of the code which checks to see if the object is still marked for deletion and restores it to `mcolItems` in the case that it is not longer marked.

Updating ApplyEdit

Like `BeginEdit`, the `ApplyEdit` method cascades the call to all the child objects. This remains true even if an object has been marked for deletion.

```
   Public Sub ApplyEdit()
     Dim objProject As Project

     If mlngEditing = 0 Then Err.Raise 445

     For Each objProject In mcolItems
       objProject.ApplyEdit
     Next
     For Each objProject In mcolDeleted
       objProject.ApplyEdit
     Next

     mlngEditing = mlngEditing - 1
   End Sub
```

At this point the `Projects` object has been updated to create the illusion that once a child object has been marked for deletion it is really gone. Behind the scenes the child object remains referenced by the `mcolDeleted` collection, but to the world outside the `Projects` object itself the object is gone.

Updating the Tasks Object

The changes to the `Tasks` object are identical to those we made in the `Projects` object. We won't walk through them in detail, but they are listed here for completeness.

First, the declarations and creating of the `Collection` object.

```
Option Explicit

Private mcolItems As Collection
Private mcolDeleted As Collection

Private mlngEditing As Long

Private Sub Class_Initialize()
  Set mcolItems = New Collection
  Set mcolDeleted = New Collection
End Sub
```

Then the `Remove` method is updated.

```
Public Sub Remove(ByVal Index As Variant)
  If mlngEditing = 0 Then Err.Raise 445

  With mcolItems(Index)
    .BeginEdit
    .Delete
    .ApplyEdit
  End With
  mcolDeleted.Add mcolItems(Index)
  mcolItems.Remove Index
End Sub
```

And `IsDirty`.

```
Public Function IsDirty() As Boolean
  Dim objTask As Task

  If mcolDeleted.Count > 0 Then
    IsDirty = True
  Else
    For Each objTask In mcolItems
      If objTask.IsDirty Then
        IsDirty = True
        Exit For
      End If
    Next
  End If
End Function
```

Finally the `BeginEdit`, `CancelEdit` and `ApplyEdit` are updated.

```
Public Sub BeginEdit()
  Dim objTask As Task

  For Each objTask In mcolItems
    objTask.BeginEdit
  Next
  For Each objTask In mcolDeleted
    objTask.BeginEdit
  Next

  mlngEditing = mlngEditing + 1
End Sub
```

```
Public Sub ApplyEdit()
  Dim objTask As Task

  If mlngEditing = 0 Then Err.Raise 445

  For Each objTask In mcolItems
    objTask.ApplyEdit
  Next
  For Each objTask In mcolDeleted
    objTask.ApplyEdit
  Next

  mlngEditing = mlngEditing - 1
End Sub

Public Sub CancelEdit()
  Dim lngindex As Long
  Dim objTask As Task

  If mlngEditing = 0 Then Err.Raise 445

  For Each objTask In mcolItems
    objTask.CancelEdit
  Next
  For lngindex = mcolDeleted.Count To 1 Step -1
    Set objTask = mcolDeleted(lngindex)
    With objTask
      If Not .IsNew Then
        .CancelEdit
        If Not .IsDeleted Then
          mcolItems.Add objTask
          mcolDeleted.Remove lngindex
        End If
      Else
        mcolDeleted.Remove lngindex
      End If
    End With
    Set objTask = Nothing
  Next

  mlngEditing = mlngEditing - 1
End Sub
```

And then our `Tasks` object, like the `Projects` object, is set up to hide any items that are removed from the collection – giving the illusion that such an object is actually gone.

Updating the ClientEdit Form

The current user interface includes code to compensate for the fact that child objects marked for deletion will be returned as members of the `Projects` object by marking them. With the changes we've now made to the `Projects` object, it will never return a reference to a child object which has been marked for deletion.

This means that we can simplify the code in the `ClientEdit` form, since it no longer needs to worry about deleted objects. In particular, the form's `ListProjects` method, which populates the `ListBox` control with the list of `Project` objects.

The code to mark a deleted object with (d) can be removed. I've shown it commented out here for clarity, but you can just remove the commented lines and change the following ElseIf to an If statement.

```
Private Sub ListProjects()
  Dim objProject As Project
  Dim lngIndex As Long

  lstProjects.Clear
  For lngIndex = 1 To mobjClient.Projects.Count
    Set objProject = mobjClient.Projects(lngIndex)
    With objProject
'       If .IsDeleted Then
'         lstProjects.AddItem .Name & " (d)"
      If .IsNew Then
         lstProjects.AddItem .Name & " (new)"
      Else
         lstProjects.AddItem .Name
      End If
      lstProjects.ItemData(lstProjects.NewIndex) = lngIndex
    End With
  Next
End Sub
```

Once that's done, save the project and recompile. We'll need to make a new copy of the DLL for binary compatibility. Now that we've added new classes to our DLL we need to update our copy so it has the correct CLSID values for the new classes.

The new Task and Tasks objects are in place and all our business objects have been updated to use state stacking to manage the OK, Cancel and Apply functionality.

Now we can move on to update the user interface of the Task Manager application so the user can interact with our new Task objects.

Updating the User Interface

Bring up the TaskManager project in Visual Basic.

The program should still work much as it did before – after all, we have only changed how the Client, Projects or Project objects work from the viewpoint of the UI developer. The state stacking enhancement only affected the *implementation* of our objects – not their *interface*. This illustrates one of the most powerful benefits of the CSLA approach – we can make fairly substantial changes to our objects and still not impact the UI itself.

However, we have added the Task and Tasks objects, and so we can enhance the UI to take advantage of these. We have also change the way in which deleted objects are handled. The user should be able to see a list of tasks associated with a project and then to add, edit or remove those tasks.

Enhancing the ProjectEdit Form

As it stands, the ProjectEdit form is very simplistic. Now we'll add some more complex functionality – basically making it very similar to the ClientEdit form. After all, now it will need to list a set of child objects and provide buttons for adding, editing and removing those objects.

Bring up the designer for the ProjectEdit form and add controls as shown in the diagram.

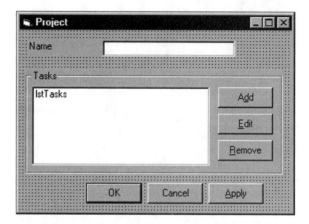

Control	Type	Value
Frame1	Frame	Tasks
lstTasks	ListBox	
cmdAdd	CommandButton	A&dd
cmdEdit	CommandButton	&Edit
cmdRemove	CommandButton	&Remove

The code behind these new controls will be very similar to the code we wrote for the ClientEdit form.

ListTasks Method

First off, let's add a routine to populate the ListBox control with a list of the child objects.

```
Private Sub ListTasks()
  Dim objTask As Task
  Dim lngIndex As Long

  lstTasks.Clear
  For lngIndex = 1 To mobjProject.Tasks.Count
    Set objTask = mobjProject.Tasks(lngIndex)
    With objTask
      If .IsNew Then
        lstTasks.AddItem .Name & " (new)"
      Else
        lstTasks.AddItem .Name
      End If
      lstTasks.ItemData(lstTasks.NewIndex) = lngIndex
    End With
  Next
End Sub
```

Note how the display is altered based on whether the Task object is new. It is nice to provide the user with a visual indication as to the status of each object, and this is one simple way of accomplishing that task.

Of course we don't need to detect objects marked for deletion, since the Tasks object is constructed to hide deleted objects from the UI, so only valid objects will be displayed.

We'll be calling this method from a number of locations in the remainder of the code.

Updating the Form_Load Routine

The first place we need to call ListTasks is from the Form_Load routine, so the ListBox gets populated with the child objects right up front.

```
Private Sub Form_Load()
  mflgLoading = True
  With mobjProject
    EnableOK .IsValid
    ' load object values into form controls
    txtName = .Name
    ListTasks
    .BeginEdit
  End With
  mflgLoading = False
End Sub
```

The Add, Edit and Remove Buttons

The code behind the cmdAdd, cmdEdit and cmdRemove buttons is virtually identical to that in the ClientEdit form that we created in Chapter 2. I won't go through it in detail since it is so similar and basic.

```
Private Sub cmdAdd_Click()
  Dim frmTask As TaskEdit

  Set frmTask = New TaskEdit
  frmTask.Component mobjProject.Tasks.Add
  frmTask.Show vbModal
  ListTasks
  Set frmTask = Nothing
End Sub

Private Sub cmdEdit_Click()
  Dim frmTask As TaskEdit

  Set frmTask = New TaskEdit
  frmTask.Component mobjProject.Tasks(lstTasks.ItemData(lstTasks.ListIndex))
  frmTask.Show vbModal
  ListTasks
  Set frmTask = Nothing
End Sub

Private Sub cmdRemove_Click()
  mobjProject.Tasks.Remove lstTasks.ItemData(lstTasks.ListIndex)
  ListTasks
End Sub
```

The common theme in both the cmdAdd_Click and cmdEdit_Click routines is the use of a new form – TaskEdit. Once we implement this new form our program will be ready.

Adding the TaskEdit Form

The `TaskEdit` form will be fairly straightforward since the `Task` object has no child objects and only a few properties. Add a new form to the project using the business form template from *Visual Basic 6 Business Objects*. If you aren't using the template, just add a regular form and insert all the code in this section. Change the form's name to `TaskEdit`.

Add controls to the form as shown in the diagram.

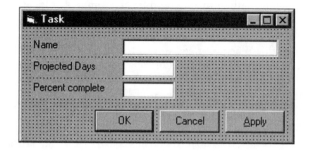

Control	Type	Value
Label1	Label	Name
Label2	Label	Projected days
Label3	Label	Percent complete
txtName	TextBox	
txtDays	TextBox	
txtPercent	TextBox	
cmdOK	CommandButton	OK
cmdClose	CommandButton	Cancel
CmdApply	CommandButton	&Apply

Now that the form's controls are ready, let's add the code.

Business Form Common Code

The basic CSLA template code gets us most of the way there. Just make the changes as shown.

```
Option Explicit

Private mflgLoading As Boolean

Private WithEvents mobjTask As Task

Public Sub Component(TaskObject As Task)
   Set mobjTask = TaskObject
End Sub
```

```
Private Sub Form_Load()
  mflgLoading = True
  With mobjTask
    EnableOK .IsValid
    ' load object values into form controls
    txtName = .Name
    txtDays = .ProjectedDays
    txtPercent = Format$(.PercentComplete, "0.0")
    .BeginEdit
  End With
  mflgLoading = False
End Sub

Private Sub cmdOK_Click()
  mobjTask.ApplyEdit
  Unload Me
End Sub

Private Sub cmdCancel_Click()
  mobjTask.CancelEdit
  Unload Me
End Sub

Private Sub cmdApply_Click()
  mobjTask.ApplyEdit
  mobjTask.BeginEdit
End Sub

Private Sub EnableOK(flgValid As Boolean)
  cmdOK.Enabled = flgValid
  cmdApply.Enabled = flgValid
End Sub

Private Sub mobjTask_Valid(IsValid As Boolean)
  EnableOK IsValid
End Sub
```

All that remains now is to add code to handle the TextBox controls.

TextBox Event Handling

The project already has two routines to take care of the details behind TextBox Change and
LostFocus events – we created these routines in Chapter 2. All we need to do is add code behind
each TextBox control's events to call these utility routines.

```
Private Sub txtDays_Change()
  If mflgLoading Then Exit Sub

  TextChange txtDays, mobjTask, "ProjectedDays"
End Sub

Private Sub txtDays_LostFocus()
  txtDays = TextLostFocus(mobjTask, "ProjectedDays")
End Sub

Private Sub txtName_Change()
  If mflgLoading Then Exit Sub

  TextChange txtName, mobjTask, "Name"
End Sub
```

```
Private Sub txtName_LostFocus()
   txtName = TextLostFocus(mobjTask, "Name")
End Sub

Private Sub txtPercent_Change()
   If mflgLoading Then Exit Sub

   TextChange txtPercent, mobjTask, "PercentComplete"
End Sub

Private Sub txtPercent_LostFocus()
   txtPercent = Format$(TextLostFocus(mobjTask, "PercentComplete"), "0.0")
End Sub
```

The `txtPercent_LostFocus` routine not only updates the display, but it also formats the value appropriately. This is a good example of keeping code to handle display issues in the UI.

Save the project at this point, as all the changes are complete.

We should be able to run the program now, working with clients, projects and tasks. While we can add and edit tasks, they are not currently saved into the database itself – only the `Client` and `Project` objects do that at this time.

In Chapter 4 we'll explore the intricacies of storing and retrieving grandchild objects into the database. For now we can be satisfied that we've demonstrated how to implement *n*-level rollback capabilities using state stacking.

Summary

The CSLA provides a good model for building applications based on both object-oriented and client/server technologies – distributed objects. However, one of the biggest drawbacks to the architecture as it was implemented in Visual Basic 6 Business Objects, and in Chapter 2, is the difficulty in handling any depth of child, grandchild and greatgrandchild objects – and so on.

In this chapter we discussed the concept of state stacking, which allows a UI-centric business object to keep *n*-levels of state data that can be used to roll back the object's state. With this technique we have, with little effort, enhanced the CSLA objects to support *n* levels of child objects.

Using this technique, we are able to add grandchild objects, such as the `Task` object, to a project. All this with no impact on the UI developer, and only some relatively minor implementation changes within the business objects themselves. Likewise, the data-centric objects are unchanged – unaffected by the new capabilities we've introduced to the UI-centric objects.

Having added UI-centric grandchild objects to our Task Manager application, we still can't persist them to the database. This is another area where the CSLA, as we've used it to date, becomes very complex. In Chapter 4 we'll explore the concept of a **superstate** – a technique to support efficient persistence of *n* levels of child objects in a client/server setting.

4

Passing Object State Across the Network

Overview

In this chapter we will continue to build on our Task Manager application by adding the ability to store `Task` objects in, and retrieve them from, the database.

In Chapter 2 we built the Task Manager application following the CSLA. The CSLA, however, didn't provide an easy way to manage the OK/Cancel/Apply functionality beyond a child object level – so we didn't add the grandchild, `Task`, objects in Chapter 2.

The concept of state stacking was introduced in Chapter 3. State stacking provides us with a powerful technique for managing OK/Cancel/Apply functionality to n levels of child objects. Using this new capability we were able to create UI-centric `Task` objects, objects that are grandchildren to the top-level parent object – `Client`.

The CSLA, as it stands, has another limitation. There is no easy way for UI-centric objects to store and retrieve data via data-centric objects when grandchild (or deeper) level objects are involved.

In this chapter I'll show why the CSLA has trouble with this concept, and we'll explore a solution that allows us to store and retrieve object families that are n levels deep, a technique called **SuperState**.

Introducing the SuperState

As we discussed in Chapter 1, a business object is composed of three main parts: interface, behavior (or implementation) and state.

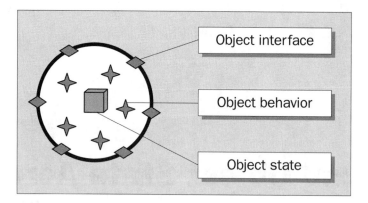

The two key design factors for a distributed object system revolve around:

❑ Where we perform the processing in our application
❑ How we move each object's state from computer to computer

The CSLA already does a good job enabling us to keep our application's processing distributed efficiently. Our UI-centric objects tend to contain processing required by the user interface, and are physically located as close to the user as possible. Likewise, the data-centric objects tend to contain processing that interacts with the application's data sources and are physically located close to those data sources.

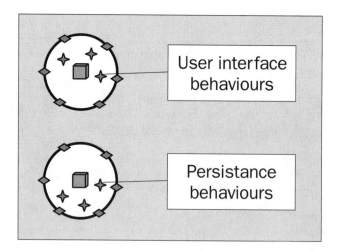

We are also able to move an object's state efficiently across the network by serializing the object's state into a byte stream – in our case a `String` variable. This is done by implementing a `GetState` method on each object.

The serialized state, in the form of a `String`, is then passed across the network, where it is deserialized – or converted from a byte stream back into detailed state data for the object.

This is illustrated in the following diagram, where we can see the interaction between the two halves of a business object – UI-centric (upper) and data-centric (lower):

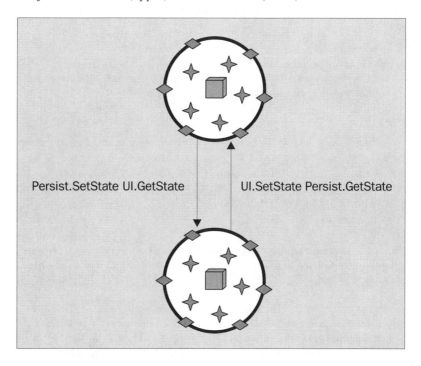

Both objects implement the `SetState` and `GetState` methods in exactly the same fashion. This makes each object symmetric with the other – both can provide state via `GetState` to be consumed by the opposing object's `SetState` method.

There are five chief ways to implement the `GetState` and `SetState` methods. These are covered thoroughly in *Visual Basic 6 Business Objects*, but we'll briefly revisit them here as well, looking at the primary techniques we can use to pass data from object to object.

Serializing Object State

While there are undoubtedly many other ways to serialize an object's state so we can pass it across a network, these are the most common and most easily implemented techniques:

- ❑ User-defined types overlaid with the `LSet` command
- ❑ `PropertyBag` objects
- ❑ Directly passing user-defined types as parameters
- ❑ Disconnected ADO `Recordset` objects
- ❑ Variant arrays

We won't go through the specific implementation of `GetState` and `SetState` methods for each of these techniques. However, each one has its own strengths and weaknesses when we discuss implementing distributed objects.

There are a number of requirements or criteria by which we can measure the effectiveness of each technique, which we shall look at before going through each technique in turn.

Requirements

One of the key requirements became quite apparent in Chapter 3 – we need to be able to stack the state of our object. Thus, whatever mechanism we might use for serialization of our object should support, or at least not interfere with, our ability to stack states.

Serialization of State

The primary requirement for stacking states is that we need a mechanism by which we can make a *copy* of the object's current state. Since the UDT/`LSet` technique we have used so far converts the object's state to a `String`, it was very easy to implement a stack by using a `Collection` object. Any technique that enables us to copy the object's state into something that can be stored in a `Collection` object will work just as well.

Performance

Performance is another obvious requirement. It is very important in any enterprise or highly scalable system that the mechanism we use to distribute our objects be as efficient as possible. Users have little patience for a slow application.

Performance comes in two 'flavors'. Obviously, we are concerned about performance in terms of converting our object's state into and out of a byte stream (the process of serialization/ deserialization). But we must also take into account the speed of access to the object's state *after* it has been deserialized. If the object's state data is stored in some format or container that slows down access to that data, then our entire application's performance will suffer.

Ease of Implementation

Another requirement of some importance is ease of implementation. In most cases, the easier a technique is to implement, the easier it is to maintain, and hence fewer bugs are inadvertently introduced into the application.

Also, an ideal solution should be mainstream – using tools and technologies that are well understood and easily accessible.

Mapping Object and Relational Models

Finally, an object's state is not the same as the tables in a relational database, which store some or all of the data. Most objects have state that is not stored in the database at all, or, alternatively, state that is stored across multiple data sources. For instance, a `Customer` object may have state data, such as last year's sales, that is a summation of a lot of data in a table, and at the same time the `Customer` object's state may come from an accounting database, a sales database and a shipping database – all on disparate back-end systems.

Object-oriented design and relational design are very different things. While there are often similarities between objects and database tables, when both the application's object model and a relational database are designed properly one will seldom, if ever, be an exact match of the other.

Therefore, a good mechanism for serializing an object's state must take into account that we'll not only be sending relational table data, but also other state data between our objects as well.

Each of the five main options we've proposed has its tradeoffs, with the `PropertyBag` being perhaps the best overall compromise. Let's quickly review each one in turn.

UDT/LSet

The UDT/`LSet` technique is the one we've used in this book so far. It was also used in *Visual Basic 6 Business Objects*. This technique uses two user-defined types (UDTs) of exactly the same length. One UDT has members that reflect the detailed state values of our object. The other UDT has one member – a single `String` variable. The `LSet` command is used to do a very fast memory copy from one UDT to the other, thus effectively converting a detailed UDT into a `String`, or a `String` into a detailed UDT.

This technique provides true serialization of an object's state data – converting the data into a simple byte stream. It works very well for state stacking, since the result of serialization is a simple `String` variable that can easily be pushed and popped on a stack of states (as we illustrated in Chapter 3).

Perhaps the biggest benefit of this technique is its performance. Gauging performance in terms of serialization/deserialization the UDT/`LSet` approach is the fastest option we have available. The next fastest, the `PropertyBag` object, is about half as fast, while all the other techniques are slower still.

> *The performance comparisons cited in this chapter were generated using a simple client/server application. An object on the server contains data, which is serialized and sent to the client. The object on the client receives the byte stream and deserializes it to restore the data into the object's local variables. This transfer is carried out using each technique. The test is intentionally simple, since the only variable we want in the application is the cost of the data transfer technique.*

If we look at performance in terms of using the state data once it has been deserialized into the object, the UDT/`LSet` technique is also excellent. Since all the data values are stored in native data types (not `Variants`, etc.), access and manipulation of the data is as fast as we'll ever get.

Where this technique falls down is with ease of implementation. While the `GetState`/`SetState` routines are trivial to create, it can be difficult to ensure that both UDTs (the detail and the overlay) are exactly the same length. Additionally, there's no provision for handling variable length data such as a memo field, or binary data, such as image or sound information.

The final criterion is whether the technique facilitates separation of the object's state from the concept of a relational table. This technique provides such separation, because the developer is required to define the object's state in the UDT, and implement code to copy values into and out of any data sources in order to serialize the data.

In terms of miscellaneous benefits, the UDT/`LSet` technique benefits greatly from the fact that the state data is converted into a `String` variable. Since such a simple, easily manipulated data type represents our object's state, we can do a great many things with great ease. For instance, we can store the state in a file, send it via MSMQ, send it over an IP socket, and more. This is true of other techniques as well – the benefit is derived by having the state in the form of a native data type within Visual Basic.

Other techniques convert the data to a Byte array. In fact, the LSet technique could also be used this way. Byte array's are sometimes less desirable than a simple String variable, however, since it may be easier to create the body of a mail message, write to a file or do other operations using a String than an array of bytes.

Overall, the UDT/LSet technique is best used when performance is the primary criterion for an application. The technique is harder to use than most others, but provides the best performance both in use of the object's state and in serialization/deserialization. This is why I've used it so far in this book – as in many cases performance is an overriding design parameter.

PropertyBag

A PropertyBag object is an object that stores values provided to it, and allows those values to be retrieved by name. Essentially it is a group of key-value pairs. We put values in with a name attached, and then retrieve those values later by using the same name. The PropertyBag object also has a Contents property, which provides us with access to the entire content of the object as a byte stream – it knows how to serialize and deserialize itself.

The PropertyBag object's methods are described in the following table:

Method	Return value	Parameters	Use
WriteProperty	None	Name, Value	This method is used to write a value into the PropertyBag object. An associated name must also be supplied – this name will be used to retrieve the value later.
ReadProperty	Value	Name	This method is used to retrieve a value from the PropertyBag object. We supply the name of the value, and the value itself is returned as a result of the method call.
Contents	Byte array (on Get)	Byte array (on Let)	This method is a property that can be either retrieved or set. When retrieved, the return value is a Byte array containing all the data contained within the PropertyBag object. This Byte array can then be set into the Contents property of another PropertyBag object – effectively cloning the original PropertyBag object's data.

The values stored in a `PropertyBag` object are of the `Variant` data type. This means that a `PropertyBag` can hold virtually any type of data, and that each value can be of a different length or type.

Visual Basic 5.0 provided the `PropertyBag` object for authors of ActiveX controls. Visual Basic 6.0 has extended the object so it is available throughout the environment – making it available for use in our objects.

> *The `PropertyBag` object has one important limitation (or feature). A value can be written to the object under a given name, then another value can be written to the object under the* same *name. In such a case, the first time a value is retrieved using that name we'll get the last value written. The* second *time the value for that name is retrieve we'll get the* first *value entered. It is not clear why the `PropertyBag` has this behavior, but it does preclude the use of `PropertyBag` objects for holding state long term. On the other hand, this behavior doesn't preclude using it for serialization and deserialization of an object's state data.*

When using a `PropertyBag` object to serialize and deserialize an object, we store the object's state data itself in `Private`, module-level variables. Then the `GetState` method just copies the `Private` variables into the `PropertyBag` object using the `WriteProperty` method and the `SetState` method copies the `PropertyBag` object's values into the `Private` object variables using the `ReadProperty` method.

Both `GetState` and `SetState` use the `PropertyBag` object's `Contents` property to retrieve and set the byte stream into the object. This allows us to serialize and deserialize state data with very little effort. We'll using this technique later in the chapter, so we'll get some good exposure to exactly how this works.

> *While the `Contents` property is an array of `Byte` values, Visual Basic can automatically coerce the `Byte` array into a `String` variable – allowing `GetState` and `SetState` to return and receive `String` parameters just like with the UDT/LSet technique. This has a small performance impact, but is sometimes worth it, since a `String` value is sometimes easier to work with than a `Byte` array, as it is an atomic, native data type.*

The `PropertyBag` technique, as with the UDT/LSet technique, allows for easy implementation of state stacking. Whether we coerce the byte stream into a `String` or leave it as a `Byte` array, it can be pushed and popped on a state stack implemented as a `Collection` object, just like in Chapter 3.

Serialization/deserialization performance of the `PropertyBag` is about half as fast as the UDT/LSet technique. However, this is still very fast, making the `PropertyBag` perfectly acceptable from a performance viewpoint in all but the most demanding cases.

Since the state data, once deserialized, is stored in module-level `Private` variables, we can use them with no performance penalty.

The `PropertyBag` technique is very easy to implement, and the `PropertyBag` object, provided with Visual Basic, is well documented. While the `GetState` and `SetState` methods end up with more code than the UDT/LSet approach, we avoid having to match lengths on UDTs – dramatically simplifying the code.

As an added bonus, we gain the ability to work with large data values such as memo fields and so forth.

> *The UDT/LSet technique requires that all* String *variables in the UDT be fixed length. This makes it very difficult, if not impossible, to work with large or variable length data such as memo-style text, images, sounds, etc.*

As with the UDT/LSet approach, PropertyBag objects require the developer to copy data into and out of the data sources to serialize and deserialize the object. This provides clear separation between the object's state data and data that is stored in databases.

Overall, the PropertyBag is typically the best choice for serialization of our objects. It has good performance, is easy to use and provides good flexibility. Essentially, for a small performance penalty, we get all the benefits of the UDT/LSet technique, plus easier use and the ability to use variable length data types.

As we continue through the book I'll use a combination of PropertyBag objects and the UDT/LSet technique. UDT/LSet still provides the best performance and so we'll use it to serialize individual objects – however, the PropertyBag makes multi-object serialization much easier, so we'll use it as well.

Direct UDT

Visual Basic 6.0 (along with an updated version of COM) allows us to pass parameters of user-defined types to and from our methods. Such UDT variables can also be placed in a Collection object.

> *These user-defined types cannot contain fixed-length strings, but they can contain variable length* String *values.*

To use direct UDTs, we need to move the declaration of the UDT itself into one of our class modules (I typically use the data-centric class). Once declared in a class module as a Public UDT, the data type can be used throughout our project. Our object simply declares a variable based on the UDT to store its state data – just like with the UDT/LSet technique.

The GetState and SetState methods become very trivial. GetState simply returns the Private UDT variable as its result, while SetState accepts a parameter typed using the UDT and just copies the parameter into the Private UDT variable within the object.

Since Visual Basic 6.0 allows a Public UDT from a class module to be placed in a Collection, it is very easy to implement state stacking as we did in Chapter 3.

Strangely enough, passing a UDT directly is slower than passing data packaged in a native String data type. The difference is enough that direct UDTs are quite a bit slower than the UDT/LSet technique – about twice as slow in fact.

The COM marshaling mechanism has to do a lot more work to safely marshal a complex UDT with many members of different data types than it does to marshal a single String variable. This results in the performance difference we're seeing.

The downside to this is shown in the poor performance. The upside however, is that COM should automatically take care of cross-platform or 32-bit to 64-bit conversions of our data. This is a potential problem with the UDT/LSet technique, where we would have to handle such conversions on our own. There's no way to know if the `PropertyBag` *object will automatically take care of this issue once 64-bit platforms become available either. Thus, direct UDT passing may be a good option if you plan to use COM to communicate across multiple operating systems, or to 64-bit computers running Windows NT – when that option becomes available.*

Also, `Public` UDTs in a class module cannot be passed as parameters using the `ByVal` keyword. Following the CSLA (and good distributed programming practices), parameters should be passed by value whenever possible – and it is usually possible.

Being unable to pass UDTs by value means that the data is not only sent across the network to the target object – but it is retrieved once the method call is complete, even if we don't use the data. To put it simply, the data is not only transferred from the server to the client, but it is also transferred from the client to the server – leading to an extra round-trip and thus more network traffic.

Once the data is inside our business object performance is great. After all, the data is local and private, just as with the UDT/`LSet` or `PropertyBag` approaches.

Direct UDTs have a huge benefit in the ease of use area. The `GetState` and `SetState` methods effectively are reduced to a single line of code each, and there is no explicit serialization or deserialization of the object's data – Visual Basic (or more accurately COM) is handling all the details.

Since the business object's data is being stored in a UDT, there is clear separation of the relational data from the object's state data, so our final requirement is met very well.

There are a couple of potentially significant drawbacks to using direct UDTs. First off, scripting languages (such as VBScript) don't understand UDTs as a data type. This means that we can't implement code in, say, ASP to retrieve and store our object's state using `GetState` or `SetState`. In Chapter 7 we'll implement a browser-based solution that does, in fact, do this very thing – this technique is inappropriate in that case.

Additionally there is a logistic concern. The ability to work with UDTs in the manner we're discussing requires updated versions of some COM DLLs. To use this technique, then, requires that all servers and client workstations be upgraded by installing these DLLs. In a small setting this may not be a problem, but in an enterprise setting such an upgrade may not be a trivial undertaking.

Direct passing of UDTs appears to be a great option at first glance. However, with the limitations on the technology, the logistic requirements for COM upgrades and the slower-than-desired performance it is probably not a good first choice. Both the `PropertyBag` and UDT/`LSet` techniques provide better performance with fewer drawbacks.

ADO Recordset

Disconnected ADO `Recordset` objects have become one of the most widely used techniques for passing data between client and server computers. Not only can they be used in the traditional application where code is written to directly interact with the data in the `Recordset`, but they can also be used to pass object state across the network.

At first glance, disconnected `Recordset` objects appear to be an ideal solution to our needs. However, as we'll see, this is perhaps the worst technique we have at our disposal when all things are considered.

When using disconnected `Recordset` objects, the typical approach is to create a `Recordset` based on a database query, then return that `Recordset` to the client-side object. The business object then uses the `Recordset` as a repository for the state data – avoiding the need to copy the data out of the `Recordset` into any other form of storage. Once the object is done working with or altering the data, the `Recordset` is sent back to the data-centric object on the application server so the database can be updated by using ADO's support for batch updates.

This seems very simple and elegant, which is why it's a frequently used technique. However, let's walk through our requirements.

Firstly, we need to implement state stacking. To stack the object's current state we are required to make a copy of the state and push it on some form of stack – in Chapter 3 we used a `Collection` to implement that stack. Unfortunately there's no easy way to copy an ADO `Recordset` object. In fact, the only way to force ADO to make a copy of a `Recordset` is to move it across processes (or across the network). Thus, to implement state stacking we'd have to create a new ActiveX EXE to house the stack of our object states. This is a lot of work, and would be quite slow since we're talking about cross-process communication.

> *At first glance it may appear that the `Clone` method will solve this problem. However, the `Clone` method does not make a copy of a `Recordset` – it merely creates a new 'cursor' we can use to access the same underlying data.*

The other alternative is to create a new `Recordset` object from scratch each time we need to stack states. The current `Recordset` data could then be copied to the new `Recordset` field-by-field to create the copy to be pushed on the stack. Obviously this is a fair bit of coding and would have a negative impact on performance.

Next on our list of considerations was performance. ADO is quite fast – remarkably so in fact. `Recordsets` flagged to use client-side cursors are automatically copied across the network – being serialized and deserialized behind the scenes. While ADO can be complex to work with, and despite having to serialize more data than previous techniques when using the `Recordset` object, this process is only about 20 times slower than the UDT/`LSet` technique.

Once the data arrives within the client-side object we need to work with it. In our previously discussed approaches the data is always stored in local, native data types and so access is as fast as we'll get. Accessing data in an ADO `Recordset` object is only about 27 times slower than accessing data from a local variable. Given the speed of data access to a local variable, this is quite inconsequential – and most impressive given the amount of work ADO must be doing behind the scenes. Thus, accessing data from an ADO `Recordset` is done at a pretty good speed.

Our next requirement is ease of use. As we noted earlier, ADO `Recordset` objects are widely used to move data across the network specifically because they are easy to use. However, given our other requirements (especially state stacking, along with some other limitations) there's a lot of extra coding that needs to be done to make `Recordset` objects work on a par with the other techniques we have at our disposal.

In the end, using disconnected `Recordset` objects is the slowest technique available, requires the most coding and is the hardest to use of all the techniques available. We've already discussed the complexities for state stacking, and we'll review some others shortly.

The final requirement is separation of object state from the concept of a relational table. One of the biggest advantages behind disconnected ADO `Recordset` objects is the ability to retrieve data directly out of the database and bring it, untouched, back to the object whose state we're restoring. However, this is *exactly* what we should not do. Such an approach directly ties the object's state to our data source – precluding the object from having state not stored in the database and potentially making it difficult to assemble an object's state from a set of widely disparate data sources.

To overcome this we can implement the data-centric object to create an ADO `Recordset` object with fields that match our object's state requirements rather than any relational table design. The data retrieved from the database is then copied into the new `Recordset` object for use by the object. This approach effectively separates the object state from relational designs – and is essentially what we're doing with all the previous techniques when we copy data from a result set into a UDT or `PropertyBag` object.

Unfortunately this approach prevents us from leveraging ADO's abilities to update disconnected `Recordset` objects directly back into the database – after all, we're no longer keeping or using the `Recordset` created from the database, but are instead using one we've created through code. To work around this, we'll end up pulling the data out of the `Recordset` object in order to update the database by calling stored procedures or manipulating another `Recordset` connected to the database.

Disconnected `Recordsets` have difficulty dealing with groups of child objects as well. This is another area where the ease of implementation is very low. While ADO does provide support for **shaped recordsets**, they don't solve all the problems we face when dealing with child objects. We still have no easy way to make a copy of the `Recordset` object to implement state stacking.

With the previous techniques, each object ends up containing its own state data in local variables. With a `Recordset` however, we'll have a single `Recordset` object containing the data for *all* the child objects – after all, we don't want to do a `SELECT` to retrieve each child object separately.

So, each child object ends up 'attached' to a row in the `Recordset`. How does each child ensure the `Recordset`'s cursor is set to the appropriate row? This is a challenge. We can use the `Clone` method on the `Recordset` to create a clone for each child object – but if we have hundreds of objects this could get real ugly, real fast.

We can give each child object a bookmark to a row (assuming our particular `Recordset` supports bookmarks – not all do). Then at the top of each method the child can set the bookmark to the right place. This works – assuming no child objects ever interact with each other.

As soon as code in one child object starts to interact with another child object, the underlying cursor location would be moved. When the thread of execution returns to the original object, the programmer would need to remember to reset the current record or we'd be manipulating the wrong row of data.

In any case, having a single `Recordset` for all child objects makes state stacking very complex. State stacking is done object-by-object, yet there's no way to stack the state for a single child object without stacking it for all child objects using `Recordset` objects.

In the final analysis, disconnected ADO Recordset objects are great for creating traditional data-oriented applications in an *n*-tier setting. However, they are very problematic if we try to use them to manage or pass the state of complex business objects in a distributed object setting.

Variant arrays

The last technique we'll discuss is perhaps the oldest – using an array of Variant values to move data between objects and across the network. This technique was popularized due to the GetRows method of Recordset and Resultset objects, which returned the entire data set in a two dimensional array of Variant values.

The typical usage of a Variant array is to retrieve the data from the database, and then use the GetRows method to convert the results into a two dimensional array. This array is then returned as a result to the client workstation, where the object makes use of the data within the array. When the data is to be updated into the database, the array is sent back across the network and a server-side object uses the data in the array to update the database itself.

This approach has some of the limitations of the disconnected ADO Recordset technique.

State stacking is very difficult. Visual Basic 6 does allow us to make a copy of an entire array into a second array declared as a **dynamic array**. A dynamic array is one declared with empty parenthesis so it has no predetermined dimensions. However, there is no easy way to make a copy of a single row from an array, short of writing code to iterate through all the array elements and copy each one. Yet, we must make copies of row-level data in order to copy the state data for any specific object. This is required to implement state stacking as in Chapter 3.

Since the array contains data for all objects, not just a single object, it is also potentially difficult to implement state stacking for individual objects. Not as hard as with Recordset objects, but still more difficult than with UDTs or PropertyBag objects.

Performance is also a problem. While the data is transferred across the network fairly efficiently, there is a lot of overhead involved in getting the data from a Recordset object into the array, and then from the array back into the database for updates.

Additionally, while the object is using the data there is a lot of overhead. Each time a value is accessed the object has to find the element in the array, then convert it from a Variant data type to the data type appropriate to how it's being used.

Overall, these combined effects leave the Variant array approach with the worst performance of any technique we are discussing here.

On the other hand, Variant arrays are very easy to work with and implement (outside of the state stacking isues). The GetRows method makes the creation of the array trivial, and the array is easily passed across the network.

The separation between object state and relational data is ambiguous at best. The use of GetRows to create the array tends to directly tie the array to the relational model – leaving little room for managing other parts of the object's state.

Perhaps even worse, the usage of the array is position-dependant. Unlike a Recordset, where values can be referenced by field name, with an array they are simply referenced by column number. A simple change to the SELECT statement that generates the original Recordset can cause client code to break – all we have to do is add a column, remove a column or change the order in which the columns are retrieved. This type of problem can be very hard to debug.

Given the performance and stability drawbacks of `Variant` arrays – and the fact that it is difficult to use them to implement state stacking – they are far from the best choice in most cases.

Summary of Options

The following table shows how each of the five main techniques stack up according to these criteria:

Technique	State stacking	Performance	Ease of use	OO/Relational separation
UDT/Lset	Easy	Very good	Poor	Good
PropertyBag	Easy	Good	Good	Good
Direct UDT	Easy	Good	Good	Good
ADO Recordset	Very difficult	Adequate	Adequate	Poor
Variant arrays	Very difficult	Adequate	Adequate	Adequate

Having reviewed all five chief techniques, we are left with the UDT/LSet technique being fastest, but somewhat difficult, and the `PropertyBag` being the overall favorite, with good performance, easy implementation and good flexibility. The direct UDT approach is also generally good – though it may require upgrades to COM on any machine using the application.

Throughout the remainder of this book, we'll use the UDT/LSet technique for individual object serialization – taking advantage of its performance. Then we'll use the `PropertyBag` option where groups of object states need to be combined – taking advantage of its flexibility and good performance.

Now that we've examined the various techniques available for moving object data across the network, let's explore some theory around distributed objects.

Passing Objects by Value

When we talk about distributing objects, our goal is to allow an object on one computer to be used by code on another computer in an efficient manner.

Conceptually, objects communicate by sending messages to one another – causing a method to be invoked when the message is received by an object.

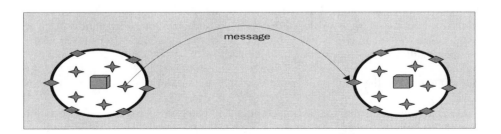

Of course this is more of a conceptual idea than reality – in most cases there aren't really *messages* being sent around. However, it is a good way to think about object communication, especially when discussing distributed objects.

In a typical object-oriented model, objects communicate with each other freely. Object-oriented designs usually assume that all method calls – or messages – have no expense in terms of performance.

In a distributed object setting this type of assumption is invalid. We have to take into account how far a message must travel to get from the calling object to the target object. The further it must travel, the worse our performance will become.

So, when one object needs to communicate with another object an evaluation needs to be made as to whether the target object should be moved physically closer to the calling object. This is a decision we must make while designing our application and its objects.

For one method call, the effort involved in moving an object rarely makes sense. However, if many method calls will be made then it frequently makes sense to move the object closer.

Moving an Object

When we talk about *moving an object*, what we're really talking about is moving the object's state from an instance of the class on one machine to an instance of the class on another machine. Another way to phrase this is *passing the object by value*.

Passing an object by value allows the object to appear to move from machine to machine around the network – thus being physically close to whatever code needs to send messages to it at the time.

In the CSLA model, we take a slightly different view. Instead of moving an object from machine to machine, we are conceptually splitting the *same object* across multiple machines. The UI-centric halves of each object typically running on the client workstation and the data-centric halves on the application server.

Instead of passing an object by value such that the same class is instantiated on each computer, in the CSLA we are instantiating the appropriate class to create either the UI-centric or data-centric object as appropriate. The concept of passing by value remains valid, we are just using objects tailored to specific requirements for supporting the user interface or data-related activities.

All of this works well, and is fairly straightforward, for a single business object. It gets more complex when we are dealing with many levels of parent-child relationships.

Defining the SuperState

By this point we should have a good understanding of the concept of state – at least as it pertains to a single object. Additionally, we've explored the concepts and techniques surrounding moving that state from machine to machine to either move the object itself or allow various facets of the object to be expressed on different machines as with the CSLA.

Now we need to expand the concept of state to encompass families of objects.

Consider the basic idea of an `Invoice` object. Such an object has `LineItem` objects that represent the various items being invoiced.

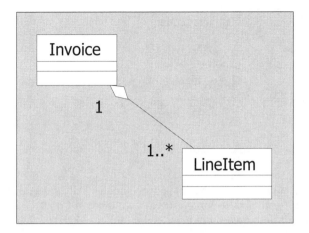

The Invoice item has state, as do each of the LineItem objects.

At the same time, it is not possible – or at least it makes no sense – to have a LineItem without an Invoice. Also, if an Invoice has LineItems, it makes no sense to just have an instance of the Invoice object without instances of those related LineItem objects.

Fundamentally, the LineItem objects may be considered *part of* the Invoice object. In Chapter 3 we explored how they are related in terms of *n*-level rollback capability as the objects' states are altered. That is part of a deeper relationship between the states of all the objects in a parent-child relationship.

This is especially apparent when we consider saving and retrieving the Invoice object in a database. We can't just save the Invoice without the LineItem objects. Likewise, we can't save a LineItem object without saving the parent Invoice object.

What we have is a transactional setting, where we must save all the objects in the family – or none of them.

Instead of viewing the LineItem objects as separate, we could more accurately view them as *part of* the Invoice object:

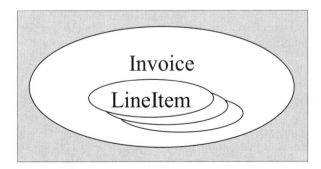

If we take this view of the objects, what does it do to our view of object state? As with all business objects, each object has its own state, as reflected by the cubes in the following diagram.

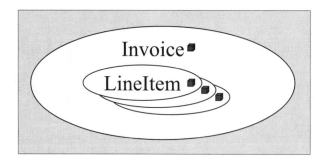

That's great when we're consider each individual object, but if we look at the `Invoice` object as a single entity that is merely composed of other objects we might take a different view. In particular, the `Invoice` object not only has a state containing its own data, but it also has a **superstate** that also includes the state data for all the objects it contains.

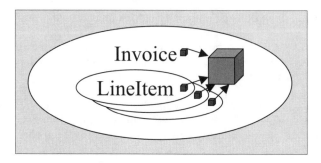

This superstate is very much like the state of an individual object, in that it contains all the data needed to recreate an equivalent instance of the object. However, where a *state* only contains a single object's data, a *superstate* actually contains all the data needed to create a new instance of an entire family of objects.

> **The superstate of an object is defined as being the combination of the object's state and the superstates of all its child objects.**

Note that the definition of superstate is recursive. It isn't enough for an object to assemble its superstate by combining its own state with that of its children. It must use the *superstates* of its children instead – thus handling the case where there are grandchild objects involved.

Using the superstate, we can efficiently transfer the state of an entire family of objects across the network. For instance, we can transfer the superstate from a UI-centric `Invoice` object and its child objects across to a data-centric `InvoicePersist` object to be saved into the database.

For a single object, the superstate is exactly the same as the object's state. Any time an object has children however, its superstate will include both the object's state and the superstate of all its child objects.

To do this, the superstate needs to be serialized into a byte stream – just like we've done with simple object states in the past. It can then be sent across the network and deserialized into an object or object family on the other side.

The following diagram illustrates this concept. At the top we have an `Invoice` object, with `LineItem` child objects. Each object has its own individual state (shown as the small cubes). However, they can all be combined to generate a single superstate (shown by the large cube). It is the superstate that must be serialized, using a method such as `GetSuperState`, so it can be efficiently sent across the network to the data-centric object at the bottom of the diagram. There it can be deserialized, using a method such as `SetSuperState`, so the individual states of each object can be manipulated.

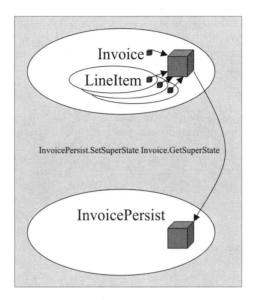

This is a variation on the model we've been discussing to date – where we serialize an object's state to send it across the network. In this case, we're just serializing the states of an entire family of objects into a single byte stream for efficient transfer.

Creating a SuperState

Now that we have the concept of a superstate, how can we build it?

Business objects, as we've been implementing them, have the ability to serialize and deserialize themselves through the `GetState` and `SetState` methods. This is a good start, since our objective is to combine the states of an entire family of objects into a single byte stream. If each object can convert its own state into a byte stream, all we need to do is come up with a way to combine those individual byte streams into a single, large byte stream.

CSLA Collection Objects

We are already doing this to some degree with our implementation of `Collection` objects following the CSLA. `Collection` objects, such as the `Projects` object, implement their `GetState` method by combining all the serialized states of their child objects, such as the `Project` objects, into a single byte stream.

This is currently done by using the `Buffer` utility object to efficiently combine those individual states into a single `String` variable. The `Buffer` object, however, has a significant limitation, in that it can only combine the states of objects that have exactly the same length. We'll see why this is important shortly.

Conceptually what we're doing with `Collection` objects is correct. The problem comes in when we introduce grandchild objects. In such a case, each child object contained by the `Collection` object will have child objects of its own. When we added the `Task` and `Tasks` objects to the Task Manager system in Chapter 3 we introduced this complication.

If the child objects have children of their own, then they will have superstates that are made up of the child object's state combined with the states of the grandchild objects. An important side effect of this is that the superstate of each child object will likely be a different length – those with more grandchild objects will be longer than those with fewer or none.

Due to the way `Buffer` is implemented we have no way to handle this, so we'll need a better solution.

Creating a GetSuperState Method

The `PropertyBag` object is a good alternative. We can use it to combine the superstate data from each child object – regardless of length. Rather than using the `Buffer` object to combine the superstates from all child objects in a `Collection` object, we can use a `PropertyBag`.

> The `PropertyBag` object allows us to store any number of arbitrarily sized values – making it ideal for assembly of a superstate.

Consider the following code that might be found in a `Collection` object:

```
Friend Function GetSuperState() As Byte()
  Dim objPB As PropertyBag
  Dim objChild As Child
  Dim lngCount As Long

  Set objPB = New PropertyBag

  ' store child items into propertybag
  With objPB
    .WriteProperty "Count", mcolItems.Count
    For Each objChild In mcolItems
      lngCount = lngCount + 1
      .WriteProperty "Item" & CStr(lngCount), objChild.GetSuperState
    Next

    ' return byte array from function
    GetSuperState = .Contents
  End With
  Set objPB = Nothing
End Function
```

This code is very similar to what we might find in a `Collection` object's `GetState` method, but there are two important differences.

First off, we're calling the `GetSuperState` method of each child object rather than the `GetState` method. We'll look at how to implement `GetSuperState` in an object shortly, but for now we can assume that `GetSuperState` returns not only the child object's state, but also the states of *its* child objects.

Secondly, we're combining all the superstate data into a `PropertyBag` object by using the `WriteProperty` method. Each child object's superstate is stored in the `PropertyBag` object using a name of `Item` combined with a number to indicate the child's position in the `Collection` object.

```
.WriteProperty "Item" & CStr(lngCount), objChild.GetSuperState
```

The total count of child objects is also stored with a name of `Count`. This will be important as we build the `SetSuperState` method – after all, we need some way to know how many child objects to pull back out of the `PropertyBag` object.

```
.WriteProperty "Count", mcolItems.Count
```

Once the `PropertyBag` contains all the child object data, we then use the `Contents` property to return all that information as a single byte stream.

```
GetSuperState = .Contents
```

This is a relatively small adaptation of the `Collection` object's original `GetState` method.

Creating a SetSuperState Method

Creating a `SetSuperState` is likewise quite similar. Consider the following code:

```
Friend Sub SetSuperState(Buffer() As Byte)
  Dim objPB As PropertyBag
  Dim lngIndex As Long
  Dim lngEdit As Long
  Dim objChild As Child

  Set objPB = New PropertyBag

  ' reset collection object
  Set mcolItems = Nothing
  Set mcolItems = New Collection

  With objPB
    ' load byte array into propertybag
    .Contents = Buffer

    ' loop through propertybag contents, loading each
    ' item into an object for the collection
    For lngIndex = 1 To .ReadProperty("Count")
      Set objChild = New Child
      objChild.SetSuperState .ReadProperty("Item" & CStr(lngIndex))
      For lngEdit = 1 To mlngEditing
        objChild.BeginEdit
      Next
      mcolItems.Add objChild
      Set objChild = Nothing
    Next
  End With
  Set objPB = Nothing
End Sub
```

As with the regular `SetState` method, this new method accepts a byte stream as a parameter. However, instead of using a `Buffer` object to decode the byte stream, this code uses a `PropertyBag` object and its `Contents` property.

I am building the various `GetSuperState` and `SetSuperState` methods throughout this book so they return and accept `Byte` array values since this is the native data type used by the `PropertyBag` object. In some cases you may need to convert this value to a `String` – especially if working in an environment that only supports simple data types (like scripting languages).

Once the `PropertyBag` object contains all the state data, we can simply loop through that data, retrieving each child object's superstate and placing it into the new child object.

```
Set objChild = New Child
objChild.SetSuperState .ReadProperty("Item" & CStr(lngIndex))
```

As with the normal `SetState` method, we need to call `BeginEdit` an appropriate number of times – this is based on the changes for state stacking we made in Chapter 3.

```
For lngEdit = 1 To mlngEditing
  objChild.BeginEdit
Next
```

Then the new child object can be placed into our underlying `Collection` and we're all set.

```
mcolItems.Add objChild
```

Conceptually this is very much like the `SetState` methods we've implemented to date, but is far more powerful since the child objects are given a superstate and not just a simple state for a single object.

Business Objects with No Children

These new `GetSuperState` and `SetSuperState` methods for a `Collection` object rely on our business objects themselves having `GetSuperState` and `SetSuperState` methods. Let's see how those may work.

The simplest case is that of a business object with no child objects of its own. In our Task Manager application this includes the `Task` objects. Most applications have many objects that have no child objects.

The superstate of an object is defined as being the combination of the object's state and the superstates of all its child objects. If our object has no children, then its superstate is nothing more than just the object's state.

This makes our job quite easy, since all CSLA business objects already have `GetState` and `SetState` methods to serialize their state. Since the superstate is the same as the state, our `GetSuperState` and `SetSuperState` methods need merely to do the same thing.

Creating a GetSuperState Method

The `GetSuperState` method returns a byte stream containing the data of the superstate. Since, in this case, the superstate is the same as the state, we can simply return the byte stream generated by the existing `GetState` method.

```
Friend Function GetSuperState() As String
  GetSuperState = GetState
End Function
```

This is, of course, the trivial case.

Creating a SetSuperState Method

Likewise, the `SetSuperState` method can just accept a parameter and pass it along to the `SetState` method.

```
Friend Sub SetSuperState(Buffer As String)
  SetState Buffer
End Sub
```

For business objects with no children, that's all we need to do. The more interesting scenario is where the business object has child objects of its own.

Business Objects with Children

If a business object has child objects then we have a bit more work to do to assemble and disassemble the superstate. We not only need to work with our object's own state, but also the superstates of all the child objects.

The fact that we are accessing the superstates of the child objects is critical. If all we used were the simple states of the child objects we'd never get their grandchild objects (should they exist). However, if we collect the superstate of each child object then we'll not only get the child's state, but also the state of all its children.

For instance, we can use a `PropertyBag` object to assemble both the current object's state together with the superstate from its child object.

```
Private Function GetSuperState() As Byte()
  Dim objPB As PropertyBag

  Set objPB = New PropertyBag
  With objPB
    ' store this object's state
    .WriteProperty "State", GetState
    ' store superstate of child object
    .WriteProperty "Child", objChild.GetSuperState
    GetSuperState = .Contents
  End With
  Set objPB = Nothing
End Function
```

This cascading effect is exactly what we want. When we assemble the superstate of any object, it will include *all* the data for its child and grandchild objects – down to *n*-levels deep. In the end, our superstate will contain the individual state data from each object in the family.

Creating a GetSuperState Method

The GetSuperState method will need to serialize the object's state, plus the collected superstates of all its child objects. Fortunately, this is not terribly difficult. The object already implements GetState, so we can easily serialize that data. Also, when an object has children, a Collection object manages the children. As we've already explored how we can create a GetSuperState method for a Collection object, we'll just leverage that knowledge here.

In fact, the technique we used in that GetSuperState implementation is very similar to what we'll do here. The PropertyBag object makes it very easy for us to bring together variable length items and then serialize them.

```
Private Function GetSuperState() As Byte()
  Dim objPB As PropertyBag

  Set objPB = New PropertyBag
  With objPB
    ' store this object's state
    .WriteProperty "State", GetState
    ' store superstate of child collection
    .WriteProperty "Children", mcolChildren.GetSuperState
    GetSuperState = .Contents
  End With
  Set objPB = Nothing
End Function
```

This routine is not terribly complex. We just create a PropertyBag object, then use its WriteProperty method to store both the results of the business object's GetState method and the results of the Collection object's GetSuperState method.

If our business object has more than one type of child object, we may have multiple Collection objects to manage them. In that case, we'd simply use the WriteProperty method to store the results from each of the Collection object's GetSuperState method.

Creating a SetSuperState Method

The SetSuperState method is just the reverse of GetSuperState. The parameter accepted by the routine is simply fed into the Contents property of a PropertyBag object, then the object's state is retrieved using the ReadProperty method, as is the superstate for the child Collection object.

```
Private Sub SetSuperState(Buffer() As Byte)
  Dim objPB As PropertyBag

  Set objPB = New PropertyBag
  With objPB
    ' restore propertybag contents
    .Contents = Buffer
    ' set this object's state from PB
    SetState .ReadProperty("State")
    ' set child collection superstate from PB
    mcolChildren.SetSuperState .ReadProperty("Children")
  End With
  Set objPB = Nothing
End Sub
```

In all these cases, we're leveraging the code already implemented within the CSLA – just extending its capabilities. It doesn't matter how the specific `GetState` or `SetState` methods for each business object are implemented – as long as they return a byte stream in some data type that can be placed into a `PropertyBag` object. Thus, the UDT/LSet, direct UDT and `PropertyBag` techniques for serializing an object's state are all good options if we want to support this approach.

At this point we've reviewed the different techniques for serializing an object's state. We've also discussed the underlying concepts behind distributed objects – at least in terms of moving objects across the network by value. Most recently we have seen how to implement `GetSuperState` and `SetSuperState` methods for each type of object we may implement following the CSLA.

Now let's return to the Task Manager application and apply these concepts so we can retrieve and store the state data from our `Task` objects.

Updating the Task Manager Application

The Task Manager application, as it stands, retrieves and stores data for the parent, `Client`, and child, `Project`, objects. It does not retrieve or store the data for the grandchild, `Task`, objects – for reasons that are probably apparent at this point. As we've seen, dealing with *n* levels of child objects requires implementation of methods to serialize and deserialize the superstate of the objects.

In fact, implementing the superstate concept will simplify the application from where it stands currently. Right now, the `Load` and `ApplyEdit` methods of the parent `Client` object have to deal directly with the state data from the `Project` objects. The `Project` objects' state data is passed to and from the data-centric `ClientPersist` object as a read-write parameter. For instance, the `Client` object's `Load` method is currently implemented as follows:

```
Public Sub Load(ID As Long)
   Dim objPersist As ClientPersist
   Dim strProjects As String

   If mcolStack.Count > 0 Then Err.Raise 445
   If Not mudtProps.IsNew Then Err.Raise 445

   mudtProps.IsNew = False

   ' code to load the object goes here
   Set objPersist = New ClientPersist
   SetState objPersist.Fetch(ID, strProjects)
   Set objPersist = Nothing
   Set mcolProjects = New Projects
   mcolProjects.SetState strProjects
End Sub
```

The highlighted lines indicate the call to the data-centric object that returns the state data for the `Project` objects, and the lines that pass that data along to the child `Collection` object.

If the `Client` object had other types of child object, we'd have more of these lines, and more parameters to the `Fetch` call.

Worse still, there's no way in this scenario to easily handle grandchild objects. Since each `Project` has its own child objects, the `Project` objects' states become very complex. Luckily we have the superstate concept, which, as we shall see, simplifies all of this.

The problem is also evident in the `Client` object's `ApplyEdit` method:

```
Public Sub ApplyEdit()
  Dim objPersist As ClientPersist
  Dim strProjects As String

  If mcolStack.Count = 0 Then Err.Raise 445

  mcolProjects.ApplyEdit
  Set objPersist = New ClientPersist
  If mudtProps.IsDeleted Then
    ' code to delete the object's data goes here
    objPersist.DeleteObject mudtProps.ID
    mcolStack.Remove mcolStack.Count
    mudtProps.IsNew = True
    mudtProps.IsDeleted = False
  ElseIf IsDirty Or mudtProps.IsNew Then
    If Not IsValid Then Err.Raise 445
    ' save object to database if appropriate
    ' save object state
    mcolStack.Remove mcolStack.Count
    strProjects = mcolProjects.GetState
    SetState objPersist.Save(GetState, strProjects)
    mcolProjects.SetState strProjects
    mudtProps.IsNew = False
  Else
    mcolStack.Remove mcolStack.Count
  End If
  Set objPersist = Nothing
  mudtProps.IsDirty = False
End Sub
```

Here, too, we are passing the `Project` objects' state data as a read-write parameter to the data-centric object's `Save` method. This requires extra code before and after the method call to handle the child object's state data.

So, let's see how we can simplify this process and, at the same time, support the retrieval and storage of the grandchild `Task` objects. To do this we'll need to change all the UI-centric business objects so they implement `GetSuperState` and `SetSuperState` methods. The data-centric objects will also need to be updated to support the superstate buffer that will be sent across the network.

To start with, we'll update the UI-centric objects.

Updating the TaskObjects Project

The `TaskObjects` project has objects with children, `Collection` objects to manage those child objects and objects with no child objects of their own. This serves well as an example here, as we'll get to implement the `GetSuperState` and `SetSuperState` methods at each level of object to see how they work in the object heirarchy.

Let's work from the bottom up – starting with the `Task` object.

Updating the Task Object

The implementation of the `GetSuperState` and `SetSuperState` methods is simplest in the `Task` object, since it has no child objects of its own. As such, its `GetSuperState` and `SetSuperState` methods will simply return the serialized state of the object itself.

```
Friend Function GetSuperState() As String
  GetSuperState = GetState
End Function

Friend Sub SetSuperState(Buffer As String)
  SetState Buffer
End Sub
```

This is trivial, since we already have `GetState` and `SetState` methods implemented to do the serialization and deserialization.

Also, we can change the scope of the `GetState` and `SetState` methods themselves. Currently they are declared using the `Friend` keyword, since the `Tasks` object interacts with them. However, the `Tasks` object will shortly be modified to use the new superstate methods, so `GetState` and `SetState` can become `Private` to the `Task` object.

```
Private Function GetState() As String
  Dim udtData As TaskData

  LSet udtData = mudtProps
  GetState = udtData.Buffer
End Function

Private Sub SetState(Buffer As String)
  Dim udtData As TaskData

  udtData.Buffer = Buffer
  LSet mudtProps = udtData
End Sub
```

> *I have not changed the `GetState` or `SetState` methods to use the `PropertyBag` technique – instead preferring to keep the performance benefits from the UDT/`LSet` technique. If you find the `PropertyBag` performance to be adequate, these routines could also be adapted to simply copy values into and out of a `PropertyBag` and module level variables in the class.*

Since we're able to leverage the code already written within the CSLA-based business object, these changes were quite trivial and we're all ready to move on to the `Tasks` object.

Updating the Tasks Object

The `Tasks` object is a `Collection` object implemented to manage the `Task` objects. The `GetSuperState` and `SetSuperState` methods for a `Collection` object are more complex than those for a simple business object.

Implementing GetSuperState

The `GetSuperState` method needs to collect all the superstates for the child `Task` objects together and return them as a single byte stream. This can be done fairly easily by using a `PropertyBag` object to collect all the superstates into properties with different names, and then returning the serialized result via the `Contents` property.

```
Friend Function GetSuperState() As Byte()
  Dim objPB As PropertyBag
  Dim lngCount As Long
  Dim objTask As Task

  Set objPB = New PropertyBag
  With objPB
    ' store total number of child objects
    .WriteProperty "Count", mcolItems.Count + mcolDeleted.Count

    ' store currently valid objects
    For Each objTask In mcolItems
      lngCount = lngCount + 1
      .WriteProperty "Item" & CStr(lngCount), objTask.GetSuperState
    Next

    ' store objects marked for deletion
    For Each objTask In mcolDeleted
      lngCount = lngCount + 1
      .WriteProperty "Item" & CStr(lngCount), objTask.GetSuperState
    Next
    GetSuperState = .Contents
  End With
  Set objPB = Nothing
End Function
```

This is essentially the same procedure that we looked at earlier in this chapter, but modified to deal specifically with the `Task` objects.

The key thing to note is that each `Task` object's `GetSuperState` method is called when building the overall superstate. This is important, since in the future some child objects may be added to the `Task` object and this code will continue to work without alteration.

Implementing SetSuperState

The `SetSuperState` method accepts a `String` parameter, which is converted to a `Byte` array and provided to a `PropertyBag` object via its `Contents` property. Once that's done the individual child objects can be created and their superstate data can be passed to their `SetSuperState` methods.

```
Friend Sub SetSuperState(Buffer() As Byte)
  Dim objPB As PropertyBag
  Dim lngIndex As Long
  Dim lngEdit As Long
  Dim objTask As Task

  Set objPB = New PropertyBag

  Set mcolItems = Nothing
  Set mcolDeleted = Nothing
  Set mcolItems = New Collection
  Set mcolDeleted = New Collection

  With objPB
    .Contents = Buffer
    For lngIndex = 1 To .ReadProperty("Count")
      ' create and load superstate for object
      Set objTask = New Task
      objTask.SetSuperState .ReadProperty("Item" & CStr(lngIndex))
```

```
      ' stack states as needed
      For lngEdit = 1 To mlngEditing
        objTask.BeginEdit
      Next

      ' place object in correct collection
      If Not objTask.IsDeleted Then
        mcolItems.Add objTask
      Else
        mcolDeleted.Add objTask
      End If
      Set objTask = Nothing
    Next
  End With
  Set objPB = Nothing
End Sub
```

Again, this is very much the same code as we built earlier in the chapter, but altered to work specifically with the Task objects.

Removing the GetState and SetState Methods

In the next section we'll be updating the Project object so that it too can build a superstate. When we do this, the Project object will be calling the GetSuperState and SetSuperState methods of the Tasks object – and it will no longer reference the GetState or SetState methods.

In fact, by the time we're done, the GetState and SetState methods on the Tasks object will be totally unnecessary. Due to this, we'll simply remove them from the class module to keep things tidy.

With that done, the Tasks object is all set. It now can serialize and deserialize the superstates of all its child objects. If those child objects had their own children we'd still be covered, since the GetSuperState and SetSuperState methods of the Task object would be providing all that data.

Next we'll update the Project object, giving us a firsthand look at how this cascading effect will work.

Updating the Project Object

The Project object is a child object of the Client object. More importantly however, it is a parent object in itself, since it has Task objects as children. Because of this, the superstate of a Project object will contain both the Project object's state and the superstates of all its child Task objects.

Since we've already updated the Task and Tasks objects to support superstates, the Project object's GetSuperState and SetSuperState methods can leverage those changes.

Implementing GetSuperState

The GetSuperState method will return a byte stream containing the Project object's state and the combined superstates of all the child Task objects. The Tasks object already has a GetSuperState method that assembles a byte stream containing all the superstates of the child objects, so the Project object's GetSuperState method needs merely to combine its own state with the byte stream returned by the Tasks object.

```
Friend Function GetSuperState() As Byte()
   Dim objPB As PropertyBag

   Set objPB = New PropertyBag
   With objPB
     ' store this object's state
     .WriteProperty "State", GetState
     ' store child collection superstate
     .WriteProperty "Tasks", mobjTasks.GetSuperState
     GetSuperState = .Contents
   End With
   Set objPB = Nothing
End Function
```

This method makes use of the `GetState` method to retrieve a serialized copy of the `Project` object's own state, and the `GetSuperState` method of the `Tasks` object. Each value is stored into a `PropertyBag` object and then the `Contents` property is used to return the combined superstate.

This superstate contains all the data for the `Project` object and its child objects. This is illustrated by the following diagram:

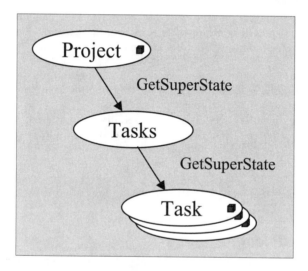

By calling `GetSuperState` recursively down the entire family of objects, we end up with a superstate that contains all their data.

Implementing SetSuperState

The `SetSuperState` method is the reverse of `GetSuperState`, accepting a byte stream in the form of a `String` value and 'unpacking' it to restore the `Project` object's own state and to provide superstate data to the `Tasks` object.

```
Friend Sub SetSuperState(Buffer() As Byte)
   Dim objPB As PropertyBag

   Set objPB = New PropertyBag
   With objPB
     .Contents = Buffer
     ' restore this object's state
     SetState .ReadProperty("State")
```

```
             ' restore superstate of child collection
        mobjTasks.SetSuperState .ReadProperty("Tasks")
      End With
      Set objPB = Nothing
   End Sub
```

The `Project` object's state is restored using the `SetState` method, while the `SetSuperState` method of the `Tasks` object is used to restore the superstates of all the child `Task` objects.

Updating GetState and SetState

Originally, the `Projects` object called the `GetState` and `SetState` methods to populate a `Buffer` object with all the child `Project` objects' data. We'll be changing the `Projects` object shortly so it no longer makes any use of the `GetState` or `SetState` methods.

`GetState` and `SetState` remain useful within the `Project` object itself, but they no longer need to be scoped with the `Friend` keyword. Instead, we can change them to be `Private`.

```
Private Function GetState() As String
   Dim udtData As ProjectData

   LSet udtData = mudtProps
   GetState = udtData.Buffer
End Function
```

```
Private Sub SetState(Buffer As String)
   Dim udtData As ProjectData

   udtData.Buffer = Buffer
   LSet mudtProps = udtData
End Sub
```

From here on out the changes will become pretty repetitive. We'll update the `Projects` object much the same way we did with the `Tasks` object, and the `Client` object will be updated as we just did with the `Project` object.

Updating the Projects Object

The `Projects` object, like the `Tasks` object, is a `Collection` object that manages child objects. The `GetSuperState` and `SetSuperState` methods will retrieve or provide superstate data from the child objects contained by the `Projects` object.

The `GetSuperState` method is identical to that in the `Tasks` object, except that the child object names have been changed to use the `Project` object.

```
Friend Function GetSuperState() As Byte()
   Dim objPB As PropertyBag
   Dim objProject As Project
   Dim lngCount As Long

   Set objPB = New PropertyBag
   With objPB
      ' store total number of child objects
      .WriteProperty "Count", mcolItems.Count + mcolDeleted.Count
```

```
            ' store superstates for valid objects
         For Each objProject In mcolItems
            lngCount = lngCount + 1
            .WriteProperty "Item" & CStr(lngCount), objProject.GetSuperState
         Next

            ' store superstates for objects marked for deletion
         For Each objProject In mcolDeleted
            lngCount = lngCount + 1
            .WriteProperty "Item" & CStr(lngCount), objProject.GetSuperState
         Next
         GetSuperState = .Contents
      End With
      Set objPB = Nothing
   End Function
```

Similarly, the `SetSuperState` method is the same with only the child names changed.

```
Friend Sub SetSuperState(Buffer() As Byte)
   Dim objPB As PropertyBag
   Dim lngIndex As Long
   Dim lngEdit As Long
   Dim objProject As Project

   Set objPB = New PropertyBag

   Set mcolItems = Nothing
   Set mcolDeleted = Nothing
   Set mcolItems = New Collection
   Set mcolDeleted = New Collection

   With objPB
      .Contents = Buffer
      For lngIndex = 1 To .ReadProperty("Count")
         ' create and set superstate for child object
         Set objProject = New Project
         objProject.SetSuperState .ReadProperty("Item" & CStr(lngIndex))

         ' state stacking
         For lngEdit = 1 To mlngEditing
            objProject.BeginEdit
         Next

         ' store the object in the appropriate collection
         If Not objProject.IsDeleted Then
           mcolItems.Add objProject
         Else
           mcolDeleted.Add objProject
         End If
         Set objProject = Nothing
      Next
   End With
   Set objPB = Nothing
End Sub
```

And, as with the `Tasks` object, the `GetState` and `SetState` methods are no longer required and can be removed. While regular objects (such as `Task` and `Project`) continue to need these two methods, the `Collection` objects (such as `Tasks` and `Projects`) do not.

At this point the `Buffer` class module is no longer required by this project. Remove it entirely from the project.

Updating the Client Object

The final object we need to update from the `TaskObjects` project is the parent `Client` object. The changes to this object are a bit different than the previous objects, since it is ultimately responsible for communicating with the data-centric `ClientPersist` object to retrieve and update the state data.

The object will need `GetSuperState` and `SetSuperState` methods, just like with our other objects. These methods will be virtually identical to those in the `Project` object, since both `Project` and `Client` have child objects.

Additionally, we'll need to update the `Load` and `ApplyEdit` methods. Both of these methods currently have code to interact with the `Client` object's state *and* the collected state of the `Project` child objects. They'll both need to be enhanced to deal with the superstate – thus also sending the `Task` object data across the network along with all the `Project` objects states.

Implementing GetSuperState

Since the `Client` object is a parent of other objects, its superstate includes not only its own state, which we can retrieve using the `GetState` method, but also the superstates of all its child objects. We've already updated the `Projects` object to assemble the superstates of all the `Project` objects into a single byte stream, so we can use that in building the `GetSuperState` method.

```
Private Function GetSuperState() As String
  Dim objPB As PropertyBag

  Set objPB = New PropertyBag
  With objPB
    ' store this object's state
    .WriteProperty "State", GetState
    ' store superstate of child collection
    .WriteProperty "Projects", mcolProjects.GetSuperState
    GetSuperState = .Contents
  End With
  Set objPB = Nothing
End Function
```

> Note that this method is scoped as `Private`, while the others up to this point have been `Friend`. `Client` is a **top-level parent** object – meaning it is not the child of any other objects. Since this is the case, the only code calling this `GetSuperState` method will be from within the `Client` object itself.

This is virtually identical to the method we implemented in the `Project` object – apart from one key difference: this method returns a `String` rather than a `Byte` array. Since this is the top-level object, it will be interfacing with external objects including the `ClientPersist` object and others later in the book. In particular, we'll be dealing with scripting languages later in the book and so it is much simpler if we deal with a simple data type such as `String` at the top level.

Because this method calls the `GetSuperState` method of its child collection, the byte stream generated will contain all the state data for all the child objects of `Client` – down to *n*-levels deep.

Implementing SetSuperState

The `SetSuperState` method will be virtually identical to the one we implemented in the `Project` object as well:

```
Private Sub SetSuperState(Buffer As String)
  Dim objPB As PropertyBag
  Dim arBuffer() As Byte

  Set objPB = New PropertyBag
  With objPB
    ' convert String to Byte array
    arBuffer = Buffer
    .Contents = arBuffer

    ' restore this object's state
    SetState .ReadProperty("State")

    ' restore superstate of child collection
    mcolProjects.SetSuperState .ReadProperty("Projects")
  End With
  Set objPB = Nothing
End Sub
```

The method just takes the parameter supplied and uses it to populate a `PropertyBag` object. The `Client` object's state is then retrieved, and the child objects' superstates are provided to the `Projects` object via its `SetSuperState` method.

Again, a key difference is that this method accepts a `String` parameter rather than a `Byte` array. This is for the same reasons as were pointed out for `GetSuperState`.

Updating Load

The `Load` method currently calls the `ClientPersist` object's `Fetch` method. That method not only accepts a parameter for the `ID` of the client to be retrieved, but it also has a read-write parameter that is used to return the state data for the `Project` objects.

The lines I'm referring to are highlighted here:

```
Public Sub Load(ID As Long)
  Dim objPersist As ClientPersist
  Dim strProjects As String

  If mcolStack.Count > 0 Then Err.Raise 445
  If Not mudtProps.IsNew Then Err.Raise 445

  mudtProps.IsNew = False

  ' code to load the object goes here
  Set objPersist = New ClientPersist
  SetState objPersist.Fetch(ID, strProjects)
  Set objPersist = Nothing
  Set mcolProjects = New Projects
  mcolProjects.SetState strProjects
End Sub
```

With the implementation of a superstate that not only handles the `Client` object's state, but also the collected states of all its child and grandchild objects, we can simplify this code quite a lot.

To start with, remove the declaration of `strProjects` – we won't be needing it any longer. Then make the changes highlighted below.

```
Public Sub Load(ID As Long)
   Dim objPersist As ClientPersist

   If mcolStack.Count > 0 Then Err.Raise 445
   If Not mudtProps.IsNew Then Err.Raise 445

   mudtProps.IsNew = False

   ' code to load the object goes here
   Set objPersist = New ClientPersist
   SetSuperState objPersist.Fetch(ID)
   Set objPersist = Nothing
End Sub
```

Notice that we've removed the second parameter to the `Fetch` method, and the code that explicitly deals with the `Projects` object. Our `Load` method is now much simpler, since all the code to deal with the child objects has been offloaded to the `SetSuperState` method.

Updating ApplyEdit

The other method that interacts with the data-centric `ClientPersist` object is the `ApplyEdit` method. This method is responsible for saving new or changed data from our objects. Like the `Load` method, this method also uses a read-write parameter to transfer the state from the `Projects` object across the network. These lines are highlighted here.

```
Public Sub ApplyEdit()
   Dim objPersist As ClientPersist
   Dim strProjects As String

   If mcolStack.Count = 0 Then Err.Raise 445

   mcolProjects.ApplyEdit
   Set objPersist = New ClientPersist
   If mudtProps.IsDeleted Then
     ' code to delete the object's data goes here
     objPersist.DeleteObject mudtProps.ID
     mcolStack.Remove mcolStack.Count
     mudtProps.IsNew = True
     mudtProps.IsDeleted = False
   ElseIf IsDirty Or mudtProps.IsNew Then
     If Not IsValid Then Err.Raise 445
     ' save object to database if appropriate
     ' save object state
     mcolStack.Remove mcolStack.Count
     strProjects = mcolProjects.GetState
     SetState objPersist.Save(GetState, strProjects)
     mcolProjects.SetState strProjects
     mudtProps.IsNew = False
   Else
     mcolStack.Remove mcolStack.Count
   End If
   Set objPersist = Nothing
   mudtProps.IsDirty = False
End Sub
```

We can simplify this code as well. First, remove the declaration for `strProjects` and then make the changes as highlighted on the next page.

```
Public Sub ApplyEdit()
  Dim objPersist As ClientPersist

  If mcolStack.Count = 0 Then Err.Raise 445

  mcolProjects.ApplyEdit
  Set objPersist = New ClientPersist
  If mudtProps.IsDeleted Then
    ' code to delete the object's data goes here
    objPersist.DeleteObject mudtProps.ID
    mcolStack.Remove mcolStack.Count
    mudtProps.IsNew = True
    mudtProps.IsDeleted = False
  ElseIf IsDirty Or mudtProps.IsNew Then
    If Not IsValid Then Err.Raise 445
    ' save object to database if appropriate
    ' save object state
    mcolStack.Remove mcolStack.Count
    SetSuperState objPersist.Save(GetSuperState)
    mudtProps.IsNew = False
  Else
    mcolStack.Remove mcolStack.Count
  End If
  Set objPersist = Nothing
  mudtProps.IsDirty = False
End Sub
```

As with the `Load` method we're able to remove all references to the `Projects` object and its related state. All those details are now handled by the `GetSuperState` and `SetSuperState` methods we've implemented.

Make sure to save all these changes to the `TaskObjects` project. We should be all set at this point – at least with our UI-centric objects.

With the changes we just made to the `Client` object, we obviously need to make some changes to the corresponding `ClientPersist` object. Additionally, we need to add further support to the `TaskServer` project so it can retrieve and store `Task` objects.

> *You'll have to recompile the `TaskObjects` DLL so the UI will take advantage of the changes we've made, but `TaskServer` needs to be updated first to take into account the changes to the parameters of the `Fetch` and `Save` methods of `ClientPersist`. If you try and compile `TaskObjects` before this you will get error messages.*

Updating the TaskServer Project

The `TaskServer` project needs some updates since we're now passing all the data for a `Client` object and all its child and grandchild objects across the network in a single byte stream.

Where the `ClientPersist` object's `Save` method was receiving two parameters – one for the `Client`'s state and one for the state of the `Project` objects – it will now receive one parameter that contains data for all the objects. Similarly, the `Fetch` method will need to produce a single return value containing state data for all the objects.

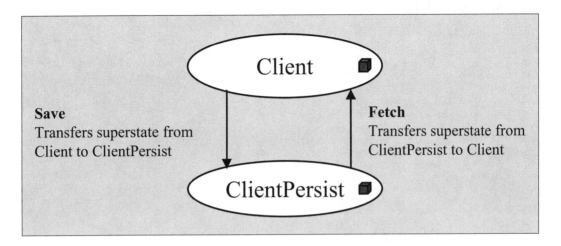

We've already updated the Client object (and its child and grandchild objects) to work with a superstate – including updating its Load and ApplyEdit methods. Now we need to make the corresponding changes in the ClientPersist object's Fetch and Save methods.

To make these changes we'll walk through the ClientPersist object and alter it so it handles the superstate concept.

Finally, we need to add a new class to the TaskServer project to take care of retrieving, saving and deleting the new Task objects. Of course we'll also want to create a new table in the database to hold the task data.

Updating the ClientPersist Object

Bring up the TaskServer project in Visual Basic and open the ClientPersist class module.

We'll need to update both the Fetch and Save methods in this module. Let's start with the Fetch method, as it is the simplest to update.

Fetch Method

Up to this point the Fetch method is implemented as a String function that returns the state data for the Client object. However, it also has a read/write parameter that is used to return the collected state data from the ProjectPersist object.

With our new approach, the Client object's Load method has been altered to expect to receive *all* the data as a return value from the ClientPersist object's Fetch method. This means that the Fetch method doesn't need to return the Project child objects' data as a separate parameter – it will be included in the superstate. This is a good thing, as it simplifies and minimizes the method call – thus increasing our overall performance and the readability of our code.

Since the return value will be generated from the Contents property of a PropertyBag object, we'll also need to declare such an object. Make the following changes.

```
Public Function Fetch(ByVal ID As Long) As String
  Dim rsClient As Recordset
  Dim strSQL As String
  Dim udtProps As ClientProps
  Dim udtData As ClientData
  Dim objPersist As ProjectPersist
  Dim objPB As PropertyBag

  Set rsClient = New Recordset
  strSQL = "SELECT * FROM CLIENTS WHERE ID=" & CStr(ID)
  rsClient.Open strSQL, DB_CONN, _
    adOpenForwardOnly, adLockReadOnly
  On Error GoTo ERRH
  If Not rsClient.EOF Then
    With udtProps
      .ID = rsClient("ID")
      .Name = rsClient("Name")
      .ContactName = rsClient("ContactName")
      .Phone = rsClient("Phone")
      .IsNew = False
      .IsDirty = False
      .IsDeleted = False
    End With
    rsClient.Close
    Set rsClient = Nothing
    LSet udtData = udtProps

    If mflgInMTS Then
      Set objPersist = mobjContext.CreateInstance("TaskServer.ProjectPersist")
    Else
      Set objPersist = CreateObject("TaskServer.ProjectPersist")
    End If
    Set objPB = New PropertyBag
    With objPB
      ' put object's state in PB
      .WriteProperty "State", udtData.Buffer
      ' put superstate of child objects in PB
      .WriteProperty "Projects", objPersist.Fetch(ID)
      Fetch = .Contents
    End With
    Set objPB = Nothing
    Set objPersist = Nothing
  Else
    ' force an error
    rsClient.MoveNext
  End If
  If mflgInMTS Then mobjContext.SetComplete
  Exit Function

ERRH:
  If Not rsClient Is Nothing Then rsClient.Close
  Set rsClient = Nothing
  Set objPB = Nothing
  If mflgInMTS Then mobjContext.SetAbort
  Err.Raise Err.Number
End Function
```

The code to retrieve the client data from the database remains consistent with our previous code. However, once the data has been retrieved we need to create an instance of the PropertyBag and use the WriteProperty method to store the state data.

The call to the `Fetch` method of the `ProjectPersist` object has also been updated. As before, this method's return value is the state of all the project data for the selected client. However, instead of returning this data via a read/write parameter we'll simply store it into the same `PropertyBag` object using the `WriteProperty` method.

By the time we're done with the modifications in this section the value returned from the `ProjectPersist` object's `Fetch` method will not only include project data, but will also include related data for each project's tasks.

Once the data is in the `PropertyBag` object, the `Fetch` method's return value is set by using the `Contents` property. The result is a byte stream containing the superstate data for the `Client` and all its child and grandchild objects.

Save Method

The changes to the `Save` method are a bit more complex. Not only does this method need to add or update the appropriate data into the database, but it also needs to return the data back to the `Client` object as a return value. This was done both via a return value from the function and a read/write parameter – similar to the `Fetch` method.

> *As discussed in* Visual Basic 6 Business Objects *and briefly touched on in Chapter 2, we need to return the object state data after the save process because some of the data may have changed. Child objects needing to be deleted will be gone, new objects will have had ID values assigned by the database and so forth. Remember, the UI-centric and data-centric objects are really two halves of the 'real' objects, so it makes a lot of sense to keep them in sync.*

Now we'll need to package all the data up into a `PropertyBag` object and return it via the function's return value – dropping the read/write parameter.

The interesting thing here is that we'll receive the contents of a `PropertyBag` object as a parameter by value, then we'll need to create another `PropertyBag` object with the updated data that will be sent back to the `Client` object via the return value of the function.

```
Public Function Save(ByVal Buffer As String) As String
    Dim rsClient As Recordset
    Dim strSQL As String
    Dim udtProps As ClientProps
    Dim udtData As ClientData
    Dim objPersist As ProjectPersist
    Dim objPB As PropertyBag
    Dim objPBOut As PropertyBag
    Dim arBuffer() As Byte

    Set objPB = New PropertyBag
    ' convert String paramter to Byte array
    arBuffer = Buffer
    With objPB
      .Contents = arBuffer
      ' get object's state from PB
      udtData.Buffer = .ReadProperty("State")
    End With
    LSet udtProps = udtData
```

```
strSQL = "SELECT * FROM CLIENTS WHERE ID=" & CStr(udtProps.ID)
Set rsClient = New Recordset
rsClient.Open strSQL, DB_CONN, adOpenKeyset, adLockOptimistic
On Error GoTo ERRH
If udtProps.IsNew Then rsClient.AddNew

With udtProps
  rsClient("Name") = .Name
  rsClient("ContactName") = .ContactName
  rsClient("Phone") = .Phone
  rsClient.Update
  If .IsNew Then
    rsClient.Bookmark = rsClient.Bookmark
    .ID = rsClient("ID")
  End If
  .IsNew = False
  .IsDirty = False
End With
rsClient.Close
Set rsClient = Nothing

Set objPBOut = New PropertyBag

LSet udtData = udtProps
If mflgInMTS Then
  Set objPersist = mobjContext.CreateInstance("TaskServer.ProjectPersist")
Else
  Set objPersist = CreateObject("TaskServer.ProjectPersist")
End If
With objPBOut
  ' store object's updated state into outbound PB
  .WriteProperty "State", udtData.Buffer
  ' store child objects and store updated superstate into outbound PB
  .WriteProperty "Projects", _
    objPersist.Save(objPB.ReadProperty("Projects"), udtProps.ID)
End With
Set objPB = Nothing
Set objPersist = Nothing

' return outbound PB as function result
Save = objPBOut.Contents
Set objPBOut = Nothing

If mflgInMTS Then mobjContext.SetComplete
Exit Function

ERRH:
  If Not rsClient Is Nothing Then rsClient.Close
  Set rsClient = Nothing
  Set objPB = Nothing
  Set objPBOut = Nothing
  If mflgInMTS Then mobjContext.SetAbort
  Err.Raise Err.Number
End Function
```

The objPB variable is a PropertyBag object used to 'decode' the value passed into the function as a parameter. In order to place the String value from the parameter into the Contents property, it first needs to be converted to a Byte array by using the arBuffer variable.

Once the `Contents` property is set, the `ReadProperty` method is first used to retrieve the `Client` object's state data, then later to retrieve the data for the child objects – to be used as a parameter to the `ProjectPersist` object's `Save` method.

The `objPBOut` variable is the `PropertyBag` object that is used to generate the return value for the function that is sent back to the UI-centric object. The `WriteProperty` method is used to store the updated client data. It is also used to store the value returned from the call to the `ProjectPersist` object's `Save` method.

Now the state data pertaining to a client will be handled as expected in the `Client` object. However, the `ProjectPersist` object is still packaging the child objects' data into a `Buffer` object, so we need to change that code to work with a `PropertyBag` as we did with the `Projects` object earlier in the chapter.

Updating the ProjectPersist Object

The `ProjectPersist` object needs to be updated in two different ways. First off, it needs to accept the contents of a `PropertyBag` rather than those of a `Buffer` object. Also, it needs to be enhanced such that its child `Task` objects are saved – by calling the `TaskPersist` object we'll be creating shortly.

Altering `PropertyPersist` to work with a `PropertyBag` object instead of a `Buffer` object is relatively straightforward. Instead of looping through the elements in the `Buffer` object, the code will just loop through the elements stored in the `PropertyBag`.

The code to save the `Task` objects will be entirely new. For each `Project` object there may be any number of child `Task` objects – but the `TaskPersist` object will take care of the details. The `ProjectPersist` object needs merely to pass the appropriate state data along.

The `Fetch` and `Save` methods will need to be updated to support `PropertyBag` containers and to handle the `Task` child objects. The `DeleteObject` method will need to be updated as well so it can make sure all `Task` objects are deleted along with the deletion of a `Project` object.

Fetch Method

The `Fetch` method is responsible for retrieving all the data about projects for a specific client. To do this, it simply performs a query against the database to retrieve all matching data. The data for a given `Project` object is then placed into a UDT, and from there into a `PropertyBag` object.

The data must go first into a UDT since that is the format used in the UI-centric object. Remember that `ClientPersist` is just one half of the real `Client` object, so we must store the object's state data in the same format in both halves of the object or they won't be able to communicate.

We'll name this new `PropertyBag` variable `objProjectPB`.

For each row of project data we also need to attempt to retrieve any related task data. This will be done using a `Fetch` method on a `TaskPersist` object. The results of this method call also need to be placed into the `objProjectPB` object.

Once a given `Project` object's data and the data from its child `Task` objects has been loaded into the `PropertyBag` object, the serialized data from that `PropertyBag` object needs to be somehow combined together with the state data from all the other `Project` objects and their children. This is handled by having a *second* `PropertyBag` object, `objPB`, into which each individual `Project` object's data is placed.

In the end the `objPB` object will contain the data for all the `Project` objects. This process is the exact reverse of the process we wrote for loading data into the UI-centric `Projects` and `Project` objects earlier in this chapter.

```vb
Public Function Fetch(ByVal Client As Long) As Byte()
    Dim rsProject As Recordset
    Dim strSQL As String
    Dim udtProps As ProjectProps
    Dim udtData As ProjectData
    Dim objPB As PropertyBag
    Dim objProjectPB As PropertyBag
    Dim lngCount As Long
    Dim objPersist As TaskPersist

    Set rsProject = New Recordset
    strSQL = "SELECT * FROM PROJECTS WHERE Client=" & CStr(Client)
    rsProject.Open strSQL, DB_CONN, _
      adOpenForwardOnly, adLockReadOnly
    Set objPB = New PropertyBag
    On Error GoTo ERRH
    Do While Not rsProject.EOF
      With udtProps
        .ID = rsProject("ID")
        .Name = rsProject("Name")
        .IsNew = False
        .IsDirty = False
        .IsDeleted = False
      End With
      LSet udtData = udtProps
      Set objProjectPB = New PropertyBag
      With objProjectPB
        ' store object's state into temporary PB
        .WriteProperty "State", udtData.Buffer

        If mflgInMTS Then
          Set objPersist = mobjContext.CreateInstance("TaskServer.TaskPersist")
        Else
          Set objPersist = CreateObject("TaskServer.TaskPersist")
        End If
        ' store child collection superstate into temporary PB
        .WriteProperty "Tasks", objPersist.Fetch(udtProps.ID)

        Set objPersist = Nothing

        ' store superstate for Project into outbound PB
        lngCount = lngCount + 1
        objPB.WriteProperty "Item" & CStr(lngCount), .Contents
      End With
      Set objProjectPB = Nothing
      rsProject.MoveNext
    Loop
    rsProject.Close
    Set rsProject = Nothing

    ' store count of Project child objects
    objPB.WriteProperty "Count", lngCount

    ' return superstates for all child objects as function result
    Fetch = objPB.Contents
    Set objPB = Nothing
```

```
   If mflgInMTS Then mobjContext.SetComplete
   Exit Function

ERRH:
   If Not rsProject Is Nothing Then rsProject.Close
   Set rsProject = Nothing
   Set objPB = Nothing
   If mflgInMTS Then mobjContext.SetAbort
   Err.Raise Err.Number
End Function
```

Once all the `Project` object data is loaded into the `objPB` variable, its `Contents` property is used to generate the return value for the function.

In many ways, this code is a combination of that we created in the `GetSuperState` methods of the `Project` and `Projects` objects. There too, we have code to combine the `Project` and `Task` object data into a byte stream – then we have code to combine each of these byte streams into a single `PropertyBag` object that comprises the superstate of the `Projects` object itself.

Save Method

The alterations to the `Save` method are a bit more substantial. Not only does this method receive and unpack the contents of a `PropertyBag`, but it also needs to build another `PropertyBag` to contain the state data *after* the database updates are made. This second `PropertyBag` is used to produce the return value for the function – sending the `Project` and related `Task` objects' data back to the `ClientPersist` object.

The variable `objPB` will act as the container for the entire byte stream containing all the `Project` objects and their child `Task` objects. Each individual `Project` object's state data will be pulled out of `objPB` and placed into the `objProjectPB` variable for processing. The `ReadProperty` method will be used on `objProjectPB` to retrieve first the individual `Project` object's state, then again to retrieve the state of all the related `Task` objects.

The `Save` method on the `TaskPersist` object is used to add or update any related `Task` object data. We'll create the `TaskPersist` object itself shortly.

Once a given `Project` object's data has been written to the database the resulting data is placed into the `objProjectPBOut` variable. The same is true with the return value from the `Save` method of the `TaskPersist` object.

All the individual `Project` superstates are then combined together into the `objPBOut` variable. When all the `Project` objects have been updated into the database, the `Save` method's return value is set by using the `Contents` property.

```
Public Function Save(Buffer() As Byte, ByVal ClientID As Long) As Byte()
   Dim rsProject As Recordset
   Dim strSQL As String
   Dim udtProps As ProjectProps
   Dim udtData As ProjectData
   Dim objPB As PropertyBag
   Dim objProjectPB As PropertyBag
   Dim objProjectPBOut As PropertyBag
   Dim objPBOut As PropertyBag
   Dim lngIndex As Long
   Dim lngCount As Long
   Dim objPersist As TaskPersist
```

```
Set objPB = New PropertyBag
Set objPBOut = New PropertyBag

' place data into PB
objPB.Contents = Buffer

Set rsProject = New Recordset

On Error GoTo ERRH
For lngIndex = 1 To objPB.ReadProperty("Count")
  ' create PB for this particular Project
  Set objProjectPB = New PropertyBag
  With objProjectPB
    ' put Project data into the PB
    .Contents = objPB.ReadProperty("Item" & CStr(lngIndex))
    ' retrieve this Project object's data from PB
    udtData.Buffer = .ReadProperty("State")
    LSet udtProps = udtData
  End With

  If Not udtProps.IsDeleted Then
    strSQL = "SELECT * FROM PROJECTS WHERE ID=" & CStr(udtProps.ID)
    rsProject.Open strSQL, DB_CONN, adOpenKeyset, adLockOptimistic
    If udtProps.IsNew Then rsProject.AddNew

    With udtProps
      rsProject("Name") = .Name
      rsProject("Client") = ClientID
      rsProject.Update
      If .IsNew Then
        rsProject.Bookmark = rsProject.Bookmark
        .ID = rsProject("ID")
      End If
      .IsNew = False
      .IsDirty = False
    End With

    Set objProjectPBOut = New PropertyBag

    LSet udtData = udtProps
    ' store project's updated data into temp PB
    objProjectPBOut.WriteProperty "State", udtData.Buffer

    If mflgInMTS Then
      Set objPersist = mobjContext.CreateInstance("TaskServer.TaskPersist")
    Else
      Set objPersist = CreateObject("TaskServer.TaskPersist")
    End If
    ' store this project's Tasks and place updated data into temp PB
    objProjectPBOut.WriteProperty "Tasks", _
      objPersist.Save(objProjectPB.ReadProperty("Tasks"), udtProps.ID)
    Set objPersist = Nothing

    ' store this project's superstate into outbound PB
    lngCount = lngCount + 1
    objPBOut.WriteProperty "Item" & lngCount, objProjectPBOut.Contents

    Set objProjectPB = Nothing
    Set objProjectPBOut = Nothing
    rsProject.Close
```

```
      Else
        DeleteProject udtProps.ID
      End If
    Next

    ' store count of Project objects into outbound PB
    objPBOut.WriteProperty "Count", lngCount

    Set objPB = Nothing
    Set rsProject = Nothing

    ' return all Project superstates as result
    Save = objPBOut.Contents
    Set objPBOut = Nothing
    If mflgInMTS Then mobjContext.SetComplete
    Exit Function

  ERRH:
    Set objPB = Nothing
    Set objPBOut = Nothing
    Set rsProject = Nothing
    If mflgInMTS Then mobjContext.SetAbort
    Err.Raise Err.Number
  End Function
```

As with the `Fetch` method, this code is like a combination of the `SetSuperState` and `GetSuperState` methods from both the `Projects` and `Project` objects earlier in the chapter.

This new code also calls a new `DeleteProject` method to remove a specific project from the database – let's look at that next.

DeleteProject Method

In the case that the specific `Project` object is marked for deletion, the `DeleteProject` method is called, so we'll need to add this `Private` method as well.

```
Private Sub DeleteProject(ProjectID As Long)
  Dim cnProject As Connection
  Dim strSQL As String
  Dim objPersist As TaskPersist

  ' delete this project from database
  Set cnProject = New Connection
  With cnProject
    .Open DB_CONN
    strSQL = "DELETE FROM PROJECTS WHERE ID=" & CStr(ProjectID)
    .Execute strSQL
    .Close
  End With
  Set cnProject = Nothing

  ' delete all tasks for this project
  ' (not needed if database does cascading deletes)
  If mobjContext Is Nothing Then
    Set objPersist = New TaskPersist
  Else
    Set objPersist = mobjContext.CreateInstance("TaskServer.TaskPersist")
  End If
  objPersist.DeleteObject ProjectID
  Set objPersist = Nothing
End Sub
```

Notice that this routine not only deletes the specific `Project` object's data, but also calls the `DeleteObject` method on the `TaskPersist` object to ensure all the child `Task` objects are removed as well.

DeleteObject Method

The changes to the `DeleteObject` method are comparatively simple. Where this method used to simply open a `Connection` object and execute a SQL `DELETE` statement, it now needs to call the `DeleteObject` method of the `TaskPersist` object once for each individual project on file. This will ensure that the task data related to each project is removed.

```
Public Sub DeleteObject(ByVal ClientID As Long)
  Dim cnProject As Connection
  Dim strSQL As String
  Dim rsProject As Recordset
  Dim objPersist As TaskPersist

  ' delete all the tasks for the projects of the specified client
  If mflgInMTS Then
    Set objPersist = mobjContext.CreateInstance("TaskServer.TaskPersist")
  Else
    Set objPersist = CreateObject("TaskServer.TaskPersist")
  End If
  strSQL = "SELECT ID FROM PROJECTS WHERE Client=" & CStr(ClientID)
  rsProject.Open strSQL, DB_CONN, _
    adOpenForwardOnly, adLockReadOnly
  Do While Not rsProject.EOF
    objPersist.DeleteObject rsProject("ID")
    rsProject.MoveNext
  Loop
  rsProject.Close
  Set rsProject = Nothing
  Set objPersist = Nothing

  Set cnProject = New Connection
  On Error GoTo ERRH
  With cnProject
    .Open DB_CONN
    strSQL = "DELETE FROM PROJECTS WHERE CLIENT=" & CStr(ClientID)
    .Execute strSQL
    .Close
  End With
  Set cnProject = Nothing
  If mflgInMTS Then mobjContext.SetComplete
  Exit Sub

ERRH:
  Set cnProject = Nothing
  If mflgInMTS Then mobjContext.SetAbort
  Err.Raise Err.Number
End Sub
```

As shown by the changes to the code, we'll simply open a `Recordset` object that contains a list of project ID values from the database. For each project ID, our code calls the `DeleteObject` method of the `TaskPersist` object.

Obviously this code, and the DeleteObject from the Client object, could be handled more efficiently via a stored procedure, triggers or other database constructs. I wrote the code in this manner to illustrate the steps and process required in the case that we are working with a database without these tools, or perhaps with multiple data sources that may not even understand SQL.

Now that we've updated the `ClientPersist` and `ProjectPersist` objects, all that remains is to implement a `TaskPersist` object. First though, we need to create a table to store the task data for our application.

Adding a Task Table

To add the `Task` table we'll use the Data View window just as in Chapter 2. Use the View | Data View Window menu option to open the window, then select the TaskMgr Data Link. Right-click on the Tables entry and choose New Table from the menu.

When prompted, name the table `Tasks` and click OK. Then enter the information to set up the table as shown in the diagram.

Column Name	Datatype	Length	Precision	Scale	Allow Nulls	Default Value	Identity	Identity Seed	Identity Increment
ID	int	4	10	0			✓	1	1
Name	varchar	50	0	0					
PercentComplete	numeric	9	18	1	✓				
ProjectedDays	int	4	10	0	✓				
Project	int	4	10	0					

Close the window. When asked, indicate that you want to save the changes, thus causing the table to be added to the database. With the table in place, we can move on to build the object that will take care of saving and retrieving task related data.

Adding the TaskPersist Object

Add a new class module to the `TaskServer` project and change its name to `TaskPersist`. If you are using MTS, as shown in this code, set the `MTSTransactionMode` property to `2-RequiresTransaction`.

ObjectContext Code

Add the following code to manage the `ObjectContext` object for our object and make it available throughout each method.

```
Option Explicit

Implements ObjectControl

Private mflgInMTS As Boolean
Private mobjContext As ObjectContext
```

```
Private Sub ObjectControl_Activate()
  Set mobjContext = GetObjectContext
  mflgInMTS = True
End Sub

Private Function ObjectControl_CanBePooled() As Boolean
  ObjectControl_CanBePooled = False
End Function

Private Sub ObjectControl_Deactivate()
  Set mobjContext = Nothing
End Sub
```

This code gets a reference to the context object when the `TaskPersist` object itself is activated, then releases that reference when the object is deactivated. With this code, we ensure that any of our object's methods have a valid reference to the context object if needed.

Fetch Method

The `Fetch` method for `TaskPersist` is quite similar to the `Fetch` method we implemented for the `ProjectPersist` object. It is simpler however, in that this code doesn't need to deal with any child objects.

The code creates a `Recordset` containing all the task data matching the appropriate project. Then we just loop through each row, loading a UDT with the data and placing that UDT into a `PropertyBag`. Once all the rows have been loaded into the `PropertyBag`, the total count of rows is also stored in the `PropertyBag` object.

```
Public Function Fetch(ByVal Project As Long) As Byte()
  Dim rsTask As Recordset
  Dim strSQL As String
  Dim udtProps As TaskProps
  Dim udtData As TaskData
  Dim objPB As PropertyBag
  Dim lngCount As Long

  ' retrieve tasks for the project
  Set rsTask = New Recordset
  strSQL = "SELECT * FROM TASKS WHERE Project=" & CStr(Project)
  rsTask.Open strSQL, DB_CONN, _
    adOpenForwardOnly, adLockReadOnly

  Set objPB = New PropertyBag
  On Error GoTo ERRH
  Do While Not rsTask.EOF
    ' put task data into UDT
    With udtProps
      .ID = rsTask("ID")
      .Name = rsTask("Name")
      .PercentComplete = IIf(IsNull(rsTask("PercentComplete")), 0, _
        rsTask("PercentComplete"))
      .ProjectedDays = IIf(IsNull(rsTask("ProjectedDays")), 0, _
        rsTask("ProjectedDays"))
      .IsNew = False
      .IsDirty = False
      .IsDeleted = False
    End With
    LSet udtData = udtProps
```

```
      ' put task UDT into propertybag
      lngCount = lngCount + 1
      objPB.WriteProperty "Item" & CStr(lngCount), udtData.Buffer
      rsTask.MoveNext
   Loop
   rsTask.Close
   Set rsTask = Nothing

   ' store count of tasks into PB and return PB contents as function result
   With objPB
      .WriteProperty "Count", lngCount
      Fetch = .Contents
   End With
   Set objPB = Nothing
   If mflgInMTS Then mobjContext.SetComplete
   Exit Function

ERRH:
   If Not rsTask Is Nothing Then rsTask.Close
   Set rsTask = Nothing
   If mflgInMTS Then mobjContext.SetAbort
   Err.Raise Err.Number
End Function
```

Once the `PropertyBag` is fully populated, its `Contents` property is used to provide the return value from the method – returning all the task data for a single project back to the `ProjectPersist` object's `Fetch` method.

Save Method

Similarly, the `Save` method accepts the contents of a `PropertyBag` object, then loops through all the elements in that object, copying each into a UDT. The data is then updated into the database.

After each element is updated into the database, the UDT is placed back into a new `PropertyBag` object so we can provide a return value from the method that contains the updated data.

```
Public Function Save(Buffer() As Byte, ByVal ProjectID As Long) As Byte()
   Dim rsTask As Recordset
   Dim strSQL As String
   Dim udtProps As TaskProps
   Dim udtData As TaskData
   Dim objPB As PropertyBag
   Dim objPBOut As PropertyBag
   Dim lngIndex As Long
   Dim lngCount As Long

   Set objPB = New PropertyBag
   Set objPBOut = New PropertyBag

   ' restore PB contents
   objPB.Contents = Buffer
   Set rsTask = New Recordset

   On Error GoTo ERRH
   For lngIndex = 1 To objPB.ReadProperty("Count")
      ' retrieve this task's data from PB
      udtData.Buffer = objPB.ReadProperty("Item" & CStr(lngIndex))
      LSet udtProps = udtData
```

```
      ' save or delete task
      If Not udtProps.IsDeleted Then
        strSQL = "SELECT * FROM TASKS WHERE ID=" & CStr(udtProps.ID)
        rsTask.Open strSQL, DB_CONN, adOpenKeyset, adLockOptimistic
        If udtProps.IsNew Then rsTask.AddNew

        With udtProps
          rsTask("Name") = .Name
          rsTask("PercentComplete") = .PercentComplete
          rsTask("ProjectedDays") = .ProjectedDays
          rsTask("Project") = ProjectID
          rsTask.Update
          If .IsNew Then
            rsTask.Bookmark = rsTask.Bookmark
            .ID = rsTask("ID")
          End If
          .IsNew = False
          .IsDirty = False
        End With
        LSet udtData = udtProps

        ' write updated task data into outbound PB
        lngCount = lngCount + 1
        objPBOut.WriteProperty "Item" & CStr(lngCount), udtData.Buffer
        rsTask.Close
      Else
        DeleteTask udtProps.ID
      End If
    Next

    ' write total number of outbound tasks into outbound PB
    objPBOut.WriteProperty "Count", lngCount

    Set objPB = Nothing
    Set rsTask = Nothing

    ' return outbound PB contents as function result
    Save = objPBOut.Contents
    Set objPBOut = Nothing
    If mflgInMTS Then mobjContext.SetComplete
    Exit Function

ERRH:
    Set objPB = Nothing
    Set objPBOut = Nothing
    Set rsTask = Nothing
    If mflgInMTS Then mobjContext.SetAbort
    Err.Raise Err.Number
End Function
```

In the case that the specific `Task` object is marked for deletion, the `DeleteTask` method is called, so we'll need to add this `Private` method as well.

```
Private Sub DeleteTask(TaskID As Long)
  Dim cnClient As Connection
  Dim strSQL As String

  ' delete single task
  strSQL = "DELETE FROM TASKS WHERE ID=" & CStr(TaskID)
  Set cnClient = New Connection
  cnClient.Open DB_CONN
  cnClient.Execute strSQL
  cnClient.Close
  Set cnClient = Nothing
End Sub
```

Once the `Save` method is complete, all the task data will be added, updated or deleted from the database and the method's return value will contain the current data as it is in the database itself.

DeleteObject Method

The final method we need to implement is the `DeleteObject` method. This method accepts a parameter indicating which `Project` object's tasks are to be deleted. Using this value, the method opens a `Connection` object and executes a SQL statement to delete the data.

```
Public Sub DeleteObject(ByVal ProjectID As Long)
  Dim cnClient As Connection
  Dim strSQL As String

  ' delete all task records for a specified project
  strSQL = "DELETE FROM TASKS WHERE PROJECT=" & CStr(ProjectID)
  Set cnClient = New Connection
  On Error GoTo ERRH
  cnClient.Open DB_CONN
  cnClient.Execute strSQL
  cnClient.Close
  Set cnClient = Nothing
  If Not mobjContext Is Nothing Then mobjContext.SetComplete
  Exit Sub

ERRH:
  Set cnClient = Nothing
  If Not mobjContext Is Nothing Then mobjContext.SetAbort
  Err.Raise Err.Number
End Sub
```

At this point we're done, so save the project and recompile it. If you are using MTS, make sure to update the DLL in MTS so the current version is invoked by the UI-centric objects.

The recompile process will generate compatibility warnings since we've changed the interfaces on our objects. In this case we know that the code using the `TaskServer` objects has been updated, so we can choose to go ahead and recompile even if it breaks compatibility.

Keep in mind that we're set to remain compatible with a copy of the `TaskServer.dll`. Once the compile is complete, make sure to update that copy of the DLL so we remain compatible with the new compile going forward.

At this point the program should run – allowing us to maintain not only client and project data, but also tasks.

Summary

In Chapter 3 we explored the concept of state stacking, solving the problem of supporting undo capability in an *n*-level family of objects. Now we've also explored one way to serialize an entire *n*-level family of objects into a single byte stream – using the concept of a superstate.

The superstate concept allows us to treat an entire family of objects as a single entity for the purpose of transferring the state across the network or sending it via any other type of message. We'll utilize this technique as we progress through the remainder of the book.

Here, at the end of Chapter 4, the Task Manager application is fully functional, allowing the user to work with client, project and task data. The application is fully *n*-tier, with objects distributed between the client workstation and the application server.

Overall, the CSLA design remains intact, we've merely enhanced it to provide more robust functionality overall. This means that our application has more capabilities, but retains its object-oriented UI-centric objects and its transactional, scalable data-centric objects.

In the next chapter we'll see how to overcome another limitation commonly encountered when developing applications using distributed objects. Visual Basic provides powerful RAD capabilities through data binding, but these are typically considered unavailable when working with business objects. Fortunately, Visual Basic 6.0 provides us with the tools required to leverage data binding in our UI design by binding controls to our business objects.

5

Binding to Business Objects

Overview

Having completed Chapter 4, we now have a fully functional application running in a physical 3-tier setting, which supports grandchild objects with both OK/Cancel/Apply functionality incorporating undo, and fully stateless and atomic data-centric objects.

In this chapter we'll shift gears a bit. Since we now have a fully functional application, utilizing the concepts of state stacking and superstates, we've pretty much covered the tools and techniques central to a basic *n*-tier application.

So far we've focused on the business objects, their state and how to manage that state within the objects and across the network. Now let's turn our focus to the user interface.

One of Visual Basic's long-time strengths has been the rapid application development (RAD) capability provided for building user interfaces. Among these capabilities is the concept of data binding – where controls on a form are linked to a `Recordset` or other representation of data from a database.

Data binding is important, because it allows a UI developer to create powerful, sophisticated interfaces with very little code. With data binding, the developer allows the various ActiveX controls and the data binding capabilities of Visual Basic to do much of the hard work that would otherwise involve writing a lot of repetitive code over and over within the UI.

Unfortunately, there is no obvious way to leverage the capabilities of data binding if the UI is being developed against business objects instead of against a representation of data such as a `Recordset`.

In this chapter we'll see how some capabilities, which were introduced in Visual Basic 6.0, allow us to create a data source that let's us do just that. This data source will allow UI components to bind directly to business objects just as though those business objects were data from a database.

Through this technique we gain all the advantages of an object-oriented design, plus the benefits of Visual Basic's RAD development using data binding.

Object-oriented design based on COM components using the CSLA provides substantial benefits, including:

- ❑ Maintainable code
- ❑ Reusable objects
- ❑ The ability to build multiple user interfaces against the same business logic
- ❑ Scalability

If we are creating a Visual Basic forms-based user interface, it would be nice if we could also take advantage of the benefits of data binding, including:

- ❑ Rapid user interface development
- ❑ Minimal code in the user interface
- ❑ Fast and easy loading of data into complex controls (such as a grid)

As we go through this chapter we'll explore a number of issues:

- ❑ The data binding architecture in Visual Basic 6
- ❑ How to create a data source in Visual Basic 6
- ❑ How to make our data source available when creating ADO Recordset objects
- ❑ Building a user interface using the data binding capabilities

In the end, we'll be in a position to take advantage of all the benefits of the CSLA and object-oriented software design – *and* all the benefits of data binding when building a Visual Basic forms-based user interface.

Visual Basic Data Binding Architecture

Visual Basic has provided data binding capabilities for many years. The feature was first added in Visual Basic 3.0, along with integrated support for JET databases via the Data Access Objects (DAO). In Visual Basic 3.0, binding was implemented using a data control, which was placed on a form. Individual controls (TextBox, grid, etc.) were then bound to the data control. The data control itself could be associated with a database and a specific query to retrieve appropriate data.

The DAO data control and associated data binding involved substantial overhead and had serious negative performance impact to applications. Due to this, most applications that needed to support many users didn't make use of the data binding technologies.

In Visual Basic 4.0 Microsoft introduced Remote Data Objects (RDO) to enhance Visual Basic's ability to interact with ODBC data sources. Along with RDO, came the RDC, or Remote Data Control. The data binding technique used for the DAO data control remained constant, but we could also bind to this new data control in the same way.

While RDO and its related data control provided better performance for ODBC data sources, much of the overhead and performance impact for applications remained. In practice, most serious applications continued to avoid the use the data binding.

There was no real impact to data binding in Visual Basic 5.0, so data binding continued to be primarily used for populating data grids or other complex controls.

Visual Basic 6.0 introduced some powerful new data binding capabilities. Because data binding in Visual Basic 6.0 is strongly integrated with OLE DB and ADO, we can now bind controls directly to `Recordset` objects or other data sources without the need for a data control at all.

With the advent of Microsoft Data Access Components (MDAC) 2.0, which ships with VB6 the terminology within the Visual Basic environment has also changed to match that of MDAC. Those controls and objects that can be bound to data are called **data consumers**. The objects providing the data to which the consumers are bound are called **data sources**.

The following table defines the main terms we'll be using throughout this chapter.

Term	Description
Data consumer	An object or control that can be bound to a data source
Data source	An object or control that provides access to data from a data provider; a data source object is typically a 'traffic cop' that selects the correct data provider to provide the data requested by the data consumer
Data provider	An OLE DB object that retrieves data from an external source and makes it available to our programs
Simple data provider	A specific type of data provider with limited capabilities – basically, simple providers only provide access to a simple two-dimensional view of data without indexing any other complex capabilities A simple data provider is a single class that implements a specific COM interface that enables it to act as a data provider

There is frequently a lot of confusion around the terms data *source*, data *provider* and the concept of a *simple provider*. To help, the following diagram illustrates the data concepts in Visual Basic 6.0.

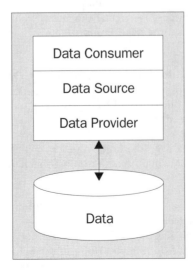

Visual Basic allows us to create our own data consumers – both ActiveX controls and non-visual objects – that can participate in data binding. But we won't discuss these capabilities in this book, as they don't help us bind to our business objects.

Visual Basic also allows us to create data sources – and this we will explore in some detail. Since data consumers are bound to data sources, if we can somehow treat our business objects as data sources then we can leverage data binding to access them.

The confusing thing is that a data *source* doesn't do much itself. It is the underlying data *provider* that interacts with the real data to make it available to our application.

Fortunately, Visual Basic enables us to build a simple data provider – thus allowing us to expose virtually any data to our data consumers as long as we can represent it as a two dimensional table of data. While we can't use Visual Basic to build full-blown data providers with advanced capabilities, we can provide access to basic tabular data.

> It is important to recognize that Visual Basic only allows us to create the simplest type of data source through the OLE DB Simple Provider (OSP) interface. Many advanced capabilities provided by other OLE DB data sources are not available using this technique. However, a simple provider is easily powerful enough to allow us to bind data consumers to our business objects.

Most data providers provide access to relational databases, files or other persistent data stores. However, it is possible to create a data provider that interacts with our business objects instead. To a data consumer there would be no visible difference, but within the data provider itself we'll interact with our objects instead of with a file or other data store.

One approach we might consider right off would be to make our business objects *themselves* into data providers. After all, why couldn't they simply expose their internal state directly through the data binding mechanism provided in Visual Basic?

This seems practical on the surface. A simple data provider is just a Visual Basic object that implements a specific COM interface. Why can't our business objects just implement this interface and become data providers? In fact they can - unfortunately, it isn't quite as simple as it at first sounds.

There's a fair amount of code involved in implementing the COM interface to become a data provider – enough to make it impractical to include that code inside each of our business objects. Were we to do so, many of our objects would have more code to support binding than they do to model our business entities and concepts.

Instead, we'll create a simple data provider object that can act as a middleman – interacting with our business objects *as they are*, yet allowing the data binding mechanism within Visual Basic to access the business objects through it.

As shown in the following diagram, our data consumers will bind to a custom data source that we'll create. This data source will use a custom simple data provider (that we'll create) to gain access to our business objects. The business objects themselves will essentially take the place of a conventional data store such as a database – at least from the viewpoint of the data consumer.

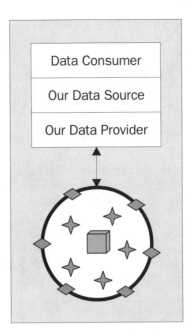

This concept obviously adds some overhead to our application – instead of directly interacting with the business objects, our UI will now go through the data binding mechanism to interact with them. However, Visual Basic 6 has improved data binding substantially when compared to previous versions, and I have found that any performance ramifications of data binding are virtually undetectable compared with an implementation where all the object interaction has been coded by hand.

Not only is performance comparable, but also the amount of repetitive, boring code that we need to write in our UI is reduced to almost nothing. Up to now we've been writing the same few lines of code behind every control on a form in order to copy values to and from the control and our business object. With data binding, the underlying technologies in Visual Basic take care of all this for us – dramatically reducing the amount of code we have to write and maintain.

Creating a Data Source in Visual Basic

In the Visual Basic books online there is a thorough example of building a data source and simple data provider (the AXData Sample program from the Creating Data Sources section). This is an excellent tutorial on the basic process of creating a data source and simple data provider to get at data from a delimited text file.

We'll build a similar data source in this chapter, but instead of using a delimited text file, our data source and simple data provider will allow data consumers to access data from business objects.

Not only will we build a simple data provider, but we'll see how to enable our provider such that we can use it to create ADO Recordset objects – something not covered in the Visual Basic books online.

The following points outline the overall process that we'll follow:

❑ We'll build an object to act as the data source
❑ We'll build two simple data provider objects by implementing the **OLE DB Simple Provider** (**OSP**) interface – one for simple COM objects and one for `Collection` objects
❑ Registry entries will be added to make our data source object act as a *provider* when opening an ADO `Recordset`
❑ Our data consumers (controls) will be bound to a `Recordset` using our objects as data providers

The fact that the registry entries allow our data source to be used as a provider when opening an ADO `Recordset` is unfortunate. This unfortunate use of terminology comes from Microsoft and appears to be unavoidable – but it sure makes it hard to discuss these concepts.

The data source object acts as a 'gateway', providing access to specific data provider objects upon request. The simple data provider objects that implement the OSP interface actually do all the hard work. These are the objects that actually interact with the data and provide information and data upon request as illustrated in the following diagram.

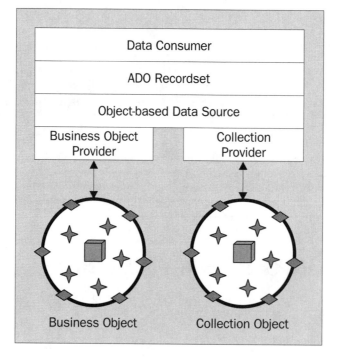

In reality, a data source object will often provide access to a number of different data provider objects that implement the OSP interface. Each of these provider objects are implemented differently, but provide similar functionality and so they are accessed via the same data source object.

This will be true in our case as well. We need to provide access to both simple business objects, such as `Client`, `Project` and `Task`, as well as providing access to the collection objects that manage the child objects – `Projects` and `Tasks`.

Most data provider objects are designed to interact with databases or files. As such, it is assumed that any information required regarding how to find or access the underlying data could be provided via a String parameter passed to the data source. Examples of such values include SQL SELECT statements, table names, file names, etc.

This is a problem in our case, since we actually need to provide our data source with a reference to a business object, and object references can't be represented by a simple String value.

To handle this requirement, we'll need to design a mechanism by which the data source DLL can be given a reference to our business objects such that they are indexed by a String value. We can then pass a String value to the data source when we want access to an object and the data source can find that object reference using the String.

To do this, we'll create a list of object references within the DLL, accessible to the data source object. Then, when the data source object is provided with the DataMember value (a String), it can cross-reference that value to find the appropriate object reference in the list. This is illustrated in the following diagram.

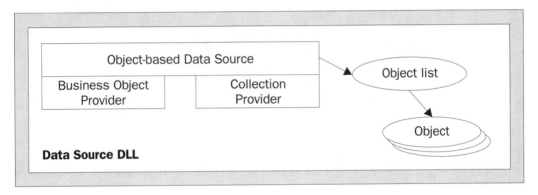

We'll also need to add another object to allow client code to add and remove object references from the list. Prior to any attempt to access the data source for a specific object, our client code will need to add that object to the list within the DLL. The Objects object will provide this access by implementing Add and Remove methods to manage these object references.

Setting up the ODSOLEDB Project

To create our data source we'll need to build a new ActiveX DLL. Open up Visual Basic to a new ActiveX DLL project.

Since this will be an Object Data Source for OLE DB, change the project's name to ODSOLEDB.

We'll also need to add some references to our project to provide the interfaces and support required by our objects. Add references to the following by using the Project | References menu option and associated dialog:

- ❑ Microsoft OLE DB Simple Provider 1.5 Library
- ❑ OLE DB Errors Type Library (Microsoft OLE DB Error Library)
- ❑ TypeLib Information

For some reason, the Microsoft OLE DB Error Library is listed under a different name until after it has been referenced – then it changes names. Thus, I've listed both names above, though only the second name is shown in the diagram here. This may depend on the version of the DLL on your system – so it may or may not happen for you.

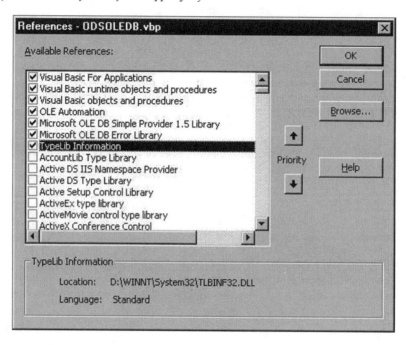

The Microsoft OLE DB Simple Provider 1.5 Library reference provides our project with everything we need to build a data source object and to implement the OLE DB Simple Provider (OSP) interface in our simple data provider objects. This reference is really the key to the project overall.

The Microsoft OLE DB Error Library reference is optional, but useful. It provides us with the standard set of OLE DB error values – some of which we may choose to raise from within our data source.

For the purposes of this book I've included minimal error checking to keep the examples as clear as possible. For a more robust application there would undoubtedly be more sophisticated error checking and many more of these constant values would be used.

The TypeLib Information reference has nothing to do with data sources in general, but is very important for our *particular* data source. This DLL provides us with the ability to examine and interact with the interfaces of objects.

In our case, we'll need to have some way to examine an arbitrary business object to identify its various properties. Each property on the object will essentially become a field in our data source. While we could hard-code these values, or add code to our business objects to provide the property names, the TypeLib Information reference will allow our data source to directly interrogate the business object for its interface – avoiding any changes to the business object.

Implementing the Object List

Before we get into building the data source object and its related simple provider objects, we need to implement a mechanism by which our client code can provide business object references to our data source DLL.

Our data source will be used by data consumers and code within the user interface. Data source objects accept a **DataMember** value when they are asked for data. Many data sources accept a SQL statement, a table name or a file name as the data member – using this value to determine the appropriate provider to return the data.

For our data source object, we'll use the `DataMember` value to determine which business object is to provide the data. Unfortunately the `DataMember` value is a `String` value – it can't be an object reference.

This means we can't directly pass a reference to our business object into the data source – all we can do is pass a `String` value so the data source object can cross reference to find the business object itself. This implies that the data source object will have a list of business objects that it can cross reference with text values – which is exactly what we're going to build now.

Adding a Global Collection

The easiest way to provide a list of object references to all the objects in a DLL is to use a `Collection` object declared as `Public` within a code module.

Add a new module to the project, using Project | Add Module, and change its name to `ODSmain`. Then add the following code.

```
Option Explicit

Public gcolObjects As Collection

Public Sub Main()
   Set gcolObjects = New Collection
End Sub
```

This simply declares a `Public` variable called `gcolObjects` – so it is available to all code within the entire project – and then implements the `Sub Main` procedure to create an instance of the `Collection` object.

We also need to choose the Project | Properties menu option and change the Startup Object to Sub Main in that dialog. If we don't do this, then our `Sub Main` procedure will never be run – after all, the default behavior is to have no startup code run when a DLL is invoked.

Adding the BusinessObjects Object

While our new `Collection` object is available throughout the `ODSOLEDB` project, it is not available from any code outside the DLL. However, as we said, our client code will need to add and remove object references from this collection. To support this requirement, we'll add a class to the project that provides that functionality – basically providing a controlled, public wrapper for the `Collection` object itself.

Select the `Class1` module and change its name to `BusinessObjects`.

To begin with, we can simply expose the number of items contained in the `Collection` by adding the following code.

```
Option Explicit

Public Function Count() As Long
  Count = gcolObjects.Count
End Function
```

We'll also provide access to specific items in the collection with an `Item` method. The key value, provided as a parameter, will be the text passed to our data source object by the code in the user interface – essentially taking the place of a table name in a regular SQL statement.

```
Public Function Item(Key As String) As Object
  Set Item = gcolObjects.Item(Key)
End Function
```

Our `Add` method will allow client code to add an item to the `Collection`. This differs from a standard `Add` method, in that the `Key` value is required in this case – and it must be a `String`. It is this value which will be used later by our data source to translate a `DataMember` value to an object reference.

```
Public Sub Add(Object As Object, Key As String)
  gcolObjects.Add Object, Key
End Sub
```

Finally, we need some way for the client code to remove the reference. Remember that any reference to an object will prevent its destruction. It is very important that the client remove all references to its objects before attempting to shut down, otherwise COM will keep the process running so the referenced objects can remain in place.

```
Public Sub Remove(Key As String)
  gcolObjects.Remove Key
End Sub
```

For simplicity of code, let's also implement a `RemoveAll` method to make it easy for a client application to just get rid of all references held by the data source.

```
Public Sub RemoveAll()
  With gcolObjects
    Do While .Count > 0
      .Remove 1
    Loop
  End With
End Sub
```

With the `Collection` object, and its public wrapper, we now have a mechanism by which a client application can provide our DLL with a reference to a business object – along with an associated `String` value. This `String` value can then be used as the `DataMember` value when the data source itself is used. The data source object will be able to use the `Collection` object to translate the `String` value back into the associated object reference.

With this infrastructure in place, we can move on to develop the data source object itself.

Implementing the Data Source Object

The data source object is the 'gateway', or entry point for all users of our simple data providers. The simple data provider objects will implement the OSP interface and interact directly with our business objects. It is the data source object that determines which simple provider is to be used and provides access to that provider upon request.

> *In a more general sense, a data source object can return any object that can be a data provider. This includes ADO Recordset objects as well as objects that implement the OSP interface. We won't explore the concept of returning an ADO Recordset in this chapter, as we'll be implementing our own simple provider objects.*

In our case, we'll use the data source object to provide access to our simple data providers. The data source object will provide some important functions:

❑ Translate the DataMember text value into an object reference to a business object
❑ Determine whether the business object is a simple object or a Collection object
❑ Invoke the appropriate simple data provider object

We will implement two of these simple provider objects:

❑ A provider to interact with a simple business object (such as Client)
❑ A provider to interact with a collection of objects (such as Projects)

The provider for simple objects will directly interact with the business object it is provided – using that object's properties as data fields to be exposed to the data consumer. The provider for Collection objects will act differently. Instead of interacting with the object itself it must interact with the *child* objects contained within the Collection.

It is the job of the data source object to determine which specific simple provider should be used and to return a reference to that provider object – with the provider object initialized and ready to be used.

Setting up the Class

Add a new class module to the ODSOLEDB project and change its name to ODS – for Object Data Source.

The key to building a data source object is to change the DataSourceBehavior property of the class to 1-vbDataSource, so make this change.

The result of this change is that the class now has an additional class-level event procedure. In addition to Class_Initialize and Class_Terminate, we can now implement a Class_GetDataMember procedure.

Handling the DataMember Parameter

The interface template for this new Class_GetDataMember procedure is:

```
Private Sub Class_GetDataMember(DataMember As String, Data As Object)
```

It accepts a `String` parameter, `DataMember`, and it returns the data provider object via the `Data` parameter.

The `DataMember` parameter is very important. When a `Recordset` object is opened there are two mandatory values, which must be provided.

```
MyRecordset.Open QueryString, ConnectionString
```

The `QueryString` parameter is often a SQL statement of some sort, while the `ConnectionString` specifies the data provider to be used along with other related data.

The `QueryString` parameter is actually passed through to the `DataMember` parameter of our data source object – via the `Class_GetDataMember` event procedure.

The `ConnectionString` parameter will merely identify our data source as the data provider to be used to populate the `Recordset`. There's nothing else we can get from this parameter via a simple data source created in Visual Basic.

Thus, the `DataMember` parameter must contain the information we need to find the appropriate business object to be used by our data source. Beyond that, we may also choose to allow the client code to restrict which fields are to be returned in the `Recordset` – just like we might with a SQL `SELECT` statement.

We could choose to do this by accepting something along the lines of a `SELECT` statement – then parsing it to find our information. Instead, we'll keep things simple and require a simpler syntax for the value.

```
ObjectName[[:Field],Field2...]
```

For instance, if we want all fields for the `Client` object, the value may be simply:

```
Client
```

But if all we want are the `ID` and `Name` fields from the `Client` object then the value would be:

```
Client:ID,Name
```

Obviously we need some way to parse the `DataMember` parameter value, splitting out the object name from the optional list of fields to be returned. Add the following code to provide this functionality.

```
Option Explicit

Private Sub ParseQuery(ByVal Query As String, _
                       ObjectName As String, Fields() As String)
  Dim lngDelimiter As Long

  lngDelimiter = InStr(1, Query, ":")
  If lngDelimiter > 0 Then
    ObjectName = Left$(Query, lngDelimiter - 1)
    Fields = Split(Mid$(Query, lngDelimiter + 1), ",")
    For lngDelimiter = LBound(Fields) To UBound(Fields)
      Fields(lngDelimiter) = Trim$(Fields(lngDelimiter))
    Next
```

```
      Else
        ObjectName = Query
        ReDim Fields(0)
        Fields(0) = "*"
      End If
    End Sub
```

This routine simply accepts the `String` value to be parsed and returns both an object name and an array containing the list of fields. If no optional fields were provided, a single asterisk is returned as a field name.

We can now start to implement the `Class_GetDataMember` method.

```
    Private Sub Class_GetDataMember(DataMember As String, Data As Object)
      Dim objBO As Object
      Dim strObject As String
      Dim arFields() As String

      ParseQuery DataMember, strObject, arFields
      Set objBO = gcolObjects.Item(strObject)
    End Sub
```

This code calls our new `ParseQuery` method to parse the `DataMember` parameter. Once we have a `String` value representing the object to be used, we can cross-reference into `gcolObjects` to find the actual object reference itself. You'll recall that `gcolObjects` is the name of the `Collection` object we declared in the BAS module to store all the object references for our data source.

At this point we should have a valid reference to a business object, along with an optional list of field names to be returned as our resultset.

Determining the Provider

As was mentioned earlier, we'll have two simple provider objects in our DLL – one for simple business objects such as `Task` and the other to handle entire collections of objects such as the `Projects` object. It is the job of the data source object to determine which simple data provider object should be initialized and returned to the calling code.

In order to determine whether to use the provider for simple objects or the one for collections we need some way to determine if the business object we're dealing with is a `Collection` object or not. To do this, we'll use the objects from the TypeLib Information reference, which we added earlier, to build an `IsCollection` method.

The TypeLib reference added a number of new objects to our project – only two of which we'll use here.

The `TLIApplication` object is the root object for the TypeLib library, so we'll use it to create the other object we'll need – `InterfaceInfo`.

The `InterfaceInfo` object allows us to write code to examine the interface of an object – determining which properties and methods are part of that interface, whether they are read-only, read-write, etc.

A read-write property is one where both the Property Let *and* Property Get *methods are implemented. A read-only property is one where only the* Property Get *method is implemented – since without a* Property Let *method there's no way to directly alter the value of the property.*

We'll use the InterfaceInfo object to examine the interface of our business object to find out of it is a Collection object or not. If an object is a Collection object it will have three key methods:

❑ Count

❑ Item

❑ NewEnum (or _NewEnum)

If our object has all three of these methods then we'll assume it is a Collection object and we'll return a True value.

```
Private Function IsCollection(BusinessObject As Object) As Boolean
  Dim objTLIApplication As TLI.TLIApplication
  Dim objInterfaceInfo As TLI.InterfaceInfo
  Dim lngIndex As Long
  Dim flgCount As Boolean
  Dim flgItem As Boolean
  Dim flgNewEnum As Boolean

  Set objTLIApplication = New TLI.TLIApplication
  Set objInterfaceInfo = _
    objTLIApplication.InterfaceInfoFromObject(BusinessObject)
  With objInterfaceInfo.Members
    For lngIndex = 1 To .Count
      If .Item(lngIndex).Name = "Count" Then
        flgCount = True
      ElseIf .Item(lngIndex).Name = "Item" Then
        flgItem = True
      ElseIf .Item(lngIndex).Name = "_NewEnum" Then
        flgNewEnum = True
      ElseIf .Item(lngIndex).Name = "NewEnum" Then
        flgNewEnum = True
      End If
    Next
  End With
  IsCollection = flgCount And flgItem And flgNewEnum
End Function
```

This routine uses the TLIApplication object to create an InterfaceInfo object for our business object. Then it loops through all the Member items in the interface, examining each one to determine its name.

If we find interface members with the names Count, Item and NewEnum (or _NewEnum) then we set flags to indicate they've been found.

We need to check for both NewEnum *and* _NewEnum *to handle both native* Collection *objects and also* Collection *objects created with Visual Basic code. Native* Collection *objects expose a* _NewEnum *method, but when we create a* Collection *object with Visual Basic we expose a* NewEnum *method instead. However, both are* Collections *and so we want to return a* True *value regardless of whether the object is native or was created within Visual Basic.*

At the end, if all three have been found, then we return a `True` value to indicate the object is a `Collection`.

We can go on and add a bit more code to our `Class_GetDataMember` procedure, since we now know which type of provider object should be used.

```
Private Sub Class_GetDataMember(DataMember As String, Data As Object)
  Dim objOSP As Object
  Dim objBO As Object
  Dim strObject As String
  Dim arFields() As String

  ParseQuery DataMember, strObject, arFields
  Set objBO = gcolObjects.Item(strObject)
  If IsCollection(objBO) Then
    Set objOSP = New CollectionProvider
  Else
    Set objOSP = New SimpleObjectProvider
  End If
  Set Data = objOSP
  Set objOSP = Nothing
End Sub
```

Once we know if the object is a `Collection` or not, we can simply create an instance of the appropriate simple provider object – either `CollectionProvider` or `SimpleObjectProvider`. The simple provider object reference is then returned to the calling code via the `Data` parameter.

Initializing the Data Provider

The last requirement our data source object needs to meet is that it must return a fully initialized simple provider object. Just creating the provider object isn't enough; we also need to make sure it is ready for use by the calling code.

In our case, this means that the provider object needs a reference to our business object. It also needs access to the optional list of fields requested by the client code.

To do this, we'll call a `LoadData` method on the provider, passing both the object and the list of fields as parameters. The `LoadData` method itself will be implemented shortly when we create each of the provider objects.

```
Private Sub Class_GetDataMember(DataMember As String, Data As Object)
  Dim objOSP As Object
  Dim objBO As Object
  Dim strObject As String
  Dim arFields() As String

  ParseQuery DataMember, strObject, arFields
  Set objBO = gcolObjects.Item(strObject)
  If IsCollection(objBO) Then
    Set objOSP = New CollectionProvider
  Else
    Set objOSP = New SimpleObjectProvider
  End If
  objOSP.LoadData objBO, arFields
  Set Data = objOSP
  Set objOSP = Nothing
End Sub
```

With this change, our data source object is ready to roll. Of course, it is useless without the associated simple provider objects, so let's move on to create them.

Implementing the Simple Provider Objects

Now that the data source object is ready for use, we need to move on and implement the underlying simple data provider objects. Each of these objects will implement the OLE DB Simple Provider (OSP) interface – enabling them to act as a data provider for our business objects.

Each provider object will be built along the same general process:

❑ Create a new class
❑ Interrogate the underlying business object for its interface
❑ Expose the business object data via the OSP interface

However, before we can get into the provider classes themselves we need to implement a helper class.

Implementing the Field Class

Each of our provider objects will provide access to a set of fields. This list of fields may be provided by the client code via the `DataMember` parameter to the ODS object, or we may find them dynamically by examining the business object's interface using the TypeLib Information library.

Regardless, we need to store some information about each field so it can be used throughout each provider. Each field will have a name accompanied by an attribute to indicate whether the field is read-only or read-write. The list of fields can be maintained in a `Collection` object, but we'll need more than a simple data type to store both the name and read/write attributes.

The code to determine the business object's interface will be divided into three general sections. The first will build the list of field names by scanning the object for all its `Property Get` methods. The second will be invoked if the UI code supplied a list of field names to use – in which case we'll build the list of field names based on that input. The third portion of the code will rescan the object's interface looking for `Property Let` methods. Any `Property Let` corresponding to a field already in the list indicates that the field is read-write – otherwise all fields are set to be read-only.

Obviously we not only need to keep a list of field names, but also store whether the field is read-only or read-write. The easiest way to handle this is to add a simple class module to the project that stores these values. Add a new class module to the `ODSOLEDB` project.

Change its name to `Field` and its `Instancing` property to **1-Private**. Add the following code.

```
Option Explicit

Private mstrName As String
Private mflgWritable As Boolean

Public Property Get Name() As String
  Name = mstrName
End Property
```

```
Public Property Let Name(Value As String)
  mstrName = Value
End Property

Public Property Get Writable() As Boolean
  Writable = mflgWritable
End Property

Public Property Let Writable(Value As Boolean)
  mflgWritable = Value
End Property
```

Not much to it, just a simple class that holds two values. We'll see how this class is used as we implement each of our simple provider objects.

Implementing the SimpleObjectProvider Class

A simple provider object is nothing more than a `Public` object that implements the OLE DB Simple Provider (OSP) interface. The OSP interface can look daunting at first glance, but upon further examination it really isn't terribly complex for the most part.

Basically, the OSP interface allows OLE DB data consumer code to interrogate our simple provider object for information about the data being provided as well as the data itself. How many rows are there? How many columns? What is the value in a specific field? Is a field read-only or read-write? And so on…

Essentially, all we need to do is write code to answer these questions on demand and we're all set. Let's see how we can do this when interacting with a simple business object.

Setting up the Class

Add a new class module to the `ODSOLEDB` project and change its name to `SimpleObjectProvider`.

Change the `Instancing` property of the class to **2-PublicNotCreatable**. This class needs to be publicly available, since it will be used by other code to provide data to our data consumers. Yet it is only created by the data source object we just built, so we need to restrict its creation.

We don't need to set the `DataSourceBehavior` property on this class. This class is *not* a data source – it is a simple data provider. The `ODS` object we've already created is the only data source object that will be in our project.

The LoadData Method

The only method on this object's native interface will be the `LoadData` method we called from the `ODS` object. This method meets the following requirements:

- ❑ Initialize the provider object
- ❑ Set up a reference to the business object we're using
- ❑ Generate a list of fields, or properties, that will be exposed by the provider

Add the following code. We'll discuss the details next.

```
Option Explicit

Private mcolFields As Collection
Private mcolListeners As Collection
Private mobjBO As Object

Public Sub LoadData(DataObject As Object, Fields() As String)
  Dim intIndex As Integer
  Dim intCol As Integer
  Dim objField As Field
  Dim objTA As TLIApplication
  Dim objTI As InterfaceInfo

  Set mobjBO = DataObject
  Set mcolFields = New Collection
  If Fields(0) <> "*" Then
    For intCol = LBound(Fields) To UBound(Fields)
      Set objField = New Field
      objField.Name = Fields(intCol)
      objField.Writable = False
      mcolFields.Add objField, Fields(intCol)
    Next
  End If

  On Error GoTo ErrorTrap
  Set objTA = New TLIApplication
  Set objTI = objTA.InterfaceInfoFromObject(mobjBO)

  With objTI
    If mcolFields.Count = 0 Then
      For intIndex = 1 To .Members.Count
        If .Members(intIndex).InvokeKind = INVOKE_PROPERTYGET Then
          Set objField = New Field
          objField.Name = .Members(intIndex).Name
          objField.Writable = False
          On Error Resume Next
          mcolFields.Add objField, .Members(intIndex).Name
        End If
        On Error GoTo ErrorTrap
      Next
    End If
    On Error Resume Next
    For intIndex = 1 To .Members.Count
      If .Members(intIndex).InvokeKind = INVOKE_PROPERTYPUT Then
        Set objField = mcolFields(.Members(intIndex).Name)
        objField.Writable = True
      End If
    Next
    On Error GoTo ErrorTrap
  End With
  Set objTI = Nothing
  Set objTA = Nothing
  Exit Sub

ErrorTrap:
  Err.Raise (E_FAIL)
End Sub
```

Note the use of the E_FAIL constant. This constant comes from the Microsoft OLE DB Error Library we referenced when we set up this project.

Now let's walk through the code to examine the interesting portions.

Referencing the Business Object

First off, there's a module-level variable to hold the reference to the business object itself.

```
Private mobjBO As Object
```

And related code to store this reference within the LoadData method.

```
Set mobjBO = DataObject
```

This covers the first requirement for the method – storing a reference to the business object that is acting as the source of our data. The second requirement, managing the list of fields provided by our object, is a bit more complex.

Adding Requested Fields

We declare a Collection object to hold the list of fields to be managed by our provider.

```
Private mcolFields As Collection
```

This will be a list of Field objects, based on the Field class we created earlier.

The first section of code checks to see if we've been provided with a list of fields to manage. If we have, then we can simply load a set of Field objects with those values. We won't know, at this point, whether the properties are read-only or read-write, so we'll just mark them as read-only for now.

```
Set mcolFields = New Collection
If Fields(0) <> "*" Then
  For intCol = LBound(Fields) To UBound(Fields)
    Set objField = New Field
    objField.Name = Fields(intCol)
    objField.Writable = False
    mcolFields.Add objField, Fields(intCol)
    Set objField = Nothing
  Next
End If
```

Having stored the object reference into the mobjBO variable, it moves on to determine if the client code has requested all fields (*) or a list of specific fields.

If a list of fields was requested, then a Field object is created for each entry in the array and is placed into the mcolFields object for later use.

There is some risk with this approach. Nothing in this code checks to ensure there actually is a property named for each field. We're assuming the calling code knows what it's doing. This is very similar to a SQL SELECT statement though – in that a SELECT statement can request fields that don't exist, and such an action will result in an error.

Dynamically Adding Fields

This next section of code is only run in the case that the client code didn't provide us with a list of fields to provide. If we were provided with a list of fields, then there's no sense trying to dynamically generate the list.

If the fields have not been provided, we use the TypeLib objects, TLIApplication and InterfaceInfo, as we did in the ODS object to interrogate the business object and find its properties.

This code runs through the object's interface to find all the Property Get procedures – essentially identifying all the potential read-only fields we might expose.

```
With objTI
  If mcolFields.Count = 0 Then
    For intIndex = 1 To .Members.Count
      If .Members(intIndex).InvokeKind = INVOKE_PROPERTYGET Then
        Set objField = New Field
        objField.Name = .Members(intIndex).Name
        objField.Writable = False
        On Error Resume Next
        mcolFields.Add objField,  .Members(intIndex).Name
        Set objField = Nothing
      End If
      On Error GoTo ErrorTrap
    Next
  End If
```

At this point we have a list of fields, all marked read-only, provided either by the client code, or dynamically by scanning the object's interface.

Identifying Read-Write Fields

Now we need to find out if any of the fields in our list are read-write. To do this, we can simply scan the object's interface again, looking for Property Let members. If a Property Let exists for any of the fields in our list, then we can mark it as being read-write.

```
For intIndex = 1 To .Members.Count
  If .Members(intIndex).InvokeKind = INVOKE_PROPERTYPUT Then
    Set objField = mcolFields(.Members(intIndex).Name)
    objField.Writable = True
  End If
Next
```

With that, we have created our list of fields based on either the values passed from the client code or by interrogating the object's interface. We've then scanned the object's interface to identify which of the fields are read-write and which should remain read-only.

At this point our provider object is fully initialized and is ready for use. The way it gets used is through the OSP interface, which we need to implement.

Implementing the OSP Interface

To be a simple provider, our object needs to implement the OLEDBSimpleProvider interface, so add the following code to the module declarations section. We'll go through each method of this interface as we add the code to our class module.

```
Option Explicit

Implements OLEDBSimpleProvider
```

Once we've added this line of code Visual Basic will require that we implement all the methods belonging to that interface. Let's walk through and implement all 14 elements of the interface.

getColumnCount

The first four methods we'll implement are used to retrieve basic information about the data we are providing.

The getColumnCount retrieves the number of columns, or fields, being provided by our object.

```
Private Function OLEDBSimpleProvider_getColumnCount() As Long
   OLEDBSimpleProvider_getColumnCount = mcolFields.Count
End Function
```

Since we have a Collection object storing the information about each of the fields we provide, this value is simply the Count property from that object.

GetRowCount

If we provide the number of columns, it isn't surprising that we also need to provide a count of the number of rows in our data set. This one is easy, since we are providing the data for a single business object – effectively one row of data.

```
Private Function OLEDBSimpleProvider_getRowCount() As Long
   OLEDBSimpleProvider_getRowCount = 1
End Function
```

When we implement the CollectionProvider object, of course, this function will return the number of objects from which we're providing data.

getEstimatedRows

Simple providers may choose to retrieve their data asynchronously. In such a case, an informative bit of information is the *estimated* number of rows that may be returned. Since our data is coming from an object that is already in memory, we won't be loading anything asynchronously and so our estimated rows will be identical to the *actual* number of rows.

```
Private Function OLEDBSimpleProvider_getEstimatedRows() As Long
   OLEDBSimpleProvider_getEstimatedRows = 1
End Function
```

As with the getRowCount method, this will always be one – after all, we only have one object.

getRWStatus

Each column, or field, in our data set might be read-only or read-write. We already identified which is which based on the code in the LoadData method. The getRWStatus method needs to simply return the appropriate response by using that data.

```
Private Function OLEDBSimpleProvider_getRWStatus _
        (ByVal iRow As Long, ByVal iColumn As Long) As OSPRW

  If mcolFields(iColumn).Writable Then
    OLEDBSimpleProvider_getRWStatus = OSPRW_READWRITE
  Else
    OLEDBSimpleProvider_getRWStatus = OSPRW_READONLY
  End If
End Function
```

Notice that both the row and column are passed as parameters. In our case, an entire column is either writable or not. However, it is possible to implement more complex scenarios where columns in specific rows may be read-only or read-write.

The OSPRW_READWRITE and OSPRW_READONLY constants are provided as part of the Microsoft OLE DB Simple Provider 1.5 Library that we referenced when we set up this project. They are used to indicate whether a field is read-write or read-only.

getVariant

The getVariant method is where much of the interesting work occurs. This is the method that is called to retrieve data from the provider for use by the calling code.

Here we discover that, although we have one row of data, we need to support the concept of the zero-th row of data. This is the row that returns the column names themselves rather than any data from our data source.

If the iRow parameter is greater than zero, then we need to return real data from our business object.

```
Private Function OLEDBSimpleProvider_getVariant _
        (ByVal iRow As Long, ByVal iColumn As Long, _
        ByVal format As OSPFORMAT) As Variant

  If iRow = 0 Then
    OLEDBSimpleProvider_getVariant = mcolFields(iColumn).Name
  Else
    OLEDBSimpleProvider_getVariant = CallByName(mobjBO, _
      mcolFields(iColumn).Name, VbGet)
  End If
End Function
```

For the column names, we can simply retrieve the Name property from our collection of Field objects.

To retrieve values from our business object itself, we'll make use of the CallByName statement (new with Visual Basic 6.0). The CallByName statement allows us to call properties and methods on an object by referencing the name of the property or method with a String variable.

Since we're retrieving data, this code uses the VbGet constant to indicate that the Property Get routine should be called.

setVariant

If we can retrieve data, we also need to be able to change it. The setVariant method works basically like the getVariant, in that we use the CallByName statement to call the appropriate Property Let routine on our business object.

However, setVariant has some extra code to notify any client that the data has changed. Part of the OSP interface (that we'll cover shortly) enables the code using our provider object to register as a 'listener'. By registering as a listener, that client has indicated that it wants to know when data supplied by our provider object is changed. Thus, when data is changed, any clients (listeners) attached to our data provider need to be notified.

We'll implement the hooks by which these listeners can attach and detach from our provider shortly. For now, just keep in mind that the list of listeners is stored in the module level variable mcolListeners. To tell the listeners about the change in data we need to add code to make the notifications as shown in the following code.

```
Private Sub OLEDBSimpleProvider_setVariant(ByVal iRow As Long, _
        ByVal iColumn As Long, ByVal format As OSPFORMAT, _
        ByVal Var As Variant)

   Dim objListener As OLEDBSimpleProviderListener
   Dim vntItem As Variant

   For Each vntItem In mcolListeners
     Set objListener = vntItem
     objListener.aboutToChangeCell iRow, iColumn      ' Pre-notification
   Next

   CallByName mobjBO, mcolFields(iColumn).Name, VbLet, CStr(Var)

   For Each vntItem In mcolListeners
     Set objListener = vntItem
     objListener.cellChanged iRow, iColumn              ' Post-notification
   Next
End Sub
```

Before any data is changed, all the listeners are notified that data is about to change by calling each of their aboutToChangeCell methods. Once the data has been changed each listener's cellChanged method is called. This communication allows the listeners to do whatever they choose, individually, in response to the data being changed in our provider.

The code to change the data itself is another call to the CallByName statement. This time we're placing data into the business object, so the VbLet constant is used, and another parameter is added to the call to contain the new data.

insertRows

Typically it is possible to add a row of data to a data set. Since our provider is interacting with just one business object, this concept has no meaning.

```
Private Function OLEDBSimpleProvider_insertRows _
        (ByVal iRow As Long, ByVal cRows As Long) As Long

   Err.Raise (E_FAIL)
End Function
```

Rather than implementing the insertRows method to insert something into our data set, we'll simply return an error result. The constant, E_FAIL, comes from the reference to the Microsoft OLE DB Error Library.

deleteRows

Likewise, deleting a row from our data set makes little sense. Again we'll simply return an error value.

```
Private Function OLEDBSimpleProvider_deleteRows _
    (ByVal iRow As Long, ByVal cRows As Long) As Long

  Err.Raise (E_FAIL)
End Function
```

> *While it could be argued that we could call the* `Delete` *method on any of our CSLA business objects to implement the* `deleteRows` *method in our provider, this is not a good general solution. So far, nothing we've done in our data source or simple provider objects has tied us to CSLA objects. By sticking with that theme, we'll end up with a data source that can be used against virtually any COM object – definitely an attractive proposition.*

find

OLE DB simple providers are quite limited compared to full-blown providers such as the SQL Server or Oracle providers. One area where they are very limited is that of performing a query. The only query capability provided by a simple provider is via the `find` method – no SQL, no `JOIN` statements – just the ability to search for a value in a column.

In our case that doesn't matter much. Since we only have one row anyway, we can just always return that row as the result of any find operation.

```
Private Function OLEDBSimpleProvider_find(ByVal iRowStart As Long, _
        ByVal iColumn As Long, ByVal val As Variant, _
        ByVal findFlags As OSPFIND, ByVal compType As OSPCOMP) As Long

  OLEDBSimpleProvider_find = 1
End Function
```

Obviously this routine can do a bit more for us in the `CollectionProvider` object later in the chapter.

addOLEDBSimpleProviderListener

In the `setVariant` method we implemented a couple of loops to call methods on each listener attached to our provider object. It is the `addOLEDBSimpleProviderListener` method which is used by those listeners to attach to our object.

Before we implement the method itself, we need to declare a module-level variable to store the list of listeners, and we need to create that `Collection` object as our provider object is created.

```
Option Explicit

Implements OLEDBSimpleProvider

Private mcolFields As Collection
Private mcolListeners As Collection
Private mobjBO As Object
```

```
Private Sub Class_Initialize()
  Set mcolListeners = New Collection
End Sub

Private Sub Class_Terminate()
  Set mcolListeners = Nothing
End Sub
```

Then we can implement the addOLEDBSimpleProviderListener method itself. This method simply accepts a reference to a callback object and adds it to the Collection.

```
Private Sub OLEDBSimpleProvider_addOLEDBSimpleProviderListener _
        (ByVal pospIListener As OLEDBSimpleProviderListener)

  Dim objOSPL As OLEDBSimpleProviderListener

  If Not (pospIListener Is Nothing) Then
    Set objOSPL = pospIListener
    mcolListeners.Add objOSPL
  End If
End Sub
```

Once the object reference is stored in the Collection, we can easily go through all the listeners to notify them as events occur in our provider – such as data changing in the setVariant method.

removeOLEDBSimpleProviderListener

This method corresponds to the addOLEDBSimpleProviderListener method. Once a listener has finished interacting with our provider object, it needs to detach by calling this method.

```
Private Sub OLEDBSimpleProvider_removeOLEDBSimpleProviderListener _
        (ByVal pospIListener As OLEDBSimpleProviderListener)

  Dim intIndex As Long

  For intIndex = 1 To mcolListeners.Count
    If mcolListeners(intIndex) Is pospIListener Then
      mcolListeners.Remove intIndex
    End If
  Next
End Sub
```

This method merely searches the list of listeners, removing the one that matches the reference passed as a parameter.

getLocale

This method is used to determine the locale of the provider. Since our underlying data source is an object, not a database, this isn't of importance to us.

```
Private Function OLEDBSimpleProvider_getLocale() As String
  OLEDBSimpleProvider_getLocale = ""
End Function
```

We'll simply return an empty string.

isAsync

As mentioned earlier, some data providers may retrieve their data asynchronously. This method allows clients to determine if our provider is doing just that.

```
Private Function OLEDBSimpleProvider_isAsync() As Long
   OLEDBSimpleProvider_isAsync = False
End Function
```

Since our data comes from a business object that's already loaded in memory, our provider will never be asynchronous so we can always return `False`.

stopTransfer

The final method we need to implement also relates to asynchronous data retrieval. If a client wants to stop the asynchronous retrieval of data it can call `stopTransfer`.

```
Private Sub OLEDBSimpleProvider_stopTransfer()
   ' Do nothing because we already have all our data
End Sub
```

In our case this has no meaning since our data is always present. However, we have to implement each method from the interface, even if the method contains no real code.

That completes the `SimpleObjectProvider` object. At this point, we have the pieces we need to support data access against pretty much any simple COM object. The next thing to do is to create a simple data provider object that can provide data access for an entire collection of objects.

Implementing a Provider Object for Collection Objects

As we've seen, a single object can be easily represented by a single row of data to be returned from a data source. Things get a bit more complex when we have an entire `Collection` object of other objects. In this case we'll end up with a number of rows of data – one for each object in the `Collection`.

There's also a possible challenge with the columns. Since a `Collection` object can technically contain quite a variety of different elements, even different types of objects, all at the same time, we need to think about how we determine the field names that will make up the columns in our data set.

With a simple OLE DB provider we are required to have a consistent set of fields for each row in the data set. While this is something we can't enforce with a standard `Collection` object, it is certainly something we can guarantee with the `Collection` objects we've implemented for the Task Manager application. So, we'll implement this simple provider object with the assumption that all the objects within a given `Collection` will be of the same type.

> *This isn't an issue with any of the `Collection` objects we've build for the Task Manager application – since our `Collection` objects ensure that only a specific type of object can be a member of the `Collection`. However, this could be a limitation if we were to try and use this data provider against any arbitrary `Collection` object where we don't control which objects may be contained.*

Setting up the Class

Add a new class module to the ODSOLEDB project. Change its name to CollectionProvider and its Instancing property to **2-PublicNotCreatable** – just as we did with the SimpleObjectProvider class.

Since a great majority of the code in this provider object will be identical to that which we just implemented, copy all the code from the SimpleObjectProvider class module into this class module. We'll just walk through the code that is changed between the two – thus saving some typing.

LoadData Method

One of the methods that we must change is the LoadData method. In the SimpleObjectProvider, the LoadData method either uses the list of fields provided by the client code, or interrogates the business object for its list of properties.

Since, in this case, the business object is a Collection object, we don't want to pull data directly out of the business object itself. Instead, we want to pull information out of the objects *contained* in the collection.

We'll still honor the optional list of fields from the client code – if provided. However, when looking at an object's interface for property information we need to look at one of the objects in the collection rather than the collection object itself.

There's another complication we need to deal with. When dealing with a single object, it is fair to assume that we actually have an object to deal with. However, with a collection of objects, there's nothing to guarantee that the Collection won't be empty. Thus, before we can interrogate one of the objects in the collection, we need to ensure there really *is* at least one object in the collection.

The lines we need to change are highlighted here.

```
Public Sub LoadData(DataObject As Object, Fields() As String)
  Dim intIndex As Integer
  Dim intCol As Integer
  Dim objField As Field
  Dim objTA As TLIApplication
  Dim objTI As InterfaceInfo
  Dim objChild As Object

  Set mobjBO = DataObject
  Set mcolFields = New Collection
  If Fields(0) <> "*" Then
    For intCol = LBound(Fields) To UBound(Fields)
      Set objField = New Field
      objField.Name = Fields(intCol)
      objField.Writable = False
      mcolFields.Add objField, Fields(intCol)
    Next
    On Error Resume Next
    Set objChild = mobjBO.Item(1)
    If Err Then Exit Sub
  Else
    On Error Resume Next
    Set objChild = mobjBO.Item(1)
```

```
      If Err Then
        Err.Raise DB_E_NOTABLE, "CustomData", _
          "No items in collection - unable to access schema"
        Exit Sub
      End If
   End If
On Error GoTo ErrorTrap
Set objTA = New TLIApplication
Set objTI = objTA.InterfaceInfoFromObject(objChild)
```

The changes center around accessing the first object contained in the collection and using that object to gain information about the interface.

If we were passed a list of fields by the client code then we definitely have a list of columns to provide – regardless of whether the collection is empty or not. Thus, even if the collection is empty and we can't access a member object we can still continue.

In fact, when writing client code it is almost always advisable to supply a list of fields when dealing with a Collection object – specifically because it is pretty common for a Collection to be empty. If no list of fields is supplied and the Collection is empty then our data provider won't be able to work with that object.

However, if no list of fields was provided *and* the collection is empty then all we can do is raise an error. There's no way to generate a list of fields to provide, so there's nothing else to do.

Implementing the OSP Interface

We have some minor changes to make in some of the methods implemented as part of the OSP interface. Additionally, we can implement the OLEDBSimpleProvider_find method now – after all, we actually have multiple rows of data to search through.

We might assume that we can now implement the OLEDBSimpleProvider_deleteRows and OLEDBSimpleProvider_insertRows methods as well. However, to implement these methods would require information that is unavailable to a generic data provider object.

In particular, we don't know what initialization requirements may exist when creating a new object. It is very common when creating a new object to call one or more methods to properly initialize that object – but we (as authors of a general data provider object) have no idea how that might work for various objects.

In fact, we really don't know how to create the object in the first place. Do we call the Add method on the Collection? Does that actually add the object, or just create a new one (like Projects or Tasks in the Task Manager application)? If we want to call New or CreateObject, how do we know what class name to use? None of this information is readily available – pretty much preventing us from implementing an insertRows method.

Likewise, we don't know how a given object may be deleted. We could call a Remove method on the Collection object, but there's no guarantee that some other methods don't need to be called either on the Collection or the child object for proper application behavior. If it is a CSLA object such a technique actually would work, though we'd also have to call ApplyEdit for the change to take effect. Overall, just calling Remove is not a safe assumption.

The point being, that our data provider object is generic – it works with virtually any Collection object and virtually any child objects. Because of this, we can't easily implement adding or deleting of child objects without understanding specifically how the collection and child objects are designed. This would limit the use of our provider to that specific type of object.

Let's go through the methods that will be changed. All the remaining methods will remain the same.

getEstimatedRows

With a single object as in the `SimpleObjectProvider`, we were guaranteed to have only one row of data. Now, however, each object contained in the collection object will be a row of data.

```
Private Function OLEDBSimpleProvider_getEstimatedRows() As Long
   OLEDBSimpleProvider_getEstimatedRows = mobjBO.Count
End Function
```

Instead of always returning the value 1, we now need to return the `Count` property from the `Collection` object.

getRowCount

As with the estimated row count, the actual row count will now be the `Count` property from our `Collection` object rather than 1.

```
Private Function OLEDBSimpleProvider_getRowCount() As Long
   OLEDBSimpleProvider_getRowCount = mobjBO.Count
End Function
```

Working with a `Collection` object is nice in this regard, since we always know that the `Count` property returns the current number of elements in the object.

getVariant

When each value is requested from our provider we need to retrieve the value from an object. When dealing with a single object we could just retrieve the value from that object using the `CallByName` statement.

The general process remains the same when dealing with a collection of objects, but instead of retrieving the value directly from the collection object, we need to get it from the appropriate member object.

```
Private Function OLEDBSimpleProvider_getVariant _
        (ByVal iRow As Long, ByVal iColumn As Long, _
         ByVal format As OSPFORMAT) As Variant

   Dim objChild As Object

   If iRow = 0 Then
     OLEDBSimpleProvider_getVariant = mcolFields(iColumn).Name
   Else
     Set objChild = mobjBO.Item(iRow)
     OLEDBSimpleProvider_getVariant = _
       CallByName(objChild, mcolFields(iColumn).Name, VbGet)
   End If
End Function
```

These changes set an `Object` variable with a reference to the appropriate member variable – as identified by the `iRow` parameter. The `CallByName` statement is then used to call the `Property Get` method on that object to retrieve the requested value.

setVariant

Similarly, when an updated value is passed to our provider we need to put it into the appropriate underlying object. This will be a member object in the collection – identified by the iRow parameter.

```
Private Sub OLEDBSimpleProvider_setVariant(ByVal iRow As Long, _
        ByVal iColumn As Long, ByVal format As OSPFORMAT, _
        ByVal Var As Variant)

    Dim objListener As OLEDBSimpleProviderListener
    Dim vntItem As Variant
    Dim objChild As Object

    For Each vntItem In mcolListeners
      Set objListener = vntItem
      objListener.aboutToChangeCell iRow, iColumn     ' Pre-notification
    Next

    Set objChild = mobjBO.Item(iRow)
    CallByName objChild, mcolFields(iColumn).Name, VbLet, CStr(Var)

    For Each vntItem In mcolListeners
      Set objListener = vntItem
      objListener.cellChanged iRow, iColumn           ' Post-notification
    Next
End Sub
```

This code is basically the same as in the SimpleObjectProvider – it is just acting on an object contained within the collection rather than on the collection object itself.

find

The final method we'll change is OLEDBSimpleProvider_find. In our previous provider object this method always returned the value 1 – after all, we only had one row of data. Now, however, we may have many rows of data – one for each member object in the collection. This means we can implement appropriate searching techniques to find elements within the collection upon request.

Implementing a find method is not terribly complex, but it does involve a lot of code. The template for this method provides the calling code with a lot of options.

```
Private Function OLEDBSimpleProvider_find(ByVal iRowStart As Long, _
        ByVal iColumn As Long, ByVal val As Variant, _
        ByVal findFlags As OSPFIND, ByVal compType As OSPCOMP) As Long
```

Our code needs to support the functionality implied by these parameters:

Parameter	Description
iRowStart	Indicates where the find function should start. This is the start row for the search.
iColumn	Indicates which column should be searched for the value.
Val	This is the value for which we are searching. How we do the matching is controlled by the compType parameter.

Parameter	Description
FindFlags	Allows the calling code to indicate the search direction (up or down) and whether the search should be case sensitive or binary.
	Case sensitive or binary searching only has meaning for columns of String values, so our code will also need to identify such columns.
compType	Provides the comparison type to be used – equal to, greater than, less than, etc.

Having looked at the template, we won't walk through all of the code in detail. The overall flow and intent should be fairly obvious by reading through the code.

```
Dim lngStop As Long
Dim intStep As Integer
Dim lngIndex As Long
Dim intCaseSensitive As Integer
Dim flgStringComp As Boolean
Dim lngResult As Long
Dim objChild As Object
Dim vntValue As Variant
Dim intCompResult As Integer

If findFlags And (OSPFIND_UP Or OSPFIND_UPCASESENSITIVE) Then
  lngStop = 1
  intStep = -1
Else
  lngStop = mobjBO.Count
  intStep = 1
End If

If findFlags And (OSPFIND_CASESENSITIVE Or OSPFIND_UPCASESENSITIVE) Then
  intCaseSensitive = vbTextCompare
Else
  intCaseSensitive = vbBinaryCompare
End If

If VarType(val) = vbString Then
  flgStringComp = True
Else
  flgStringComp = False
End If

lngResult = -1
For lngIndex = ilngStart To lngStop Step intStep
  objChild = mobjBO.Item(lngIndex)
  vntValue = CallByName(objChild, mcolFields(iColumn).Name, VbGet)

  If flgStringComp Then        ' doing string compares
    intCompResult = StrComp(vntValue, val, intCaseSensitive)
    Select Case compType
    Case OSPCOMP_DEFAULT, OSPCOMP_EQ
      If intCompResult = 0 Then
        lngResult = lngIndex
        Exit For
      End If
    Case OSPCOMP_GE
      If intCompResult >= 0 Then
        lngResult = lngIndex
```

```
                Exit For
              End If
            Case OSPCOMP_GT
              If intCompResult > 0 Then
                lngResult = lngIndex
                Exit For
              End If
            Case OSPCOMP_LE
              If intCompResult <= 0 Then
                lngResult = lngIndex
                Exit For
              End If
            Case OSPCOMP_LT
              If intCompResult < 0 Then
                lngResult = lngIndex
                Exit For
              End If
            Case OSPCOMP_NE
              If intCompResult <> 0 Then
                lngResult = lngIndex
                Exit For
              End If
            End Select
          Else                          ' normal (non-string) compare
            Select Case compType
            Case OSPCOMP_DEFAULT, OSPCOMP_EQ
              If vntValue = val Then
                lngResult = lngIndex
                Exit For
              End If
            Case OSPCOMP_GE
              If vntValue >= val Then
                lngResult = lngIndex
                Exit For
              End If
            Case OSPCOMP_GT
              If vntValue > val Then
                lngResult = lngIndex
                Exit For
              End If
            Case OSPCOMP_LE
              If vntValue <= val Then
                lngResult = lngIndex
                Exit For
              End If
            Case OSPCOMP_LT
              If vntValue < val Then
                lngResult = lngIndex
                Exit For
              End If
            Case OSPCOMP_NE
              If vntValue <> val Then
                lngResult = lngIndex
                Exit For
              End If
            End Select
          End If
      Next lngIndex

      OLEDBSimpleProvider_find = lngResult
```

One of the team on this book found that the OPSFIND_UPCASESENSITIVE constant wasn't defined. While this didn't happen to me, if it happens to you the value is 3. There are so many versions of OLE DB floating around out there, it can be hard to predict what exists on any given computer...

With this method implemented, our data source DLL is complete.

Save and compile the DLL before moving on to the next and final step.

It is recommended that you also make a copy of the DLL and then use the Project | Properties dialog to set the Version Compatibility setting to Binary Compatibility so it remains compatible with the copy. This will ensure that the CLSID values for each class remain constant with subsequent recompiles, ensuring that the component a lot easier to maintain and more useful.

Registering the Data Source

Having built a data source DLL with its associated simple provider objects, we are almost ready to roll. Only one step remains. While our DLL is set up to provide data services within the context of OLE DB, it is currently registered merely as a COM component – not as a data provider of any sort.

For our component to be recognized by OLE DB and ADO as a valid data source we need to add a few entries to the system registry. The easiest way to do this is to create a REG file, which can then simply be run to add the required entries. To do this we have to:

- ❑ Generate a GUID value
- ❑ Create a REG file
- ❑ Register the provider

It is not strictly necessary to add these registry entries. As it stands, our data source can be used via the DataAdaptor and BindingCollection mechanisms provided with Visual Basic. However, these mechanisms are somewhat limited and are certainly non-standard when compared to simply opening an ADO Recordset object.

I won't discuss the DataAdaptor or BindingCollection here, since by adding these registry entries we'll be able to use our data source DLL pretty much like any other data provider one might use with ADO.

Generating a GUID Value

One element we'll need to build the REG file is a GUID, or globally unique identifier. GUID values are unique across time and space, not just on one computer or one network. This is important, since we may deploy our new data source component across many computers and we can't risk having conflicts of its ID value on *any* computer.

There are different ways to generate a GUID value. The easiest is to use the graphical GUIDGEN or DOS UUIDGEN programs provided on the Visual Studio CDs under the \common\tools directory.

Alternatively, it is possible to write a bit of Visual Basic code to generate a GUID by calling the CoCreateGuid and StringFromGUID2 APIs found in OLE32.DLL. However, by far the easiest approach is to simply use GUIDGEN.EXE.

To use this GUIDGEN to create a GUID value, simply run the program (either off the CD, creating a shortcut or copying the program to a location of your choice). As shown in the diagram, click the Registry Format option and then click the New GUID button.

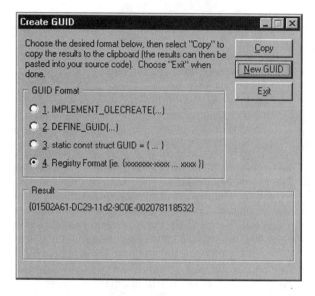

The Result frame will display the newly generated GUID value – using the format required for a registry entry, since that was the option we selected. Then click the Copy button to copy the value into the Windows clipboard.

From the clipboard you can paste the value anywhere you choose using standard pasting techniques (Edit | Paste, *Ctrl-V*, etc.).

Once we've got a GUID, we can proceed to build the REG file itself.

Creating the REG File

A REG file is essentially a text file containing a set of registry entries that we want placed in the registry. The file itself can be created with Notepad or any other text editor. Enter the following.

> **It is very important that you use the GUID value you generated rather than the one shown in this example.**

```
REGEDIT4

[HKEY_CLASSES_ROOT\ODSOLEDB]
@="Business Object Data"

[HKEY_CLASSES_ROOT\ODSOLEDB\CLSID]
@="{C88A04B1-DB20-11d2-9C0D-002078dc2942}"

[HKEY_CLASSES_ROOT\CLSID\{C88A04B1-DB20-11d2-9C0D-002078dc2942}]
@="ODSOLEDB"
```

```
[HKEY_CLASSES_ROOT\CLSID\{C88A04B1-DB20-11d2-9C0D-002078dc2942}\InprocServer32]
@="d:\\Program Files\\Common Files\\System\\OLE DB\\MSDAOSP.DLL"
"ThreadingModel"="Both"

[HKEY_CLASSES_ROOT\CLSID\{C88A04B1-DB20-11d2-9C0D-002078dc2942}\ProgID]
@="ODSOLEDB.1"

[HKEY_CLASSES_ROOT\CLSID\{C88A04B1-DB20-11d2-9C0D-
002078dc2942}\VersionIndependentProgID]
@="ODSOLEDB"

[HKEY_CLASSES_ROOT\CLSID\{C88A04B1-DB20-11d2-9C0D-002078dc2942}\OLE DB Provider]
@="Business Object Data"

[HKEY_CLASSES_ROOT\CLSID\{C88A04B1-DB20-11d2-9C0D-002078dc2942}\OSP Data Object]
@="ODSOLEDB.ODS"
```

These entries identify a new data provider named ODSOLEDB, or Business Object Data. An intermediate DLL, supplied by Microsoft, is referenced to sit between our simple provider objects and ADO or other data consumer objects – MSDAOSP.DLL.

The following table describes the function of each entry.

HKEY_CLASSES_ROOT\ODSOLEDB	Maps the name ODSOLEDB to a more human readable name
HKEY_CLASSES_ROOT\ODSOLEDB\CLSID	Maps the name ODSOLEDB to a class ID value (our GUID)
HKEY_CLASSES_ROOT\CLSID\{guid}	Maps the class ID (our GUID) back to the name ODSOLEDB
HKEY_CLASSES_ROOT\CLSID\{guid}\ InprocServer32	Specifies the DLL to be invoked when our data provider is requested
HKEY_CLASSES_ROOT\CLSID\{guid}\ ProgID	Specifies the PROGID (name) of our DLL
HKEY_CLASSES_ROOT\CLSID\{guid}\ VersionIndependentProgID	Specifies the PROGID (name) of our DLL without version information
HKEY_CLASSES_ROOT\CLSID\{guid}\ OLE DB Provider	Specifies the human-readable name of our provider
HKEY_CLASSES_ROOT\CLSID\{guid}\ OSP Data Object	Specifies the specific PROGID of our data source class

Most COM objects are invoked via either CLSID value or PROGID value. Most of the registry entries we're making here map the CLSID to the PROGID and the PROGID to the CLSID. There's an additional version independent PROGID value specified so the user can choose to just get the most recent version available. This is just like creating an Excel Application object. We can use the PROGID:

```
Set objExcel = CreateObject("Excel.Application.8")
```

Or we can use the version independent PROGID if we just want the current version:

```
Set objExcel = CreateObject("Excel.Application")
```

The more interesting entry is the one for `InprocServer32`. This entry tells COM that the `MSDAOSP.DLL` is to be invoked any time someone requests the use of our OLE DB provider. `MSDAOSP` is an adapter for OLE DB simple providers, making them available for use as though they were a full-blown OLE DB data provider.

The `OSP Data Object` registry entry is used by `MSDAOSP` to find and invoke our specific data source object. The following diagram illustrates the parts of the infrastructure connecting a data consumer with our simple data provider object.

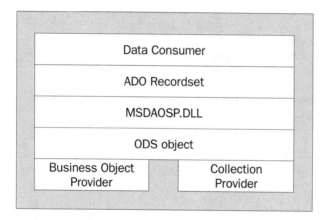

Now save the file as `ODSOLEDB.REG`. Make sure to set the Save files as type option of the save dialog to All files or Notepad will automatically append a `.TXT` to the end of the filename.

Registering the Provider

The REG file extension is marked such that the REGEDIT application is run when we simply double-click on the REG file that we have just created. The REGEDIT application will make the entries into the registry as specified in the text file.

> **Any time you alter the registry you should make sure to have a current Emergency Repair disk or other backup of the registry available in case something goes wrong.**

At this point our data source DLL is a fully functional, fully accessible data provider. We can use it to create ADO Recordset objects that interact with our business objects instead of a persistent data store.

We can now open an ADO Recordset with code similar to the following:

```
rs.Open "MyObject", "Provider=ODSOLEDB"
```

Of course this assumes that we've used the Add method of the BusinessObjects object in our DLL to add a reference to some business object under the name MyObject prior to attempting to open the Recordset.

Alternatively, we might specify a list of fields we want in our Recordset with code like this:

```
rs.Open "MyObject:Field1,Field2,Field3", _
   "Provider=ODSOLEDB"
```

Let's see how this works by updating the Task Manager application's user interface to utilize data binding technology.

Updating the Task Manager Application

Now that we have a data source that allows us to bind data consumers to business objects using standard binding techniques, it would be practical to convert our existing Task Manager application's user interface to be data bound instead of relying on code to move data into and out of each control on the forms.

Currently each form has code in the Form_Load procedure to populate all the controls on the form from data stored in the business object being edited. This code will be replaced with code that uses data binding to bind each control to a data source acting on that business object.

Interestingly enough, the code to set up the data binding is longer and more involved than the code we currently have in each Form_Load procedure. However, by using data binding there's a lot of code that we can eliminate from elsewhere in the application.

Each control's Change and LostFocus events are currently implemented to interact with the business object as well. The Change events are used to move data from the control into the appropriate property of the business object. The LostFocus event is used to update the control with the latest value from the object – ensuring that the object and control are continually in sync.

All of this code can be eliminated once data binding is in place. The data binding mechanism will take care of updating our object with the value in each control, and conversely it will also ensure that our controls are in sync with the object.

Adding References

Before we get into updating the forms themselves, we need to add a couple of references to our TaskMgr project. Bring up the TaskMgr project in Visual Basic and choose the Project | References menu option.

Referencing ADO

The obvious reference that we need is to the Microsoft ActiveX Data Objects 2.1 Library. If we're going to be working with OLE DB data sources, the way to do it is via ADO – thus requiring this library reference. Our project now has access to ADO Recordset and Connection objects among others.

> *Visual Basic will also automatically add a reference to the* Microsoft Data Binding Collection *library when we first run our program. You can add this manually if you'd like, otherwise it will be added for us – just don't be surprised to see it referenced later on.*

Referencing ODSOLEDB

What is a bit unusual is that the project will also need a reference to the ODSOLEDB.DLL itself. This is not typical – most data providers don't require a client program to make a reference, as ADO and OLE DB take care of all those details behind the scenes.

With the ODSOLEDB provider however, we must give the data source a reference to each business object that will be used. This is done by creating an instance of the BusinessObjects class and calling its Add method for each business object. In order to do this, we need a reference to the DLL itself.

This reference is technically not required for the DLL to act as a data source – just for this one requirement of interacting with the BusinessObjects object.

So we need to add a reference to ODSOLEDB to the project. And now we're ready to go through each form and update it to utilize data binding.

Data Binding in ClientEdit

In Visual Basic, open the ClientEdit form.

Often, data binding is done at design time using the graphical form designer and a data control. With our data source however, this isn't practical. Our data source requires access to an instance of a class – an object – with which it will work. Something must instantiate this object prior to any attempts to use the data source, and this means our program must be running.

> **All data binding with the ODSOLEDB data provider must be done in code at run-time.**

Thus, we need to bring up the code window for the ClientEdit form, where we'll make our changes. The changes we'll make to this form are basically the same as with each of the other forms.

Declaring Recordset Variables

If we're going to bind the form's controls to data, the easiest way to do it is to open ADO Recordset objects and bind to them. References to such objects should be held in module level variables so they remain valid throughout the life of the form.

The ClientEdit form interacts with two different types of 'data'. It interacts with the data from the Client object and it interacts with the data from the Projects object.

The Projects object is really the container, which takes care of all the Project child objects on behalf of the Client object. So, we could say that the form is interacting with all the Project child objects, however, it does so via the Projects object.

Because of this, the form will require a Recordset object to represent the Client object, and another Recordset object to represent the Projects object (providing access to each of the Project objects contained within). The first step is to declare the variables for these objects.

```
Option Explicit

Private mflgLoading As Boolean

Private WithEvents mobjClient As Client
Private mrsClient As Recordset
Private mrsProjects As Recordset
```

We'll use these variables as we update the Form_Load procedure.

Updating Form_Load

Of all the routines we need to update, Form_Load will require the most changes.

Up to this point, this method has been responsible for copying values from each of the Client object's properties into the form's controls for display. While this will remain true, we'll be accomplishing this goal in an entirely new way by using data binding.

Make the changes as shown, then we'll walk through what they mean.

```
Private Sub Form_Load()
  Dim objDS As BusinessObjects

  mflgLoading = True
  With mobjClient
    EnableOK .IsValid
    .BeginEdit
  End With

    ' Register our business objects with the
    ' data source
    Set objDS = New BusinessObjects
    objDS.Add mobjClient, "Client"
    objDS.Add mobjClient.Projects, "Projects"

    Set mrsClient = New Recordset
    mrsClient.Open "Client:Name,ContactName,Phone", _
      "Provider=ODSOLEDB"
    Set txtName.DataSource = mrsClient
    txtName.DataField = "Name"
    Set txtContactName.DataSource = mrsClient
    txtContactName.DataField = "ContactName"
    Set txtPhone.DataSource = mrsClient
    txtPhone.DataField = "Phone"

    Set mrsProjects = New Recordset
    mrsProjects.Open "Projects:Name,ID", "Provider=ODSOLEDB"
    With lstProjects
      Set .RowSource = mrsProjects
      .ListField = "Name"
      .BoundColumn = "ID"
    End With

    objDS.RemoveAll
    Set objDS = Nothing
  mflgLoading = False
End Sub
```

First off, we can see that the code which used to initialize the controls on the form has been removed.

```
With mobjClient
  EnableOK .IsValid
  .BeginEdit
End With
```

The remainder of the code is all new. In general, this code uses the BusinessObjects object to provide the ODSOLEDB data source with references to the Client and Projects objects. Then two Recordset objects are created: one for the Client object – to which the related controls are bound; the other for the Projects object – to which the lstProjects control is bound.

Referencing the Business Objects

Before the ODSOLEDB data source can be used to open a Recordset object it must have references to any business objects that are going to be used to provide data. In this case, that means the Client object and its related Projects object.

These references are added by calling the Add method of the BusinessObjects object, which we designed into the data source DLL.

```
Set objDS = New BusinessObjects
objDS.Add mobjClient, "Client"
objDS.Add mobjClient.Projects, "Projects"
```

Each object reference is given a name, which will be used as we open each Recordset object.

Notice that, at the very end of the Form_Load procedure we also use the RemoveAll method to remove all the references to our business objects.

```
objDS.RemoveAll
```

This may appear odd, since the data source obviously continues to use these objects once the form is loaded. The thing is, that each Recordset object will have a reference to the object it needs. The DLL in general no longer requires a reference since each specific provider is already initialized. Thus, this is an excellent place to clean up the references so we don't forget to handle it later.

Binding to the Client Object

The ClientEdit form has three controls which are connected to the Client object. To bind these to that object, we'll need to open a Recordset object based on the Client object, then bind the controls to that Recordset.

Opening the Recordset is relatively straightforward. The Open method's first parameter would typically be a SQL SELECT statement, but in our case it is the name of the business object as it is registered in the BusinessObjects object, with an optional list of fields to return. The second parameter is the name of the OLE DB provider – in this case our new ODSOLEDB provider.

```
Set mrsClient = New Recordset
mrsClient.Open "Client:Name,ContactName,Phone", _
  "Provider=ODSOLEDB"
```

Once we have an open `Recordset`, each control can be bound to it. This is done by setting the `DataSource` property to the `Recordset` object and the `DataField` property to the field name for the control.

```
Set txtName.DataSource = mrsClient
txtName.DataField = "Name"
```

This shows how the `txtName` control is bound to the `Recordset`. All the other controls are handled in a similar fashion.

Binding to the Projects Object

The next section of code opens a `Recordset` object to reflect the `Projects` object from the `Client`. Since the `Projects` object is a collection of other objects, the `ODSOLEDB` data source will use the `CollectionProvider` object to provide the data.

```
Set mrsProjects = New Recordset
mrsProjects.Open "Projects:Name,ID", "Provider=ODSOLEDB"
```

In this case it is important that we specify the optional list of fields after the object name in the `Open` method call. This is because there may be *no* `Project` objects in the collection – in which case the `CollectionProvider` object can't dynamically generate a list of field names. By providing a list of field names, our `CollectionProvider` object will use them rather than relying on dynamic discovery.

Now we are ready to bind the `lstProjects` control to the `Recordset` object. So far our form has made use of a `ListBox` control – one of the standard controls in the toolbox. However, there is another list control called the `DataList` which is optimized for use with ADO `Recordset` objects. Before binding our control let's switch the form to make use of this new control.

Remove the `lstProjects` control from the form. Right-click on the toolbox and choose the **Components...** menu option – then select the **Microsoft DataList Controls 6.0 (OLEDB)** entry. Using the new `DataList` control in the toolbox, add the control in the same location as the `ListBox` we just removed. Name this control `lstProjects`.

With this done, the code to bind the new `lstProjects` control to the `Recordset` object will work nicely.

```
With lstProjects
  Set .RowSource = mrsProjects
  .ListField = "Name"
  .BoundColumn = "ID"
End With
```

With the `DataList` control, the `RowSource` is used instead of the `DataSource` for the data being displayed. Likewise, the `ListField` property indicates the column to be displayed rather than the `DataField`. The `DataSource` and `DataField` properties are used to allow the `DataList` control to update data in a separate `Recordset` – so we can populate the `DataList` from one source and use it to update a second source.

In our case we're just using the control as a display, so we don't need to worry about the `DataSource` and `DataField` properties.

The BoundColumn property is typically used as the key field to tie the DataList controls display data together with the data it is to update – essentially a foreign key between the RowSource and DataSource data sources. However, it is also a useful replacement for the ItemData property in the regular ListBox – allowing the DataControl to retain a unique key value for each entry in the list.

In our original code there was a call to a ListProjects method, which loaded the data from the Projects object into the lstProjects control. Not only has that method been replaced here in Form_Load, but it also needs to be replaced throughout the form.

Adding a Form_Unload Method

Now that we have module-level Recordset objects opened from the Form_Load, we need to implement a Form_Unload to close these Recordset objects.

```
Private Sub Form_Unload(Cancel As Integer)
  mrsClient.Close
  Set mrsClient = Nothing

  mrsProjects.Close
  Set mrsProjects = Nothing
End Sub
```

This closes both the mrsClient and mrsProjects objects and dereferences them by setting the variables to Nothing.

Removing the ListProjects Method

The ListProjects method has been responsible for loading the names of all the Project objects into the lstProjects control. Now that the control is bound to a Recordset, this method is no longer required.

However, we know that the list of Project objects will change from time to time – once a new Project is added, or one is removed, for instance. In such cases the code in the form would call the ListProjects method to refresh the display to match the contents of the Projects collection.

This requirement remains. However, instead of refreshing the display by hand, we can simply force the Recordset object to refresh itself based on the Projects object by calling the Requery method.

```
mrsProjects.Requery
```

This will cause the Recordset object to requery its underlying data source – in this case our Projects object – to ensure that its data is correct. The data binding technology will automatically cause any controls bound to the Recordset object to be refreshed once this is complete.

Essentially then, we can go through the code in the form replacing any calls to the ListProjects method with calls to the Recordset object's Requery method. For instance, in the cmdAdd_Click event procedure we'll make the following change.

```
Private Sub cmdAdd_Click()
  Dim frmProject As ProjectEdit

  Set frmProject = New ProjectEdit
  frmProject.Component mobjClient.Projects.Add
  frmProject.Show vbModal
  mrsProjects.Requery
End Sub
```

The same change needs to be made to the following methods.

❑   cmdEdit_Click

❑   cmdRemove_Click

❑   cmdApply_Click

Finally the ListProjects method itself can be removed from the module since it is no longer called from anywhere in the application – all the display updates are handled by data binding.

Implementing the SelectedItem Method

Both the Edit and Remove buttons cause our application to interact with whichever item is currently selected in the lstProjects list. When lstProjects was a ListBox control we made use of the ItemData property to store an index value so the code could easily find the correct element in the Projects object.

Things aren't quite so simple when working with the DataList control, since there is no ItemData property.

Instead, when we bound the Projects data to the DataList control we specified the BoundColumn property of lstProjects to be ID – the unique key value for each child object. So, this value is easily accessible for the currently selected item in the control, giving us a way to find the correct child object.

Both the Edit and Remove buttons make use of the positional index of the item in the Collection however, so we need some way to figure out that value. This can be done by scanning through the Projects object to find the member object with the same ID property as the one selected in the lstProjects control.

Implementing SelectedItem

Since we'll have to do this same thing later in the ProjectEdit form when working with the Tasks object, let's generalize this into a centralized SelectedItem function.

In the TUImain code module add the following.

```
Public Function SelectedItem(List As DataList, _
                             BoundCollection As Object) As Long
  Dim lngIndex As Long

  With BoundCollection
    For lngIndex = 1 To .Count
      If .Item(lngIndex).ID = Val(List.BoundText) Then
        SelectedItem = lngIndex
        Exit For
      End If
    Next
  End With
End Function
```

This function returns the positional index of the item within the `Collection` object. It accepts a `DataList` control and the `Collection` object as parameters, then scans through the object to find the item with the `ID` that matches the value from the `BoundText` property of the `DataList` control.

The `BoundText` value is whatever value is in the `BoundColumn` for the currently selected item in the list. In our case, it will be the `ID` property value for the currently selected `Project` object.

Updating the Edit Button

Where the Edit button used the `ItemData` property from the `ListBox` control to find the selected item, we can now use the new `SelectedItem` method to provide the same functionality.

```
Private Sub cmdEdit_Click()
  Dim frmProject As ProjectEdit

  Set frmProject = New ProjectEdit
  frmProject.Component _
    mobjClient.Projects(SelectedItem(lstProjects, mobjClient.Projects))
  frmProject.Show vbModal
  mrsProjects.Requery
End Sub
```

The `lstProjects` control and the `Projects` object from our `Client` object are the parameters, and the function returns the positional index of the selected item within the `Projects` object so it can be edited.

Updating the Remove Button

Likewise, the `Remove` button has code that references the `ItemData` property. It too needs to be changed to use the new `SelectedItem` method.

```
Private Sub cmdRemove_Click()
  mobjClient.Projects.Remove SelectedItem(lstProjects, mobjClient.Projects)
  mrsProjects.Requery
End Sub
```

Now, after replacing the `ListBox` with a `DataList`, setting up the data binding, replacing the `ListProjects` method with a call to `Requery` and implementing the `SelectedItem` method we have completely switched the handling of the `lstProjects` control to use data binding technologies.

In fact, the entire form is now data bound to the `Client` and its `Projects` object, eliminating the need for any code to copy data into or out of the fields on the form.

Removing the Change and LostFocus Procedures

The final step in converting the `ClientEdit` form to use data binding is to eliminate the extra code that's no longer needed. We've already eliminated the need for the `ListProjects` method since the `lstProjects` control is bound to a `Recordset`. Now we can go through and remove the various `Click` and `LostFocus` methods for the data bound controls on the form.

Since the `txtName`, `txtContactName` and `txtPhone` controls are now bound to a `Recordset` object, they are automatically kept in sync with the contents of that data source. The code we have implemented in each control's `Change` and `LostFocus` events is now extraneous.

Remove the following routines from the module.

- ❑ txtName_Change
- ❑ txtContactName_Change
- ❑ txtPhone_Change
- ❑ txtname_LostFocus
- ❑ txtContactName_LostFocus
- ❑ txtPhone_LostFocus

Now the ClientEdit form is set up for data binding. Overall we've reduced the amount of code involved in implementing the form, by removing the ListProjects, Change and LostFocus methods – even though the Form_Load is more complex and we've added a SelectedItem method to the project. The benefits are greater with more complex forms and more complex objects, as we save a few lines of code for each control on the form.

Now we'll go through the ProjectEdit and TaskEdit forms, converting them to use data binding as well.

Data Binding in ProjectEdit

Having gone through the process of changing the ClientEdit form to use data binding in detail, the steps required to change a form to use the new technology are probably fairly apparent. In fact, the changes to the ProjectEdit form are virtually identical.

We'll need to replace the lstTasks ListBox control with a DataList control, change the Form_Load method to bind all the controls to Recordsets and eliminate the ListTasks, Change and LostFocus methods. Once that's done the ProjectEdit form will use data binding just like the ClientEdit form does now.

First off, bring up the ProjectEdit form in Visual Basic and replace the ListBox control named lstTasks with a DataList control by the same name. Then open the ProjectEdit form's code window and make the following changes.

Recordset declarations to start with.

```
Option Explicit

Private mflgLoading As Boolean

Private WithEvents mobjProject As Project
Private mrsProject As Recordset
Private mrsTasks As Recordset
```

Then the Form_Load method needs to be changed to open a Recordset for the Project and another for its Tasks. Each control on the form is then bound to the appropriate Recordset object.

```
Private Sub Form_Load()
  Dim objDS As BusinessObjects

  mflgLoading = True
  With mobjProject
    EnableOK .IsValid
    .BeginEdit
  End With
```

```
    ' Register our business objects with the
    ' data source
    Set objDS = New BusinessObjects
    objDS.Add mobjProject, "Project"
    objDS.Add mobjProject.Tasks, "Tasks"

    Set mrsProject = New Recordset
    mrsProject.Open "Project", "Provider=ODSOLEDB"
    Set txtName.DataSource = mrsProject
    txtName.DataField = "Name"

    Set mrsTasks = New Recordset
    mrsTasks.Open "Tasks:ID,Name", "Provider=ODSOLEDB"
    With lstTasks
      Set .RowSource = mrsTasks
      .ListField = "Name"
      .BoundColumn = "ID"
    End With

    objDS.RemoveAll
    Set objDS = Nothing
    mflgLoading = False
  End Sub
```

The `ListTasks` method can now be removed from the module. Replace all calls to `ListTasks` with a call to `mrsTasks.Requery` instead. This impacts the following procedures.

- ❑   `cmdAdd_Click`
- ❑   `cmdEdit_Click`
- ❑   `cmdRemove_Click`

Also, both the **Edit** and **Remove** buttons need to be changed to use the `SelectedItem` method instead of relying on the `ItemData` property from `lstTasks`.

```
    Private Sub cmdEdit_Click()
      Dim frmTask As TaskEdit

      Set frmTask = New TaskEdit
      frmTask.Component mobjProject.Tasks(SelectedItem(lstTasks, mobjProject.Tasks))
      frmTask.Show vbModal
      mrsTasks.Requery
    End Sub

    Private Sub cmdRemove_Click()
      mobjProject.Tasks.Remove SelectedItem(lstTasks, mobjProject.Tasks)
      mrsTasks.Requery
    End Sub
```

Finally the `txtName_Change` and `txtName_LostFocus` event procedures can be eliminated since their function is provided by the data binding technology.

Now all that remains is to implement data binding in the `TaskEdit` form and we're all done.

Data Binding in TaskEdit

The `TaskEdit` form is the easiest to update, since it doesn't have to deal with any child objects. This means it only has a single `Recordset` object to deal with – the one representing the `Task` object being edited.

We'll need to update the `Form_Load` method to set up the data binding, and then remove the `Change` and `LostFocus` event procedures, by which time we will be pretty much done.

However, this form does have one unique and interesting feature that requires a bit of extra implementation. The `PercentComplete` field is a numeric value that is currently formatted to appear nicely on the form. Fortunately Visual Basic 6.0 provides a new capability to allow a user interface to format data bound values for display – so we'll see how that fits into the picture.

Switching to Data Binding

By now, switching a form to use data binding should be old hat. We'll just run through the changes to code very quickly.

First add a declaration.

```
Option Explicit

Private mflgLoading As Boolean

Private WithEvents mobjTask As Task
Private mrsTask As Recordset
```

Then update the `Form_Load` method.

```
Private Sub Form_Load()
  Dim objDS As BusinessObjects

  mflgLoading = True
  With mobjTask
    EnableOK .IsValid
    .BeginEdit
  End With

  Set objDS = New BusinessObjects
  objDS.Add mobjTask, "Task"

  Set mrsTask = New Recordset
  mrsTask.Open "Task", "Provider=ODSOLEDB"
  Set txtName.DataSource = mrsTask
  txtName.DataField = "Name"
  Set txtDays.DataSource = mrsTask
  txtDays.DataField = "ProjectedDays"
  Set txtPercent.DataSource = mrsTask
  txtPercent.DataField = "PercentComplete"

  objDS.RemoveAll
  Set objDS = Nothing
  mflgLoading = False
End Sub
```

Then remove the `Change` and `LostFocus` event procedures and we're all set. All, that is, except for figuring out how to format the `PercentComplete` property value.

Formatting Numeric Values

Visual Basic 6.0 introduced the concept of a **format object**. This object sits between a bound field and the data source to which it is bound, allowing us to format an object for display and then unformat it before it is returned to the data source.

In fact, Visual Basic uses a standard format object on our behalf to handle most common data binding needs. This is available directly through the Visual Basic IDE in the Properties window for each control that can act as a data consumer.

> *Some controls, such as the Microsoft Hierarchical FlexGrid don't provide the nice graphical technique shown here – instead the format object has to be invoked through code. We won't cover that approach here, since the graphic approach will work fine for our purposes.*

Bring up the `TaskEdit` form in Visual Basic and select the `txtPercent` control on the form designer.

In the Properties window there is a `DataFormat` property. Click on it and a button should appear to provide us access to the data formatting options.

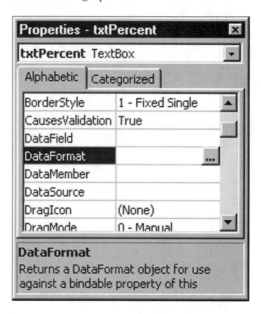

Click on the button to bring up a formatting dialog. This dialog is very similar to formatting dialogs found in other applications such as Microsoft Excel, allowing us to format text, numeric, dates and other types of data. In our case, select the Number option and increase the Decimal places to 1.

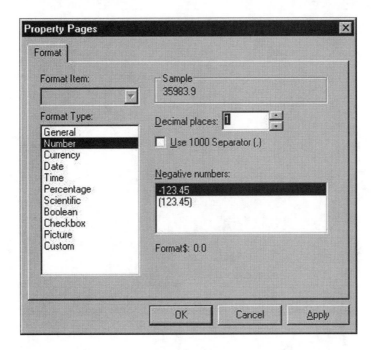

That's all there is to it. Now this new format (essentially "0.0") will be used for any data bound to the txtPercent control – including the data from our Task object.

At this point our changes are complete and the Task Manager application is now using data binding – against business objects instead of tables in a database.

Summary

One of the greatest strengths Visual Basic offers is the RAD support for the concept of data binding. Traditionally we had to give up that RAD capability when developing applications based on business objects, since data binding was designed to work with representations of data, not objects.

As we've seen in this chapter, Visual Basic 6.0 allows us to implement our own data sources – including data sources that can provide data binding capabilities to business objects. This means that we can now implement RAD style user interfaces even in applications that are based on business objects.

This technique may be useful regardless of whether an application is designed following the CSLA or not, since it allows us to use data binding against virtually any object or collection of like objects.

We were able to implement this change with no change to the TaskObjects or TaskServer DLLs. What data binding brings is another option when designing and building a user interface with business objects.

In the next chapter we'll revisit the concept of object state. To date we've been working with applications in a synchronous, connected fashion. In Chapter 6 we'll see how Microsoft Message Queue (MSMQ) fits into the CSLA to provide asynchronous capabilities to our application.

Using Microsoft Message Queue

Overview

Our Task Manager application illustrates a powerful model for application development, taking advantage of both object-oriented programming concepts and client/server transactional design. In the last chapter we even implemented data binding in the user interface. In this chapter we'll return to state management – exploring how Microsoft Message Queue (MSMQ) can be used to provide an asynchronous, queued mechanism for passing object state across the network.

So far in this book our UI-centric business objects have communicated with the data-centric objects by using distributed COM (DCOM). DCOM provides a synchronous, connection-based technology by which objects can communicate.

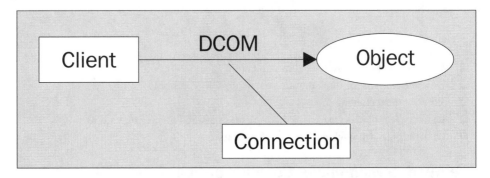

As shown in the diagram, when we communicate with an object via DCOM, a connection is established between the machine running the client code and the machine running the object. This connection is maintained as long as the client code keeps a reference to the server-side object.

Due to the connection-based nature of DCOM, the client-side code, such as that found in our UI-centric objects, can only communicate with the server-side objects if a connection can be made between the client workstation and the server machine. If either the network or server are down then no communication is possible and our application won't run.

Additionally, every time the client code calls a method on the object the client is suspended until that method completes. There is no direct provision for the client to call the method and then keep on working *while* the object completes the method. In most cases this is desirable behavior, since our client code can make a method call and know that the method will be complete (including returning any results) before any other client code will execute.

> *Certainly there are techniques we can use to simulate asynchronous method calls through DCOM – the point here is that it is not something directly provided by the technology.*

Since method calls via DCOM are synchronous, server-side methods, such as the `Fetch` method of a data-centric business object, can both accept parameters and return a result.

There are times when we may not want, or may not have, a synchronous, connection-based method call. In such cases we have to look at asynchronous methods of communication. In this chapter we will be looking at asynchronous method calls, and how to implement this using Microsoft Message Queue server (MSMQ).

The following diagram illustrates how MSMQ sits between the client code and the object on the server – eliminating the need for a continual connection between the two machines.

Asynchronous method calls allow work to be done in the background, but there's no implied mechanism to control *how many* method calls may be in the background at any given time. With queuing however, we have a mechanism to store asynchronous method calls until we can get to them – implying that there is a level of control over how many might be processed at any given time.

In this chapter we'll look at:

- ❑ Why we need asynchronous communication
- ❑ Different options for implementing asynchronous communication
- ❑ Why we need queuing
- ❑ Different techniques we can use to implement queued messaging with MSMQ
- ❑ Updating the task tracking app. to use MSMQ

Why We Need Asynchronous Communication

Sometimes it doesn't matter whether or not a method is completed immediately – as long as it is completed at some point in the future everything will be fine. Other times we simply cannot physically guarantee a connection for a method to complete.

Server Unavailability

At times an application may need to operate even if the network or server are unavailable. Perhaps the application is working with a local store of data, but also needs to post changes to a central database. With queued messaging, the application can continue to run against the local data even if the central server is unavailable.

One good way to implement such a scheme is to have a local data store on the client workstation against which the application runs. This allows the user to work with the data as needed – even performing multiple edits of the data over time – without any difficulty.

The trick is to ensure that the data on the workstation gets updated to the central server once the client workstation is connected to the network. This is easily handled through queued messaging.

Each time the application updates data on the client workstation's data store, it can also send a queued message to the server indicating the ID value or other unique key to find the updated data. Once the client workstation reconnects to the network, these queued messages will be delivered to the server, and the server can then update the changed data from the client into the central database.

Background Processing

There are also situations, where synchronous communication is possible. However, it is preferable for the communications to take place asynchronously.

Consider an order entry system, for example. If the user entry application interacts primarily with a customer and part list database to enter the order, but also needs to update a shipping database we can use queuing to make the application more robust. While the customer data and part list may be required for the application to operate, we can queue messages to the shipping department so the application can continue to run even if the shipping database is unavailable.

Another example where asynchronous method calls may make sense is for activity logging, where an action should complete immediately and a log should be made that the activity was done – but the log entries can be written later.

Long-running Methods

Other times we know that a method will take a long time to complete and we don't want to lock up the entire application until it completes. In these cases an asynchronous method call would be preferable.

An example here may be report generation or the running of a long utility. If the report or utility takes minutes to complete it may be preferable to allow the user to continue working in the application while the report or utility runs in the background.

Large or Complex Environments

For most practical purposes, queued messages are most useful in larger applications. A large, complex application is more likely to have direct dependencies on some servers, and indirect dependencies on other servers – and it's the indirect dependencies where queuing will often make sense. The combination of asynchronous methods and queued messaging can be particularly powerful.

Also, by combining asynchronous method calls with queuing we can implement a form of load control on our server. Better still, multiple servers can receive messages from a single queue – allowing an application to easily spread server processing across multiple machines.

Since our Task Manager application is not terribly large, and at least as it stands there are no indirect dependencies for data, it doesn't seem to lend itself well to asynchronous or queued messaging. Thus, for this chapter, we'll need to use our imagination – envisioning the Task Manager application as being much larger and more complex than it really is.

In particular, such an application may tie into an employee database so tasks can be assigned to individuals. It may also tie into cost accounting, payroll, email and a variety of other complex back-end systems. As we explore MSMQ and how it can be integrated into an application designed using the CSLA keep in mind that, while we're stretching it with the Task Manager application, the techniques and concepts may apply to many larger real-world applications.

Microsoft Message Queue

Microsoft Message Queue (MSMQ) runs as a **service** under Windows. Microsoft introduced it in the Windows NT4 Option Pack (which is available for download from the Microsoft site). It will also become part of Windows 2000 Server. The MSMQ client software is also available for Windows 95 and 98, making it widely applicable for use by our applications. It exposes a set of objects that client applications and components can use to create messages and queues. It also handles the delivery of the messages to the appropriate queue, along with methods that can search through queues and retrieve messages from queues.

> *Since there are books out there that cover MSMQ in some detail, I won't attempt to go through every permutation or capability of the tool in this one chapter. Instead I'll focus on some ways that it can fit nicely into the design of a CSLA-based application. If you want to find out more about it, pick up a copy of MTS MSMQ with VB and ASP (ISBN 1-81001-46-0), from Wrox Press.*

Before we get into how to use MSMQ with CSLA-based applications, let's take a quick overview of the tool and its general capabilities.

MSMQ provides an easy, reliable tool we can use to implement asynchronous, queued communication between objects. In fact, it's more basic than that since MSMQ is essentially nothing more than a way to send arbitrary data from one application to another in an asynchronous and queued manner.

MSMQ Overview

While message queuing has nothing to do with managing email, and the messages it uses are not email messages, the easiest way to appreciate how MSMQ works is by comparing it to email.

The principles behind message queuing are very simple. If you want to pass a message to another application, you can simply wrap it up in a special package a put it into a message queue. The receiving application can then retrieve the waiting messages when it likes. The message stays in the queue until it has been picked up.

MSMQ can also provide:

- ❑ **Guaranteed once-only delivery**. A message can be marked as undelivered until it reaches the server. When it is received, intact by the server, then it is flagged as received. If it is not received the sending application can either try to resend or notify the failure of delivery.

❑ **Prioritization and routing of messages**. MSMQ provides exactly the same kind of services as you get on email. For example, you can mark a message as urgent, so that it is delivered first. It can also be configured to route messages depending on rules.

❑ **Message and system security**. MSMQ requires the applications to identify themselves to the server before sending and receiving messages. They can also be encrypted or digitally signed to prevent unauthorized interception.

❑ **Disparate system integration**. MSMQ stores the data in a format that the sender and recipient are agree on, so it does not matter what the recipients environment looks like – it can convert the data into whatever format is suitable after receipt.

*While MSMQ only directly supports Windows NT and Windows 9x, a company called **Level 8 Systems** manufactures a range of components that can access message queues on other systems. For more information, check out their web site at* `http://www.level8.com`

MSMQ Architecture

I won't go into all the gory details of MSMQ architecture in this book. However, it is important that we have a basic grasp of the elements of an MSMQ solution so we can see where the various parts of our application fit in.

On a basic level, MSMQ has *clients* and *servers*. However, there are two types of client and several types of server that may be involved in an MSMQ environment.

MSMQ Servers

First off, let's briefly look at the different types of server. The server architecture assumes that there is a hierarchical structure to our enterprise and to our network. The basic concept is that within our overall enterprise there may be one or more sites (or locations). Each site manages its own queuing to minimize the traffic across our enterprise WAN (or distributed LAN).

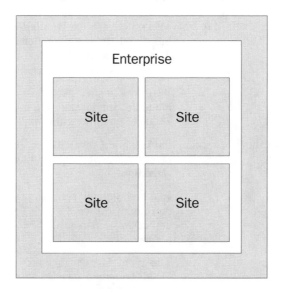

At least one MSMQ server will exist within each site to manage the queuing within that area. These servers are called **Site Controllers** and can be a Primary or a Backup to provide redundancy.

Additionally, within one site there will be a special server known as the **Primary Enterprise Controller**. This server is the Site Controller for that site, but it is also an enterprise-wide resource that coordinates communication between all the Site Controllers across the organization.

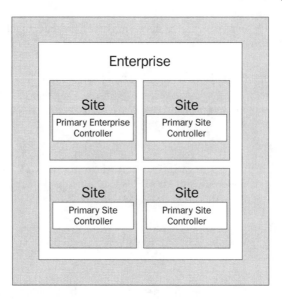

The various types of server are described in the following table.

Server	Description
Primary Enterprise Controller	This server acts as the Site Controller within its site, but also maintains the enterprise configuration database and coordinates communication between all the Site Controllers in the enterprise.
Primary Site Controller	Within each site, the Primary Site Controller maintains the local configuration database and manages queuing within that site.
Backup Site Controller	Backup Site Controllers exist to pick up if the Primary server should fail – providing higher levels of reliability.
Routing Server	In a high volume setting, or a very large enterprise, there may also be Routing Servers, which are dedicated to managing the routing of messages around the network.
Connector Server	This type of server manages connections to non-MSMQ queuing services – acting much like a gateway.

The server computers manage the queues and the routing of messages.

The benefits of this architecture to the developer are huge. We don't need to worry about where a server is or how to reach it through the network. All we need to do is send our message by specifying the destination server's name – and MSMQ takes care of figuring out how to get the message to that server.

Of course this implies that we have clients to create the messages or all of this infrastructure may be meaningless.

MSMQ Clients

Each server may manage messages from many client machines. Before a workstation can send messages via MSMQ however, there must be some client software installed on each client workstation to allow an application to actually create and send a message.

MSMQ supports two types of client installation – independent and dependent.

Independent Client

An **independent client** is pretty much a full installation of MSMQ. Such a client can create and modify queues, just like a server.

The major advantage of an independent client is that the MSMQ services are useable regardless of whether the client has a connection to an MSMQ server or not. This means that an application running on a laptop, for instance, would need an independent client installation so it can continue to function even when the laptop isn't connected to the network.

The *real* queue doesn't reside on the client of course – it resides on a server within the enterprise. However, an independent client has the ability to store messages bound for a queue even if that queue is not available at the moment. This is a required type of installation for any disconnected client that needs to send messages while not connected to the network.

Obviously there are some serious design ramifications to the disconnected client model. If the client workstation is not physically connected to the server then all the data and processing capabilities our application requires to operate must be present on the client workstation itself.

Then, while the application is running, messages can be sent using MSMQ. The MSMQ independent client software stores these messages until the next time the workstation is connected to the network. At which time the messages are automatically forwarded to the MSMQ server to be delivered to the appropriate queue.

An application designed for such a disconnected scenario must not require any response, data or services from any server to operate. The application must operate independently from any server-based processing.

Dependent Client

A **dependent client** is quite a bit different. Such a client has no access to MSMQ services unless a direct connection to an MSMQ server is available.

This type of client involves a smaller installation on the workstation, since the client doesn't need to be able to create or work with queues when the MSMQ server is unavailable – thus the code required on the client is much less.

At the same time, applications running on a dependent client will not operate if the MSMQ server is unavailable. This can limit the utility of using MSMQ – at least in terms of gaining up-time for our application – since if the server is down, then so is our application.

However, many of the advantages of MSMQ remain valid – we still gain asynchronous processing and can implement load throttling or load balancing for our server-side work.

Now that we have a basic grasp of the various types of servers and clients supported by MSMQ, let's take a look at the programming model we'll be using when interacting with MSMQ from code.

MSMQ objects

MSMQ provides a set of objects that we can use in our programs to take advantage of its services. We'll discuss the key objects in more detail later, but the following table provides a summary of the objects available.

Object	Description
MSMQApplication	This object provides global functionality – essentially it appears to exist for consistency with other applications such as Word or Excel that expose an Application object.
MSMQCoordinatedTransaction Dispenser	If we're running in the context of a DTC transaction, this object can be used to gain access to the underlying DTC transaction dispenser.
MSMQEvent	This object describes an interface to be used to describe events for MSMQ. We'll implement this later in order to receive events as MSMQ receives messages.
MSMQMessage	This object represents a message. It can be sent to a queue or retrieved from a queue – either way our application will use this object any time we are dealing with a message.
MSMQQuery	This object is used to look up public queues. If we need to find a queue based on certain criteria – this is how it's done. When this object's LookupQueue method is called, we'll get an MSMQQueueInfos object back that contains a list of queues matching the criteria.
MSMQQueue	This object represents an open queue. Once we've opened a queue we will have one of these objects and can then use it to retrieve messages out of that queue. It is also used as a parameter for the MSMQMessage object's Send method when we want to send a message to this queue.

Object	Description
`MSMQQueueInfo`	This object represents the meta-data around a queue. We will use it when creating, deleting or opening a queue.
	Where the `MSMQQueue` object represents the queue in terms of sending or retrieving messages, this object allows us to manipulate the queue object itself.
`MSMQQueueInfos`	This object is a collection of `MSMQQueueInfo` objects. It is returned as a result from the `LookupQueue` method on the `MSMQQuery` object.
`MSMQTransaction`	This object is returned from either the `MSMQCoordinatedTransactionDispenser` or `MSMQTransactionDispenser` and represents the transaction in progress (if any). It has methods to commit or abort the transaction.
`MSMQTransactionDispenser`	If we're running in the context of a transaction, this object will provide us access to the underlying MSMQ transaction dispenser.

In this chapter we won't explore everything there is to know about MSMQ – that would take far more than a single chapter. However, we will cover the basic uses of a number of these objects. We'll see how to:

- ❑ Create a queue
- ❑ Open an existing queue
- ❑ Send a message
- ❑ Read a message from a queue
- ❑ Detect when a message has arrived in a queue

To do all these things we only need to deal with a few key objects from all those available. We'll discuss the key ones, `MSMQMessage` and `MSMQQueue`, shortly. First, it is important to understand where to get MSMQ and what tools are available to us for administration.

MSMQ Availability and Tools

MSMQ is widely available, and provides a set of administrative tools we can use to help manage queues and monitor activity.

MSMQ Availability

MSMQ is available on the Windows NT Option Pack CD and will be part of the Windows 2000 installation. The Windows NT Option Pack CD is freely available to licensed owners of Windows NT and includes a number of server enhancements – including MSMQ.

To do everything described in this chapter you'll need to install MSMQ off the CD and also apply the Windows NT 4.0 Service Pack 4 (SP4) after installing MSMQ. Without SP4, passing objects by value (which we'll get into later) won't work from Visual Basic.

All the work I did throughout this chapter was done under Windows NT. However, if you aren't running under Windows NT you can still install the independent client for Windows 9x and work with the queues on your server.

> **Regardless, you must have Windows NT Server running a Primary Enterprise Controller somewhere on your network or MSMQ will not operate.**

There is an SP4 update for Win9x that should be on your CD in the following directory:

```
<CD Drive>:\SUPPORT\MSMQ.95\MQ95SP4.EXE
```

You'll want to apply that as well to ensure everything runs properly.

MSMQ Explorer

The primary administrative tool provided by MSMQ is the MSMQ Explorer.

Interestingly enough, while the independent client under Win9x allows applications to work with queues – there is no MSMQ Explorer provided for the Win9x environment. This means that we have to go to an MSMQ server machine to use this tool.

The following diagram shows the explorer in my environment, where my Primary Enterprise Controller (PEC) is a machine named ss3test.

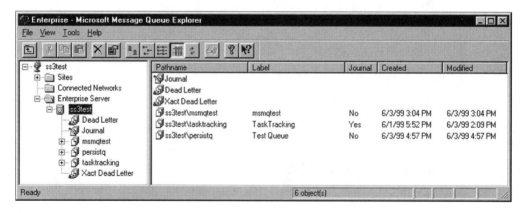

All the queues currently set up on my server are listed, with their details shown in the right-hand pane.

From here we can create new queues, remove existing queues and perform other administrative functions such as setting security, limiting the space a queue can consume on disk and so forth.

Additionally, we can right-click on a specific queue and choose the `Properties` menu option. This will bring up the properties dialog for the queue, including a tab for `Status`.

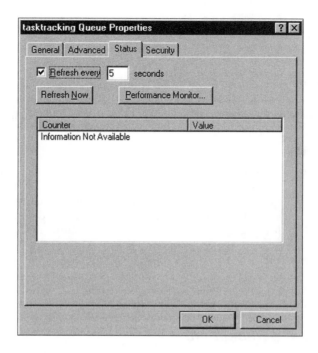

This tab shows statistical information about the queue – including the number of bytes of data in the queue. Information like this can be very valuable as you troubleshoot an application – allowing you to ensure that messages of the appropriate size are arriving in the queue, etc.

MSMQ Messages

The data sent through MSMQ is sent inside a construct called a **message** – represented by the MSMQMessage object. A message not only contains the data, but also includes some meta-data such as a label, the priority of the message, the time it was sent and so forth. Some of the most commonly useful properties of an MSMQMessage object are:

Property	Description
Body	The actual data being sent in the message – at most 4 MB of data per message
BodyLength	The number of bytes of data contained in the body of the message
Label	An arbitrary text label for the message – this label is assigned by the sending application
AppSpecific	An arbitrary numeric value attached to the message – this value is assigned by the sending application
Priority	The priority of the message – higher priority messages will be inserted at the top of the queue, thus typically being processed before lower priority messages

As we have seen, there's more to MSMQ than simple delivery of messages. So, let's take a look at some of the more powerful and commonly used capabilities provided by the tool and how they are implemented. We'll briefly look at:

❑ Express or recoverable message delivery
❑ Optional guaranteed once-only delivery
❑ Integration with MTS transactions so a message is only sent if an MTS transaction completes

The Delivery Property

Each message has a `Delivery` property that is used to tell MSMQ whether a message should be delivered as rapidly or as safely as possible. If this property is set to `MQMSG_DELIVERY_EXPRESS` (the default), then the message will be sent as fast as possible, with minimal regard for reliability. In particular, the message will never be written to disk, but is instead stored in memory. Because of this, if any server crashes while the message is stored in its memory then the message will be lost.

If the `Delivery` property is set to `MQMSG_DELIVERY_RECOVERABLE` then the message will be written to disk on each server as it moves from the sender to the receiver. This prevents the message from being lost in the case of a machine failure – but slows down the delivery process since the message must be stored and removed from disk on each machine as it is moved across the network.

Transactional Message Reception

Setting the `Delivery` property to `MQMSG_DELIVERY_RECOVERABLE` has a potential side effect that may not be ideal. In particular, since the message is written to disk on the server, an ill-timed server crash can actually cause the message to be delivered more than one time.

To avoid this, a message can be received within the context of an MTS transaction. The transactional support and integration between MSMQ, MTS and DTC (the Distributed Transaction Coordinator) will ensure that a message is only delivered one time and that it is removed from the queue's disk cache once it has been delivered.

Transaction Message Transmission

It is also possible to *send* a message within a transaction. The benefit here is that the message will only be sent in the case that the entire transaction is completed. Within a given MTS transaction there may be some database writes, MSMQ messages sent, etc. However, if any one of these operations signals a failure by calling `SetAbort` then none of it will be committed – the database changes will be rolled back and the MSMQ message will not be sent.

> **If a message is transactional, it can only be sent to a transactional queue.**

Any time a message is sent from within a transaction its `Delivery` property will be forced to the `MQMSG_DELIVERY_RECOVERABLE` value.

MSMQ Queues

Within MSMQ, messages are delivered to queues. Once in a queue, a message can be retrieved by an application designed to process the messages.

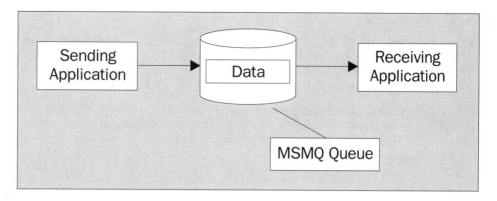

Queues act as both the address to which a message may be sent, and a storage mechanism where messages reside until they are processed.

Public and Private Queues

An MSMQ queue can be either public or private. Public queues are visible and available to any MSMQ application on the network. Private queues can only be accessed by the application that created the queue or applications that are given the information about the private queue.

Public queues are used to allow applications to send data to a known location for processing. For instance, a public queue might be set up to allow an application to generate reports on a centralized server. Any client can send a message to the report generation queue, since it is publicly accessible.

Private queues are typically used for various types of responses within a queued application. In the report example above, the sending machine may create a private queue and send its addressing information along with the message requesting the report. Once the report has been generated, the report processing application can send a message back to the sender's private queue indicating that the report is complete.

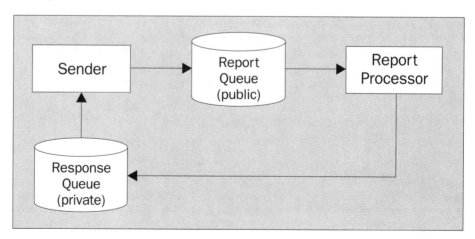

No one else can send messages to that private queue, since only the sender and the report processor have that queue's addressing information.

Transactional Queues

Queues may be marked as transactional, meaning that they will only accept messages sent within a transaction and a transaction is required to read the messages from the queue. This impacts the Delivery property of a message, since all messages routed through a transactional queue will be forced to use the MQMSG_DELIVERY_RECOVERABLE value for this property.

To make a queue transactional, it has to be marked as so when it is created. This is done by setting the IsTransactional parameter to True when the Create method is called.

Creating a Queue in Visual Basic

MSMQ uses some support objects to provide administrative capabilities such as locating and creating queues. Perhaps the most important is the MSMQQueueInfo object, since it is the object that allows us to create a queue or gain a reference to that queue once it is created.

Public Queue

The code to create a public queue programmatically is quite short (do not enter this code).

```
Dim objQI As MSMQQueueInfo

Set objQI = New MSMQQueueInfo
With objQI
  .PathName = "myserver\myqueue"
  .Create
End With
```

This code creates a queue named myqueue on the server named myserver. The server name can be the NetBIOS machine name, a fully qualified DNS name or a period (".") to indicate the local machine.

The queue is non-transactional (we come on to transactional queues next), so messages sent or received through this queue will not have transactional protection and thus may be lost (if the message Delivery property is set for express delivery), or delivered more than once (if the Delivery property is set for recoverable delivery).

The PathName property can be more complex than shown here. The first word in the path must specify the server that will host the queue, but beyond that there are few limitations on the path name. For instance, the following may be appropriate for a report generation queue in our Task Manager application.

```
.PathName = "myserver\TaskTracker\reports"
```

Microsoft recommends keeping the path name to 64 characters or less to achieve best performance and to ensure that the Active Directory administrative tools can properly display the name.

If the queue is being created on the same machine where the application is running, then the server name can be replaced with a '.' – simplifying the code since we don't have to figure out the name of the machine.

```
.PathName = ".\TaskTracker\reports"
```

This technique is typically more useful for private queues than for public queues.

Transactional Queue

The queue created by the code we've just seen is a public queue (we'll cover private queues shortly), but it is not transactional. To make a transactional queue, we'd change the `Create` method call as shown.

```
.Create True
```

By passing the `True` value to the `IsTransactional` parameter (which is the first parameter for the `Create` method) we've indicated that the queue should only accept messages sent within a transaction and that a transaction will be required when reading messages from the queue.

In this case, messages are guaranteed to be delivered once and once only.

Private Queue

Public queues can easily found and accessed by virtually any MSMQ application by using the `MSMQQuery` object's `LookupQueue` method. Private queues are not available for searching, so only the creating program knows it exists. The creating program can provide access information to other applications, allowing them to use the queue – but applications can't just browse for private queues.

Creating a private queue is virtually identical to creating a public queue. The only difference is the presence of a special keyword in the `PathName` property of the queue.

To create a public queue the `PathName` is built using the server name followed by a path of our choosing. To create a private queue, the `PathName` is built using the local server name and the reserved word `'PRIVATE$'` followed by our path.

For instance, to create a private queue we could use the following code. The line showing the pathname is highlighted.

```
Dim objQI As MSMQQueueInfo

Set objQI = New MSMQQueueInfo
With objQI
    .PathName = ".\PRIVATE$\myqueue"
    .Create
End With
```

This is essentially the same code as we would use to create a public queue, but because of the `PRIVATE$` keyword the queue's information won't be published such that it is searchable – making it a private queue.

Overall MSMQ is a very powerful tool. As with any tool, it is most powerful when used in appropriate scenarios. In the next section we'll examine some architectural considerations and approaches that impact how and when MSMQ should be used.

Architectural Approaches

From a very basic viewpoint, MSMQ is a tool that allows an application on one machine to send a message into a queue. Then a second application (possibly on another machine) can read the messages out of that queue and do whatever it wants with each message, whenever it gets around to it. MSMQ is a great way to send uni-directional messages from a sender to a processor.

While this may be a simplistic view of the tool, it is a valuable way to think about MSMQ as we evaluate how it fits into any given architecture.

Referencing the MSMQ Library

Before we can use MSMQ from a Visual Basic program, we must use the Project | References menu option to add a reference to the Microsoft Message Queue Object Library. This is illustrated in the following diagram.

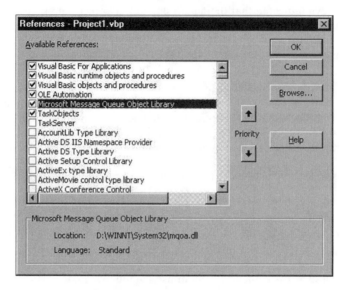

Once this reference has been added to a Visual Basic project, all the MSMQ objects and services will be available to our code.

Basic Components

Any time we use MSMQ, we are transmitting a message from one application to a queue, where it is then picked up by another application to be processed. This implies that there's always at least one sender and one receiver for our messages.

Sender

The sender is an application that creates an MSMQMessage object, sets its properties and then sends it to one or more queues. The steps to do this are as follows.

1. Obtain an MSMQQueue object for the destination queue
2. Create an MSMQMessage object
3. Populate the MSMQMessage object
4. Use the MSMQMessage object's Send method to send the message to the queue

In many applications there will be multiple senders for a single queue. For instance, each client workstation may be sending messages to a single queue to request that reports be generated. Or perhaps a group of MTS servers are all sending messages to a queue that is recording an audit log of activity.

A sending application can be written to send either raw data (up to 4 MB) in the body of the message, or it can be written to send an entire object.

Sending Data

The code to send raw data in a message is fairly straightforward and follows the steps listed above.

```
Dim objQI As MSMQQueueInfo
Dim objQ As MSMQQueue
Dim objM As MSMQMessage

' Create MSMQQueueInfo and use it to open an MSMQQueue object
Set objQI = New MSMQQueueInfo
objQI.PathName = "myserver\myqueue"
Set objQ = objQI.Open(MQ_SEND_ACCESS, MQ_DENY_NONE)

' create and initialize a message object
Set objM = New MSMQMessage
With objM
  .Label = "Test Message"
  .Body = "Here is the body of the message to be processed"

   ' send the message to the queue we opened earlier
  .Send objQ
End With
```

The code creates an `MSMQQueueInfo` object and uses it to open an `MSMQQueue` object based on the `PathName` property. In this case, it is opening a queue on `myserver` with the name `myqueue`. The parameters to the `Open` method indicate the following:

Parameter	Meaning
MQ_SEND_ACCESS	Indicates that we are opening the queue for the purpose of sending a message
MQ_DENY_NONE	Indicates that we don't want exclusive access to the queue – we are not denying use of the queue to other users

With the queue available, the code then creates a new instance of an `MSMQMessage` object and sets its `Label` and `Body` properties. The `Body` property is typed as a `Variant`, so it can hold virtually any type of data – text, binary, whatever. In this case we're providing a simple string.

Once the message is ready, the `Send` method is called, causing the message to be sent to the specified queue.

This approach to sending messages is very powerful because it provides us with almost unlimited flexibility. Any data we can store in a `Variant` data type can be easily placed into a message body and sent to a queue.

With flexibility comes extra work however. We also have to write a program to read the messages out of the queue and process them as appropriate. This implies that we have to be able to unpack the data stored in the message body and decipher it.

Thus, we can't simply throw data into the message body. Instead we need to take care to ensure we can retrieve the data from the message body in an intelligent and efficient manner. This can be done using a number of techniques for managing the contents of a message's body, including:

❑ Using the Contents property of a PropertyBag object
❑ The UDT/LSet technique we're using for serializing objects
❑ Creating a delimited string

Basically, any approach that allows us to easily pack and unpack a series of data values into a single stream of data will work just fine.

Sending Objects

While sending an arbitrary stream of data as the body of a message is very flexible and powerful, it can also be challenging. Suppose the data is large and complex – such as the result set from a database query, or the combined data from a Collection object. Converting such data into a data stream, and then reconstituting it back into a useful form on the receiving end is not trivial.

Fortunately MSMQ provides an easy answer to this problem. Or perhaps it is better to say COM provides an easy answer. Two well-known COM interfaces that an object can choose to implement are IPersistStream and IPersistStorage. These interfaces are used to request that an object serialize its data and expose it to the client program. Collectively I'll refer to them as the IPersist interface.

MSMQ makes use of these interfaces if an object supports them. This means that, if an object implements one of these interfaces, we can simply assign the object to the Body property of a message and MSMQ will take care of the rest.

Many objects support these interfaces, including:

❑ ADO Recordset objects
❑ PropertyBag objects
❑ Any Visual Basic object with the Persistable property set to 1-Persistable

Since an ADO Recordset object implements the IPersist interface, the code to send a Recordset in a message is quite straightforward.

```
Dim objQI As MSMQQueueInfo
Dim objQ As MSMQQueue
Dim objM As MSMQMessage

' Create MSMQQueueInfo and use it to open an MSMQQueue object
Set objQI = New MSMQQueueInfo
objQI.PathName = "myserver\myqueue"
Set objQ = objQI.Open(MQ_SEND_ACCESS, MQ_DENY_NONE)

' create and initialize a message object
Set objM = New MSMQMessage
With objM
  .Label = "An ADO Recordset"
  .Body = rsMyRecordset

  ' send the message to the queue we opened earlier
  .Send objQ
End With
```

The key point of interest is the line that assigns the `Body` property.

```
.Body = rsMyRecordset
```

Notice that all we're doing here is assigning a `Recordset` object directly to the `Body` property. MSMQ is intelligent enough to realize that we've assigned an object, so it determines whether the object supports the `IPersist` interface. If so, the object's data is requested and stored in the body of the message.

In fact, it is not just the data that is stored. MSMQ also stores enough information about the object (its PROGID) so it can create a new instance of that object within the receiving application – as we'll see shortly.

The ability to simply send an entire complex object within the body of a message is very powerful. However, it is important to remember that a lot of work is going on behind the scenes. Such simple looking code is deceptive – all the complex data from the `Recordset` object is still being converted to a byte stream before it is placed in the body of the message.

Just because we didn't have to write the hard code, doesn't mean it doesn't exist. Even more importantly, there is a performance impact to consider. The one line of code we write will cause a lot of work to be done – and that work may take substantial amounts of time.

Receiver

Now that we've seen how to send messages, either using simple data or by sending entire objects, we can examine how to receive these messages.

A message is sent from a sender into a queue. Once in the queue, another program – the receiver – must read the message from the queue and then process the message as appropriate.

Receiver as an NT Service

It is very likely that we'll want our receiver application to continue to run on the server regardless of whether someone is logged into the machine or not. After all, we don't want to stop receiving messages just because no one is logged into the server.

Since MSMQ provides no mechanism for launching an application when a message arrives in a queue, it is up to us to ensure that an application is actually running to read messages from the queue.

If an application runs on the server even when no one is logged in, it is typically implemented as a **Windows NT service**. Receiver applications are ideally implemented to be a Windows NT service since they should continue to run even when no one is logged into the server.

Unfortunately there's no direct or easy way to build a Windows NT service using Visual Basic.

The Windows NT Resource Kit provides the SRVANY utility – a tool that allows us to make a Visual Basic application into an NT service. Unfortunately, at this stage it is very primitive and limited, although it can work in some cases.

The Microsoft MSDN Library also includes an ActiveX control – NTService – that can be used to make a Visual Basic application work as an NT service. This approach is more robust, but requires a subscription to MSDN to gain access to the control.

Creating an NT service from within Visual Basic is something not recommended by Microsoft and isn't within the scope of this book. If you do decide to build a receiver application as an NT service check out *Professional NT Services* from Wrox Press (ISBN 1-861001-30-4), which has a chapter on MSMQ and the Agent Usage Pattern.

While it would be ideal if our receiver application were a Windows NT service, we won't create a service in this chapter. We will, however, create an application to act as a receiver and you can adapt it to be a service if you choose.

Receiving a Message

When creating a receiver application we'll obviously need to know when a message has arrived in the queue. We can choose to explicitly read messages in the queue or we can have MSMQ raise an event each time a message arrives in the queue so we know when to go get it.

There are some differences between receiving data and receiving an object. We'll take a look at each in turn to see how it works.

Yet another interesting capability is to be able to read a message in the queue without removing the message from the queue. This is done with the Peek method – allowing us to peek at the contents of the queue without affecting them.

For now we'll stick with the Receive method, which not only reads the message from the queue, but also removes it from the queue.

> *Once the message has been removed from the queue it is gone – unless we're reading messages within a transaction. If we are within a transaction the message may be placed back into the queue in the case that the transaction fails and is not committed.*

Receiving a message follows a comparable set of steps to sending a message.

1. Obtain an MSMQQueue object for the receiver's queue
2. Call the queue's Receive method to read an MSMQMessage object
3. Use the contents of the message object to do any processing

These basic steps remain constant whether we're retrieving a message that contains data or one that contains an object.

Receiving Data

In our earlier example we saw how to send a message with an arbitrary stream of data. Receiving such a message is fairly straightforward.

```
Dim objQI As MSMQQueueInfo
Dim objQ As MSMQQueue
Dim objM As MSMQMessage


' Create MSMQQueueInfo and use it to open an MSMQQueue object
Set objQI = New MSMQQueueInfo
objQI.PathName = "myserver\myqueue"
Set objQ = objQI.Open(MQ_RECEIVE_ACCESS, MQ_DENY_NONE)
```

```
' retrieve the first message from the queue
' the following line will wait until a message is available to be read
Set objM = objQ.Receive
With objM
   Debug.Print .Label
   Debug.Print .Body
End With
```

We gain a reference to the queue in the same way as when we went to send a message – using the MSMQQueueInfo object and the appropriate path name. Once we have a reference to the queue, the Receive method is used to return a fully populated instance of an MSMQMessage object.

> Note, as shown here the **Receive** method will wait forever until it receives a message, so be cautious or add a timeout value as a parameter of the **Receive** method.

Once we have the message object, the Body property can be used to retrieve the data from the object. Given the data, we can implement whatever processing is appropriate. In this simple case the code just prints the contents into the Immediate window.

Receiving Objects

Receiving an object is a bit more interesting. The code to receive the object is quite comparable to receiving simple data, although the implications are interesting.

```
Dim objQI As MSMQQueueInfo
Dim objQ As MSMQQueue
Dim objM As MSMQMessage
Dim rsNewRecordset As Recordset

' Create MSMQQueueInfo and use it to open an MSMQQueue object
Set objQI = New MSMQQueueInfo
objQI.PathName = "myserver\myqueue"
Set objQ = objQI.Open(MQ_RECEIVE_ACCESS, MQ_DENY_NONE)

' Receive the first queued message and process it
Set objM = objQ.Receive
With objM
   Debug.Print .Label
   Set rsNewRecordset = .Body
   Debug.Print rsNewRecordset.RecordCount
End With
```

Notice that the use of the Body property now involves the Set statement.

```
Set rsNewRecordset = .Body
```

MSMQ not only stored the data from the Recordset object, it also stored information about the Recordset object itself so it can create a new instance of the appropriate object when the Body property is accessed.

This does imply that the machine where the receiving code is running has access to the appropriate COM server (DLL or EXE) so it can create an instance of the appropriate object. If not, the call to the Body property will fail.

Of course we either need to know the type of object to expect in order to declare the object variable to hold the new reference. Either that, or we can use the `Object` data type and hope to figure out what kind of object it is later – which is probably not the best approach.

As I said, the implications are interesting. This technique allows us to very easily transfer a complex object into a message such that MSMQ will automatically reconstitute the object for the receiving application.

Of course, it is up to the receiving application to figure out what to do with the object once it is reconstituted. Also note that this technique literally reconstitutes an object with the exact same class – it doesn't provide a mechanism by which we can send data from one class (such as a UI-centric object) to another class (such as a data-centric object).

We'll get further into the design ramifications later in this chapter as we see how to integrate MSMQ with the CSLA.

Using the MSMQEvent Class

The code shown above receives a message explicitly, when it is told to. It can be placed behind a button or anywhere else where we want our receiving application to read a message from the queue.

The thing about receiving messages is that there's no way to predict when a message may arrive. In many, if not most, cases we'll only want to attempt to read a message from the queue if we know there's a message waiting to be read.

Fortunately MSMQ provides a mechanism by which our application can be notified any time a message arrives in the queue. This is handled through the normal COM event technology – accessed within Visual Basic by using the `WithEvents` keyword.

One of the classes available once we've referenced the MSMQ library is `MSMQEvent`. This type of object has no properties or methods - the entire purpose for its existence is to raise events into our application.

An `MSMQEvent` object will raise two events – `Arrived` and `ArrivedError`. The `Arrived` event will fire when a message arrives in the queue, while `ArrivedError` will be raised in the case that a message arrives abnormally – with some error occurring in the delivery.

To receive these events, our application will need a form or class module. In that module, there will need to be a couple module-level declarations.

```
Option Explicit

Private mobjQ As MSMQQueue
Private WithEvents mobjMQEvents As MSMQEvent
```

Then in the `Form_Load` or `Class_Initialize` the code will need to create the `MSMQEvent` object, as well as gain a reference to the appropriate queue. Using these two references, we can tell the queue to raise events to our application.

```
Dim objQI As MSMQQueueInfo

' Create MSMQQueueInfo and use it to open an MSMQQueue object
Set objQI = New MSMQQueueInfo
objQI.PathName = "myserver\myqueue"
Set mobjQ = objQI.Open(MQ_RECEIVE_ACCESS, MQ_DENY_NONE)
```

```
' Enable notification for message arrival
Set mobjMQEvents = New MSMQEvent
mobjQ.EnableNotification mobjMQEvents
```

The last line is key – it calls the `EnableNotification` method of the queue object so the queue knows to raise events into our application.

Since we are declaring the `mobjMQEvents` object using the `WithEvents` keyword we can add code to receive any events it may raise. The key event to receive is the `Arrived` event. By using the code from the previous section we can automatically read any message as it arrives.

```
Private Sub mobjMQEvents_Arrived(ByVal Queue As Object, ByVal Cursor As Long)
    Dim objQI As MSMQQueueInfo
    Dim objQ As MSMQQueue
    Dim objM As MSMQMessage
    Dim rsNewRecordset As Recordset

    ' Create MSMQQueueInfo and use it to open an MSMQQueue object
    Set objQI = New MSMQQueueInfo
    objQI.PathName = "myserver\myqueue"
    Set objQ = objQI.Open(MQ_RECEIVE_ACCESS, MQ_DENY_NONE)

    ' Receive and process a message
    Set objM = objQ.Receive
    With objM
      Debug.Print .Label
      Set rsNewRecordset = .Body
      Debug.Print rsNewRecordset.RecordCount
    End With

    ' Reenable the event notification mechanism
    mobjQ.EnableNotification mobjMQEvents
End Sub
```

Notice the last line in the method. All the rest of the code is directly from the previous section, where we examined how to read a message that contains an object. This last line, however, is new.

```
mobjQ.EnableNotification mobjMQEvents
```

The `MSMQEvent` object only receives one event when a message arrives. Then it automatically disconnects and won't receive any further messages unless we reset the process by calling the queue object's `EnableNotification` method again.

At first glance this seems like an odd way to handle things, but it is really quite convenient. We never want to have an `Arrived` event fire off while we are in the middle of handling a previous `Arrived` event. This could rapidly cause our application to be processing many messages at the same time – leading to unforeseen consequences. Eventually our application may even run out of stack space if messages are arriving faster than they can be processed.

By disabling the event mechanism when an event arrives, we are guaranteed not to receive another `Arrived` event until *we* choose to reset the event mechanism. As soon as the event mechanism is reset the queue is checked for existing messages and the arrival event will be fired – ensuring that we're always notified when there are pending messages.

Application Models

We've seen the code to send a message, read a message and how to receive an event each time a message arrives in a queue. That covers the basics, but doesn't necessarily illustrate how MSMQ might fit into an application's architecture.

Queued messages can be very powerful, but it is important to think through how they might fit into an application before implementing them. Not all applications can benefit from this technology, nor does it fit every situation where asynchronous processing or load balancing is required.

Bi-directional Communication

The first, and perhaps most important, consideration is that MSMQ is primarily designed around the concept of one-way messaging.

While MSMQ does have some facilities for bi-directional messaging (via response queues), one must be *very* cautious in making a decision to use it in such a scenario. MSMQ makes no guarantee that a message will be processed in a timely fashion, so a client that sits and waits for a response could wait for a long, long time.

If we implement an application to send a message and then do nothing while it waits for a response, then the application is really flying in the face of MSMQ's design. This is potentially risky, since it is possible that the server is down, or that the queue has a backlog of messages and so our application could wait for a response message for minutes, hours or even days. This may tend to irritate the user.

> If our application *requires* a timely response to a message, it should be designed to use a synchronous technology such as DCOM, or, as we'll see in Chapter 7, Remote Data Services.

There are cases, however, where an application needs a response to a message, but can be designed so that the response isn't immediately required.

For instance, an application may need to store some data or send an email message, but not necessarily before any other work can be completed. At the same time, the user may wish to know when that work has been completed – perhaps for peace of mind, or because then they'll know they can do something else following on from that task.

In such a case, the application can be designed to require a response message, while also allowing the user to use the application in the meantime. This way the user can continue to be productive, and yet they can be notified when the response message arrives – after the server-side processing is complete. To implement such bi-directional communication, however, the sender and receiver need to do some extra work.

Updating the Sender for Bi-directional Communication

The sender of the message will now also be the receiver of a response. This means that the sender must create a queue to receive that message, and then listen for the arrival of a message on that queue. This new queue is called a **response queue**.

Typically this response queue will be a private queue. It doesn't need to be publicly available, since the only program that will be sending a message to it is the server program processing the sender's original message.

The sender also needs to continue to operate while waiting for the response message to arrive. Typically this will be handled through the MSMQEvent object and its Arrived event. The sender application can continue to interact with the user and do anything else that's required, and when the response message arrives in its private queue the Arrived event will fire and the program can take appropriate steps.

Only one question remains – how does the receiver application know which private queue should receive the response message? MSMQ provides a property on the MSMQMessage object for this very purpose – the ResponseQueueInfo property.

As we noted, the sending application will probably create a private queue to receive the response message. To create this queue we might use code like the following.

Declare the MSMQQueueInfo, MSMQQueue and MSMQEvent objects at a module level.

```
Private mobjResponseQI As MSMQQueueInfo
Private mobjResponseQ As MSMQQueue
Private WithEvents mobjResponseQE As MSMQEvent
```

Then create the response queue in code somewhere before sending any messages to the server.

```
' Create MSMQQueueInfo and use it to create a private queue
Set mobjResponseQI = New MSMQQueueInfo
With mobjResponseQI
  .PathName = ".\PRIVATE$\responsequeue"
  .Create

  ' open the newly created queue
  Set mobjResponseQ = .Open(MQ_RECEIVE_ACCESS, MQ_DENY_NONE)
End With

  ' enable arrival event notification for the private queue
Set mobjResponseQE = New MSMQEvent
mobjResponseQ.EnableNotification mobjResponseQE
```

This code also creates the MSMQEvent object and sets it up so we'll receive an Arrived event any time a message arrives in the response queue.

When we then send the message to the server, we'll use this MSMQQueueInfo object to populate the ResponseQueueInfo property of the message – something like the following.

```
Dim objQI As MSMQQueueInfo
Dim objQ As MSMQQueue
Dim objM As MSMQMessage

' Create MSMQQueueInfo and use it to open a queue
Set objQI = New MSMQQueueInfo
objQI.PathName = "myserver\myqueue"
Set objQ = objQI.Open(MQ_SEND_ACCESS, MQ_DENY_NONE)

' Create a new message and initialize it
```

```
Set objM = New MSMQMessage
With objM
   ' store the private queue info into the message
   Set .ResponseQueueInfo = mobjResponseQI
   .Label = "My message label"
   .Body = "The body of the message is here"

   ' send the message
   .Send objQ
End With
```

With that done, we can implement code to respond to the `Arrived` event so the application knows when the server has sent a response message.

```
Private Sub mobjResponseQE_Arrived(ByVal Queue As Object, ByVal Cursor As Long)
   Dim objM As MSMQMessage

   ' receive and process the message
   Set objM = Queue.Receive(receivetimeout:=0)
   MsgBox objM.Body

   ' reenable message arrival notification
   mobjQ.EnableNotification mobjResponseQE
End Sub
```

In this simple code we're just popping up a message box displaying the body of the message – obviously the application could do whatever is appropriate with the response message.

Notice the use of the `receivetimeout` parameter on the `Receive` method. By setting this to 0 we are indicating that the method should return immediately regardless of whether or not a message is found in the queue.

Even with the `Arrived` event, there might not be a message in the queue. This is because MSMQ supports multiple readers for a given queue and so some other receiver application could have got to the message before we did.

This type of approach is powerful, because the sending application is not tied up waiting for the response message. The user can still work with the application and be productive, and yet the application can be notified when a response message arrives.

Of course this does mean that the sending application cannot be dependent on the response from the server. For all we know, the server may be very busy, the queue may be very full – any number of things. The response message may not arrive for minutes or even hours – so if the sending application needs the response then this would not be an appropriate implementation and DCOM or another synchronous technology would be a better choice.

Updating the Receiver for Bi-directional Communication

The server-side receiver application will also need some changes. We've already seen how to update the sending application to create a response queue and use the message object's `ResponseQueueInfo` property to pass the response queue's address to the receiving application.

Now let's see how the receiving application is updated to not only receive the message from the sender, but also to turn around and send a response message when appropriate.

A typical receiver application will be set up to respond to the Arrived event on its queue, where it can process the message as needed. Now we need to add code to this procedure to determine whether or not the message requires a response. Then, if it does, to send a response message.

```
Private Sub mobjMQEvents_Arrived(ByVal Queue As Object, ByVal Cursor As Long)
  Dim objQI As MSMQQueueInfo
  Dim objQ As MSMQQueue
  Dim objM As MSMQMessage
  Dim objRQ As MSMQQueue
  Dim objRM As MSMQMessage

  ' Create MSMQQueueInfo and use it to open an MSMQQueue object
  Set objQI = New MSMQQueueInfo
  objQI.PathName = "myserver\myqueue"
  Set objQ = objQI.Open(MQ_RECEIVE_ACCESS, MQ_DENY_NONE)

  ' receive a message, indicating that we want the queue info
  Set objM = objQ.Receive WantDestinationQueue:=True
  With objM
    Debug.Print .Label
    Debug.Print .Body

    ' if there is a response queue included, generate a response
    If Not .ResponseQueueInfo Is Nothing Then
      ' open the reponse queue
      Set objRQ = .ResponseQueueInfo.Open(MQ_SEND_ACCESS, MQ_DENY_NONE)

      ' create and populate the response message
      Set objRM = New MSMQMessage
      objRM.Label = "RE: " & .Label
      objRM.Body = "This is the response message body"
      objRM.ResponseQueueInfo = .DestinationQueueInfo
      objRM.CorrelationId = .Id

      ' send the response message
      objRM.Send objRQ
    End If

  End With

  ' reenable message arrival notification
  mobjQ.EnableNotification mobjMQEvents
End Sub
```

Looking through the code, there are quite a few changes compared with receiving a message and not worrying about a response message. Let's walk through the changes.

First off, when we read the message from our queue there's a new parameter added to the Receive method call. The WantDestinationQueue parameter is passed as True – indicating that we not only want to retrieve the message, but also that the message should also contain information about the queue from which it was read. We'll see why this is important shortly – but for now consider the thought that the sender may have sent the same message to a number of queues, in which case it might be important to indicate which queue has sent the response message.

Next, we've added a check to determine whether the message's ResponseQueueInfo property references an object or if it is Nothing. If it references an object, then we know that the sender must expect a response message.

```
If Not .ResponseQueueInfo Is Nothing Then
```

The next few lines should look, for the most part, pretty familiar. They open the response queue, create a new message object, populate the message and send it to the response queue.

```
Set objRQ = .ResponseQueueInfo.Open(MQ_SEND_ACCESS, MQ_DENY_NONE)
Set objRM = New MSMQMessage
objRM.Label = "RE: " & .Label
objRM.Body = "This is the response message body"
objRM.ResponseQueueInfo = .DestinationQueueInfo
objRM.CorrelationId = .Id
objRM.Send objRQ
```

There's no magic to the `Label` or `Body` properties used in this example – they could be anything appropriate for your specific application. In this case I've simply provided some basic text values.

The `ResponseQueueInfo` parameter is new – or at least different. Since this is a response message, one might wonder why it would have anything in its `ResponseQueueInfo` parameter at all. We're certainly not expecting to send a response to our response

This code follows a basic MSMQ convention however.

> **The convention is that a response message will use the `ResponseQueueInfo` parameter of a *response* message to hold information about the queue that received the *original* message and sent the reply.**

This is why we used the `WantDestinationQueue` parameter on the `Receive` method to ensure that we not only retrieved the message but also the information about the queue itself. Without that parameter, the `DestinationQueueInfo` property of the original message object wouldn't contain a valid reference.

By returning the queue information about the receiver's queue back to the sender, we are allowing the sender to determine which queue actually ended up processing its message and sending the response.

The `CorrelationId` is also new. This is another MSMQ convention for providing valuable information back to the sender of the original message. It is very possible that the sender has sent a number of messages for processing – each expecting a response message. Therefore, it is important that the sender have some way of identifying which specific message has been responded to.

Each message has a unique id value assigned by MSMQ when the message was first created. This value is available via the message object's `Id` property. By setting the `CorrelationId` property of the response message to the original message's `Id` value, we provide a mechanism by which the sender of the original message can correlate the response back to the original message it sent.

Obviously there are a lot of options available in MSMQ – more than can possibly be covered in a single chapter. Fortunately there are other books available that cover MSMQ itself in substantially more detail, so we won't dig any deeper than this here. If you do want to read more about MSMQ, pick up a copy of MTS MSMQ with VB and ASP (ISBN 1-861001-46-0) from Wrox Press.

At this point we should have a basic grasp of the concepts involved when building bi-directional applications based on MSMQ. The real key is to remember that a response may not occur rapidly – our application *must* assume that a response could take minutes, hours or even days to arrive.

So far in this chapter we've implicitly assumed that messages were being sent from a client to a server of some sort. While this is certainly one valid use of MSMQ, it is definitely not the only option. Not only that, but there are various configurations of the client-server communication model itself.

We've discussed how to implement a sender and a receiver – in general terms. So, now let's take a look at some of the possible ways we can mix this sender-receiver combination.

Server-Server Communication

One of the most useful ways to leverage MSMQ is for server-to-server communication. There are many scenarios in which a client requests a service from a server, and that server in turn needs to invoke services on other servers.

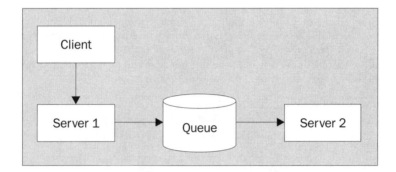

In many cases there's no need for the client or the first server to wait for the second server's work to complete. Consider scenarios such as audit logging, updating a non-operational data store, sending notification email messages, and others. These are often good candidates for this type of server-to-server queuing.

For a more complex example, consider something like an MRP (materials resource planning) system. Most such systems generate the MRP data via a complex series of calculations – often run in a batch nightly or weekly. In a synchronous world, there's no realistic way that the MRP requirements can be recalculated even for one part when a sales order or completion of a work order is entered.

With queuing, however, it is very practical. The client application may allow the user to enter a sales order or complete a work order – updating the related data into the database immediately, just like any other conventional application.

Then, as the server updates the database with the new data, it could also send a message to a queue on another server. This other server would read that queue and update the MRP requirements data for any parts affected by the new data. These calculations – while sometimes lengthy – would have minimal impact on the user who entered that new data.

Additionally, we now have a way to control the system-wide impact of such MRP recalculations. The receiving application could process one message at a time, or more messages at a time if the system (database, etc.) can handle the load. Alternatively, at times of peak load the MRP processing could be temporarily suspended – allowing all the inbound messages to simply queue up for later processing.

Server-to-server communication through MSMQ seems natural. Logistically it tends to be easy to install and maintain MSMQ on a server machine. If every application server has MSMQ installed, then we can easily leverage all the capabilities of the tool, since our application design can assume that messages can be sent from server to server as needed.

Let's now contrast this with sending messages from client workstations, where we may need to install an MSMQ client on hundreds or thousands of client workstations – possibly widely dispersed geographically.

Client-Server Communication

Another common way to think about using MSMQ is for client-to-server communication. Interestingly enough, this is often not the best choice.

Most client-to-server communications have synchronous requirements. A user is requesting data for display, or has entered data that is to be updated into the database – probably with the expectation that the data will be there immediately. These are not scenarios where MSMQ tends to be useful, since they assume synchronous, immediate communication.

A common case where MSMQ may seem more attractive is where a client is frequently disconnected from the network and the application is used offline. In such a case changes are often entered while offline to be updated to a central database when the client workstation is reconnected to the network.

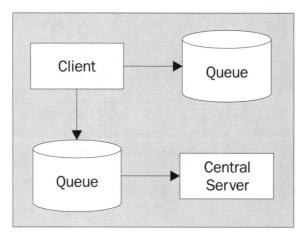

MSMQ may or may not make sense here. In many cases, the user will expect to be able to enter data, save it, and then bring that data back up for editing – all without ever reconnecting to the central server. If the *only* place the updated data is stored is in a queued message, the user won't be able to update it once they've saved it.

One solution is to send a message as well as store the changes in a local database. It is worth remembering, however, that subsequent changes to the data will also generate queued messages – meaning that our central server may get an entire series of messages to update the same data. Since MSMQ has no guarantee that such messages will arrive in a specific order, this could make our receiving application quite complex.

> **In many disconnected scenarios, database synchronization makes more sense than using MSMQ.**

Still, there are scenarios where queued client to server communication makes sense.

In our offline scenario, the client application may provide a separate function so the user can indicate a final 'commit' – causing not only the local store of data to be updated, but also causing a queued message to be sent. The local data would then be flagged for read-only until the next time the data is updated into the central server.

Other possible scenarios include applications that are otherwise totally self-contained on the client workstation, but wish to keep a centralized log or journal of activities.

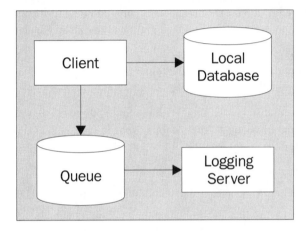

Alternatively, our application may require synchronous client/server communication with its main server, but may also support queued communication with other servers.

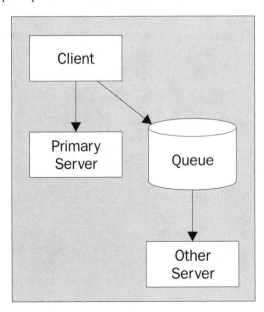

This last scenario is often interchangeable with server-to-server communications since the primary server could as easily send the message to the other server instead of to the client. However, allowing the client to send the queued message may help reduce some load on the primary server – possibly useful if that server is near its capacity.

While there are certainly other variations, such as server-to-client messaging or client-to-client messaging, what we've covered here are the most common scenarios. But enough theory – let's get back to practical application and see how MSMQ can integrate with CSLA-based applications.

Integration with the CSLA

The CSLA has a basic structure composed of four segments, or tiers – the user interface, UI-centric objects, data-centric objects and data services. So far, all communications between these tiers have been synchronous.

In fact, it is not immediately obvious where MSMQ might fit into the overall architecture. For instance, it seems unlikely that the user would attempt to bring up a form to edit a business object and then wait patiently while the request for the object's data is queued behind dozens of other similar requests.

However, while loading data may be a synchronous event, updating data into the database could be queued. The updates probably won't be immediately available, but for some applications this is acceptable.

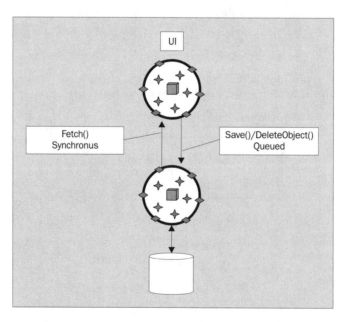

The real benefit here is a potentially large performance gain. If it takes a long time to update data into the database, queuing the updates can provide the user with the appearance of speed, since the `ApplyEdit` method call returns immediately – even though the updates take just as long.

There are three ways we might queue the call to the data-centric object's `Save` or `DeleteObject` methods. We could:

1. Make the UI-centric object persistable – causing it to implement an `IPersist` interface so MSMQ can send the object directly

2. Send just the UI-centric object's state in the body of a message

3. Create a new type of object to contain the state and relay the call to the appropriate data-centric object's method

If we just send the object's state in the body of the message, then the receiver of the message can get that state out of the message and do whatever seems appropriate with it. In many cases, this state data will simply be used as a parameter to a data-centric object's `Save` or `DeleteObject` method.

Were we to create a new type of object for our message we could combine these two effects. Such an object would reflect the desired action – be that to update data or perhaps delete it. Within this new object would be the UI-centric object's state, as well as any data needed to determine the appropriate data-centric object and method to call.

Let's take a look at the mechanics used in these three techniques.

> **For the moment we will be using generalize CSLA code fragments, rather than implementing them in the Task Manager project.**

1) Persistable UI-centric Objects

If we make a UI-centric object persistable then we can send the object itself in the body of an MSMQ message object. The object will then be reconstituted on the server, where we can work with it. Note that the UI-centric object itself will be reconstituted on the server, implying that our UI-centric DLL must be present on the server as well.

Overall this is probably not the best way to integrate MSMQ into a CSLA application. This implementation is somewhat inefficient, since it forces us to reconstitute the UI-centric business objects on the server, and it also forces us to alter the interface of our top-level parent object. Anything that causes us to alter an object's interface requires carefully consideration, since it may cause serious deployment issues in the case that the UI-centric business objects are already installed on client workstations.

Making the UI-centric Object Persistable

Visual Basic 6.0 added the `Persistable` property to all publicly creatable class modules. Setting this value to 1-Persistable at design time allows us to implement two new class methods.

Method	Use
`Class_ReadProperties`	Automatically called to restore the object's data when it is being instantiated (or deserialized)
`Class_WriteProperties`	Automatically called to save the object's data when it is being persisted (or serialized)

Both of these new methods accept a `PropertyBag` as a parameter. The `PropertyBag` object is created by the Visual Basic runtime before the method is called – which means the code in each method merely needs to either place values into the `PropertyBag` object or retrieve them from the `PropertyBag` and store them locally.

This appears to work well, since our CSLA objects (as of Chapter 4) use `PropertyBag` objects to build their superstates. We already have implemented virtually everything we need for an object to implement these two methods. Unfortunately, as we'll see later, this isn't really an ideal solution overall.

Not every CSLA object needs to be persistable. In fact, only top-level parent objects (such as the `Client` object in our Task Manager application) need to implement these methods. After all, it makes no sense to send a child object across the network without its parent – most child objects can't exist on their own, so serializing them independently makes little sense.

Besides, we have implemented the superstate concept, so when we send the superstate of an object across the network, all its child objects' states are transferred as well. Thus, by making the top-level parent object persistable, we automatically provide a mechanism for transferring the child objects.

Regardless of whether an object is a top-level parent or not, the technique used to make it persistable remains the same. We'll walk through the concept here, and then actually implement it for the `Client` object later in the chapter. Though we won't use this technique for transferring the object through MSMQ, it is still worth seeing it done in case you wish to use this approach in a different setting.

Within a UI-centric object we already have two `Private` methods – `GetSuperState` and `SetSuperState`. These methods serialize and deserialize our object's data – just like the `Class_ReadProperties` and `Class_WriteProperties` methods will. In fact, we'll leverage our existing code to implement the new methods.

Implementing Class_WriteProperties for an Object

In general, the steps to make a CSLA object persistable are fairly straightforward. To make a CSLA UI-centric business object persistable, change the class module's `Persistable` property to 1-Persistable. Then implement the `Class_WriteProperties` method such that it loads the `PropertyBag` object with data – by moving the appropriate lines from the `GetSuperState` method.

> *Remember that these are generalized code fragments to illustrate the concepts; they are not alterations to the Task Manager project.*

```
Private Sub Class_WriteProperties(PropBag As PropertyBag)
   With PropBag
      .WriteProperty "State", GetState
      .WriteProperty "Children", mcolChildren.GetSuperState
   End With
End Sub
```

Notice that the `WriteProperties` method accepts a `PropertyBag` object as a parameter. When this method is called intrinsically by Visual Basic (when our object is being serialized), Visual Basic supplies the `PropertyBag` object. However, there's nothing to stop us from calling this method as well – provided that we create a `PropertyBag` object for use as a parameter.

We'll do exactly that by updating the `GetSuperState` method to call `Class_WriteProperties` instead of loading the `PropertyBag` object itself.

```
Private Function GetSuperState() As String
   Dim objPB As PropertyBag

   Set objPB = New PropertyBag
   Class_WriteProperties objPB
   GetSuperState = objPB.Contents
   Set objPB = Nothing
End Function
```

For the most part this method should look familiar – after all, it's pretty much the same as the ones we implemented in the `Client` and `Project` objects in Chapter 4. However, we've replaced the code that explicitly loads the `PropertyBag` object with a simple call to the `Class_WriteProperties` method.

Implementing Class_ReadProperties

The `Class_ReadProperties` method is created in a similar fashion – by borrowing a few lines from the `SetSuperState` method. The new method is implemented like this.

```
Private Sub Class_ReadProperties(PropBag As PropertyBag)
   With PropBag
      SetState .ReadProperty("State")
      mcolChildren.SetSuperState .ReadProperty("Children")
   End With
End Sub
```

The code to retrieve values from the `PropertyBag` has been taken from the `SetSuperState` method. That method needs to be changed as well.

```
Private Sub SetSuperState(Buffer As String)
   Dim objPB As PropertyBag
   Dim arBuffer() As Byte

   Set objPB = New PropertyBag
   arBuffer = Buffer
   objPB.Contents = arBuffer
   Class_ReadProperties objPB
   Set objPB = Nothing
End Sub
```

As with the `GetSuperState` method, this should look quite familiar. The only difference from Chapter 4 is that this method now calls the `Class_ReadProperties` method instead of explicitly loading the `PropertyBag` object itself.

With these changes we can easily convert any UI-centric business object such that it implements the `IPersist` interface – allowing MSMQ to directly include the object in a message body.

Placing an Object into a PropertyBag

In fact, there are a number of tools and technologies that work well with persistable objects – including the `PropertyBag` object. After making a UI-centric object persistable we can write client code as follows.

```
Dim objPB As PropertyBag
Dim objClient As Client
Dim objClone As Client
```

```
Set objClient = New Client
objClient.Load 1
Set objPB = New PropertyBag
objPB.WriteProperty "Object", objClient

Set objClone = objPB.ReadProperty("Object")
```

This bit of code creates a new `Client` object and puts it into a `PropertyBag` object. Then we can simply clone the object by setting a different `Client` object variable to the `ReadProperty` method of the `PropertyBag`.

This is the same concept as placing an object into the `Body` property of an MSMQ message object and then having the object recreated once the message is read from the queue.

Sending the Message

Following the idea that only an update or delete operation will be queued, we'll want to update the UI-centric object's `ApplyEdit` method to send a queued message rather than directly interacting with the data-centric object.

> **This only applies to top-level parent objects, since they are the only objects that interact with data-centric objects in any case.**

The `ApplyEdit` method will be changed quite a bit. After all, as it stands the method assumes that our objects will be updated to include any changes made by the data-centric business object. However, with this new approach we won't be waiting for the data-centric processing to occur, so we won't have access to any of the changes that might be made.

> **Essentially we must assume that our UI-centric objects will no longer reflect the actual data stored in the database.**

The affected lines are highlighted in the following code. Don't make these changes to the Task Manager application – we're just discussing the theory at this point.

```
Public Sub ApplyEdit()
    Dim objQI As MSMQQueueInfo
    Dim objQ As MSMQQueue
    Dim objM As MSMQMessage

    If mcolStack.Count = 0 Then Err.Raise 445

    mcolChildren.ApplyEdit

    Set objQI = New MSMQQueueInfo
    objQI.PathName = "myserver\myqueue"
    Set objQ = objQI.Open(MQ_SEND_ACCESS, MQ_DENY_NONE)
    Set objM = New MSMQMessage

    If mudtProps.IsDeleted Then
        ' code to delete the object's data goes here
```

```
      With objM
         .AppSpecific = 1
         .Body = CStr(mudtProps.ID)
         .Send objQ
      End With
      mcolStack.Remove mcolStack.Count
      mudtProps.IsNew = True
      mudtProps.IsDeleted = False
   ElseIf IsDirty Or mudtProps.IsNew Then
      If Not IsValid Then Err.Raise 445
      ' save object to database if appropriate
      ' save object state
      mcolStack.Remove mcolStack.Count
      With objM
         .AppSpecific = 2
         .Body = Me
         .Send objQ
      End With
      mudtProps.IsNew = False
   Else
      mcolStack.Remove mcolStack.Count
   End If
   mudtProps.IsDirty = False
End Sub
```

The first new code creates and opens a queue object and a new message object.

```
Set objQI = New MSMQQueueInfo
objQI.PathName = "myserver\myqueue"
Set objQ = objQI.Open(MQ_SEND_ACCESS, MQ_DENY_NONE)
Set objM = New MSMQMessage
```

Then we've simply replaced the code that calls the `objPersist` object with code to send an appropriate message. We're making use of the `AppSpecific` property on the `MSMQMessage` object – this property allows us to send any application specific numeric value we choose along with the message. For deletion, we'll set the `AppSpecific` value to 1 and send the object's `ID` value in the body of the message.

```
With objM
   .AppSpecific = 1
   .Body = CStr(mudtProps.ID)
   .Send objQ
End With
```

If we're saving the object we'll set the `AppSpecific` value to 2 and set the body of the message to our object itself – thus invoking the persistable nature of the UI-centric object.

```
With objM
   .AppSpecific = 2
   .Body = Me
   .Send objQ
End With
```

The result is that we're sending a message that contains the entire superstate of our object, so that the receiver of the message can simply set an object variable to the `Body` of the message to reconstitute the UI-centric object.

Having looked at the UI-centric processing, let's look at how this message gets processed at the other end.

Receiving the Message

To receive messages from the queue we'll need to create a whole new application. This can be a Standard EXE project – and it will be run on a server machine that has access to the MSMQ queue where we're sending our messages.

We've already explored the basic concepts behind receiving messages, so we won't rehash them in detail here. Instead we'll focus on the particulars of receiving the messages sent from a UI-centric object as we just discussed.

In this implementation we'll assume that the MSMQEvent object is being used so we can just respond to the Arrived event when a message is placed in the queue. This also assumes that the receiver application has references to both the UI-centric and data-centric DLLs, since it will make use of both the UI-centric and data-centric objects.

> *If this looks like a generally bad idea – it probably is. Remember, this isn't the ideal approach – though it certainly can be made to work.*

It is implied, then, that the machine where this application is running has the UI-centric DLL installed, and at the very least has access to the server where the data-centric objects are running – if they are not directly running on this same machine.

The Arrived event routine will look something like the following.

```
Private Sub mobjQE_Arrived(ByVal Queue As Object, ByVal Cursor As Long)
  Dim objM As MSMQMessage
  Dim objObject As UIObject
  Dim objPersist As ObjectPersist

  Set objPersist = New ObjectPersist
  Set objM = mobjQ.Receive
  With objM
    If .AppSpecific = 1 Then   ' deleting
      objPersist.DeleteObject Val(.Body)
    Else                       ' saving
      Set objObject = .Body
      objPersist.Save objObject.GetSuperState
      Set objObject = Nothing
    End If
  End With
  Set objM = Nothing
  Set objPersist = Nothing

  mobjQ.EnableNotification mobjQE
End Sub
```

As written, this routine assumes the queue is only receiving messages for a specific type of business object. If a single queue will be receiving multiple types of business object then the AppSpecific property value will need to not only indicate whether to delete or save the object, but will also need to indicate the specific type of object contained in the message.

The code simply checks the AppSpecific property to see if it is 1 or 2. If it is 1 then the message is requesting a delete operation, so the data-centric object's DeleteObject method is called.

```
objPersist.DeleteObject Val(.Body)
```

If the `AppSpecific` property is 2, then the message is requesting a save or update. This is a bit more complex. First off, the `Body` property contains the actual UI-centric object, so we need to reconstitute it before doing anything else.

```
Set objObject = .Body
```

Once that's done we can use this object's superstate as a parameter to the `Save` method of the data-centric object.

```
objPersist.Save objObject.GetSuperState
```

The problem here is that the `GetSuperState` method on all UI-centric objects is a `Private` method. Unfortunately the data-centric `Save` method requires that value as a parameter, so we'll need to change the UI-centric object's interface so the `GetSuperState` method is `Public`.

Notice that even though the `Save` method returns an updated superstate for the UI-centric object we ignore it. There's no point in getting that value, since there's nowhere to put it. While we could send it back to the client in a response message, there's no guarantee that it hasn't been a long time since the original message was sent and so the user may be performing an entirely different task than they were when they sent the message.

With relatively few changes to our UI-centric object and no changes to the data-centric object we have added queued updates to a CSLA application. Unfortunately this technique required a change to the interface of our UI-centric object – a potential logistical nightmare. We are also forced to reconstitute the UI-centric object on the server, for no other reason than to retrieve its superstate – a seemingly wasteful approach.

Also, our receiver application could get pretty complex were we to send updates for a variety of business objects into the same queue for processing. The `AppSpecific` property on each message would quickly become complicated since it would need to encode both the type of object and type of operation to be performed. Additionally, this is not terribly extensible since the actions are hardcoded directly into the receiving application.

Let's take a look at another approach that avoids some of these issues.

2) Sending Raw State Data

Instead of making our UI-centric object persistable and then sending the object itself through the body of a message, we could just send the UI-centric object's superstate data. This approach has the benefits of not requiring any changes to the UI-centric object's public interface, and the UI-centric object doesn't have to be reconstituted on the server – thus increasing overall performance.

The coding changes for this approach are similar (though simpler) than those we just looked at for making an object persistable.

Changes to the UI-centric Object

Since we aren't making the UI-centric object persistable, we don't need to worry about the `Persistable` property in this case. We also don't need to change the `GetSuperState` or `SetSuperState` methods.

Instead we can move directly to the coding changes in `ApplyEdit` so it sends a message to a queue rather than directly communicating with the data-centric object. The affected line has been highlighted in the following code.

```
Public Sub ApplyEdit()
  Dim objQI As MSMQQueueInfo
  Dim objQ As MSMQQueue
  Dim objM As MSMQMessage

  If mcolStack.Count = 0 Then Err.Raise 445

  mcolChildren.ApplyEdit

  Set objQI = New MSMQQueueInfo
  objQI.PathName = "myserver\myqueue"
  Set objQ = objQI.Open(MQ_SEND_ACCESS, MQ_DENY_NONE)
  Set objM = New MSMQMessage

  If mudtProps.IsDeleted Then
    ' code to delete the object's data goes here
    With objM
      .AppSpecific = 1
      .Body = CStr(mudtProps.ID)
      .Send objQ
    End With
    mcolStack.Remove mcolStack.Count
    mudtProps.IsNew = True
    mudtProps.IsDeleted = False
  ElseIf IsDirty Or mudtProps.IsNew Then
    If Not IsValid Then Err.Raise 445
    ' save object to database if appropriate
    ' save object state
    mcolStack.Remove mcolStack.Count
    With objM
      .AppSpecific = 2
      .Body = GetSuperState
      .Send objQ
    End With
    mudtProps.IsNew = False
  Else
    mcolStack.Remove mcolStack.Count
  End If
  mudtProps.IsDirty = False
End Sub
```

These changes are very similar to those we made when passing the object itself. In fact, the changes for deleting the object are identical – we still set `AppSpecific` to 1 and pass the object's `ID` property in the body of the message.

The code that sends the save/update message is just changed a tiny bit.

```
    With objM
      .AppSpecific = 2
      .Body = GetSuperState
      .Send objQ
    End With
```

Instead of passing `Me` to the `Body` property, we're now passing the return value from the `GetSuperState` method. The body of this message will contain only the state of our object, not the object itself.

Of course my references to passing 'the object itself' throughout this chapter are actually inaccurate. What's really happening is that MSMQ uses the IPersist interface to retrieve the object's serialized data, and it also stores information about the object's class so it can instantiate a new object of the same class when needed. It then uses that new object's IPersist interface to give it the serialized data from the message. However, it is much easier to just describe this process as passing the object rather than passing its state.

With these changes, when ApplyEdit is called a message will be queued up to delete or update the object's data. At some later point, a receiver application will read the messages in the queue and use the data-centric objects to actually do the updates.

Receiving the Message

The receiver application will also be very similar to what we've seen so far. Since the message will contain the state of the UI-centric object rather than the object itself, there will be some differences, compared to the receiver we built in the previous section.

The new Arrived event routine will look something like the following.

```
Private Sub mobjQE_Arrived(ByVal Queue As Object, ByVal Cursor As Long)
  Dim objM As MSMQMessage
  Dim objPersist As ObjectPersist

  Set objPersist = New ObjectPersist
  Set objM = mobjQ.Receive
  With objM
    If .AppSpecific = 1 Then   ' deleting
      objPersist.DeleteObject Val(.Body)
    Else                       ' saving
      objPersist.Save .Body
    End If
  End With
  Set objM = Nothing
  Set objPersist = Nothing

  mobjQ.EnableNotification mobjQE
End Sub
```

The code to call DeleteObject is unchanged, only the call to the data-centric object's Save method is different.

Now, instead of instantiating the UI-centric object on the server and calling its GetSuperState method, we can simply pass the contents of the message's Body property as a parameter to the Save method. This is quite a bit simpler and faster than our previous approach.

Overall, passing a UI-centric object's state is easier and more efficient than passing the object itself. However, this approach still doesn't address the complexities we'll face if a single queue will be receiving messages dealing with a variety of different business objects. The AppSpecific property will probably still need to be used to indicate not only whether to delete or update, but also which business object's state is contained in the body of the message.

3) Action-based Objects

The last technique for sending messages that we'll cover is the use of action-based message objects. Instead of passing the UI-centric object itself, or even its raw state data, we can send a new type of object that not only contains the state data, but also the knowledge about what kind of action to take on the server.

The whole point behind this approach is to simplify the receiving application. So far, our receiving application code has assumed that the queue would only be receiving messages for a single type of business object.

In reality, it is most likely that a queue will be used to receive messages for a great number of different business objects – with the expectation that the receiving application will figure out the appropriate action to take for each object.

This can be handled by encoding more data into the `AppSpecific` property on the message. For instance, we might have something like this.

AppSpecific value	Object	Action
1	SalesOrder	Delete
2	SalesOrder	Update
3	Customer	Delete
4	Customer	Update

Unfortunately, this can get messy pretty quick. Even if we use constants for the `AppSpecific` property values to make our code readable, it isn't all that easy to add a new type of action or a new business object – in either case we need to update the receiver application itself.

Many other possible solutions exist – for example we could create new queues any time we need to add new functionality that requires a different receiver application. Virtually all solutions involving code values, multiple queues and so forth end up getting messy though.

Action-based message objects provide an answer to this problem. If the action to be performed is handled by an object specifically designed to do that work, then the receiving application can be generalized to merely read messages from the queue – allowing the action-based message to do whatever processing is appropriate for the specific action.

One powerful way to implement this type of object within the context of the CSLA is to treat it as a proxy object for the data-centric object. In fact this is very much like the way COM itself is designed and the reason the same object can be run in-process, locally and remotely without changes.

Rather than having the UI-centric object ever talk directly to the data-centric object like this:

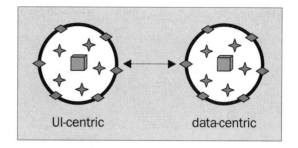

By providing a proxy for the data-centric object, we can shield the UI-centric object from any knowledge about whether its data is moved around synchronously or via queued messages.

> *This is also a very powerful technique for creating disconnected client applications. With virtually no change to the UI-centric or data-centric objects, we can update or enhance the data-centric proxy object to detect whether the workstation is offline or online and store the data in the appropriate location.*

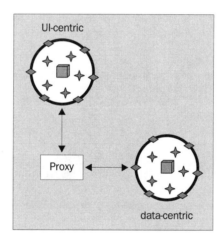

This new proxy object can take care of all our queuing details – simplifying the addition of queued messaging support to UI-centric objects and making it very easy to create a generic message receiver application.

In order to support queuing, the code that implements the sending of messages must reside on the client. Were it to reside on the server, then messages could only be sent when the server is available – exactly the byte of situation MSMQ is trying to overcome.

Creating a Proxy Object

As we've seen, MSMQ makes it very easy to send an object itself through a message – as long as the object is persistable and the COM component containing the class is installed on both client and server.

This is what we'll do with our new proxy object. This object will exist in a new ActiveX DLL and it will be persistable. Typically this DLL will have a project name ending in 'ProxyServer'. For instance, this type of DLL for our Task Manager application would have the name TaskProxyServer – as we'll see later in the chapter. The actual proxy objects will typically have a name ending in 'Proxy' – for instance ClientProxy.

On the client side – where the UI-centric object will use it – the proxy object will implement the same interface as the data-centric object it represents. The implementation of the actual methods will be quite a bit different however.

Note however, that we *will not* use the Implements keyword for this purpose. This is because the interface of the data-centric object accepts its parameters with the ByVal keyword – which makes great sense for passing parameters across the network. Our proxy object, on the other hand, will be running in the same process as the UI-centric object and so using ByVal will add a lot of unneeded overhead to our application.

Thus, we'll directly implement the Fetch, Save and DeleteObject methods as our proxy object's native interface. These methods will basically have the same interface as the data-centric object would have, but without the ByVal keyword.

Making the Object Persistable

Since this object will be passing itself as the body of a MSMQ message, we'll need to make it persistable by setting the class module's Persistable property to 1-Persistable.

Then we'll need to implement the Class_ReadProperties and Class_WriteProperties methods. To make our object self-contained, it will need to know two things – the data being affected and the action to take.

This data can be stored in module-level variables until requested, so we'll just declare them.

```
Option Explicit

Private mstrBody As String
Private mstrAction As String
```

Then the two new methods can simply read and write values from these variables.

```
Private Sub Class_ReadProperties(PropBag As PropertyBag)
  With PropBag
    mstrBody = .ReadProperty("Body")
    mstrAction = .ReadProperty("Action")
  End With
End Sub

Private Sub Class_WriteProperties(PropBag As PropertyBag)
  With PropBag
    .WriteProperty "Body", mstrBody
    .WriteProperty "Action", mstrAction
  End With
End Sub
```

With this code, our object is now persistable and can be passed in the body of an MSMQ message object.

Fetch Method

The Fetch method will be pretty simple, since that method's function will remain synchronous. All this routine will do is relay the method call on to the data-centric object.

```
Public Function Fetch(ID As Long) As String
  Dim objPersist As ObjectPersist

  Set objPersist = New ObjectPersist
  Fetch = objPersist.Fetch(ID)
  Set objPersist = Nothing
End Function
```

This code is quite redundant as compared to the code in the UI-centric object's Load method. However, by using this proxy object we can gain the ability to change to queued messaging, a local data store, or any other variation with no impact to the UI-centric object.

SendMessage Method

Both the Save and DeleteObject methods will end up sending a queued message. However, in both cases that message will contain this proxy object in the body of the message itself. Given how we made this object persistable, the Save and DeleteObject methods will just need to set the module-level variables for the message content and action – then we can have a private method do the actual send.

The SendMessage method is this central method.

```
Private Sub SendMessage()
  Dim objQI As MSMQQueueInfo
  Dim objQ As MSMQQueue
  Dim objM As MSMQMessage

  Set objQI = New MSMQQueueInfo
  objQI.PathName = "myserver\myqueue"
  Set objQ = objQI.Open(MQ_SEND_ACCESS, MQ_DENY_NONE)
  Set objM = New MSMQMessage
  With objM
    .Body = Me
    .Send objQ
  End With
End Sub
```

This method contains the code we've seen in the ApplyEdit method in the last couple of sections. It just opens a queue, creates a message and sends the message to the queue.

Notice that the only thing sent in the message is Me – this object. Of course we know that this object, when serialized, will provide the values of both the mstrBody (which will be made up from the data in the buffer) and the mstrAction (to determine the required action) variables.

Given the way this is implemented, it is important to remember that the DLL containing the proxy object will need to be installed on both the client workstation (where the UI-centric objects are installed) and the server machine where we'll be receiving messages from the queue.

Save Method

With the SendMessage method implemented, the Save method becomes quite simple to implement. All we need to do is store the Buffer parameter and set the mstrAction variable, then call SendMessage.

```
Public Function Save(Buffer As String) As String
  mstrBody = Buffer
  mstrAction = "Save"
  SendMessage
  Save = Buffer
End Function
```

Notice that the `Save` method, as a function, needs to return a value. We return the `Buffer` itself in this case, since we have nothing else to return. The other option would be to return an empty string, but that would require changes in the UI-centric object to handle that case – by returning the `Buffer` we avoid changing the UI-centric object.

DeleteObject Method

Similar to the `Save` method, the `DeleteObject` method just needs to set the `mstrBody` and `mstrAction` variables and call the `SendMessage` method.

```
Public Sub DeleteObject(ID As Long)
  mstrBody = CStr(ID)
  mstrAction = "Delete"
  SendMessage
End Sub
```

In this case the only bit of data required is the object's `ID` – passed as a parameter. The action is set to the text `Delete` and the message is sent.

Updating the UI-centric Object

Now that we have a proxy object, we can update the UI-centric object to make use of the proxy instead of directly interacting with the data-centric object.

Any routines where the UI-centric object interacts with the data-centric object will need to be updated. However, this is a one-time update. Once this change has been made, we can then change the proxy object – radically altering how our data is stored and retrieved – with absolutely no impact on the UI-centric object – a technique which is very powerful.

The only two methods in a UI-centric object that interact with the data-centric object are the `Load` and `ApplyEdit` methods. These are only in the top-level parent object – since all child objects rely on their parent to handle loading and saving of data.

Before making coding changes, we'll need to make changes to the DLL references in our UI-centric project. As it stands, a UI-centric DLL has a reference to the data-centric DLL. Now it will need a reference to the proxy DLL instead.

Once these references have been changed we can move on to alter the `ApplyEdit` and `Load` methods of our UI-centric object so they take advantage of this new proxy object.

ApplyEdit Method

The `ApplyEdit` method in a standard UI-centric top-level parent object creates a reference to the data-centric business object and then calls the `DeleteObject` or `Save` methods as appropriate. The only change we need to make is such that the correct object is created for the `objPersist` variable and we're all set.

```
Dim objPersist As ObjectProxy

Set objPersist = New ObjectProxy
```

This means that with the previous change to the project's references, we need to change just two lines in the `ApplyEdit` method and it is ready to roll.

Load Method

The same is true of the `Load` method. It also just creates a reference to the data-centric object and calls its methods. Now it will just need to create a reference to the proxy object instead – the remainder of the code is unchanged.

```
Dim objPersist As ObjectProxy

Set objPersist = New ObjectProxy
```

With these simple changes, our UI-centric object will now rely on the proxy object to handle all the details of storing and retrieving data. This means we can easily change the proxy object from storing in a central database to storing in a local data store – or in this example we have changed from synchronous updating of data to using queued messages.

Receiving a Message

One of the major reasons for going down the road of implementing an action-based proxy object was to simplify the application that receives messages. The receiver application is a new component in our CSLA architecture. Its job is simple – it just receives messages from the queue and allows the action-based objects in each message to do the appropriate processing on the server.

Let's see how that is accomplished.

Implementing the Receiver

The receiving applications we've seen so far have been responsible for both reading the message from the queue and for performing appropriate actions based on that message. This is a potentially limiting approach, since any time we want to take a different action or add a new type of message we have to change the receiving application itself.

The action-based message objects provide a less monolithic approach to processing messages in a queue. With these new objects, we can change the receiving application to merely read the messages from the queue – allowing the action-based object in the body of each message to do the real work.

In this case, the receiving application can implement its `Arrived` event method as follows. The line where all the interesting work occurs is highlighted.

```
Private Sub mobjQE_Arrived(ByVal Queue As Object, ByVal Cursor As Long)
  Dim objM As MSMQMessage
  Dim objProxy As Object

  Set objM = mobjQ.Receive

  Set objProxy = objM.Body

  Set objProxy = Nothing
  Set objM = Nothing

  mobjQ.EnableNotification mobjQE
End Sub
```

This code just reads the message from the queue and instantiates the action-based proxy object contained in the message body.

What may not be immediately clear from this code is that the proxy object's Class_ReadProperties method is also called as the object is instantiated – allowing us to make the proxy object react to the fact that it has come into existence.

Updating the Proxy Object

If we return to the proxy object that we examined earlier in this section we see that it does implement very basic Class_ReadProperties and Class_WriteProperties methods. Since the only time that this object will ever be instantiated using the Class_ReadProperties method is when it is read from the queue, we can add code to this method to take whatever steps seem appropriate based on the data contained in the object.

This is illustrated in the following diagram.

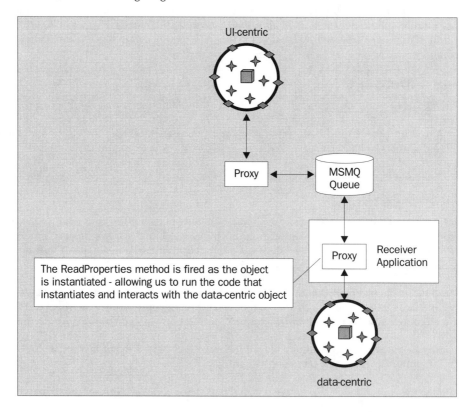

The ReadProperties method is fired as the object is instantiated - allowing us to run the code that instantiates and interacts with the data-centric object

If this approach seems too unclear or hard to read, we might also add a new method to the proxy object – such as DoAction. This method would be called within the Arrived event code after the object is instantiated – potentially making the code easier to read. The drawback to this approach is that the DoAction method would also be visible to the author of the UI-centric object and so it's not as tidy as we might like.

The `Class_ReadProperties` method would likely be enhanced to handle both the delete and save actions.

```
Private Sub Class_ReadProperties(PropBag As PropertyBag)
  Dim objPersist As ObjectPersist

  Set objPersist = New ObjectPersist

  With PropBag
    Select Case .ReadProperty("Action")
    Case "Save"
      objPersist.Save .ReadProperty("Body")
    Case "Delete"
      objPersist.DeleteObject Val(.ReadProperty("Body"))
    End Select
  End With

  Set objPersist = Nothing
End Sub
```

Instead of copying the values from the `PropertyBag` object into the module-level variables, this code simply uses those values to do the appropriate action.

A data-centric object is created then, based on the `Action` entry in the `PropertyBag`, its `Save` or `DeleteObject` method is called, passing the `Body` entry from the `PropertyBag` as a parameter.

The nice thing about this approach is that we can easily add new actions, change existing actions or add entire new proxy objects to our overall application without changing the application actually reading messages from the queue. All the real work is done within specialized, action-based proxy objects contained within the body of each message.

It is this approach which provides the most functionality with the least impact to existing UI-centric objects. So, now let's apply this technique to our Task Manager application.

Updating the Task Manager Application

The Task Manager application currently relies entirely on synchronous communication between the UI-centric and data-centric objects. If we use some imagination we might consider a scenario where this application is used so heavily, and where the data update process takes so long, that it makes more sense to change the update process so it is handled by queued messages instead of synchronous method calls.

In this spirit then, we'll enhance the Task Manager application to send queued messages to handle any saving or deleting of data. To do this, we'll use the action-based proxy object technique we just covered, since it is the most powerful and flexible approach.

Creating the Receiver

The first thing to do is create a receiver application. Once this application is created it can work with any business objects in our application (or other applications), since it offloads all the application-specific work to the proxy objects.

As noted earlier in the chapter, a receiver application would ideally be implemented as a Windows NT service. Unfortunately Visual Basic doesn't provide any easy or reliable way to do this, so we won't cover it here. However, since this program is independent of any specific business application, we could implement it using C++ and still have our proxy objects be implemented in Visual Basic. For now, we'll simply implement this program using Visual Basic.

We've already covered the code to read a message from the queue and process it via a proxy object, so we'll go through this pretty fast.

Creating the Queue

The first thing to do is create the queue for our application. This can be done using the MSMQ Explorer application or via code. In this case, let's use the Explorer.

Open the MSMQ Explorer application and select the server (under Enterprise Server) that will host the queue. Then right-click on the server name and choose New | Queue...

This will bring up a dialog where we can enter the new queue name. Type in TaskTracking and click OK.

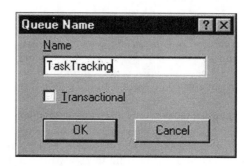

This will create a queue on the server so we can use it within our application.

In this case, to keep things as simple as possible, we're using a non-transactional queue. Were we to mark this as a transactional queue, both our sending and reading processes would need to be transactional. This would impact our architecture somewhat, as the ClientProxy and Receiver classes we'll be implementing shortly would need to be running in MTS.

Still, the basic approach remains valid, so we'll follow the simpler approach for the purposes of this chapter.

Now that we have a queue, we can move on to implement the receiving application itself.

Creating the Receiver Application

The receiver application will be a Standard EXE, so bring up Visual Basic and open a new project of this type. Change the project name to TaskReceiver.

Use the Project | References dialog to add a reference to the MSMQ library – Microsoft Message Queue Object Library. Notice that we don't need to add a reference to the TaskServer DLL or the TaskProxyServer DLL (which we'll create shortly). This is because all the information needed to reinstantiate the proxy object will be contained in the MSMQ message so we don't need to worry about it.

Now we can move on to create the code to work with the TaskTracking queue we just created.

The Receiver Object

Add a standard class module to the project and change its name to `Receiver`. This will be the heart of our application.

The class will need two module-level variables, to hold references to the queue and to the `MSMQEvents` object. While we're there, let's add an event of our own so it is easy to tell our program when a message has been processed.

```
Option Explicit

Public Event Arrived()

Private WithEvents mobjQE As MSMQEvent
Private mobjQ As MSMQQueue
```

In the `Class_Initialize` routine we need to open the queue for reading. In this code I've used a local queue, indicated by the period (".") in the pathname. You'll want to change this to the appropriate server name in your environment.

```
Private Sub Class_Initialize()
  Dim objQI As MSMQQueueInfo

  ' Create MSMQQueueInfo and use it to open an MSMQQueue object
  Set objQI = New MSMQQueueInfo
  With objQI
    .PathName = ".\TaskTracking"
    Set mobjQ = .Open(MQ_RECEIVE_ACCESS, MQ_DENY_NONE)
  End With

  ' enable message arrival notification
  Set mobjQE = New MSMQEvent
  mobjQ.EnableNotification mobjQE
End Sub
```

In the `Class_Terminate` we need to clean up.

```
Private Sub Class_Terminate()
  Set mobjQE = Nothing
  mobjQ.Close
  Set mobjQ = Nothing
End Sub
```

There will be two times where we need to process messages. One is when the `Arrived` event fires to indicate that a new message is in the queue, the other is when our program first starts up. It is very possible that there will already be messages in the queue when our program starts – in which case the `Arrived` event won't fire.

To take care of this, we'll create a `CheckMessages` method that reads messages from the queue until it is empty. Then we can use this method as our program starts up, and when the `Arrived` event fires.

```
Public Sub CheckMessages()
  Dim objM As MSMQMessage
  Dim objProxy As Object
```

```
      On Error Resume Next
      Do While True
          ' read the message from the queue
          Set objM = mobjQ.Receive(ReceiveTimeout:=10)
          ' if message read failed just exit - there was no message in the queue
          If Err Then Exit Do

          ' instantiate the proxy object - causing its ReadProperties event to fire
          Set objProxy = objM.Body

          Set objM = Nothing

          ' if we processed a message fire the Arrived event for our monitoring
          If Not objProxy Is Nothing Then RaiseEvent Arrived
          Set objProxy = Nothing
      Loop

      ' reenable message arrival notification
      mobjQ.EnableNotification mobjQE
  End Sub
```

This code is pretty similar to what we've seen so far in the chapter. However, in this case we're reading messages in a loop – using the `ReceiveTimeout` parameter so we don't wait forever for a message to arrive.

If we have multiple simultaneous applications reading from the queue (which may occur in a high-volume setting), it is possible for the `Arrived` event to fire, but for there no longer to be a message in the queue. I've implemented rudimentary error trapping for this case in the `CheckMessages` method.

Also note that we raise our own `Arrived` event to tell our program that we've processed an event. We'll use this shortly as we build a simple display to show how many messages have been processed.

Once we're done receiving messages, we need to reset the event reception mechanism so the `Arrived` event will fire if any further messages arrive.

The final method we need to implement is the routine that responds to the `Arrived` event.

```
  Private Sub mobjQE_Arrived(ByVal Queue As Object, ByVal Cursor As Long)
      CheckMessages
  End Sub
```

Since all the hard work is done in the `CheckMessages` method, this routine is quite simple.

All that remains now is to build a simple display to show how many messages have been processed.

A Simple Display

This project will already have a form module. Change its name to `ReceiveDisplay` and its `Caption` to `Task Receiver`. We'll use this form as a basic display so we can tell how many messages the program has processed.

Add two Label controls and a CommandButton as shown.

Type	Name	Value
Label	Label1	Messages received
Label	lblCount	0
CommandButton	cmdClose	Close

Bring up the form's code window. We'll need a variable to hold a reference to the Received object.

```
Option Explicit

Private WithEvents mobjReceiver As Receiver
```

Since this is declared using the WithEvents keyword we can implement a routine to respond to the Arrived event and keep a count of the number of messages processed.

```
Private Sub mobjReceiver_Arrived()
   lblCount = Format$(Val(lblCount) + 1)
End Sub
```

In the Form_Load method we can simply create an instance of the Receiver object and then call its CheckMessages method.

```
Private Sub Form_Load()
   Set mobjReceiver = New Receiver
   mobjReceiver.CheckMessages
End Sub
```

The call to CheckMessages is important, as this will cause the Receiver object to read any messages that might already be in the queue.

That completes the receiver application. We can save and compile it at this point. Of course this application doesn't really do much without the existence of an action-based proxy object.

Creating the Proxy Object

The proxy object will need to exist on both the client workstation and the server where our recently completed receiver application will be running. The easiest way to handle this is to place the object in its own ActiveX DLL so we can install it where it is needed.

315

Open a new ActiveX DLL project in Visual Basic and change the project name to
`TaskProxyServer`.

The proxy object will need to directly interact with the data-centric objects in `TaskServer`, so use
the Project | References dialog to add that reference. While we're there, we can also add a reference
to the MSMQ library, since this object will also be sending queued messages.

The ClientProxy Object

The project will already have a class module, so change its name to `ClientProxy` and set its
`Persistable` property to 1-Persistable.

> **Our Task Tracking application only has one top-level parent object –**
> `Client`. **If it had more such objects, we'd create a proxy class for each one.**

We've already covered the basic steps required in building a proxy object, so I won't rehash the
details. The first step in the process is to handle the demands of the UI-centric `Client` object.

```
Option Explicit

Private mstrBody As String
Private mstrAction As String

Public Function Fetch(ID As Long) As String
  Dim objPersist As ClientPersist

  Set objPersist = New ClientPersist
  Fetch = objPersist.Fetch(ID)
  Set objPersist = Nothing
End Function

Public Function Save(Buffer As String) As String
  mstrBody = Buffer
  mstrAction = "Save"
  SendMessage
  Save = Buffer
End Function

Public Sub DeleteObject(ID As Long)
  mstrBody = CStr(ID)
  mstrAction = "Delete"
  SendMessage
End Sub

Private Sub SendMessage()
  Dim objQI As MSMQQueueInfo
  Dim objQ As MSMQQueue
  Dim objM As MSMQMessage

  ' Create MSMQQueueInfo and use it to open an MSMQQueue object
  Set objQI = New MSMQQueueInfo
  objQI.PathName = "myserver\TaskTracking"
  Set objQ = objQI.Open(MQ_SEND_ACCESS, MQ_DENY_NONE)

  ' create and initialize a message object
  Set objM = New MSMQMessage
  With objM
    .Body = Me
```

```
      ' send the message
      .Send objQ
   End With
End Sub

Private Sub Class_WriteProperties(PropBag As PropertyBag)
   With PropBag
      ' store the superstate (or other data) provided by the UI-centric object
      .WriteProperty "Body", mstrBody
      ' store the action that is to be performed
      .WriteProperty "Action", mstrAction
   End With
End Sub
```

The `Fetch` method directly interacts with the `ClientPersist` object – employing synchronous communications. The `Save` and `DeleteObject` methods simply send this object as the body of a MSMQ message so our receiver application can process them.

Note that the pathname for the queue uses the server name `myserver`. You'll need to change this to be the appropriate server name for your environment.

Then all that remains is to implement the code which will be invoked by the receiver application when the `ClientProxy` object is reinstantiated on the server.

```
Private Sub Class_ReadProperties(PropBag As PropertyBag)
   Dim objPersist As ClientPersist

   Set objPersist = New ClientPersist

   With PropBag
     ' retrieve and check the action to be performed
     Select Case .ReadProperty("Action")
     Case "Save"
       ' call the data-centric object to save the data
       objPersist.Save .ReadProperty("Body")
     Case "Delete"
        ' call the data-centric object to delete the object
        objPersist.DeleteObject Val(.ReadProperty("Body"))
     End Select
   End With

   Set objPersist = Nothing
End Sub
```

This code also interacts with the `ClientPersist` object to either save or delete the object as appropriate. Note that there's nothing here that requires this code to be running on the same machine as the `TaskServer` DLL – thus we can place the application to read from the queue on a different machine from where the data-centric objects themselves are running. This can be used to increase scalability if desired.

Now save and compile this project. Be sure to set the compatibility option to Binary Compatibility and use a copy of the DLL as the compatibility source.

Install the DLL on the machine where the receiving application will be running and on each client workstation.

The application to receive messages on the queue is now fully ready for use. All that remains is to update the Client object to use the proxy object instead of directly interacting with the ClientPersist object.

Updating the TaskObjects Project

We're almost done at this point, all that remains is to make some changes to the TaskObjects project. This DLL no longer requires a reference to TaskServer, but does need a reference to TaskProxyServer. Also we'll need to update the Client object's Load and ApplyEdit methods to use the proxy object.

Changing the References

Open the TaskObjects project in Visual Basic and bring up the References dialog.

Remove the reference to the TaskServer DLL, because we won't be directly interacting with the data-centric objects any more, since the ClientProxy object will take care of that for us. Add a reference to the TaskProxyServer DLL so our code can make use of the ClientProxy object.

Updating the Client Object

Open the code window for the Client class. We'll need to update both the Load and ApplyEdit methods so they don't create ClientPersist objects, but rather create ClientProxy objects. In the end, this only involves changes to four lines of code – and no changes to the Client object's public interface.

```
Public Sub ApplyEdit()
  Dim objPersist As ClientProxy

  If mcolStack.Count = 0 Then Err.Raise 445

  mcolProjects.ApplyEdit
  Set objPersist = New ClientProxy
  If mudtProps.IsDeleted Then
    ' code to delete the object's data goes here
    objPersist.DeleteObject mudtProps.ID
    mcolStack.Remove mcolStack.Count
    mudtProps.IsNew = True
    mudtProps.IsDeleted = False
  ElseIf IsDirty Or mudtProps.IsNew Then
    If Not IsValid Then Err.Raise 445
    ' save object to database if appropriate
    ' save object state
    mcolStack.Remove mcolStack.Count
    SetSuperState objPersist.Save(GetSuperState)
    mudtProps.IsNew = False
  Else
    mcolStack.Remove mcolStack.Count
  End If
  Set objPersist = Nothing
  mudtProps.IsDirty = False
End Sub
```

```
Public Sub Load(ID As Long)
   Dim objPersist As ClientProxy

   If mcolStack.Count > 0 Then Err.Raise 445
   If Not mudtProps.IsNew Then Err.Raise 445

   mudtProps.IsNew = False

   ' code to load the object goes here
   Set objPersist = New ClientProxy
   SetSuperState objPersist.Fetch(ID)
   Set objPersist = Nothing
End Sub
```

At this point our Task Manager application should run just fine. We can bring up a client and its related data, change it and then save it back into the database. The save (or delete) operation will be handled via queued messages, providing the illusion of high performance to the user, although they might not really update the database for some time.

There are potential drawbacks to this approach. In particular, there's a window of time between when the user clicks the OK button to when the database is actually updated that users may access 'old' data from the database. This is a consequence of using queued database updates and is something to be evaluated before choosing queued updates for your specific application.

Summary

Microsoft Message Queue (MSMQ) is a very powerful and flexible technology for sending asynchronous, queued messages from one application to another. In this chapter we've discussed a number of different issues and techniques surrounding its use, but there are certainly many others to consider.

In the end, we've implemented a powerful framework using action-based proxy objects to send messages from UI-centric objects to the server where they can be processed. This is a very extensible approach that requires few changes to our UI-centric objects and no changes at all to the data-centric objects.

The same basic technique can be used for server-to-server communication as well – providing a flexible mechanism by which servers can send messages to each other to request services or work to be performed.

MSMQ is a good addition to our toolkit when building CSLA-based applications.

In the next chapter we'll continue to focus on managing state in various environments. In particular, Chapter 7 will cover managing state in a browser-based world – including discussions on storing state in the browser, on the web server and passing state from client to server across HTTP.

7

Distributed Objects and the Web

Overview

Browser-based development is becoming more and more common – and more and more powerful – all the time. However, browser-based development has relied historically on non-object based technologies – although object-oriented concepts are rapidly creeping into the mix. In this chapter we'll explore some techniques we can use to leverage distributed object concepts when developing applications for the web.

When creating applications, web developers have many issues to deal with, and none is as pervasive as managing state. In the context of a browser-based application, state is considered to be the data used by the application, entered by the user, stored in a database, etc.

If we create a series of three pages that collect a set of related information from the user, then all the data from all three pages would be considered the state of that user's session within the application. The challenge web developers face is how to manage this state.

Note that we're not talking about objects at all here – this is basic web development. The challenge is that browsers forget everything from page to page. So when our three page application moves from page one to page two, we lose all of page one's data – unless it is stored somewhere temporarily.

There are three main options:

- ❑ Store the data in a cookie (file) on the client
- ❑ Store the data somewhere on the web server
- ❑ Write the data to a temporary location in the database

Contrast this with more typical forms-based application development. These applications typically store this type of state data on the client (in application variables) until the user is done with all data entry. Of course this type of application doesn't forget everything as we move from form to form like a browser will.

If our application is using distributed objects then the state data will typically be contained in objects – very possibly on the client workstation. However, with traditional applications we can keep an object reference as the user moves from form to form. This isn't so easy with a browser, where it forgets data – including object references – as the user moves from page to page.

We already know how to store data in a database – with or without objects – so we won't cover that option in this chapter. Still, this option is probably the best option in a load balanced network. In such a setting, each time the user requests services from a server they may be routed to a different server (be it a web server or an application server). This precludes storing any data on these servers – pretty much forcing us to store data only at the database level.

We will, however, discuss how to store object state in the web server. If we're building a browser-independent application, where we can't make any assumptions about the user's browser and thus can't send much more than simple HTML, then our objects and other code will remain on the web server. Storing object state in the web server may seem simple, but it isn't as straightforward as one might hope, as we'll see in this chapter.

We'll also discuss storing object state in the browser – without using a cookie. There are ways to keep object references around even when the user moves from page to page – allowing us to write VBScript or JavaScript in our web pages that interacts with our UI-centric business objects. In such a scenario we become tied to a specific browser, but we gain more client-side functionality. This means we can create powerful and highly interactive user interfaces based on our objects, which are entirely browser-based.

Of course, if our UI-centric objects are running on a client workstation within the browser they'll still need to communicate with the data-centric objects on our servers – even if there's a firewall in the way. Fortunately, we can use Remote Data Services (RDS) to communicate from UI-centric to data-centric objects over HTTP – bypassing firewalls and providing the same level of functionality that we have implemented so far using DCOM.

Let's start by exploring the issues around keeping object state in the web server.

Object State and IIS

When building most Internet applications a primary design requirement is to reach as many browsers as possible. In most cases this means using only the most basic HTML to generate the user interface – making no assumptions about the user's browser or computer platform.

With this type of scenario, it is impractical to distribute objects (or other forms of business logic) out to the actual client workstations. However, we can distribute objects as far as the web server itself. In *Visual Basic 6 Business Objects* we explored this concept to some degree – building HTML-based user interfaces with both Active Server Pages (ASP) and Visual Basic 6's new IIS Application based on the WebClass.

In either case, the ASP or WebClass code acts as a proxy for the user's actual interface – interacting with the UI-centric business objects in much the same way as a traditional form-based user interface.

The following diagram illustrates this scenario. We have a client workstation running a browser and displaying HTML to generate the interface displayed to the user. The browser sends requests to the web server via HTTP and those requests are then handled by an ASP script, a WebClass application or any other COM-aware server-side development tool – for example ColdFusion. The web server application in turn instantiates a COM object and uses that object to perform business processing.

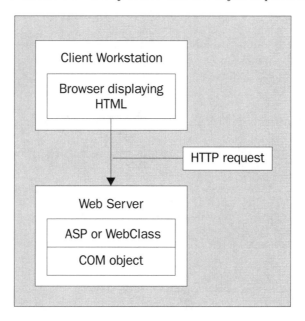

The CSLA architecture works relatively well in this configuration, since we can easily leverage our UI-centric business objects on the web server from ASP or WebClass code. To the UI-centric object, the ASP or WebClass code appears to be the user interface – thus this code effectively becomes a proxy for the real user interface.

However, scalability is limited because of the stateless nature of this type of application. The UI-centric objects only exist as long as a single ASP page or WebClass is being processed. Once the processing is complete and the result has been sent back to the user's browser, all the UI-centric object data is either lost, or perhaps saved into a database. Either way, it is no longer directly available from the web server.

Storing Data in IIS

ASP and the WebClass environment both provide a Session object. This object exists throughout the life of a single session for a single user – where a session may span many different web pages over a period of time.

The Session object manages the whole session concept for us. It typically writes a cookie to the client workstation with a unique ID value. Each time that browser reconnects to the web server that cookie is retrieved and the original session is located based on the ID it contains.

In the end, this means that we can write server-side code in ASP or a WebClass with assurance that we'll have the exact same Session object from page to page as long as the user is interacting with our site. This point of continuity is key.

Again, this assumes that we aren't using a web server farm or some other clustering technology. In such a case, we can't always dictate that the same server will handle the user requests time after time.

Using the Session Object

The Session object has the ability to store an arbitrary collection of values – which we can retrieve and manipulate within our code. Combine this with the fact that the Session object is maintained from page to page and we have a powerful tool by which we can store application data in the web server.

In an ASP page, for instance, we might write code something like this.

```
<%
  Session("ClientID") = txtID.value
  Session("ClientName") = txtName.value
%>
```

This code stores two values from controls on the HTML page into the Session object's collection of values. We can then write more code on another page to retrieve those values – after all, the Session object remains available over a period of time.

```
<%
  Response.Write "ID: " & Session("ClientID") & "<P>"
  Response.Write "Name: " & Session("ClientName") & "<P>"
%>
```

The Session object's collection of values is really a collection of Variant data types – very similar to the Collection object in Visual Basic. Thus we can store virtually any type of data and then retrieve it on subsequent pages as they are processed. This is true in both ASP and WebClass objects.

Storing Object References in the Session Object

Given that the Session object's collection of values is of type Variant it follows that it can store references to COM objects. After all, that is one of the valid Variant types.

Following this train of thought, it seems that we should be able to simply hold a reference to the UI-centric objects used by our application and thus have access to those objects throughout the life of the user's session. In fact, this is true and we can do such a thing.

```
<%
  objClient.Name = txtName.value
  Set Session("Client") = objClient
%>
```

Then later, on a subsequent page, we can retrieve and use that object reference.

```
<%
  Set objClient = Session("Client")
  Response.Write "Name: " & objClient.Name & "<P>"
%>
```

It is certainly true that this will work – and it is easy to implement and easy to read. Unfortunately, there is a serious drawback that renders this technique virtually useless for all but the smallest applications. To understand why, we must consider how IIS utilizes COM threads and also how Visual Basic COM objects interact with the threads on which they run.

IIS manages a pool of threads on which it runs ASP pages or `WebClass` objects. Ideally, any time a page needs to be processed it is assigned to a free thread, processed by that thread, then the thread is released for use by another page.

For this to occur, all code running within the context of each page needs to be **thread neutral**. This means that none of the code that is run can interact with thread local storage – a section of memory unique to each individual thread. The reason may be obvious, were some code to store a value into memory associated with a specific thread, then that code *must* run on that thread in the future or the value will be unavailable.

And here's where the problem comes into play. Visual Basic COM objects *always* use thread local storage. Thus, Visual Basic objects *must* run on the exact same thread each time they perform any action, a concept directly in conflict with the desire of IIS to manage a pool of interchangeable threads.

When IIS assigns a thread to a page, all code for that page – including COM objects – runs on that thread.

To boil this down, if a `Session` object contains a reference to a COM object that isn't thread neutral (such as a Visual Basic object), then all processing for all the pages in that entire session must run on the same thread. Since IIS only manages a limited number of threads in its pool, we are almost guaranteed to have some pages queue up while waiting for their thread to become free – while other threads may be sitting idle but unusable.

Keep in mind that this isn't a problem for all applications. A certain number of users can be supported before thread contention starts to cause serious performance problems. The exact number of users depends on how often the users do something that causes interaction with the server, how many users there are at any time and how long it takes to process the average page on the server.

Storing Object State in the Session Object

There is an alternative. Rather than holding a direct reference to an object – and suffering all the threading problems that entails – we could just hold a reference to the object's state. More accurately, we could hold a reference to its superstate – thus also getting all child object state in a single statement.

Consider code such as the following:

```
<%
  objClient.Name = txtName.value
  Session("ClientState") = objClient.GetSuperState
%>
```

This code stores a simple `String` variable – containing the object's superstate – into the `Session` object. There are no threading issues or anything else here, since we're just storing a simple data type. Simple data types can be stored in the `Session` object without tying us to a single thread.

Later, on a subsequent page, we can create a new instance of the UI-centric object, and then reload it and its child objects by using that superstate data:

```
<%
  Set objClient = Server.CreateObject("MyCOMServer.Client")
  objClient.SetSuperState = CStr(Session("ClientState"))
  Response.Write "Name: " & objClient.Name & "<P>"
%>
```

The end result is that we can take a snapshot of the object, store it, and then recreate the object exactly as it was.

There's no doubt that this is not a perfect solution. The ideal solution is to simply keep an object reference to the UI-centric objects – no unloading and reloading of data at all. However, as we've seen, that isn't always practical, so this is a viable alternative.

Advantages

The primary advantages of this approach are performance and ease of implementation.

Performance is good because the state data is not written to disk – it is kept in memory. While we do have to recreate the objects for each page, they are created out of data in memory rather than hitting a disk subsystem or traversing the network to retrieve the data from another machine.

The approach is easy to implement. All we need to do is make the `GetSuperState` and `SetSuperState` methods on the top-level parent object into `Public` methods and store the state instead of an object reference.

Additionally, there's no cleanup. One problem often encountered when storing temporary state data to disk is that the user can always navigate away from our site in the middle of things – leaving us hanging with useless data sitting on disk. This often requires writing cleanup batch jobs or finding other solutions – extra work with no business purpose. Since this approach keeps the temporary data in memory, when the session times out (and is released) the memory is automatically released as well – giving us free cleanup.

Drawbacks

Of course, there are a couple of drawbacks as well. First off, we do have to serialize and deserialize the UI-centric object and all of its child objects each time a page is processed. This isn't free – though it is a lot cheaper that storing data to disk.

Also, we are consuming memory on the web server. Typically this isn't a problem, since even a relatively complex family of objects will have a superstate of only a few thousand bytes. However, if we also have a few thousand concurrent users then this can add up.

It is important to do some multiplication during the technical design phase of a project to determine how much server memory this type of approach will consume. In most cases there won't be a problem, but it is important to consider this issue.

Server Farms

In a high-scalability scenario you may also have server farms set up – a group of web servers that are essentially interchangeable, set up so users are spread across these servers for load balancing.

By keeping session-oriented data on a web server, we are effectively dictating that a user, once they've started using the application, will remain connected to the same server. After all, it's that server which has the required session data in memory.

In a server farm setting it is quite common to force a user to interact with the same server for the entire life of a session – thus allowing the application to store that user's state data on the web server. Such a choice can, however, degrade the ability of the server farm to perform load balancing, since a user is stuck on the same server even if that server becomes overly busy.

To avoid this, we are pretty much forced to store the user's state data in the database – retrieving it each time a new request comes in to the web server.

By choosing to store our object's superstate data in the `Session` object we have dictated that the user will continue to use the same web server during the life of the session. While we do need to keep in mind the potential load balancing impact of this choice, we can bask in the knowledge that many sites do exactly this and continue to work just fine.

Updating the Task Manager Application

Let's assume for a moment that hundreds, if not thousands, of people working on projects around the world will use our Task Manager application. They'll be retrieving and entering data in high volumes, requiring a scalable solution – and since they'll be scattered around the globe, perhaps using many different computer platforms and browsers, a browser independent solution makes sense.

Due to the browser independent requirement, we can't distribute objects beyond the web server. For all we know, the user is running Lynx under Unix – no objects, no graphics, nothing but text.

Because of the scalability requirement, we need to implement something that is fast – preferably keeping data available from page to page as the user moves through the application.

While this may appear contrived, requirements of this type are very common, and fortunately we have a solution: keep the UI-centric objects on the web server and store the superstate data in the `Session` object between pages of the application.

Enhancing the UI-centric Objects

Before we can store any superstate data, we need to enhance our top-level parent object such that its `GetSuperState` and `SetSuperState` methods are `Public`.

Only the top-level parent, `Client`, needs to be updated. All its child objects are essentially *part of* the parent object and thus their state data is included in the top-level parent's superstate. We have no reason to directly access the superstate data of any child objects – they'll come and go based on what we do to the parent object.

Open the `TaskObjects` project in Visual Basic and bring up the `Client` class module.

The changes we'll make appear trivial – just change the `Private` keyword to `Public` for the two methods.

```
Public Function GetSuperState() As String
```

```
Public Sub SetSuperState(Buffer As String)
```

The unfortunate part of this is that we've changed the object's public interface. This means updating the compatibility on the server and re-deploying the objects to all client workstations.

On the other hand, if the only user interface for the application is browser-based, then only the web servers need to be updated.

Save and compile the project.

Implementing the ASP Pages

In the interest of simplicity and clarity, I won't implement a full-blown browser-based UI for the application in this chapter. Instead, we'll create some basic pages so the user can browse through a client's project details – demonstrating how object state is maintained from page to page. The basic concepts shown here would be quite easy to extend into a much more powerful interface.

default.htm

This first page will be a simple launch point; not only for this new user interface but also for the one we'll create in the next section of this chapter. This file, as well as the others we'll create, needs to be placed in a virtual directory set up as a web site under IIS or Microsoft Peer Web Services (PWS).

Setting up such a directory is beyond the scope of this book – there are many books on ASP that cover these details very well, such as *Beginning ASP 2.0* (ISBN 1-861001-34-7), or *Professional Active Server Pages 2.0* (ISBN 1-861001-26-6), both from Wrox Press. Alternatively you can put the files in a folder under the `InetPub\wwwroot` folder created when you installed either IIS or PWS.

In my case I've set up a site called `tasktrack`. It is in the directory for this site that I'll place all the files.

Open a new file, named `default.htm`, and enter the following HTML.

I just use Notepad to create HTML and ASP files. They are simple text files, so no particular tool is required. If you are having trouble saving the file with the appropriate extension, just put the file name in quotes when you save it.

```
<HTML>
<BODY>
<A href="aspstart.asp">Launch ASP server-based task tracking UI</A><P>
<A href="mainframe.htm">Launch browser-based task tracking UI</A><P>
</P>
</BODY>
</HTML>
```

This simple HTML creates a basic page with two links. The first is for the pages we're about to create, the second will be used in the next section of this chapter.

aspstart.asp

Our start page links to an ASP page named `aspstart.asp`. This page will take the place of the Visual Basic start form in our new form-based interface. The Visual Basic form prompted the user for the ID number of a client, and then accessed that client through another form. We'll emulate that behavior here. The page we are going to create will simply look like this.

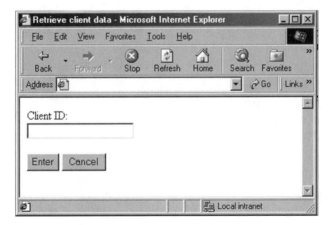

Open a new text file and save it as `aspstart.asp`. Add the following code.

```
<HTML>

<HEAD>
<TITLE>Retrieve client data</TITLE>
</HEAD>

<BODY>
<FORM ACTION="getclient.asp" METHOD="post" id=form1 name=form1>
  Client ID:<BR>
  <INPUT name=txtID><P>
  <INPUT TYPE=submit VALUE="Enter" id=submit1 name=submit1>
  <INPUT TYPE=reset VALUE="Cancel" id=reset1 name=reset1>
</P></FORM>
</BODY>
</HTML>
```

This page is just an HTML form with a single text entry control and buttons to submit or cancel the entry. If the user submits the entry, the form's contents are sent to the server – invoking a page named `getclient.asp`.

So far we haven't done anything with either the UI-centric objects or the `Session` object. However, behind the scenes the `Session` object has already interacted with the browser to create the appropriate cookie file and so all subsequent pages will interact with that exact same `Session` object.

getclient.asp

The `getclient.asp` form is quite a bit more interesting. It is on this page that we first create a UI-centric business object and display its data. Moreover, this page stores that object's superstate into the `Session` object for use by subsequent pages.

Create a file called `getclient.asp` and enter the following code.

```
<HTML>
<%
Set objClient = Server.CreateObject("TaskObjects.Client")
lngID = Request.Form("txtID")
on error resume next
objClient.Load CLng(lngID)

if err = 3021 then
%>
    <HEAD>
    <TITLE>Client not found</TITLE>
    </HEAD>
    <BODY>
    Client not found in the database.
    </BODY>

<%    elseif err <> 0 then
%>
    <HEAD>
    <TITLE>Client not found</TITLE>
    </HEAD>
    <BODY>
    An error has occured while retrieving the client<br>
    The error number is <% =err %><br>
    </BODY>

<% else
    Session("ClientState") = objClient.GetSuperState
%>
    <HEAD>
    <TITLE>Client <% =objClient.Name %></TITLE>
    </HEAD>
    <BODY>
    Client ID:
    <% =objClient.ID %><P>
    Client name:
    <% =objClient.Name %><P>
    Client phone:
    <% =objClient.Phone %><P>
```

```
    <HR><P>
    <TABLE border=1 cellPadding=1 cellSpacing=1 width=75%>
      <TR>
        <TD><STRONG>Project name</STRONG></TD>
      </TR>

      <% For Each objProject In objClient.Projects %>
        <TR>
          <TD><A href="getproject.asp?project=<%=objProject.ID%>">
            <% =objProject.Name %></A>
          </TD>
        </TR>
      <% Next %>
    </TABLE></P><BR>
    </BODY>
  <% end if %>
  </HTML>
```

The first section of this code creates an instance of the `Client` object and calls its `Load` method using the value entered by the user on the previous page.

```
Set objClient = Server.CreateObject("TaskObjects.Client")
lngID = Request.Form("txtID")
on error resume next
objClient.Load CLng(lngID)
```

I've also implemented error handling, so if the object fails to load we return a page indicating that the client wasn't found. On the other hand, if no error is encountered then the code proceeds to build a page that displays the client's detail and a list of associated projects.

Before generating the display, we store the `Client` object's superstate in the `Session` object.

```
Session("ClientState") = objClient.GetSuperState
```

This is the key to what will follow. Note that as we build a list of projects for display that each one is also a link to the `getproject.asp` file.

```
<A href="getproject.asp?project=<%=objProject.ID%>"><% =objProject.Name %></A>
```

The `ID` property is passed as a parameter on the URL so the next page knows which project is to be displayed.

getproject.asp

When the user clicks on one of the project links from the previous page, this new page is invoked on the web server. Remember that, outside of the `Session` object, the web server remembers nothing from any previous pages.

Fortunately, we saved the `Client` object's state data in the `Session` object, so it is available in this new page. This means we can reload the `Client` object without talking to the database or any other machine – giving us very good performance for this page.

331

Create a `getproject.asp` file and enter the following code.

```
<HTML>
<%
Set objClient = Server.CreateObject("TaskObjects.Client")
objClient.SetSuperState Session("ClientState")
%>
<HEAD>
<TITLE>Client <% =objClient.Name %></TITLE>
</HEAD>
<BODY>
Client name:
<% =objClient.Name %><P>
<%
  lngProject = Request.QueryString.Item(1)
  For Each objTemp In objClient.Projects
    if objTemp.ID = CLng(lngProject) then
      Set objProject = objTemp
      exit for
    end if
  next
%>
Project name:
<% = objProject.Name %><P>

<HR><P>
<TABLE border=1 cellPadding=1 cellSpacing=1 width=75%>
  <TR>
      <TD><STRONG>Task name</STRONG></TD>
      <TD><STRONG>Projected days</STRONG></TD>
      <TD><STRONG>Percent complete</STRONG></TD>
  </TR>

  <% For Each objTask In objProject.Tasks %>
    <TR>
      <TD><% =objTask.Name %></TD>
      <TD><% =objTask.ProjectedDays %></TD>
      <TD><% =objTask.PercentComplete %></TD>
  </TR>
  <% Next %>
</TABLE></P><BR>
</BODY>
</HTML>
```

The first few lines are where we recreate the `Client` object.

```
Set objClient = Server.CreateObject("TaskObjects.Client")
objClient.SetSuperState Session("ClientState")
```

Firstly, the code creates a new instance of the `Client` object itself. This is required since the last `Client` object was destroyed as soon as the `getclient.asp` page was done processing – IIS keeps nothing around from page to page.

The new `Client` object is totally blank of course. Normally we'd call the `Load` method to load its data from the database. In this case however, we can simply call its `SetSuperState` method to deserialize the state data stored in the `Session` object.

Once that's done, all we need to do is loop through all the `Project` objects for the client to find the one with the `ID` passed as a parameter on the URL.

```
lngProject = Request.QueryString.Item(1)
For Each objTemp In objClient.Projects
  if objTemp.ID = CLng(lngProject) then
    Set objProject = objTemp
    exit for
  end if
next
```

Once we have a reference to the right `Project` object the rest is pretty straightforward HTML to display the data.

These few pages are pretty simple, but the concept should be clear. We could have just as easily built pages that edit the object data and then at some point provide the user with a button that runs an ASP page which calls the `ApplyEdit` method – saving the object's data back into the database.

While this technique provides a highly scalable, browser independent solution, it is still only providing a batch-oriented user interface. There's no real intelligence on the client machine, so the user doesn't get rich feedback while entering or interacting with our data. In the next section we'll explore how to distribute our UI-centric business objects all the way out to the client workstation – within the browser – to implement a robust interface comparable to anything we'd create with a Visual Basic form.

Distributing Objects to the Browser

With the advent of JavaScript, VBscript and the Document Object Model we are beginning to gain the ability to create robust user interfaces in the context of a browser. Prior to these technologies, it has been relatively difficult to put any intelligence or user interaction inside the browser itself.

Even with client-side scripting on the browser, there is little support for the concept of object-oriented programming. Most scripting capabilities are on a par with the capabilities we enjoyed with Visual Basic 3 – that is, focused on building code to directly manipulate views of data.

Wouldn't it be great if there were some way to leverage all the business logic from our UI-centric objects within a browser-based interface? Wouldn't it be even better if, at the same time, we had a way for these objects to remain loaded in memory as the user moves from page to page within our application? Fortunately, there is a way to do just this.

We can design a DHTML page with scripting code that interacts with COM objects on the client. All we need to do is to have the browser download and install our UI-centric business objects on the user's workstation. With our UI-centric objects on the client, the script code in our DHTML pages can interact with these objects just like the code in a conventional Visual Basic form.

Of course, there are some limitations. Since the intent is to run the UI-centric objects on the client workstation within the browser, we are dictating that the client workstation must be able to install and run the COM DLL containing the objects. This means a Win32 platform such as Windows 9x or Windows NT.

Additionally, the Document Object Model (DOM) is far from standard across browsers (although Internet Explorer 5 is the first browser to implement the W3C DOM, which we can hope will become standard in all new browsers). This means that, at the moment, script implemented in one browser may not work in another.

The HTML pages that we'll be creating will only serve Internet Explorer – other pages would need to be created to use the business objects from other browsers, since they'd have different DOM implementations.

Storing Data Across Pages

There is a relatively obscure technique available to script developers that allows the script to pass data from page to page without resorting to sending the data to the server or storing it in a cookie file.

The concepts and techniques used in this section will work for VBScript, JavaScript and when building the new DHTML Applications available in Visual Basic 6.

Using a Frame to Store Data

This technique requires the use of frames. The basic concept is that any web page displayed to the user is displayed within a frame. However, there's also a second frame – possibly invisible – that remains constant even as the user moves from page to page in the main frame.

Within the context of this second frame we can store and retrieve data via the DOM – allowing script within the pages displayed in the main frame to keep data in memory from page to page. This is illustrated in the following diagram, where the larger frame is used to display the user's web pages, and the smaller frame is used to hold references to COM objects via the <OBJECT> HTML tag.

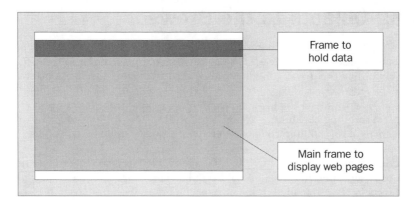

To implement frames in HTML we must first create a **frameset** page. This page doesn't actually display any data, but rather sets up how many frames there will be and where they'll be located in the browser's display.

For instance, we may have a frameset page such as the following:

```
<HTML>

<HEAD>
<TITLE>Task Tracking</TITLE>

<FRAMESET>
  <FRAME ID=frmData src="data.htm">
  <FRAME ID=frmMain src="display.htm">
</FRAMESET>
</HEAD>
</HTML>
```

If the `data.htm` page contains some hidden fields, we can then store data in them from script in the `display.htm` page.

I won't go into more detail on this here, because there's an easier, though similar, way to store the data from page to page.

Storing Data in the Frameset Page

Just because the frameset page doesn't display anything to the user doesn't mean it's useless. In fact, it can be used to store data all by itself. The frameset page is the one page guaranteed not to disappear as the user moves from page to page within the other frames – making it the ideal location to store data.

Instead of having a frameset create multiple frames, we can just create one frame to cover the entire browser display area.

```
<HTML>

<HEAD>
<TITLE>The Application</TITLE>

<FRAMESET>
  <FRAME ID=frmMain src="display.htm">
</FRAMESET>
</HEAD>
</HTML>
```

From the user's viewpoint it appears that they are viewing a normal page with no frames at all. However, 'underneath' the display there really is a frame – and an associated frameset page. This frameset page remains constant as the user moves from page to page within the single display frame.

This means that script in the pages displayed in the main frame can interact with objects that may exist within the frameset page itself.

The implication is that there'll be some objects in the frameset page that can actually contain that data. In the example shown above we haven't included anything in the page that can store data. However, the frameset page can contain the <OBJECT> tag – allowing us to add an object for use by our scripting code.

Were we to have such an object, the frameset page may appear as follows.

```
<HTML>

<HEAD>
<TITLE> The Application </TITLE>

<OBJECT ID=Session
  CLASSID="CLSID:43A467AF-IB5E-11D3-A074-00902707906A"></OBJECT>

<FRAMESET>
  <FRAME ID=frmMain src="display.htm">
</FRAMESET>
</HEAD>
</HTML>
```

Then, within the `display.htm` page we could create script code to interact with this object. Here is some VBScript code that calls a method on this object.

```
window.Parent.document.Session.TheMethod
```

Assuming the object referenced on the frameset page is designed to store and retrieve data, we can use it from the script in our pages as a data repository – kind of like the `Session` object available through ASP, but on the client instead of the server.

Before we try to implement pages that store data in the frameset, let's create an object to act as a data repository.

Creating the Session Object

If we are to store arbitrary data from page to page, providing easy storage and retrieval, we'll want to build an object geared around that purpose. Considering the objects available natively within Visual Basic, the `Collection` object comes to mind as an easy to use repository of arbitrary data. When we think about it, the ASP `Session` object is essentially a collection of values as well – lending weight to the thought that perhaps our data repository object should act like a `Collection`.

Objects referenced by the `<OBJECT>` tag in a document are COM objects – typically housed in a DLL. They can be created using Visual Basic by using an ActiveX DLL project.

The DLL we'll create will only have one class – the one to store our data.

However, it isn't quite that easy. There are complicating factors imposed on us by the browser environment – in particular the Refresh button on the toolbar.

If the user refreshes the page, all data on that page is lost as the page is reloaded. This includes the frameset page – implying that the object reference held by that underlying page is lost and recreated as part of the refresh process.

On the surface this appears to be a serious problem – one that could be a showstopper. After all, we can't afford to have a simple mouseclick or keypress cause all our data to be lost. Luckily there's a straightforward answer.

Just because a refresh causes the *object* to be released, doesn't mean that the DLL itself is released. In fact, Internet Explorer will keep the DLL loaded in memory during a refresh, even though all the objects are destroyed.

Therein lies the answer – since as long as the DLL remains loaded, any global variables remain valid. This means that we can store the data itself in a global `Collection` object – then implement a class module that delegates to that object to store and retrieve data.

Even though our custom `Collection` object may be destroyed if the user refreshes the page, the underlying Visual Basic `Collection` object will remain valid since it won't be destroyed unless the DLL is unloaded.

The DLL won't be unloaded unless the user moves off our frameset (releasing the `<OBJECT>` tag) or the browser is closed down – also releasing the tag.

Creating the DLL

Open Visual Basic and create a new ActiveX DLL project. Change the project name to `BrowserObjects`.

The Global Collection Object

Add a BAS module to the project and change its name to `BOmain`. This module will contain the global variable for the `Collection` that will contain all our data. We'll also need a `Sub Main` procedure to instantiate the object as the DLL is initialized. Enter the following code.

```
Option Explicit

Public gcolItems As Collection

Public Sub Main ()
  Set gcolItems = New Collection
End Sub
```

Make sure to use the project's properties dialog to set the Startup Object to Sub Main or this code will never be run.

Now all we need to do is implement a custom `Collection` object to expose this global object to the client code. This will be a pretty basic custom object, since we're really trying to expose the full potential of the `Collection` object itself.

The Custom Collection Object

Change the name of `Class1` to `Session`. The name `Session` seems to make sense, since in many ways we'll be using this object much like the ASP `Session` object – essentially providing the concept of a session in the browser instead of on the server.

Add the following code – we'll go through in it detail below.

```
Option Explicit

Public Function Count() As Long
  ' delegate to the global collection
  Count = gcolItems.Count
End Function

Public Function NewEnum() As IUnknown
  ' delegate to the global collection
  Set NewEnum = gcolItems.[_NewEnum]
End Function

Public Function Item(ByVal Index As Variant) As Variant
  If VarType(gcolItems(Index)) = vbObject Then
    ' if the item is an object, use Set to return the reference
    Set Item = gcolItems(Index)
  Else
    ' if not an object, just return the value
    Item = gcolItems(Index)
  End If
End Function
```

```
Public Sub Add(Value As Variant, Optional Key As String)
  ' delegate to the global collection
  If Len(Key) > 0 Then
    gcolItems.Add Value, Key
  Else
    gcolItems.Add Value
  End If
End Sub

Public Function CreateObject(ProgID As String, Optional Key As String) As Object
  Dim objNew As Object

  ' create a new object using the supplied PROGID
  Set objNew = VBA.CreateObject(ProgID)

  ' add the new object to the global collection
  If Len(Key) > 0 Then
    gcolItems.Add objNew, Key
  Else
    gcolItems.Add objNew
  End If

  ' return a reference to the new object
  Set CreateObject = objNew
  Set objNew = Nothing
End Function

Public Sub Remove(ByVal Index As Variant)
  On Error Resume Next
  ' delegate to the global collection
  gcolItems.Remove Index
End Sub
```

Use the **Tools | Procedure Attributes** menu option and click on the **Advanced** button. Change the **Procedure ID** of the `Item` procedure to **(default)** and click **Apply**. Then change the **Procedure ID** of the `NewEnum` procedure to **−4** and click the **Hide this member** option. These changes are required to make this object work and act just like a `Collection` object.

For the most part this code is a basic implementation of a user collection based on the Visual Basic `Collection` object. Usually however, we build a user collection with the intent of restricting the types of values it can hold. In this case we're emulating the `Collection` object's behavior almost entirely. Due to this there are a couple of interesting changes.

First off, the `Item` method needs to detect whether the element being retrieved is an object or not. If it is, the `Set` keyword must be used, while if it is not then a direct assignment is required.

```
Public Function Item(ByVal Index As Variant) As Variant
  If VarType(gcolItems(Index)) = vbObject Then
    Set Item = gcolItems(Index)
  Else
    Item = gcolItems(Index)
  End If
End Function
```

Also, the `Add` method allows an optional key value. Our code needs to handle the fact that there may or may not be a key value present.

```
Public Sub Add(Value As Variant, Optional Key As String)
  If Len(Key) > 0 Then
    gcolItems.Add Value, Key
  Else
    gcolItems.Add Value
  End If
End Sub
```

The `Remove` method is a bit of a departure from standard. It ignores the error in the case that the client code attempts to remove an element that doesn't exist. This is just for simplicity of the scripting code we'll use in the browser. Rather than making the scripting code trap this error each time, we can simply trap it here – allowing the scripting code to call `Remove` without fear of failure.

```
Public Sub Remove(ByVal Index As Variant)
  On Error Resume Next
  gcolItems.Remove Index
End Sub
```

Finally, we have an entirely new and different method – `CreateObject`. This is important because we need to provide a mechanism by which the script code running in the browser can create arbitrary objects and add them to the `Session` object. For instance, the script code will need to create a UI-centric business object if we're to build an interface based on our object model.

```
Public Function CreateObject(ProgID As String, Optional Key As String) As Object
  Dim objNew As Object

  Set objNew = VBA.CreateObject(ProgID)
  If Len(Key) > 0 Then
    gcolItems.Add objNew, Key
  Else
    gcolItems.Add objNew
  End If
  Set CreateObject = objNew
  Set objNew = Nothing
End Function
```

In many ways this method is like the `Add` method in that it adds a new element to the `Collection` with an optional key value. However, instead of accepting the object as a parameter, it accepts the `ProgID` value (`servername.classname`) and uses it to create a new instance of the class.

With this code entered, save and compile the DLL.

Be sure to make a copy of the DLL and set the **Version Compatibility** setting to **Binary Compatibility**. Our web pages will be using the CLSID for the `Session` class to create an instance of the object and this will ensure that this value doesn't change if we decide to recompile the DLL at some future point.

Finding the CLSID

Now that the DLL has been compiled, we'll need to find the CLSID that was assigned to the `Session` class. This can be done a couple ways, including the use of the `regedit.exe` application.

Run this application, then choose the **Edit | Find** menu option. Enter `BrowserObjects.Session` and click **Find Next**.

There may be multiple entries for this progid in the registry. Continue searching, opening out the main folder, until you find an entry that appears as shown in the diagram.

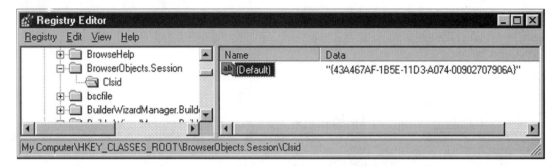

The GUID value for your class will be different than for mine, but the remainder of the display should be similar.

It is this CLSID GUID value that you will need when building an HTML page that makes use of this object.

Keep the `regedit.exe` program open, we're not done with it yet.

Marking the Object Safe for Scripting and Initialization

The `Session` object we've just created will be used within an HTML page – loaded using the `<OBJECT>` tag. Because of this, we'll want to mark it as being safe-for-scripting and safe-for-initialization. If we don't mark it this way, our users will get warnings each time the browser attempts to create an instance of the object – and that can get annoying.

> **Users can avoid this type of message by setting their browser security to Low – but that is not recommended!**

If we're deploying the `Session` object's DLL using the Visual Basic Package and Deployment Wizard (see Appendix B), we can allow the wizard itself to mark the DLL as needed. Just make sure you change the settings in the wizard as appropriate when it prompts you.

However, if we're not using the wizard – for instance on our development workstation – then we'll need to add a couple registry entries of our own.

Since we already know the CLSID for the `Session` object, use `regedit.exe` to do a search for that CLSID value. You should find a display that appears similar to the following diagram.

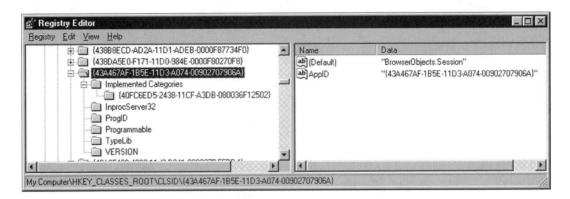

We need to add two sub-keys to the Implemented Categories key. Right-click on that key and choose the New | Key menu option.

Set the key's name to the following.

```
{7DD95801-9882-11CF-9FA9-00AA006C42C4}
```

This is a special key name that is used to indicate that an object is safe for scripting. With this key in place, we won't receive warnings that our component may be unsafe for use by scripting langauges.

Then repeat the process to add a key with the following name.

```
{7DD95802-9882-11CF-9FA9-00AA006C42C4}
```

This is also a special key name. It is used to indicate that an object is safe for initializing. These two special key names combined indicate that a component is safe for creation and use within a scripting environment such as Internet Explorer.

> **Note that we haven't added any *values*, just keys.**

Once this is done our `Session` object will be considered safe and the browser will not bring up warning dialogs each time an instance of the object is created by our script code.

Building a Frameset Page

With our `Session` object built and ready to go, we can create a pretty generic frameset page for use in building any application that utilizes this new object. This file can be built using Notepad or any HTML editor. For now I'll just show you the principles, we'll make our proper framest page a bit later:

```
<HTML>

<HEAD>
<TITLE>My Application</TITLE>

<OBJECT ID="Session"
CLASSID="CLSID:43A467AF-IB5E-11D3-A074-00902707906A"
CODEBASE="BrowserObjects.CAB#version=1,0,0,8">
```

```
  </OBJECT>

<FRAMESET>
  <FRAME ID=frmMain src="firstpage.htm">
</FRAMESET>
</HEAD>
</HTML>
```

The CLSID value used in the <OBJECT> tag is the one from our Session object – we located this GUID value earlier in the chapter.

The <OBJECT> tag shown here is built assuming that we've used the Visual Basic Package and Deployment Wizard to build an Internet distribution CAB file. I'm not going to go into the CODEBASE keyword, distribution, CAB files and everything related to them in detail since there are books dedicated to these concepts. If you don't want to worry about deployment and CAB files, the OBJECT tag could be changed to look like this.

```
<OBJECT ID="Session"
CLASSID="CLSID:43A467AF-IB5E-11D3-A074-00902707906A">
</OBJECT>
```

To customize this page for use with any application, simply change the TITLE tag to fit your application and change the FRAME tag to point to the appropriate first page to be displayed.

In most cases this frameset page itself will be named default.htm as it needs to be the first page loaded for the entire application. All other pages are loaded inside this single frame that consumes the entire display area.

Updating the Task Manager Application

At this point we've discussed the basic concept behind maintaining data and objects within the browser as the user navigates from page to page. We've also built a new Session object to support this concept and we've seen how to build the frameset page on which our web pages would be based.

Now let's quickly build a set of pages to view information from our Task Manager application using these new concepts. These pages will essentially provide the same functionality as those we built earlier in this chapter, using ASP.

> *The concepts and techniques shown here could just as easily be used to create HTML pages that edit the data rather than simply displaying it, but we'll stick with displaying to help keep things simple.*

Since the UI-centric objects will be used just like they are in a conventional forms-based UI, no changes are required to them at all. The same is true with the data-centric objects, which are being used by the UI-centric objects, not by the UI directly, so no change to them is needed.

This means we can simply move onto building the UI itself.

The UI can be built using DHTML and browser scripting with VBScript or JavaScript. It could also be created using the new DHTML Application available with Visual Basic 6. DHTML with VBScript is a perfectly acceptable choice when working within Internet Explorer (and it is an essentially familiar language to any Visual Basic developer), so we'll create this application with that technology.

If we choose to implement the UI using the Visual Basic 6 DHTML Application, the Session *object and frameset page will be the same as shown here – but instead of DHMTL pages being displayed in the frame, we'd display the DHTML Application pages.*

We've already built the start page for the tasktrack site. It has two links – one for the ASP pages we already built, and one for this new application. The link for this application goes to a page called mainframe.htm, which will be the start page for our new set of pages.

Creating the mainframe.htm Page

Open a new file in the same directory as the ASP files we created earlier in this chapter and name it mainframe.htm. You can use Notepad, any other text editor or an HTML editor of your choice.

Enter the following code, substituting the CLSID you found earlier for the one shown in the OBJECT tag:

```
<HTML>

<HEAD>
<TITLE>Task Tracking</TITLE>

<OBJECT ID="Session"
CLASSID="CLSID:43A467AF-IB5E-11D3-A074-00902707906A">

</OBJECT>

<FRAMESET>
   <FRAME ID=frmMain src="input.htm">
</FRAMESET>
</HEAD>
</HTML>
```

This is the same basic page that we saw earlier in this chapter – it is a simple frameset page that has an <OBJECT> tag to load the Session object we built.

This page uses a file named input.htm to populate the single frame. It is this new page that the user actually sees and with which they interact.

Creating the input.htm Page

The input.htm page is the first visible page of our application. It is the first page the user actually sees – even though the mainframe.htm page was really loaded behind the scenes.

Create a new file in the same directory as the mainframe.htm file and name it input.htm.

Note that the script code in this document will be run *on the client* under Internet Explorer. Since we are targeting IE, we can (and are) using VBscript and the IE Document Object Model. It may be possible to implement equivalent functionality in other browsers by using a scripting language supported by that browser and also using that browser's DOM.

Enter the following code.

```
<HTML>

<HEAD>
<META Content="VBScript">
<TITLE>Retrieve client data</TITLE>
<SCRIPT ID=clientEventHandlers LANGUAGE=VBScript>
<!--

function LoadClient()
  Set objSession = window.Parent.document.Session

  objSession.Remove "Client"
  Set objClient = objSession.CreateObject("TaskObjects.Client","Client")

  objClient.Load CLng(txtID.value)
  window.Parent.frames.item("frmMain").navigate("getclient.htm")
end function

//-->
</SCRIPT>

</HEAD>
<BODY>

  Client ID:<BR>
  <INPUT id=txtID><P>
  <INPUT id=btnLoad name=button1 style="LEFT: 11px; TOP: 77px"
    type=button value=Load onclick=LoadClient()>
  <INPUT TYPE=reset VALUE="Cancel" id=reset1 name=reset1>

</BODY>
</HTML>
```

This creates a page that appears very similar to the first page presented in our ASP solution. It has a single text entry field, a button to load the data and a button to cancel the operation.

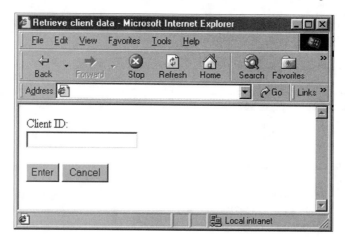

The Load Button

When the user clicks on the Load button, its onclick event will fire. The <INPUT> tag that creates this button has an attribute indicating that the onclick event should cause the LoadClient method to be run.

```
<INPUT id=btnLoad name=button1 style="LEFT: 11px; TOP: 77px"
  type=button value=Load onclick=LoadClient()>
```

So, when the user clicks this button, the LoadClient method will be run.

The LoadClient Method

The LoadClient method is also in the HTML, marked by the <SCRIPT> tags.

```
<SCRIPT ID=clientEventHandlers LANGUAGE=VBScript>
<!--

function LoadClient()
  Set objSession = window.Parent.document.Session

  objSession.Remove "Client"
  Set objClient = objSession.CreateObject("TaskObjects.Client","Client")

  objClient.Load CLng(txtID.value)
  window.Parent.frames.item("frmMain").navigate("getclient.htm")
end function

//-->
</SCRIPT>
```

This method is where the interesting work is done. The first line gets a reference to the Session object from the mainframe.htm page. This object is created based on the <OBJECT> tag in that page and appears as an object or element from that page.

Getting to the Session Object

To reach the Session object we're using the Document Object Model (DOM) as implemented by Internet Explorer 4.0.

```
Set objSession = window.Parent.document.Session
```

Previous versions of IE didn't support the DOM, and there's no guarantee that future versions will be the same – welcome to the world of browser-based development.

The window element indicates the current page's window. Its Parent property gets us to the current page's parent object – which is the frameset page. After all, our current page is contained within that frameset page. The document property then gets us to the frameset page's document where the <OBJECT> tag resides. Once we're there, we can get to any object in the frameset page by using its ID value. The <OBJECT> tag set the ID to Session, so that's the name we use here to get at the object.

Creating the Client Object

Now that we have a reference to the `Session` object, the script code can ensure that there's not already a `Client` object in the collection by using the `Remove` method. Recall that we designed our `Remove` method to ignore errors, catering for the situation where the collection is empty. Then the `CreateObject` method can be used to create a new `Client` object and add it to the session.

Once a `Client` object has been created, the script simply calls its `Load` method to load the object with the appropriate client data.

```
objClient.Load CLng(txtID.value)
```

Note that the `CLng` method is used to convert the value entered by the user into a `Long`. This is required because all values in VBScript are `Variant`, but our Visual Basic object is strongly typed. We'll get an error if we don't convert the `Variant` elements to the correct type before passing them to our object.

Navigating to the getclient Page

With the `Client` object fully populated and stored in the `Session` object, we can navigate to the next page. In fact, it is important that the frameset page remain in place, and that we simply navigate to a new page *within* the frame. As long as the frameset page remains in place so will any objects it references – such as our `Session` object.

The navigation is handled by some script code that accesses elements in the DOM.

```
window.Parent.frames.item("frmMain").navigate("getclient.htm")
```

Again, the `window.Parent` elements get us a reference to the `mainframe.htm` page itself, since that is the parent of the currently displayed page. As a frameset page, `mainframe.htm` has a `frames` collection we can use to get at any frame it contains. In this case we'll get access to the `frmMain` frame and call its `navigate` method to make that frame display the next page in our application.

Creating the getclient.htm Page

The `getclient.htm` page will display the information from the `Client` object – including listing all the `Project` objects in its `Projects` collection.

Since this page will be created entirely by client-side script, it will be a bit different from pages we've built using ASP. Instead of mixing HTML and code the way ASP does it, this page will use pure script to generate the display seen by the user.

Create a new file named `getclient.htm` and add the following code:

```
<HTML>
<HEAD>
<TITLE>Client display</TITLE>
</HEAD>

<SCRIPT LANGUAGE=VBScript>
<!--

Sub Window_OnLoad()
  Set objClient = window.Parent.document.Session("Client")
  strTop = _
    "Client ID: " & objClient.ID & _
    "<P>" & _
    "Client name: " & objClient.Name & _
    "<P>" & _
    "Client phone: " & objClient.Phone & _
    "<P>"
  spnTop.InnerHTML = strTop

  strTbl = "Projects:<BR>" & _
    "<SELECT NAME='selPrj'>"
  For Each objProject In objClient.Projects
    strTbl = strTbl & _
      "<OPTION VALUE='" & objProject.ID & "'>" & _
      objProject.Name
  Next
  strTbl = strTbl & "</SELECT>"
  spnTable.innerHTML = strTbl
End Sub

sub LoadProject()
  for i=0 to selPrj.length - 1
    if selPrj.options(i).selected then
      ID = selPrj.options(i).value
      exit for
    end if
  next
  Set objSession = window.Parent.document.Session
  objSession.Remove "ProjectID"
  objSession.Add ID, "ProjectID"
  window.Parent.frames.item("frmMain").navigate("getproject.htm")
end sub

-->
</SCRIPT>

<BODY>
<SPAN id=spnTop></SPAN>
<HR><P>
  <SPAN id=spnTable></SPAN><P>
  <INPUT type=button value='Show detail' onclick=LoadProject()>
</P>
</BODY>
</HTML>
```

When this page is invoked it should look something like the following diagram.

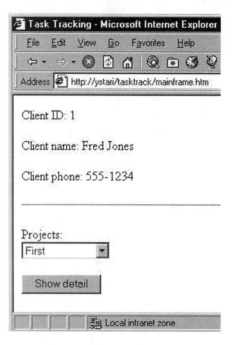

Notice the combo box above the button – this takes the place of the <SPAN> tag in the HTML – it is dynamically replaced by the Window_onLoad procedure.

Document Body and innerHTML

We'll examine the scripting code in this document momentarily. First though, let's take a look at the BODY of the message, since it is somewhat unique in appearance.

The BODY of this page is quite small – the only thing it actually displays is a single button.

```
<BODY>
<SPAN id=spnTop></SPAN>
<HR><P>
  <SPAN id=spnTable></SPAN><P>
  <INPUT type=button value='Show detail' onclick=LoadProject()>
</P><P></P>
</BODY>
```

This seems pretty odd at first glance. The trick is with the <SPAN> tag. Both <SPAN> and <DIV> tags have a property through the DOM called innerHTML. Script code can dynamically replace whatever might be contained within a <SPAN> or <DIV> tag at runtime by setting the innerHTML property to a String value containing valid HTML.

All the real work to create the display for the user occurs as the page is loaded – when the Window_OnLoad event fires.

Displaying Client Information

The `Window_OnLoad` event fires as the page is being loaded. The first thing the script does is to get a reference to the `Client` object from the `Session` object.

```
Set objClient = window.Parent.document.Session("Client")
```

This is pretty similar code to what we saw in the `input.htm` page – walking up the DOM to the frameset page to get to the `Session` object, then retrieving the `Client` item from the collection.

In this routine we've placed script code to build a valid HTML `String` value to display all the `Client` object's data. This value is then assigned to the SPAN with an `id` of spnTop.

```
strTop = _
  "Client ID: " & objClient.ID & _
  "<P>" & _
  "Client name: " & objClient.Name & _
  "<P>" & _
  "Client phone: " & objClient.Phone & _
  "<P>"
spnTop.InnerHTML = strTop
```

Once this is done, a similar approach is taken to display the names of all this client's projects.

Displaying Project Names

The project names could be displayed in an HTML table as they are in our ASP application. However, that approach is less than optimal in this case, since our UI-centric objects are on the client workstation rather than on the web server.

A table of hyperlinks back to another page doesn't help us much here. The purpose of a link is to tell the web server to retrieve another page. In many cases we'll also pass a parameter so the web server can generate the page as appropriate. With all our data on the client however, the web server shouldn't be generating a dynamic page – in fact a web server should be unnecessary, file-based URLs should work just fine since the code is contained in the page itself to be run within the browser.

This means that we should have script code in the browser to figure out which element the user clicked on and then to take appropriate steps. Such an approach is much more like a conventional form-based UI, where the UI determines what the user did and instigates appropriate actions based on that input.

Given the rich object and event model provided by the DOM, it would seem that we could just display a table of project names, then have an `onclick` event run a routine in our browser – much like we did with the **Load** button in the last page.

Unfortunately, HTML added to a page using the `innerHTML` property of a SPAN or DIV doesn't work the same as elements that were on the page from the beginning. Thus, these new elements don't get the same event handling and we can't simply detect the `onclick` event and react to the user's input.

However, there is a relatively good solution to this problem. Instead of building a table, we can create a list of project names with the SELECT tag. This will cause them to list in something like Visual Basic's ComboBox control. The code to do this is shown on the next page.

```
strTbl = "Projects:<BR>" & _
  "<SELECT NAME='selPrj'>"
For Each objProject In objClient.Projects
  strTbl = strTbl & _
    "<OPTION VALUE='" & objProject.ID & "'>" & _
    objProject.Name
Next
strTbl = strTbl & "</SELECT>"
spnTable.innerHTML = strTbl
```

Though we can't react instantly to the fact that the user clicked on an element in the list, we can create script code for the Show detail button to determine which element was clicked and to then take appropriate action.

Selecting a Project

The Show detail button is part of the original page – it is not added via the innerHTML property of a SPAN tag. This means its event handling mechanism is fully operational and we can have its onclick event run a method within our page.

With the project names listed in a SELECT tag, our code can scan the list of projects to find which one is selected, then load the getproject.htm page to display details about that project.

```
function LoadProject()
  for i=0 to selPrj.length - 1
    if selPrj.options(i).selected then
      ID = selPrj.options(i).value
      exit for
    end if
  next
  Set objSession = window.Parent.document.Session
  objSession.Remove "ProjectID"
  objSession.Add ID, "ProjectID"
  window.Parent.frames.item("frmMain").navigate("getproject.htm")
end function
```

The first bit of code here simply runs through the list of elements in the SELECT tag to find the one that is selected. That value is stored in a variable named ID.

The script then gets a reference to the Session object and uses it to store the ID value with the key of ProjectID. Once this value has been stored we simply navigate the frame's display to the getproject.htm page. That page will retrieve this ID from the Session object and can then display the appropriate Project object's data.

Creating the getproject.htm Page

This page follows the pattern of the previous page. The BODY of the page is basically just a <SPAN> tag and the Window_OnLoad event is used to build a valid HTML String value to be placed in that tag's innerHTML property.

Create a new file named `getproject.htm` and enter the following code.

```
<HTML>
<HEAD>
<TITLE>Project display</TITLE>
</HEAD>

<SCRIPT LANGUAGE=VBScript>
<!--

Sub Window_OnLoad()
  Set objClient = window.Parent.document.Session("Client")
  ID = window.Parent.document.Session("ProjectID")

  For Each objProject in objClient.Projects
    if CLng(objProject.ID) = CLng(ID) then
      exit for
    end if
  next

  strTop = _
    "<a href=getclient.htm>" & _
    "Client ID: " & objClient.ID & _
    "</a><P>" & _
    "Client name: " & objClient.Name & _
    "<P>" & _
    "Project ID: " & objProject.ID & _
    "<P>" & _
    "Project name: " & objProject.Name & _
    "<P>"
  spnTop.InnerHTML = strTop

  strTbl = _
    "<TABLE border=1 cellPadding=1 cellSpacing=1 width=75%>" & _
    "<TR bgColor=Orange>" & _
    "   <TD><STRONG>Task name</STRONG></TD>" & _
    "   <TD><STRONG>Projected days</STRONG></TD>" & _
    "   <TD><STRONG>Percent complete</STRONG></TD>" & _
    "</TR>"

  For Each objTask In objProject.Tasks
  strTbl = strTbl & _
    "<TR>" & _
    "<TD>" & objTask.Name & "</TD>" & _
    "<TD>" & objTask.ProjectedDays & "</TD>" & _
    "<TD>" & objTask.PercentComplete & "</TD>" & _
    "</TR>"
  Next

  strTbl = strTbl & "</TABLE>"
  spnTable.innerHTML = strTbl
End Sub

-->
</SCRIPT>

<BODY>
<SPAN id=spnTop></SPAN>
<HR><P>
  <SPAN id=spnTable></SPAN>
</P><BR>
</BODY>
</HTML>
```

Chapter 7

All the interesting portions of this page are in the `Window_OnLoad` event procedure. Let's walk through that code.

Retrieving the Project Object

The first thing the code does is to retrieve a reference to the appropriate `Project` object.

```
Set objClient = window.Parent.document.Session("Client")
  ID = window.Parent.document.Session("ProjectID")

  For Each objProject in objClient.Projects
    if CLng(objProject.ID) = CLng(ID) then
      exit for
    end if
  next
```

The `Session` object contains a reference to the `Client` object. The `Session` object also contains a numeric `ID` value under the key `ProjectID`. This `ID` value represents the project selected by the user on the previous page, so we can use it to identify which `Project` object corresponds to that selection by simply looping through the `Projects` collection.

In the end, we have an `objProject` variable that can be used by the remainder of the code to display detailed information.

Displaying Project Information

The next bit of code is very similar to that from the previous page. We simply build a `String` value of HTML and put it into the `innerHTML` property of the `spnTop` element in the body of the document.

```
strTop = _
    "<a href=getclient.htm>" & _
    "Client ID: " & objClient.ID & _
    "</a><P>" & _
    "Client name: " & objClient.Name & _
    "<P>" & _
    "Project ID: " & objProject.ID & _
    "<P>" & _
    "Project name: " & objProject.Name & _
    "<P>"
  spnTop.InnerHTML = strTop
```

This not only displays some `Client` object information, but also displays the information about the selected `Project` object.

Displaying a List of Tasks

Finally, we need to display a list of task details from the `Tasks` collection for this `Project` object. If we want to allow the user to drill down to a specific `Task` object's detail we'll want to use a `SELECT` tag as on the previous page. In this case however, I've opted to display all the information in an HTML table.

```
strTbl = _
    "<TABLE border=1 cellPadding=1 cellSpacing=1 width=75%>" & _
    "<TR bgColor=Orange>" & _
    "  <TD><STRONG>Task name</STRONG></TD>" & _
    "  <TD><STRONG>Projected days</STRONG></TD>" & _
    "  <TD><STRONG>Percent complete</STRONG></TD>" & _
    "</TR>"
```

```
For Each objTask In objProject.Tasks
strTbl = strTbl & _
  "<TR>" & _
  "<TD>" & objTask.Name & "</TD>" & _
  "<TD>" & objTask.ProjectedDays & "</TD>" & _
  "<TD>" & objTask.PercentComplete & "</TD>" & _
  "</TR>"
Next

strTbl = strTbl & "</TABLE>"
spnTable.innerHTML = strTbl
```

This code simply builds a `String` value containing the HTML for a table containing all the information from the `Task` objects. That value is then assigned to the `innerHTML` property of the `spnTable` element.

In the end, the user simply sees a page displaying the project information and a list of tasks associated with the project they selected.

The beauty of this whole user interface is that the web server did nothing but provide simple HTML pages to the browser. No processing, data access or dynamic page generation occurred on the web server – it was all handled by the client workstation in the browser.

Such an approach can allow us to create much more scalable applications overall, since much of the web server's work has been offloaded to individual client workstations. We've effectively spread the processing load of dynamic web page creation across as many client workstations as are using the application.

Additionally, the UI-centric objects are located right there on the browser. This means that an entry screen in the browser can use the UI-centric object's business logic and processing to create a powerful user interface that feels as responsive to the user as a conventional forms-based interface. No more batch-oriented data entry!

There's one final consideration. As it stands, our UI-centric objects are still using DCOM – or maybe even MSMQ if you've made the changes from Chapter 6 – to communicate with the data-centric business objects.

In many browser-based settings this can be problematic since there is often a firewall between the client workstation and any of the servers used by our application. Fortunately there's an easy answer to this problem – Remote Data Services.

Using Remote Data Services

Remote Data Services (RDS) is a technology available to client workstations running Internet Explorer. RDS was introduced as a technology to allow script code running in a browser to request an ADO Recordset object from the web server.

However, RDS has evolved and is far more powerful than that – in fact it is now a technology by which code running on a client workstation can call methods on COM objects running on a web server – over HTTP.

Since method calls via RDS are over HTTP, they bypass most firewall security – allowing us to create powerful UI components that interact with server-side objects while avoiding many security complications.

Obviously there are potential issues with allowing applications on a client application to invoke an object through the firewall via HTTP. As we'll see, we do get to choose *which* objects can be invoked in this manner, but it is largely up to us to implement security to prevent unauthorized use of our objects.

Additionally, it is quite common to have load balanced server farms for web applications. Since HTTP requests are spread across the servers in such farms, we can gain a form of automatic load balancing merely by routing our method calls via HTTP. For this reason RDS may be attractive even within an organization's *local* network.

How RDS Works

The syntax of such a method call is very similar to that of a DCOM method call, but instead of using DCOM, the call is handled by RDS and is sent over HTTP – bypassing most firewalls and providing a mechanism by which applications on a client can interact with server-side objects without conflicting with most security mechanisms.

The following diagram shows a client workstation running either script within a browser or a full-blown client application. The code running on the client workstation interacts with a COM object on the web server via the HTTP protocol.

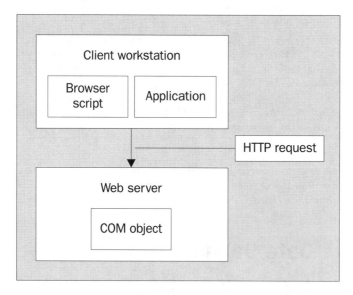

To take advantage of this technology, the client application (or browser-based script) makes use of the Microsoft Remote Data Services Library. This is automatically available to script within the browser, but we need to add a reference to this library for any Visual Basic components that will make use of this functionality.

The DataSpace Object

The client-side code creates an RDS `DataSpace` object to manage the communications from the client's end of things. The `DataSpace` object has a `CreateObject` method, which is used to create an instance of the server-side object.

> **More accurately, the `CreateObject` method creates a client-side proxy object and sets things up so RDS knows what server-side object to create. The object isn't really created until a method is called.**

The client code then calls methods on the server-side object just like it would using DCOM. For instance, an RDS-aware `Load` method in a UI-centric object might appear something like this.

```
Public Sub Load(ID As Long)
  Dim objDS As DataSpace
  Dim objPersist As ObjectPersist

  Set objDS = New RDS.DataSpace
  Set objPersist = objDS.CreateObject("ObjectServer.ObjectPersist", _
    "http://myserver")
  Fetch = objPersist.Fetch(ID)
  Set objPersist = Nothing
  Set objDS = Nothing
End Sub
```

If this seems too easy to be true – well, it really is this easy.

RDS is nearly transparent to a COM developer. For the most part the only thing to change is the way we create the server-side object since we need to use the `DataSpace` object's `CreateObject` instead of the `New` keyword or the built-in `CreateObject` method provided by Visual Basic. Also, instead of a traditional server name, we need to provide an HTTP server name – the name of the web server that will be hosting the server-side object.

The `DataSpace` object also provides the `InternetTimeout` property so we can indicate how long the client should wait for a response. In the volatile world of the Internet this is a very valuable capability.

Server-side Atomic Methods Required

There is one catch. The server-side object exists only for the duration of each method call. If we call a method, and then immediately call a second method then we will have created *two* server-side objects. One gets created to service the first method call and is destroyed. Then a second is created to service the second method call and is destroyed.

This means that the server-side object cannot preserve any data from one method call to the next – meaning that methods are totally atomic, even if they aren't designed that way. This can be a problem if we're converting an application that's not designed this way. Fortunately the CSLA design already specifies that server-side components have totally atomic methods, so we're all set!

Server-side Security

We've bypassed most firewall type security with RDS since the request to the server is over HTTP and the response appears to be similar to any other data being sent from the web server to a client. However, we obviously don't want to bypass *all* security. It would be a problem if RDS allowed a client to create any arbitrary object on the server.

RDS provides a mechanism to help us out. We need to tell RDS which specific classes on our server are available for creation by clients. It will only create classes from that specific list – everything else is off-limits.

This list of classes is stored in the registry, where we create a set of sub-keys – each one being the PROGID of a class that can be created via RDS. The registry entries for each class are added under HKEY_LOCAL_MACHINE in the SYSTEM\CurrentControlSet\Services\ W3SVC\Parameters\ADCLaunch key.

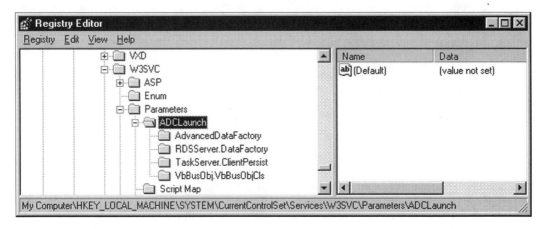

As shown in the diagram, the sub-key entered for each class is its PROGID – the servername.classname that we'd use to instantiate an object using CreateObject in Visual Basic.

For our CSLA-based applications, we'll typically add one such entry for each data-centric business object – thus allowing the UI-centric objects to interact with them via RDS.

No other changes are required on the server-side objects. As long as they are designed with atomic methods and are stateless then they are all set.

Updating the Task Manager Application

In Chapter 6 we added the TaskProxyServer project to the mix – shielding our UI-centric objects from the code to handle MSMQ. This change is strategically valuable here as well, since it is in the implementations of Fetch, Save and DeleteObject within the ClientProxy object that all our code changes will take place.

We'll also need to add registry entries for the TaskServer.ClientPersist object on the server so RDS knows it is a valid object to create.

Once that's done, our UI-centric objects will access their data-centric counterparts over HTTP. Very little impact to our code, but a huge benefit in an environment where firewalls or scalability are a consideration.

Updating the ClientProxy Object

First off, open Visual Basic and bring up the `TaskProxyServer` project. We'll make all our actual code changes in the `ClientProxy` object.

Referencing the RDS Library

Before we can use RDS, it is important to add a reference to the Microsoft Remote Data Services Library as shown in the diagram.

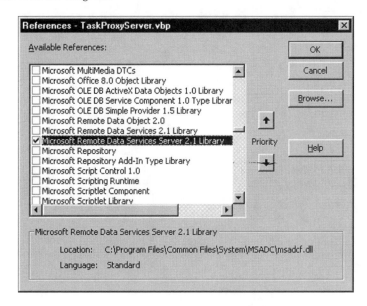

Note that there's no reference to the MSMQ library. We'll be altering the code to use RDS exclusively, so there's no reason to retain the reference to MSMQ.

We've also removed the reference to the `TaskServer` component. By removing this reference our method calls will be late bound, so we'll need to change the `Dim` statements in our code to declare the `objPersist` variables as type `Object`.

The benefit to doing this is that we don't need to distribute the `TaskServer` type library to the client workstations. There is a logistic benefit to taking this approach, since it further decouples the code running on the client from the code running on the server – making long-term maintenance of the application easier.

Updating the Code

Open the code window for the `ClientProxy` class module and remove the declarations we added for MSMQ – we won't be needing them for RDS.

```
'Private mstrBody As String
'Private mstrAction As String
```

Also remove the `SendMessage`, `Class_ReadProperties` and `Class_WriteProperties` methods, as they won't be used any longer either. Change the Persistable property to 0-NotPersistable.

Then we can move on to update the routines that remain.

Updating the Fetch Method

To start with, let's update the `Fetch` method. This method was unchanged when we implemented MSMQ in Chapter 6, so it best illustrates how we can change a method from using DCOM to RDS. The DCOM version of this routine appears as follows.

```
Public Function Fetch(ID As Long) As String
  Dim objPersist As ClientPersist

  Set objPersist = New ClientPersist
  Fetch = objPersist.Fetch(ID)
  Set objPersist = Nothing
End Function
```

Since we've removed the reference to the `TaskServer` component, our declaration will need to change to be of type `Object`. Also we'll update the code to create an RDS `DataSpace` object and use it to create the `ClientPersist` object. Make the following changes.

```
Public Function Fetch(ID As Long) As String
  Dim objDS As DataSpace
  Dim objPersist As Object

  Set objDS = New RDS.DataSpace
  Set objPersist = objDS.CreateObject("TaskServer.ClientPersist", _
    "http://myserver")
  Fetch = objPersist.Fetch(ID)
  Set objPersist = Nothing
  Set objDS = Nothing
End Function
```

You'll need to replace `myserver` with the name of your development web server, and from this point forward our UI-centric `Client` object will retrieve its data over HTTP instead of over DCOM.

> Note that we've changed the declaration of `objPersist` to be of type `Object`. This makes the interaction with this object be late bound, but avoids any requirement to register the server-side component on the client workstation.

The other two methods will look very similar.

Updating the Save Method

The `Save` method as it stands is using MSMQ. Because of this, it doesn't actually return any updated data from the `Save` method of the data-centric object – after all, MSMQ is asynchronous.

RDS is synchronous – just like DCOM. This means that the `Save` method will once again be returning updated data. As with the `Fetch` method, the `Save` method will be almost identical to DCOM-based code except the `ClientPersist` object will be created using the `DataSpace` object's `CreateObject` method.

```
Public Function Save(Buffer As String) As String
  Dim objDS As DataSpace
  Dim objPersist As Object

  Set objDS = New RDS.DataSpace
  Set objPersist = objDS.CreateObject("TaskServer.ClientPersist", _
    "http://myserver")
  Save = objPersist.Save(Buffer)
  Set objPersist = Nothing
  Set objDS = Nothing
End Function
```

As you might predict, the `DeleteObject` method will end up appearing quite similar.

Updating the DeleteObject Method

The `DeleteObject` method will be changed in the same ways as the previous two methods.

```
Public Sub DeleteObject(ID As Long)
  Dim objDS As DataSpace
  Dim objPersist As Object

  Set objDS = New RDS.DataSpace
  Set objPersist = objDS.CreateObject("TaskServer.ClientPersist", _
    "http://myserver")
  objPersist.DeleteObject ID
  Set objPersist = Nothing
  Set objDS = Nothing
End Sub
```

Now save and recompile the `TaskProxyServer` project.

Deploying TaskProxyServer

The `TaskProxyServer` DLL must be installed on the client workstation for this to work properly.

If we are deploying a conventional forms-based application this DLL should be part of the client install. This will be handled automatically by the Package and Deployment Wizard, since it will detect that the `TaskObjects` DLL depends on the `TaskProxyServer` DLL.

If our client-side application is running within a browser (by using the frameset technique discussed earlier for instance), then we'll need to ensure that the `TaskProxyServer` is included in the CAB file used to deploy the UI-centric objects. Again, the Package and Deployment Wizard should take care of these details for us (see Appendix B).

All that remains at this point is to add the server-side registry entries so RDS knows it is allowed to create the `ClientPersist` object. Without that change the code we just updated would fail due to RDS and its internal security.

Making TaskServer Available via RDS

The `TaskServer` component doesn't need any code changes to work with RDS.

The `ClientPersist` object's methods are already atomic and the object is stateless – meaning it will work great with RDS. While these requirements are certainly a limitation in some cases, they fit exactly with the way a CSLA-based application is designed.

This means that all we need to do is add a registry entry so RDS will allow client code to create an instance of the `ClientPersist` object.

This can be done with any registry editing tool – in this case I'll use `regedit.exe`. Open up the program and choose the Edit | Find menu option. Search for the text `adclaunch`. We're looking for the key named as follows.

```
HKEY_LOCAL_MACHINE\SYSTEM\CurrentControlSet\Services\ W3SVC\Parameters\ADCLaunch
```

Right-click on the `ADCLaunch` entry and choose the New | Key menu option. Change the name of the new key to `TaskServer.ClientPersist` – the `PROGID` of the `ClientPersist` data-centric business object.

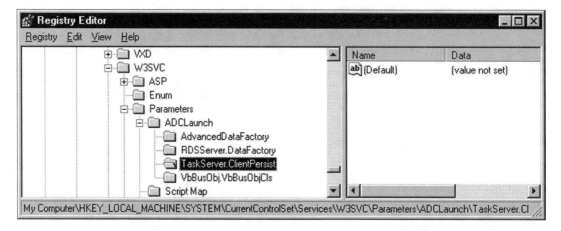

With this key added to the registry, RDS will now allow clients to create the `ClientPersist` object and call its methods. This means that the code changes we made to the `ClientProxy` object will now work and we can run our script-based browser application from earlier in this chapter and have the communications run over HTTP.

> *To really test this requires at least two machines – one running the client software and one acting as the server, running IIS. If you* really *want to prove it works you'll want to make sure you are going through a firewall that screens out everything but HTTP traffic.*
>
> *However, for a simple test, it is probably enough to just set the second parameter on the* `CreateObject` *call (in the* `ClientProxy` *object) to an empty string – thus indicating that the server-side objects should be invoked on the current machine.*

It also means that we can run our form-based user interface from earlier in the book and have *its* communications run over HTTP. Such a scenario is powerful to consider, since it means we could distribute a conventional client application, but have it utilize HTTP-based communication with the server-side objects to take advantage of a web farm to distribute the load across multiple servers, or to provide for Internet-based communication for roving users such as a sales force.

Summary

Internet development and related technologies are evolving rapidly becoming more and more robust all the time. Already we have some capabilities that allow us to develop Internet applications that take advantage of distributed object architectures.

If we are concerned about browser independence, perhaps needing to reach users who may be using unknown browsers, we can distribute our objects only as far as the web server. However, by storing serialized object state in the ASP Session object we can provide better performance and easier maintenance for our application than storing that same state in a cookie on the client or in temporary tables in a database.

In the case that the browser is known to be Internet Explorer 4.0 or higher, our options are greatly enhanced. Using the `BrowserObjects.Session` object created in this chapter we have an elegant mechanism by which state data – including business object references – can be maintained on the client as the user moves from page to page.

This technology can allow us to build browser-based applications that are as robust and highly interactive as a conventional forms-based user interface. It can also be used in conjunction with Visual Basic 6 DHTML Applications, leveraging the best of a browser-based interface with the power of both Visual Basic and distributed objects.

Finally, if we have UI-centric objects running within the browser on a client workstation they'll need an Internet-friendly way to communicate with the data-centric business objects running on the server. This functionality is easily provided using Remote Data Services (RDS).

RDS not only allows our objects to communicate through firewalls by using HTTP, but we can also leverage web server farms to spread our server-side load across multiple servers – with no extra effort on our part.

Additionally, we can use RDS from more traditional user interfaces – allowing roving users or others who use our application from outside the firewall to have all the functionality a user would find over a LAN with the objects running DCOM.

We can use these techniques and concepts to create powerful Internet or intranet applications that leverage all the power, capabilities and reuse inherent in the CSLA – and exploit all that Internet technologies have to offer.

Implementing a Load Balancing Cluster

Overview

Perhaps the most common reason for moving to a multi-tier architecture and employing the use of distributed objects is to gain a high degree of scalability for our applications.

We can gain a lot of scalability through the use of Microsoft Transaction Server (MTS), database connection pooling and efficiently managing the passing of data between the tiers of our application – in short, all of the techniques that we used in *Visual Basic 6 Business Objects* and those we've seen up to now in this book.

However, there may come a time when your application needs to support so many concurrent users that a single application server in the middle tier simply can't handle the load. In such a case there are two main options – get a bigger application server or implement clustering to spread the load across more than one machine.

While purchasing a larger server machine may solve the problem, there are limits to how much throughput is possible on a single Windows NT server. Eventually, even with a larger server machine, we may find that we can't support all the users with reasonable performance.

There are various technologies and techniques we can use to spread an application's processing across multiple servers. In this chapter we'll briefly discuss a couple of the primary techniques at our disposal. Then we'll use Visual Basic to actually implement a simple load balancing server for use with our Task Manager (or any other) application.

Although there are a number of available and future technologies that provide load balancing capabilities, it is still worth creating clustering software ourselves, even if for no other reason than to gain an in-depth understanding of the many issues involved.

Load Balancing

The concept of load balancing is fairly basic. The idea is simply that a request from a client may be handled by one of a number of possible server machines.

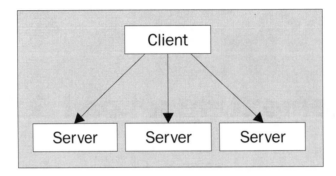

If there is some mechanism by which client requests are funneled to the server most able to do the work – or handle the load – then we have **load balancing**. (If all clients spread their work across the possible servers then we have **load sharing**.)

Load Balancing Techniques

There are some key issues we need to address to implement load balancing. We need some technique to determine which server will handle each client request. Also, we need to decide if our load balancing will be static over the lifetime of a client application (that is, for all the requests made by a single client), or dynamic for each client request.

Before we get into the development of our particular load balancing cluster, we'll discuss the various design options available. Additionally, we'll briefly discuss a couple commercial options that are available today. While developing a load balancing cluster on our own is an interesting exercise, we may prefer a vendor-supported option in some environments.

Determining the Server

There are a number of ways by which we can determine which client requests goes to which server. The following is a list of the common approaches.

- ❑ Round Robin – Requests are handled by each server in turn, one after another
- ❑ Server response – Requests are handled by the server that currently has the best response time
- ❑ Connection count – Requests are routed to the server with the least number of existing connections
- ❑ Random – Requests are handled by a random server
- ❑ Static rating – Requests are handled proportionally to the rating of each server; the highest rated server gets the most requests, etc.

The server to be used is often determined by a specific machine (the **cluster router**) whose job is to field requests from clients and to implement the appropriate algorithm:

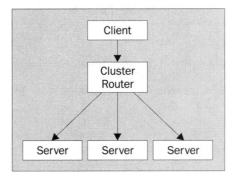

This cluster router may create an object on the client's behalf, returning a valid reference to the client. Alternatively, the router may simply return the name of the server on which the client is to create the object, allowing the client to create its own object. The diagram shown here illustrates the former approach.

We'll also discuss the use of MSMQ to implement load balancing – which will use a different technique. Instead of the client determining which server will handle the request, the client will simply send the request to a queue and the servers will determine which is to handle the message containing the request.

The technique that we'll implement in this chapter will use a cluster router to tell the client the name of the server. The client will then create the object on that server. Such an approach minimizes the load on the cluster router, providing the best overall performance for the cluster under high loads.

Static vs Dynamic Balancing

There are also a couple of ways we can handle individual requests – method calls – from the client:

- ❑   Static Load Balancing
- ❑   Dynamic Load Balancing

Static Load Balancing

In this model a client establishes a connection to a server using any of the load balancing techniques listed above. Once the connection is made, the client's requests will go only to that server until the application is closed. This approach has the lowest overhead to implement, since each client only interacts with the cluster router once – from then on it continues to use the same server. Additionally, this approach could allow our application to maintain some state data on the server, since a single server will be used throughout the life of the application.

The drawback is that a given server may end up with a lot of clients running objects on it. If many clients are idle, more objects will be created on that server. Then, later, all those clients may become busy – overloading the server.

Dynamic Load Balancing

In this case the client does not retain a connection to a specific server. Rather, a connection (and object) is created each time the client needs the server to do work. In this case, the client may use one server for one request, and another server for the next. This has the potential benefit of continually rebalancing the load across the servers.

The drawback to this approach is that it incurs more overhead. Each method call now requires that the client first ask the cluster router where the object should be created, and then create the object before calling a method. This means that each method requires an extra two calls across the network (counting the response from the cluster router).

Consequently, since the client may use services from many servers over time, no state data may be maintained on the server. We can't predict which specific server the client will be using at any given point in time.

Choosing an Approach

The choice between static or dynamic load balancing should be made based on the characteristics of our application.

If our application frequently creates server-side objects during its normal course of operation – then static load balancing may make sense. The overhead of constantly re-evaluating which server should service each request could become overwhelming in such a case.

However, most applications don't fit that model. Typically an application spends much of its time waiting for the user to interact with our UI-centric objects – not interacting with server-side objects at all. In such a case, a dynamic model is often preferable, since it provides the best overall performance when the application actually does need to interact with a server-side object.

In this chapter we'll implement a load balanced cluster that utilizes dynamic load balancing. This provides the best overall cluster performance, overhead notwithstanding.

Load Balancing Technologies

There are a number of existing technologies that provide load sharing or load balancing capabilities. Other load balancing capabilities may become available in the future, through COM+ or other means. In the following sections we will examine a few of these technologies, including MSMQ, the Windows Load Balancing Service (WLBS), hardware-based solutions and COM+ dynamic load balancing.

Using MSMQ

In Chapter 6 we explored various ways by which we can utilize Microsoft Message Queue (MSMQ). This technology provides us with a way to implement both asynchronous and queued messaging.

We also saw that queuing is typically not an ideal solution for client to server communication when the client needs a response back immediately. Since most client to server communication *does* require a response from the server, MSMQ is often not a choice that leaps to mind.

What we didn't explore in detail is the ability of MSMQ to send a response message back to a queue on the client workstation. This can allow us to simulate a synchronous method call using queuing technology. Although it is a bit of a hack, it can still be an effective approach.

One interesting aspect of MSMQ queues is that they can be serviced by more than one server. In other words, a single queue can have many servers reading its messages – each server providing the same set of functionality.

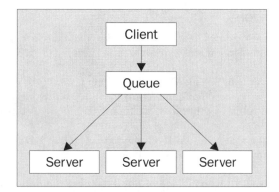

Interestingly enough, this looks very similar to the load balancing diagram we saw earlier in the chapter. In fact, this is a technique that does implement a form of load sharing. Since a number of servers are reading and processing messages from the queue, the processing of various requests from the clients will be spread amongst all those servers.

This type of load sharing is nice because it leverages existing technologies. Unfortunately, it requires that each client workstation set up a queue to receive responses from the servers, and we need to change our client application to simulate a synchronous call by entering a wait loop until a response from the server arrives in the client's queue.

Windows Load Balancing Service

Windows NT Server Enterprise Edition provides the Windows Load Balancing Service (WLBS). This service performs a type of load balancing at a network level.

When a client attempts to establish a TCP/IP connection to a WLBS cluster, the cluster chooses one machine and establishes the IP connection to that server. Once an IP connection has been established to a server, that server supports the connection until the client disconnects.

WLBS determines server load based on the number of connections existing to each server.

This type of clustering is designed with the assumption that it will be used for stateless server-side activities, since the client workstation will talk to a number of servers over time. Any time the client disconnects, it may be switched to another server without warning upon its next connection.

Typically a client won't retain a connection to the server for longer than a single method call or request – so we can expect that we'll be moved from server to server quite frequently.

Since this technology operates at the IP level, anything we use that establishes an IP connection from the client to the server can be load balanced. Obvious examples include HTTP requests from a browser, SMTP requests from e-mail systems and so forth.

Since Remote Data Services (RDS) uses HTTP as its underlying protocol, and as HTTP is based on IP connections, we gain automatic load balancing for all RDS-based applications.

In Chapter 7 we saw how easy it is to have an application designed following the CSLA use RDS instead of DCOM for server communications. By combining RDS with WLBS we have an easy and powerful way to implement load balancing for our applications.

Hardware-based Solutions

Along the same lines as the Windows Load Balancing Service, there are network routers that will balance a TCP/IP connection load across a number of servers.

The concept and result is very similar to WLBS. As a client attempts to establish an IP connection to a server, the router hardware causes that connection to be established to the server with the least load at the time (or using round robin or other load balancing techniques – this varies by the product).

Any technology we are using that relies on IP connections (such as RDS) will allow us to take advantage of this type of hardware-based load balancing.

Hardware-based solutions have the advantage of not degrading the performance of a server machine. With WLBS there is a server machine managing the routing of each IP connection request. A hardware-based solution relies on a dedicated router to take care of those details, leaving our servers fully available to handle the work requested by our client workstations.

Unfortunately, most hardware-based solutions require the purchase of a relatively expensive, specialized router, while WLBS is included with Windows NT Server Enterprise Edition for no extra charge.

COM+ Dynamic Load Balancing

Microsoft has indicated that COM+ will provide a form of dynamic load balancing. Few details are public at this time, so it is a difficult topic to discuss in any depth.

However, I feel it important to mention that COM+ will be providing some form of dynamic load balancing, presumably at the COM level. Given that COM+ is the next step in the evolution of COM, this form of clustering will undoubtedly become commonly used as COM+ becomes available and accepted across the industry.

Having briefly discussed the most common options for load balancing available today, let's dive into the details and explore the issues involved in implementing a load balancing cluster. Though you may choose to use an existing or future technology for your application, there is a lot of benefit to be gained in seeing just how load balancing is implemented, since most technologies are just a variation on the basic theme.

Implementing a Cluster

In this section we'll implement a COM-based load balanced cluster. This cluster will provide a high degree of scalability and a higher degree of fault tolerance than we find when working with a single server machine.

Earlier in the chapter we discussed some of the common issues surrounding load balancing technologies. Now we need to determine what load balancing algorithm to use, whether the balancing will be static or dynamic and on what general technology our cluster will be based.

Each choice will affect the specific implementation of the cluster, providing its own set of strengths and weaknesses, as we've already seen. Since the intent of implementing the cluster software is to explore some of the basic issues and concepts around this type of software, we'll choose an approach that is powerful, yet relatively easy to implement. Certainly other choices could be made, potentially creating a cluster that is better suited to your application's requirements.

In a dynamic load balancing scenario there are three different types of machine involved, and we'll need to implement software to run on each of these machines:

- Client workstations
- Worker servers – that actually handle the requests from the clients
- Cluster routers – that direct the client requests to the right worker servers

There are also four main functions that must be implemented in a load balancing solution:

- Monitor each server's status
- Implement a cluster router
- Allow the client to access the cluster
- Enable the cluster to answer client requests

Each worker server needs to monitor its own status and provide that information to all cluster routers. The monitoring process ensures that each worker server is actually running, and also allows the cluster routers to determine how much load each worker server can handle. This last part can be done in a variety of ways, including monitoring the response time or number of connections to a server. In our case we'll take a simpler approach – assigning each worker server a static rating value. The higher the rating, the more processing the server will be assigned.

The second major function involves the cluster routers. The routers need to monitor all the worker servers, keeping track of whether each one is actually running. The cluster routers also need to be aware of changes in each worker server's rating. These ratings may change over time based on varying workloads – affecting how much more work will be directed to each worker server. We'll implement a monitor application that continually tracks the worker servers so we know they're running and have up to date rating values for each.

Each client needs to implement some functionality to find out which worker server should handle its requests. The cluster router will actually keep track of which worker servers have the lowest work load, but it will be up to the client to ask for that information.

Ideally this would be transparent to client applications – or as close as possible. Obviously we can't alter the functionality of Visual Basic's `New` or `CreateObject` statements, but we will create a client-side COM DLL that implements a `CreateObject` lookalike method. In this way our client applications will need to only change one line of code to switch from regular object creation to using our load balanced cluster.

Finally, the cluster server needs to answer client requests regarding which worker server should be used. The cluster server will already be monitoring each worker server's status, so it should have all the information it needs to determine the best server for each client. We'll build our client-side COM DLL to communicate with the cluster server whenever the client needs to determine which worker server to use.

The following diagram illustrates the overall architecture of this solution. The client application wants to invoke a component on a server. To do this, it uses the Cluster DLL to ask the Cluster Router which Worker Server to use. The client then creates a Worker Component (a server-side DLL specific to this application) on the Worker Server indicated.

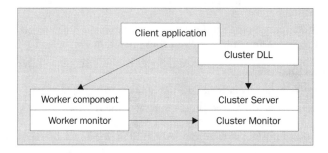

There are two general event flows here. One for the cluster itself, and one when a client needs a server-side object to do some work.

First, let's take a look at how the cluster components fit together. While the cluster is running, the Cluster Monitor component is continually maintaining a list of all the worker servers and their ratings. This is done by relying on the Worker Monitor component, on each worker server, to maintain that server's rating and update the cluster monitor. Each Worker Monitor is responsible for continually updating the Cluster Monitor with current information. The Cluster Monitor knows a Worker Server is unavailable if it hasn't received a recent rating updated from that server.

This is illustrated in the diagram opposite.

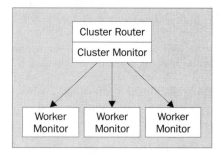

Given that the Cluster Router and Worker Servers are continually interacting, we can assume that the Cluster Router knows which Worker Servers should get the most work assigned at any given point in time. Now we can take a look at how the client interacts with the cluster.

When a client application needs an object reference on a server, it uses the Cluster DLL component's `CreateObject` method instead of either `New` or the regular `CreateObject`. That method asks the Cluster Router component for the name of the worker server on which to create the object, as illustrated in the diagram opposite.

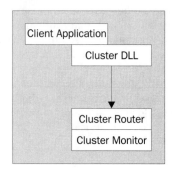

The Cluster Router component relies on the Cluster Monitor to keep the list of worker server ratings up to date, so it can provide appropriate information back to the Cluster DLL component regarding which Worker Server should be used.

Finally, the client will end up with a reference to a server-side object on the appropriate Worker Server. At this point, the client can interact with that object just as though it were created outside of any clustered environment.

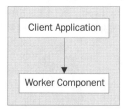

The process of monitoring all the Worker Servers and the process of servicing each client request are interrelated, but generally operate independently of each other. That means that the cluster monitoring process continues in the background of all the servers regardless of whether there are clients using the cluster or not. The client request process is designed with the assumption that the worker server ratings are continually updated behind the scenes.

Obviously, there is a certain level of overhead implied by the interaction between the Worker Servers and the Cluster Routers. The more often each Worker Server updates the Cluster Router the more accurate our information about that Worker Server's availability and rating – but also the more network and CPU processing overhead is consumed.

The question of how often to update the ratings is a tough one. The longer we wait, the less accurate our data. The more often we update, the more overhead we create. In the solution we'll develop in this book, our Worker Servers will update their data every half-second – ensuring that the Cluster Router will know within half a second if a Worker Server has crashed or been taken off line.

To handle the background monitoring of the worker servers and provide that information to the client workstations, we'll need to implement three components.

- ❑ **Worker Monitor** – will report on the worker machine's rating
- ❑ **Cluster Monitor** – will keep track of all the work server's ratings and whether they are currently available
- ❑ **Cluster Server** – will provide this information to the client workstations upon request

The Worker Monitor

Each worker server will have a rating. The higher the rating, the more client requests will be directed to that machine.

> *The rating value in our case will be a static number, but it could be changed to reflect the number of connections to the machine, the machine's response time, CPU utilization, etc. You'll see in the code where the rating is sent to the cluster monitor, and that could be changed from a static value to something more complex.*

Every so often, half a second in our case, the worker monitor component will send its current rating to the cluster monitor. This does two things. First off, it ensures that the cluster monitor always has a current rating value. Secondly, it allows the cluster monitor to know that the worker server is still alive. We're basically implementing a half-second heartbeat message for our servers.

Since our rating value will be static, it really isn't necessary to update it continually. However, by implementing this model we can easily change to a dynamic rating system later.

More important, however, is the fault tolerance we gain through this approach. If a worker server crashes or is taken down, the cluster server will know about it in less than a second. Subsequent client requests can then be routed to other worker servers, avoiding the one that is now offline.

Of course, users who are in the middle of an interaction with the server as it goes down will be affected, though subsequent requests will be rerouted. This provides a pretty high degree of fault tolerance – comparable to most other clustering solutions available today.

Setting up the Project

Let's move on and actually implement the Worker Monitor. Since this component will be used by the Cluster Monitor on a different machine, we need to implement the Worker Monitor component such that it can be invoked across the network.

When the Cluster Monitor starts up, it will create a Worker Monitor on each worker server. Once created, each Worker Monitor will update the Cluster Monitor with the worker server's rating every half-second.

There are two ways to handle this. We can create an ActiveX EXE and use the `dcomcnfg` utility to allow access, or we can create an ActiveX DLL and let MTS take care of those details. The MTS approach is generally easier and more reliable, so we'll build this project as an ActiveX DLL and use MTS.

> *An ActiveX EXE is a COM server that runs in its own process. As such, it can be invoked by code on the same machine or on another machine across the network. In order to invoke an object in an ActiveX EXE across the network, we need to use the `dcomcnfg.exe` administrative utility to set up security and other parameters indicating how the object can be accessed.*

Open Visual Basic and create a new ActiveX DLL project. Change the project name to `WorkerMonitor`. Since this component will be running in MTS the Threading Model should be set to Apartment Threaded – which it is by default.

Creating the Monitor Class

Select the `Class1` module and change its name to `Monitor`. This class will implement three methods:

- ❑ `Initialize`
- ❑ `Shutdown`
- ❑ `SendStatus`

The Cluster Monitor component (residing on the Cluster Router server) will create an instance of this class on each worker server. It will then call an `Initialize` method on the `Monitor` object to provide the `Monitor` object with a reference back to the Cluster Monitor.

As the Cluster Monitor component shuts down it will need to call a `Shutdown` method on the `Monitor` object so all references are released. The Cluster Monitor and Worker Monitor components will have a circular reference to each other, so it is vitally important that they properly release object references before shutting down or they'll hang in memory forever.

Finally, the `Monitor` object will periodically need to send the worker machine's rating back to the Cluster Monitor. This will be handled by a `SendStatus` method – called from a `Timer` control, which we'll add later.

Declarations

The `Monitor` object will retain a reference back to the Cluster Monitor so it can send the rating value over time, and it will need to keep the rating value for the worker server. We'll also add a constant value to store the number of ticks between sending updates to the Cluster Monitor.

Add the following code to the `Monitor` class module.

```
Option Explicit

Private mobjCaller As Object
Private mlngRating As Long

Private Const REPORT_INT = 500
```

Referencing the Windows Scripting Host

Our rating values will be a static number. To add a level of flexibility, this value can be stored in the registry and retrieved as our object is initialized.

In the past, accessing the registry required API calls. However, Microsoft has released the Windows Scripting Host – allowing us to create VBScript programs that run within the Windows environment. A nice side effect is that the scripting host *library* is also available – and it allows us to perform many system level operations very easily using Visual Basic, including interacting with the registry.

> *The Windows Scripting Host is free and can be downloaded from Microsoft's web site at* `http://msdn.microsoft.com/scripting/`. *Not only does it allow us to access the registry, but also network resources, printers, the Windows shell and other capabilities. To read more about the Windows Scripting Host, pick up a copy of* Windows Scripting Host Programmer's Reference (ISBN 1-861002-65-3) *from Wrox Press.*

With the scripting host installed on your computer, simply add a reference to the Windows Scripting Host Object Model Ver (1.0).

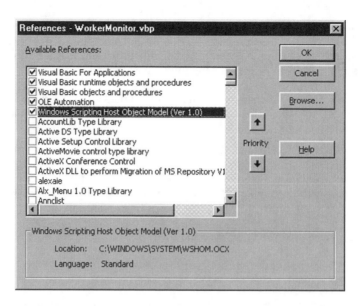

We'll use the scripting host in our other components as well, since it makes it so easy to handle registry interaction.

Initialize Method

Once the Cluster Monitor has created an instance of the `Monitor` object on a worker server, it will call the `Initialize` method. This method does a couple of things. First off, it initializes the `Monitor` object overall – retrieving the server's rating and starting the `Timer` control that triggers sending the rating back to the Cluster Monitor. It also records a reference back to the Cluster Monitor component so we have some way to actually send the updated rating value.

Enter the following code.

```
Public Sub Initialize(Caller As Object)
   Dim objShell As IWshShell_Class

   ' create the windows shell object from the scripting host library
   Set objShell = New IWshShell_Class

   ' retrieve the server's rating value from the registry
   mlngRating = _
      objShell.RegRead("HKEY_LOCAL_MACHINE\Software\Wrox\Cluster\ServerRating")
   Set objShell = Nothing

   ' store a reference to the cluster monitor (our caller)
   Set mobjCaller = Caller

   ' load the form with our timer control
   Load AppMain

   ' add a reference to this object to the timer form
   AppMain.Register Me

   ' send an initial status back to the cluster monitor
   SendStatus
End Sub
```

The first bit of code uses the Windows Scripting Host library to retrieve the rating for this server from the registry.

```
Dim objShell As IWshShell_Class

Set objShell = New IWshShell_Class
mlngRating = _
   objShell.RegRead("HKEY_LOCAL_MACHINE\Software\Wrox\Cluster\ServerRating")
Set objShell = Nothing
```

The `IWshShell_Class` provides the `RegRead` method. This method accepts a registry key and returns the value stored at that location.

If there's no value in the registry this code will raise an error and the application will fail. Adding the registry entry should be part of the installation for any worker server.

Before running this component on any worker server we'll need to make sure we add a DWORD value under the `HKEY_LOCAL_MACHINE\Software\Wrox\Cluster\` registry key.

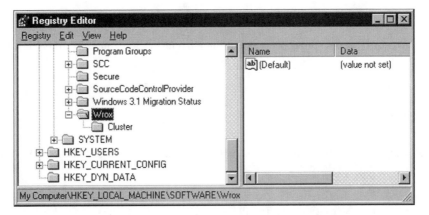

Set the value name to `ServerRating`, and set it's value to some numeric value. For my testing I used 10 for my Pentium 150 and 20 for my Pentium 200 – causing the Pentium 200 to get twice the load of the P150. This can be done using `regedit.exe` or any other registry editing tool.

The diagram opposite shows an entry of 20 being added using the `regedit.exe` tool.

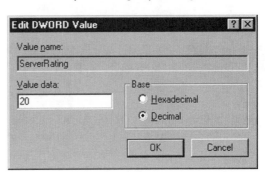

The method then stores a reference to the object passed as a parameter for later use:

```
Set mobjCaller = Caller
```

This object reference will point back to an object in the Cluster Monitor component so we can send the rating value.

Then the code loads a form named AppMain, provides the form with a reference to the Monitor object and starts a Timer control.

```
' add a reference to this object to the timer form
AppMain.Register Me

' enable the timer on the form so it fires every half-second
With AppMain.Timer1
  .Interval = REPORT_INT
  .Enabled = True
End With
```

We'll create the form shortly, but the basic idea is that the Timer control will fire every so often (500 ticks in this case – where there are 1000 ticks in a second). Each time the Timer fires, it will call the SendStatus method on our object so we send the current rating value up to the Cluster Monitor component.

Finally we directly call SendStatus once, ensuring that the Cluster Monitor starts out with a rating value.

Shutdown Method

The Shutdown method is quite simple. This method will be called by the Cluster Monitor component as it is shutting down.

It is very important that this occur. The Cluster Monitor component holds a reference to our Monitor object – that's why it exists after all. However, the Monitor object also holds a reference back to the Cluster Monitor – forming a circular reference. Since objects never go away until their reference count reaches zero, circular references can be tricky. The objects need to mutually agree to release the references to each other before they can shut down.

Enter the following code.

```
Public Sub Shutdown()
  AppMain.Deregister
  Set mobjCaller = Nothing
End Sub
```

The Shutdown method tells the AppMain form to drop its reference to the Monitor object and releases the reference to the Cluster Monitor – leaving no circular references so everything will close properly.

SendStatus Method

Finally, when the `Timer` on the `AppMain` form fires it will call a `SendStatus` method to tell our object to update the Cluster Monitor with the rating value.

```
Friend Sub SendStatus()
  mobjCaller.UpdateStatus mlngRating
End Sub
```

This routine simply calls an `UpdateStatus` method on the object provided as a parameter to the `Initialize` method. We'll implement this method when we create the Cluster Monitor component.

Creating the AppMain Form

Our component needs to periodically update the Cluster Monitor with the current rating value. This requires some form of timer functionality – either via a `Timer` control or an API call. In this case we'll take the simple route and use the `Timer` control provided with Visual Basic.

Add a form to the project and change its name to `AppMain`.

Add a `Timer` control to the form, leaving its name as `Timer1`. Also set its `Enabled` property to `False`. We don't want it accidentally firing until we've initialized the object.

Registering and Unregistering the Monitor Object

The whole reason for this form is to host the `Timer` control. The whole reason for the control is so it can call a method on our `Monitor` object. In order to call the method, we'll need a reference to the object – which is where the `Register` and `Deregister` methods come into play.

The `Register` method will accept and store a reference to the `Monitor` object in a module-level variable. Add the following code to `AppMain`:

```
Option Explicit

Private mobjClient As Monitor

Public Sub Register(Client As Monitor)
  Set mobjClient = Client
End Sub
```

The `Deregister` method simply releases this reference and unloads the form. When this method is called we know that we're shutting down and won't need the form.

```
Public Sub Deregister()
  Set mobjClient = Nothing
  Unload Me
End Sub
```

With these two methods maintaining the reference to our `Monitor` object, all that remains is to implement the code in the `Timer` control itself.

The Timer Control

The `Timer` will be started by the `Initialize` method of the `Monitor` object. Each time it fires, all we need to do is call the `Monitor` object's `SendStatus` method.

```
Private Sub Timer1_Timer()
  Timer1.Enabled = False
  mobjClient.SendStatus
  Timer1.Enabled = True
End Sub
```

Of course, it is always important to disable the timer before doing any work and then enable it when we're done to avoid re-entrancy problems.

Building the Component

With the coding done, save and compile the DLL. We'll see how to install it on individual worker servers in the next section.

First, make sure to make a copy of the DLL and set up Binary Compatibility against that copy.

> Any time we create a component for use in MTS it is critically important that we are properly using Binary Compatibility.

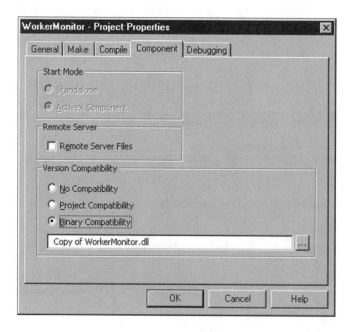

Installing the Component

With that done, we are ready to install the DLL on each worker server. If our worker servers already have the Visual Basic runtime and other related support files (including the Windows Scripting Host), we can simply drag the DLL into the MTS explorer on the worker server. MTS will take care of registering the component so it is available through COM.

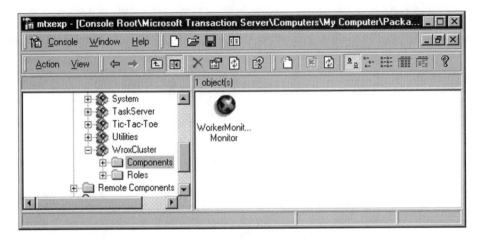

Don't forget to add the registry entry for the server rating on each worker server as well. We discussed this registry value earlier. The `WorkerServer` component won't run without this entry in place.

If a worker server doesn't already have the Visual Basic runtime and other related support files you'll need to create a setup file using the Package & Deployment Wizard. The details of how to do this are covered in Appendix B.

The Cluster Monitor

Now that our worker servers are ready to report their status, we can implement a monitor to run on the cluster server. The cluster server is the machine that coordinates which client requests go to which worker server. Before the cluster server can provide information to the client, however, it must monitor the current status of each worker server.

This is handled through the Cluster Monitor component, as shown in the following diagram.

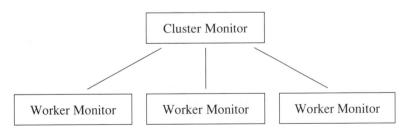

As shown in the diagram, there is a single cluster monitor that keeps track of all the worker servers. The danger with such a model is that a single cluster server is also a single point of failure. If this server goes down, then the entire cluster becomes unavailable. To help mitigate this effect, we can have multiple cluster servers, each monitoring all the worker servers. If one cluster server fails, then clients can use a different cluster server to find out which worker server should be used for each request.

In the following diagram we have two separate cluster servers, each running a cluster monitor to keep track of the status of the worker servers. With this configuration, if a cluster server becomes unavailable, clients can simply use the other cluster server to find out which worker server should be used.

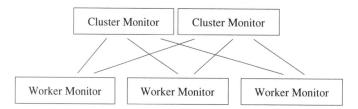

This technique can also be used to spread the load of routing client requests across multiple cluster servers in the case that a single cluster server becomes overloaded. The actual choice of which cluster server to use will be determined by the individual client – as we'll see when we implement the DLL that runs on the client workstation later in this chapter.

We already know some things about the monitor component that will run on the cluster server, since it interacts with the `WorkerMonitor` DLL that we just finished. This new component must be able to start up an instance of the `Monitor` class on each worker server and pass that `Monitor` object a reference to itself so the `Monitor` object can call back with updated rating information.

We also know that this new component will be used by the Cluster Server component (which we'll create next) when a decision as to which worker server is best must be made. The data collected by the Cluster Monitor must be easily available to the Cluster Server. To take care of this, we'll implement a chunk of shared memory using a **memory mapped file**.

A memory mapped file is a Windows operating system concept that allows us to share a single range of memory between different processes (or COM apartments) on the same computer. Normally in Windows, the memory used by each process is entirely isolated from the memory used by any other process. This is usually a good thing – since it makes it virtually impossible for the actions of one application to interfere with the actions of another.

However, there are times when we *do* want to share memory between processes (or COM apartments). Memory mapped files are one powerful technique to do just that. We'll explore memory mapped files later in the chapter – creating a Visual Basic class module to deal with all the details.

Finally, we know that this new component must run independently of any given client. We want to know the status of all the worker servers at all times, so we're ready for any incoming client request. Ideally this would mean that we'd be building a Windows NT service so it would run all the time, regardless of someone being logged into the server.

As we discussed in Chapter 6 however, Visual Basic doesn't provide any direct way to create a robust NT service. Because of this, we'll just implement this program as a regular application. If you desire to build a service out of it, you may try using one of the options discussed in Chapter 6.

Setting up the Project

If this application is to run independently, it needs to be an EXE of some form. Since it will be providing references to its objects so that the `Monitor` object on each worker server can call back into the application, it should be an ActiveX EXE.

Open Visual Basic and create a new ActiveX EXE project. Change the project name to `ClusterMonitor`.

Since this application will also need to read entries from the registry, add a reference to the Windows Scripting Host Object Model (Ver 1.0) by using the Project | References menu option.

Also, we'll be interacting with the `Monitor` object we created in the `WorkerMonitor` project. To make this easier, add a reference to the `WorkerMonitor` DLL.

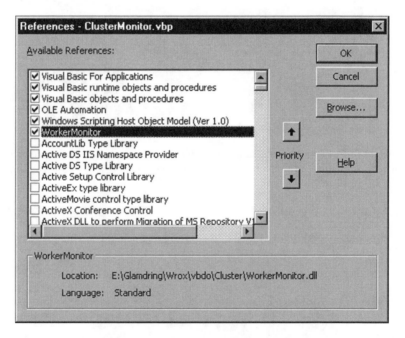

> **The WorkerMonitor DLL needs to be registered on each cluster server machine to make this reference.**

Now we're ready to create the code.

Creating the CSMain Module

Since this is an ActiveX EXE, our two startup options are none or `Sub Main`. As we start up, we'll definitely need to do some work, so `Sub Main` is the clear choice.

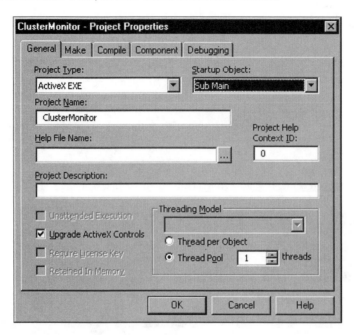

Add a new BAS module to the project and change its name to `CSMain`. We'll use this module both for the `Sub Main` procedure and also to hold some global variables for use throughout the application.

```
Option Explicit

Public Const REPORT_INTERVAL = 550

Public gcolServers As Collection
Public gobjMM As MemoryMap

Public Sub Main()
  MonitorDisplay.Show
End Sub
```

The REPORT_INTERVAL constant will be used by a `Timer` control similar to the one in the `WorkerMonitor` application. Notice that the value is larger than the one in the `WorkerMonitor` application. This is important, because we'll be using the timer in *this* application to expire worker servers that haven't reported in recently and we want to ensure that we don't expire them too fast.

Depending on the speed of your network (and its typical load), you may need to make this number larger to account for network latency.

The `gcolServers` variable will be used to maintain a list of worker server connections. As we establish connections to each `Monitor` object this `Collection` will hold the references.

Finally the `gobjMM` variable will hold the reference to our shared memory map. We'll get into the specifics of this memory map and why we need shared memory shortly.

Then the `Sub Main` procedure itself simply shows a form. There's no pressing need for a UI in this type of application, but it is nice to see that it is working. In any case, we need some container for our `Timer` controls and we might as well use it as a status display since we've got it. Most of the initialization of the application will be handled in the `Form_Load` routine.

Creating the ClusterSvr Class

This application will most likely be communicating with several worker servers. To keep track of those servers and their current status, we'll create a `ClusterSvr` object for each worker. This `ClusterSvr` object will maintain the reference to the `Monitor` object on its worker server and will receive the rating values sent from the `Monitor` object back to this application.

Choose the `Class1` module and change its name to `ClusterSvr`.

Change its **Instancing** property to **2-PublicNotCreatable**. It should be public, because we'll be passing a reference back to this object across to the worker server's `Monitor` object. However, we don't want anyone outside of this application actually creating a `ClusterSvr` object.

Declarations

The class will need some module level declarations.

```
Option Explicit

Private mobjServer As WorkerMonitor.Monitor
Private mlngStatus As Long
Private mdtUpdate As Date
Private mstrServer As String
```

The `mobjServer` variable will maintain our reference to the `Monitor` object on the appropriate worker server. Remember, there'll be one `ClusterSvr` object for each worker server.

The `mlngStatus` variable will store the latest rating value provided by the worker server, while the `mdtUpdate` variable will keep track of the last time we received such a value. This way, if we don't hear from the worker server within a certain amount of time we can assume that it has crashed or otherwise become unavailable – allowing us to force its rating to zero so no client requests are sent to it.

Finally, the `mstrServer` variable just keeps track of the name of the worker server. We'll need this information throughout the application.

Attach Method

Since the primary purpose of the `ClusterSvr` object is to create and maintain a reference to a worker server, it makes sense to have an `Attach` method so we know the server to which we should attach.

```
Friend Sub Attach(Server As String)
  mstrServer = Server
  mdtUpdate = Now

  On Error Resume Next

  ' create a Monitor object on the indicated worker server machine
  Set mobjServer = CreateObject("WorkerMonitor.Monitor", Server)

  If Err Then
    ' if we get an error trying to talk to the worker server
    ' set its rating to zero to mark it as unavailable
    mlngStatus = 0
  Else

    ' given a Monitor object on the worker server, initialize it with
    ' a reference to this ClusterSvr object
    mobjServer.Initialize Me
    If Err Then
      ' if this operation fails, release the reference and set the rating
      ' to zero to mark the worker server as unavailable
      Set mobjServer = Nothing
      mlngStatus = 0
    End If
  End If

End Sub
```

Notice that the scope of this method is `Friend`. Since the `ClusterSvr` object is `PublicNotCreatable`, we need to be careful about what we expose to the outside world. Most of the methods we'll be implementing in this class are only used by other parts of the `ClusterMonitor` application, so they'll be scoped using the `Friend` keyword.

This method accepts the server name as a parameter and stores it into the `mstrServer` variable for later use. We also initialize the `mdtUpdate` variable so we have a known starting point for timing out the server if it doesn't provide us with rating information.

Next, `CreateObject` is used to create an instance of the `Monitor` object on the worker server. The ability to specify the server name on which to create an object is new with Visual Basic 6 and is critical for what we are doing here.

If any errors are encountered while attempting to create the `Monitor` object, we'll simply force that server's status to zero, thus ensuring that no client requests will be sent in that direction. The server is still left in the list of potential servers, because we'll be implementing a retry function later on. This way, if the server comes up later, we'll notice that it is there and begin using it.

This is important for fault tolerance. We must assume that a server might not be there when we start up, and may come online later. Alternatively a server may crash and get a rating of zero, but then come back online and we'll want to start using it again.

If, on the other hand, a `Monitor` object is successfully created, then we need to call its `Initialize` method. This method accepts a parameter so the `Monitor` object can call back with rating information, so we provide it with a reference to the `ClusterSvr` object itself.

It is also possible that the `Initialize` method will fail. Since we didn't explicitly trap any errors in that method, those errors will be raised back to the `ClusterSvr` object where we can deal with them. If the `Monitor` object's `Initialize` method fails we also need to ensure that the server's rating is zero. After all, something went wrong, so we sure don't want to be sending client requests that direction.

UpdateStatus Method

If the `Initialize` method succeeds, the `Monitor` object will begin sending rating information for that server back to our `ClusterSvr` object. This is done by the `Monitor` object calling an `UpdateStatus` method on our `ClusterSvr` object.

```
Public Sub UpdateStatus(NewStatus As Long)
   mlngStatus = NewStatus
   mdtUpdate = Now
End Sub
```

This method is `Public` because it will be used by the `Monitor` object on the worker server.

The method doesn't do a lot – it just records the new rating value provided via the parameter and then updates the `mdtUpdate` variable. By updating this variable to `Now`, we are indicating that we have heard from this worker server and so we know that it hasn't crashed or become unavailable.

Status Property

Now that the `Monitor` object is updating us with the worker server's rating, we can implement a property on the `ClusterSvr` object to report on that server's status.

There are two things going on here. First off, we want to return the rating value we got from the worker server. However, we don't want to return that value if we haven't heard from the server in a while. In that case we must assume that the server has crashed or become unavailable.

```
Friend Property Get Status() As Long
   If DateDiff("s", mdtUpdate, Now) > REPORT_INTERVAL / 1000 + 1 Then
      Status = 0
   Else
      Status = mlngStatus
   End If
End Property
```

Keeping in mind that our `REPORT_INTERVAL` constant is in *ticks* for use by a `Timer` control, we need to convert it back to seconds. We also want to leave a bit of leeway before timing out a worker server, because there could be delays due to processor or network load.

In the end, the `DateDiff` method returns the number of seconds since the last rating value was received. If that value is greater than one second more than our reporting interval then we'll assume the worker server has crashed.

If this seems like a short timeout, consider why we're using clustering in the first place. The whole idea is that we've got so many requests coming in to our servers that a single server can't handle them. By the time this is the case, we are pretty much guaranteed that there are many requests coming in each second. Were we to wait longer, say 5 seconds, before marking a worker as being offline then we'd be routing client requests to a dead-end for that whole time.

Even with this solution we have a one second interval where we could send some requests to a dead server. We'll address this when we build the client-side DLL later in the chapter.

Shutdown Method

If the `ClusterMonitor` application is closed it is important that the `Monitor` objects are also shut down. We have a circular reference here, with the `ClusterSvr` object holding a reference to a `Monitor` object, and that `Monitor` object holding a reference back. If we don't manually release these references then the objects will never shut down.

The `Shutdown` method on the `ClusterSvr` object calls the `Shutdown` method on the `Monitor` object and then releases the reference to that `Monitor` object.

```
Friend Sub Shutdown()
  If Not mobjServer Is Nothing And Status > 0 Then
    mobjServer.Shutdown
    Set mobjServer = Nothing
  End If
End Sub
```

The tricky part of this is that the worker server may have crashed somewhere in here – or perhaps we never did get a reference to the `Monitor` object in the first place.

If we never got a reference, then `mobjServer` will be `Nothing` – so we handle that.

If we did get a reference, but then the server crashed, we should be able to check the `Status` property to find out. If it is zero then we know that the server is offline so there's no point trying to call the `Shutdown` method on the `Monitor` object.

In fact, attempting to call that method could cause our `ClusterMonitor` to hang for many seconds before COM gets around to telling us that the method call failed.

ServerName Property

The last thing we need to code is a simple property to return the worker server's name.

```
Friend Property Get ServerName() As String
  ServerName = mstrServer
End Property
```

This will be used by other code in our application.

Adding the MonitorDisplay Form

The `MonitorDisplay` form serves two purposes. First, it contains the `Timer` controls that drive the application. Second, it provides a monitor display to show which worker servers are online.

Most of the activity in this application occurs due to `Timer` controls. These could be replaced with API calls, but I have opted for the easy, standard approach by using controls.

Add a new form to the project and change its name to `MonitorDisplay`. Add controls to the form as shown in the diagram and described in the table below.

Type	Name
ListBox	`lstServers`
Timer	`Timer1`
Timer	`Restart`

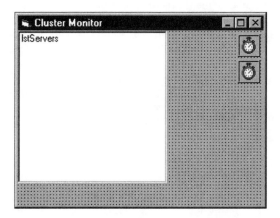

Set the `Enabled` properties of the two `Timer` controls to `False`. We don't want them doing anything until the application is ready.

Also set the `Sorted` property of the `ListBox` to `True` so it will be easier to pick out the worker servers that are unavailable.

For appearances, add a `Form_Resize` method so the `ListBox` control always consumes the entire display area.

```
Option Explicit

Private Sub Form_Resize()
  lstServers.Move 1, 1, ScaleWidth, ScaleHeight
End Sub
```

Then we're ready to add the code to make things work.

Initializing the Application

The first thing that happens when this form is invoked is that the `Form_Load` method is run. It just calls an `Initialize` method to set up the application.

```
Private Sub Form_Load()
  Initialize
End Sub
```

We need to do quite a bit as this program starts up. To start with, we need to get a list of the worker servers, attaching a `ClusterSvr` object to each one.

Once that's done we need to initialize the shared memory we'll be using to provide information about the worker servers out to the Cluster Server component. After this, the code also starts up the `Timer` that updates this shared memory based on the status information kept in the `ClusterSvr` objects.

Finally the `Restart` timer is started. When this fires it will trigger a process by which we attempt to attach (or reattach) to any servers that have a rating of zero.

```
Private Sub Initialize()
  Dim objShell As IWshShell_Class
  Dim lngCount As Long
  Dim lngIndex As Long

  ' create a collection to hold a list of the worker servers
  Set gcolServers = New Collection

  ' access the registry to get a list of the worker servers
  Set objShell = New IWshShell_Class
  With objShell
    lngCount = .RegRead("HKEY_LOCAL_MACHINE\Software\Wrox\Cluster\ServerCount")
    For lngIndex = 1 To lngCount
      ' for each worker server, call the AddServer method
      AddServer _
        objShell.RegRead("HKEY_LOCAL_MACHINE\Software\Wrox\Cluster\Server" & _
        CStr(lngIndex))
    Next
  End With
  Set objShell = Nothing

  ' create an initialize the memory map we'll use for communication with
  ' the Cluster Server component
  Set gobjMM = New MemoryMap
  gobjMM.Initialize "WroxCluster", 32768

  ' enable the timer that refreshes the data in the shared memory map
  With Timer1
    .Interval = REPORT_INTERVAL
    .Enabled = True
  End With
  Timer1_Timer

  ' enable the timer that retries connections to offline worker servers
  With Restart
    .Interval = 60000
    .Enabled = True
  End With
End Sub
```

Again we use the `IWshShell_Class` object from the Windows Scripting Host to access the registry. It is in the registry that the names of the worker servers are stored.

Before attempting to run the `ClusterMonitor` application on a server, the registry on that machine must be updated with appropriate entries under the `HKEY_LOCAL_MACHINE\Software\Wrox\Cluster` key.

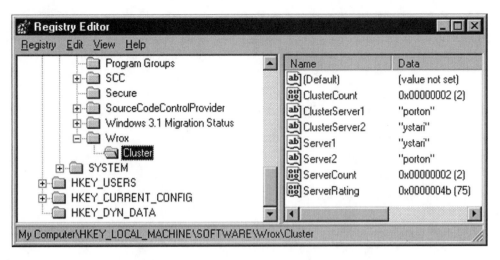

The `ServerCount` value indicates the number of worker servers, with each server's name stored under a `Server#` value, where `#` is replaced with `1...n`, where `n` is the value of the `ServerCount`.

For each worker server listed in the registry, an `AddServer` method is called.

AddServer Method

The `AddServer` method attempts to attach our application to a `Monitor` object on the specified worker server.

```
Private Sub AddServer(Server As String)
   Dim objServer As ClusterSvr

   Set objServer = New ClusterSvr
   objServer.Attach Server
   gcolServers.Add objServer, Server
End Sub
```

This is relatively straightforward, since the `ClusterSvr` object we've already implemented handles most of the work. The `AddServer` method just needs to create a `ClusterSvr` object and call its `Attach` method.

Once the `ClusterSvr` object has attached to the worker server, we just add it to the `gcolServers` object so we have a list of all the connections that have been made.

Note that the `ClusterSvr` object is added to the `Collection` even if it didn't establish a connection to the `Monitor` object. In such a case, the `ClusterSvr` object will always be returning a rating of zero anyway, so no client requests will be routed there. However, this is important because the `Restart` timer method will run through and attempt to reconnect to these zero rated servers every so often – providing a mechanism by which a crashed or unavailable server can become available later.

Form_Unload Method

If the user closes the form we need to ensure that everything is cleaned up appropriately. This primarily means running through the ClusterSvr objects and calling each one's Shutdown method.

```
Private Sub Form_Unload(Cancel As Integer)
  Dim lngIndex As Long
  Dim objServer As ClusterSvr

  ' disable the timers as we close down
  Timer1.Enabled = False
  Restart.Enabled = False

  ' for each worker server, call the Shutdown method to close all connections
  For lngIndex = gcolServers.Count To 1 Step -1
    Set objServer = gcolServers(lngIndex)
    objServer.Shutdown
    gcolServers.Remove lngIndex
  Next
End Sub
```

Once the Shutdown method has been called the ClusterSvr object is removed from the Collection – releasing the last reference to it and allowing it to terminate.

After all the objects have been properly shut down, the form will finish unloading – ending the application.

Updating Server Status

Most of the work in the ClusterMonitor application occurs in the Timer1_Timer method. This event fires based on the REPORT_INTERVAL constant – set to just longer than the interval for the Timer control in each WorkerMonitor.

Each time this routine runs, it scans through the list of ClusterSvr objects, recording the status values of each into a PropertyBag object. This is done because it is very easy to convert a PropertyBag object into a Byte array – exactly what we need for writing into a chunk of shared memory. The Cluster Server component can then very easily retrieve the data from shared memory to reconstitute a PropertyBag object with all the status data.

Additionally, every 5 times through the list we'll update the ListBox control's contents. We don't want to do this each time because there's too great a performance hit involved up updating the UI that often.

```
Private Sub Timer1_Timer()
  Dim objPB As PropertyBag
  Dim objServer As ClusterSvr
  Dim lngCount As Long
  Static intDisplay As Integer

  ' stop the timer to prevent reentrancy problems
  Timer1.Enabled = False

  ' create a new PropertyBag to store the worker server ratings
  Set objPB = New PropertyBag
```

```
         ' blank the listbox control
      If intDisplay = 0 Then lstServers.Clear
      With objPB
         ' store the number of worker servers
         .WriteProperty "ServerCount", gcolServers.Count
         lngCount = 0
         For Each objServer In gcolServers
           lngCount = lngCount + 1
           ' store this worker server's name and rating
           .WriteProperty "ServerName" & CStr(lngCount), _
             objServer.ServerName
           .WriteProperty "ServerStatus" & CStr(lngCount), _
             objServer.Status

           ' update the listbox display
           If intDisplay = 0 Then _
             lstServers.AddItem Format$(objServer.Status, "0000") & _
               " (" & objServer.ServerName & ")"
         Next
      End With

      ' write the PropertyBag into the shared memory mapped file
      gobjMM.SetData objPB

      ' update the display counter - we'll only update the listbox every 5th time
      intDisplay = intDisplay + 1
      If intDisplay = 5 Then intDisplay = 0

      ' reenable the timer so it fires again
      Timer1.Enabled = True
   End Sub
```

Each worker server's name and current rating are stored into the `PropertyBag` for use by the Cluster Server component we'll create later.

First we store the number of worker servers being monitored.

```
       .WriteProperty "ServerCount", gcolServers.Count
```

Then we loop through all the `ClusterSvr` objects, writing the server name and rating of each worker server into the `PropertyBag` object.

```
       For Each objServer In gcolServers
         lngCount = lngCount + 1
         ' store this worker server's name and rating
         .WriteProperty "ServerName" & CStr(lngCount), _
           objServer.ServerName
         .WriteProperty "ServerStatus" & CStr(lngCount), _
           objServer.Status
```

We also update the `ListBox` control's display with the worker server information.

```
       If intDisplay = 0 Then _
         lstServers.AddItem Format$(objServer.Status, "0000") & _
           " (" & objServer.ServerName & ")"
```

This is only done every fifth time through the process for performance reasons. While a visual monitor display is useful, there is a cost associated with constantly repopulating the ListBox control. To minimize this cost, we don't update the display as often as we update the worker server data.

Near the bottom of the routine, notice the interaction with the shared memory.

```
gobjMM.SetData objPB
```

The SetData method accepts a PropertyBag object as a parameter and safely writes it into an area of shared memory. This is a fairly complex thing to do, which is why the entire shared memory concept will be encapsulated within the MemoryMap class.

Restarting Offline Servers

The last thing we need to do in the form is handle the Restart timer. As we've noted, it is possible for a worker server to be unavailable for a while, and then become available later. In that case, we'd like to add it back into the list of valid servers.

We don't want to do this too often, as it can be very time consuming. Attempting to communicate with a server that is offline takes a long time. We make the call and wait for COM to timeout our request – returning with an error many seconds later. This routine is coded to only go off every 5 minutes through the use of a Static counter variable (since a Timer control can't be set for that long).

```
Private Sub Restart_Timer()
  Dim lngIndex As Long
  Dim objServer As ClusterSvr
  Static intCount As Integer

  ' the timer fires every minute. This block of code counts to five,
  ' so we only try to restart worker servers every 5 minutes
  intCount = intCount + 1
  If intCount < 5 Then Exit Sub
  intCount = 0

  ' stop the timers to prevent them from firing while we restart any
  ' worker servers
  Timer1.Enabled = False
  Restart.Enabled = False

  ' loop through all the worker servers
  For lngIndex = gcolServers.Count To 1 Step -1
    Set objServer = gcolServers(lngIndex)

    ' if a worker server is unavailable, try to reconnect to it
    If objServer.Status = 0 Then
      ' remove the worker server from our list
      gcolServers.Remove objServer.ServerName
      ' readd the server to our list - causing a reconnect attempt
      AddServer objServer.ServerName
    End If
    Set objServer = Nothing
  Next

  ' restart the timers to restore normal operation of this application
  Restart.Enabled = True
  Timer1.Enabled = True
End Sub
```

The code in the routine is not terribly complex. We simply loop through the list of `ClusterSvr` objects. If any of them have a `Status` of zero then we'll remove it from the list of servers and call the `AddServer` method.

`AddServer` will create a new `ClusterSvr` object and attempt to connect to the worker server. If it succeeds then we'll have another server for use by our clients. If not, then we'll be back where we started, with a `ClusterSvr` object returning a `Status` of zero. In five minutes we'll try again.

At this point the bulk of our application is ready to roll. In fact, the only thing we haven't resolved is how (and why) to implement shared memory.

This is a good point at which to save the project. We're about to create a class module that will make several Windows API calls. Calling into the Windows API is typically a tricky thing to do, potentially causing our application, Visual Basic or even possibly Windows to lock up or crash.

Handling Shared Memory: The MemoryMap Class

Before getting into *how* to implement shared memory, let's discuss *why* we need it.

Why Shared Memory

Each time a client wants to know the name of a server on which it can create an object, it will ask the Cluster Server component (which we'll write next). That component needs to get the worker server ratings from the `ClusterMonitor` component we are writing now, since it is the component that collects all that data.

If we only had to worry about sporadic requests from clients, we might just have the clients ask the `ClusterMonitor` directly. However, we're writing all this stuff because we have a lot of clients – so we can expect to have many client requests coming in each second.

To handle this kind of load, there should be a number of threads allocated to dealing with client requests. In C++ we'd just spin up some threads within the `ClusterMonitor` and all would be well. Each thread in the process could directly access the memory of the process to get at the worker server ratings. To use multiple threads in Visual Basic, however, means that we'll also be using COM apartments.

Each Visual Basic thread runs in a **single-threaded apartment**. Each such apartment looks (to the thread) like an isolated process – no memory is shared across apartments. This means that we could have many threads, but they'd have no way to get at the list of worker server ratings since each is isolated into its own apartment.

Getting at this data via COM method calls will reduce us to one-at-a-time processing. This is definitely not scalable.

Wouldn't it be nice if we could have some memory available to all the threads of our Cluster Server component? Then they could all just skim through the worker server ratings concurrently – providing very high scalability.

Better still, what if we share the same memory among not only the Cluster Server component's threads, but also with the `ClusterMonitor` component? Then the `ClusterMonitor` can update the memory as it gets new data (which we've already seen), and all the threads in the Cluster Server component can read that data.

In this scenario we'll have a single *writer* (ClusterMonitor) and many concurrent *readers* (all the threads in the Cluster Server component).

Memory Mapped Files

Though there are a number of ways to share memory between threads and between processes within the Windows environment, one stands out as the simplest – **memory mapped files**.

A memory mapped file may be either a physical file (on disk) which is mapped into the computer's memory so it appears as a pool of bytes – not like a disk file at all. Or it can be created without the physical file – in which case it is just a pool of bytes.

Mapping a physical file is a good way to gain access to large amounts of data on disk since only the parts of the file currently in use are physically loaded into the computer's memory. If we're not directly interacting with other parts of the file, it is stored on disk, not in memory at all.

This capability, while very powerful, isn't what we need for our current application. Instead, we're just looking for a way to efficiently share memory between processes – thus a memory mapped file created without a physical file will work just fine.

Memory mapped files are created through the use of some Win32 API calls.

API	Description
CreateFileMapping	Opens a handle to a memory mapped file
MapViewOfFile	Maps a file into the current process (or COM apartment's) memory – accepts a handle opened by CreateFileMapping
UnmapViewOfFile	Removes a file mapping from the process (or COM apartment's) memory
CloseHandle	Closes a handle – in this case used to close the handle from CreateFileMapping
CopyMemory	An alias for RtlMoveMemory – copies data from one memory location to another

In our case we don't really care about any physical file – instead we just want a chunk of memory to be shared. Either way, the API calls involved are not complex – as far as API calls go anyway.

Synchronization

The most complex thing about shared memory is the need to synchronize the various processes and threads that use it.

We can't allow alterations to the shared memory when any thread is in the middle of reading from it. Likewise, we can't allow any thread to read the memory while it is being altered.

The possible scenarios here can become complex. Fortunately, we have a single writer with multiple concurrent readers – a relatively straightforward case.

I'm not going to get into all the gory details of synchronization here – there are entire books written to deal with multi-threading issues and so forth. Instead, let's just look at the specific solution for our case.

We need a single gateway through which all threads pass before they can use the shared memory. In this way, the writer can close the gate to prevent any readers from coming in, and then open it when the writing is done.

This can be handled by a synchronization object called a **mutex**. A mutex can only be held by a single thread. If it is held, then any subsequent threads that attempt to access it go into a wait state until it is available.

The writer can grab the mutex and hold it as long as it is writing to the memory. This means no other threads can grab the mutex during that time.

Each reader can try to grab the mutex. But if the writer is already writing, then the reader will have to wait until the mutex becomes available. However, if the mutex is free, then the reader knows it is safe to proceed.

It can then immediately release the mutex for the next reader. After all, we're not trying to prevent multiple reads – just concurrent writes and reads.

Only one thing remains then. Suppose a reader is already reading when the writer grabs the mutex. Since the writer has the mutex we don't have to worry about new readers entering the memory– but that doesn't preclude existing readers from already being there.

This can be solved by using another synchronization object – a **semaphore**. Unlike a mutex, a semaphore can be set up to allow many threads to hold it. The semaphore keeps a count of the number of threads that hold it – meaning we can tell when it is in use.

We can have all readers grab the semaphore before they read from the shared memory and release it when they are done reading. Essentially this means that the semaphore will provide us with a count of the number of readers currently in the process of reading from the shared memory.

Once the writer has grabbed the mutex, it just has to wait until the semaphore indicates that all the readers are done. Then it can do its writing and release the mutex – allowing readers to resume their work.

The API calls to handle a mutex include the following.

API	Description
CreateMutex	Opens a handle to a mutex object.
WaitForSingleObject	Grabs the mutex – waits until the mutex is free if needed.
ReleaseMutex	Releases the thread's hold on the mutex, making it available for use by another thread.
CloseHandle	Closes a handle – in this case used to close the handle from CreateMutex.

The Win32 API calls used to interact with a semaphore follow.

API	Description
CreateSemaphore	Opens a handle to a semaphore object – also used to set the semaphore's initial count value to the maximum number of threads that can hold it at any given time.
OpenSemaphore	Opens a handle to an existing semaphore object.
WaitForSingleObject	Grabs the semaphore – decrementing the semaphore count value. If the semaphore count reaches zero, this call will wait until the count goes above zero and then it decrements it.
ReleaseSemaphore	Releases the thread's hold on the semaphore, incrementing the semaphore count value.
CloseHandle	Closes a handle – in this case used to close the handle from CreateSemaphore.

By using the technique described here we can ensure that the shared memory is not being altered at the same time it is being read. At the same time, we are able to allow many threads to read from the shared memory at the same time.

Creating the Class

That's enough theory – it's time to build the class. Add a new class module to the project and change its name to MemoryMap.

Change its **Instancing** property to **1-Private**. While we'll also be using this class in the Cluster Server component, we'll just include the module into that project as well.

Declarations

Since we're using so many API calls, there are a lot of API declarations in this module.

```
Option Explicit

Private Const SYNC_WAIT = 1000              ' how long to wait for a semaphore

Private Const FILE_MAP_WRITE = &H2          ' map a memory mapped file for write
Private Const PAGE_READWRITE = 4&           ' mark a page for read-write access
Private Const ERROR_ALREADY_EXISTS = 183&   ' error when a memory mapped file
                                            ' already exists as we try to create it

Private Const WAIT_OBJECT_0 = 0&            ' indicates we got a mutex/semaphore

' this API creats a memory mapped file
Private Declare Function CreateFileMapping Lib "kernel32" Alias
"CreateFileMappingA" _
   (ByVal hFile As Long, ByVal lpFileMappingAttributes As Long, ByVal _
   flProtect As Long, ByVal dwMaximumSizeHigh As Long, ByVal dwMaximumSizeLow _
   As Long, ByVal lpName As String) As Long
```

```
' this API unmaps a view of a memory mapped file
Private Declare Function UnmapViewOfFile Lib "kernel32" (ByVal lpBaseAddress _
   As Long) As Long

' this API maps a view of a memory mapped file - allowing us to use it
Private Declare Function MapViewOfFile Lib "kernel32" (ByVal _
   hFileMappingObject As Long, ByVal dwDesiredAccess As Long, ByVal _
   dwFileOffsetHigh As Long, ByVal dwFileOffsetLow As Long, ByVal _
   dwNumberOfBytesToMap As Long) As Long

' this API closes a handle
Private Declare Function CloseHandle Lib "kernel32" (ByVal hObject As Long) _
   As Long

' this API copies bytes of data from one location in memory to another
Private Declare Sub CopyMemory Lib "kernel32" Alias "RtlMoveMemory" _
   (Destination As Any, Source As Any, ByVal Length As Long)

' this API creates a mutex synchronization object
Private Declare Function CreateMutex Lib "kernel32" Alias "CreateMutexA" _
   (ByVal lpMutexAttributes As Long, ByVal bInitialOwner As Long, _
   ByVal lpName As String) As Long

' this API releases a mutex synchronization object
Private Declare Function ReleaseMutex Lib "kernel32" (ByVal hMutex As Long) _
   As Long

' this API creates a semaphore synchronization object
Private Declare Function CreateSemaphore Lib "kernel32" Alias _
   "CreateSemaphoreA" (ByVal lpSemaphoreAttributes As Long, _
   ByVal lInitialCount As Long, ByVal lMaximumCount As Long, _
   ByVal lpName As String) As Long

' this API releases a semaphore synchronization object
Private Declare Function ReleaseSemaphore Lib "kernel32" _
   (ByVal hSemaphore As Long, ByVal lReleaseCount As Long, _
   lpPreviousCount As Long) As Long

' this API opens an existing semaphore synchronization object
Private Declare Function OpenSemaphore Lib "kernel32" Alias _
   "OpenSemaphoreA" (ByVal dwDesiredAccess As Long, ByVal bInheritHandle _
   As Long, ByVal lpName As String) As Long

' this API causes our application to wait until it gains access to an object
Private Declare Function WaitForSingleObject Lib "kernel32" (ByVal _
   hHandle As Long, ByVal dwMilliseconds As Long) As Long
```

Additionally, we need to declare some actual module level variables to hold the handles and addresses for our mutex, semaphore and memory mapped file objects.

```
Option Explicit
```

```
Private mlngMappingHandle As Long
Private mlngMappingAddress As Long
Private mlngMutexHandle As Long
Private mlngSemaphoreHandle As Long
```

We'll see how these are used as we walk through the rest of the code.

Initialize Method

Before using the shared memory, we need to initialize all our objects – the memory mapped file, the mutex and the semaphore. This is handled through the `Initialize` method.

If you aren't used to dealing with API calls this may appear daunting. It isn't really too difficult though.

The memory mapped file, mutex and semaphore each require a unique name. Interestingly enough, the names must be unique even across these different types of object. To take care of this, we accept a name as a parameter and then append a suffix for each type of object.

Also, when a memory mapped file is first opened we need to indicate the maximum number of bytes we'll be writing into it. This too is a parameter provided by the calling code. Having a large number here isn't necessarily a bad thing, since the memory is virtual. No physical memory is actually consumed until we write into it.

Enter the following code, and then we'll walk through it section by section.

```
Public Sub Initialize(ShareName As String, MaxLength As Long)
   Dim lngMapErr As Long

   ' open a handle for a memory mapped file
   mlngMappingHandle = CreateFileMapping(-1, 0, PAGE_READWRITE, 0, _
     MaxLength, ShareName & ".map")
   If mlngMappingHandle = 0 Then Exit Sub
   lngMapErr = Err.LastDllError

   ' map a view of the memory mapped file so we can use it
   mlngMappingAddress = MapViewOfFile(mlngMappingHandle, FILE_MAP_WRITE, 0, 0, 0)
   If mlngMappingAddress = 0 Then
      ' if we couldn't map a view, close the handle and quit
      CloseHandle mlngMappingHandle
      Exit Sub
   End If
   If Not lngMapErr = ERROR_ALREADY_EXISTS Then _
      CopyMemory ByVal mlngMappingAddress, 0, 4

   ' create (or open) a mutex
   mlngMutexHandle = CreateMutex(0, False, ShareName & ".mtx")
   If mlngMutexHandle = 0 Then
      ' if we couldn't create or open the mutex close all handles and quit
      UnmapViewOfFile mlngMappingAddress
      CloseHandle mlngMappingHandle
      Exit Sub
   End If
```

```
      ' attempt to open a semaphore
   mlngSemaphoreHandle = OpenSemaphore(-1, False, ShareName & ".sem")
   If mlngSemaphoreHandle = 0 Then
     ' if the semaphore doesn't exist, create the semaphore
   mlngSemaphoreHandle = CreateSemaphore(0, 100, 100, ShareName & ".sem")
   If mlngSemaphoreHandle = 0 Then
     ' if we couldn't create the semaphore close all handles and quit
     UnmapViewOfFile mlngMappingAddress
     CloseHandle mlngMappingHandle
     CloseHandle mlngMutexHandle
     Exit Sub
   End If
   End If
 End If
End Sub
```

The first section of code opens the memory mapped file. If it doesn't exist then the code creates it, otherwise it will just open the existing memory. To do this, we'll use the `CreateFileMapping` API.

Parameter	Meaning
Hfile	Handle to the physical file to be mapped. Use −1 to indicate that there is no physical file to be mapped.
LpFileMappingAttributes	Accepts a structure indicating security attributes to use when mapping to the file. Passing a 0 indicates that we don't wish to restrict access to the memory.
FlProtect	Accepts a value indicating how the memory is to be accessed. PAGE_READWRITE indicates we want read-write access to the memory.
DwMaximumSizeHigh	The maximum size of a memory mapped file is specified by two 32-bit values. This number indicates the upper 32-bits of that number. Since the memory we need is less than 4 gigabytes, this value will be zero.
dwMaximumSizeLow	The maximum size of a memory mapped file is specified by two 32-bit values. This number indicates the lower 32-bits of that number. This value is Used to indicate sizes up to four gigabytes – in our case we'll set it to the `MaxLength` value passed as a parameter.
LpName	Name of the file mapping object.

Here is the section of code that opens a handle for a memory mapped file:

```
mlngMappingHandle = CreateFileMapping(-1, 0, PAGE_READWRITE, 0, _
   MaxLength, ShareName & ".map")
If mlngMappingHandle = 0 Then Exit Sub
lngMapErr = Err.LastDllError
```

If the API call returns zero, then it failed. Otherwise it will return a numeric value – the handle of the file mapping we just created.

If the API call succeeds, it means that either we created the memory mapped file *or* that we have opened an existing memory mapped file of the same name. To find out whether we created or opened the memory mapped file, we need to check `Err.LastDllError`. If this returns `ERROR_ALREADY_EXISTS` then we know that an existing file was opened. We'll store this value into a variable, since we'll need it shortly.

The next section of code maps the memory mapped file so we can use it as though it were just regular memory. To do this, we'll use the `MapViewOfFile` API.

Parameter	Meaning
hFileMappingObject	Handle of the memory mapped file opened with `CreateFileMapping`.
dwDesiredAccess	A value indicating the access level we desire for the memory. The value `FILE_MAP_WRITE` indicates we want to be able to write to the memory.
dwFileOffsetHigh	We can specify the location in the file where we want to start mapping the memory. This is done with two 32-bit values. This is the high value for use in extremely large files – in our case it will be zero.
dwFileOffsetLow	This is the low 32-bits of the start position for mapping the memory. Since we want to start at the beginning of the memory mapped file, this value will be zero.
dwNumberOfBytesToMap	We can map just part of the memory mapped file. However, in our case we want access to the entire mapped area, so we'll set this value to zero – indicating that we want full access.

Here is the section of code to map the memory mapped file:

```
mlngMappingAddress = MapViewOfFile(mlngMappingHandle, FILE_MAP_WRITE, 0, 0, 0)
If mlngMappingAddress = 0 Then
  CloseHandle mlngMappingHandle
  Exit Sub
End If
If Not lngMapErr = ERROR_ALREADY_EXISTS Then _
  CopyMemory ByVal mlngMappingAddress, 0, 4
```

If we succeed in mapping the memory then the API will return the memory address where the file has been mapped. We can use this memory address to access the data stored in the memory mapped file. If the API fails it will return the value zero.

Once we've mapped the file into our memory space, we need to determine if the file already existed or if we created it. This is done by checking the `Err.LastDllError` value from the `CreateFileMapping` API call – and we stored that value in the variable `lngMapErr`. The `ERROR_ALREADY_EXISTS` value indicates that the file already existed – meaning we opened an existing file. If, on the other hand, we created the memory mapped file then we need to initialize it by writing zero into the first 4 bytes of the memory.

These first four bytes will be used as a length counter for the actual data we store – since there's nothing in there yet the value should be zero. The value will be a Long (or four bytes) so we write four zeros.

Once the memory mapped file is open we need to create or open the mutex that will be used to prevent readers from coming in while the writer is writing.

To do this, we'll use the CreateMutex API.

Parameter	Meaning
lpMutexAttributes	A structure containing security attributes if we wish to restrict who can use the mutex. If we don't wish to restrict usage, we can just pass a zero.
BInitialOwner	A boolean indicating if we want immediate ownership of the mutex. In our case we don't – we won't own it until we try to access the memory – we we'll pass a False value.
LpName	The name of the mutex object. This name must be unique (including unique among semaphore objects, memory mapped file, objects, etc.). This name is used to gain access to existing mutex objects.

Here is the code to create or open the mutex:

```
mlngMutexHandle = CreateMutex(0, False, ShareName & ".mtx")
If mlngMutexHandle = 0 Then
  UnmapViewOfFile mlngMappingAddress
  CloseHandle mlngMappingHandle
  Exit Sub
End If
```

Notice that if this fails we just close the memory mapped file and quit.

Finally the semaphore that will keep a count of the number of readers it created. In this case it is created with an initial value of 100, meaning that no more than 100 concurrent readers will be allowed.

To do this, we'll use the OpenSemaphore and CreateSemaphore APIs. First, here is the OpenSemaphore API:

Parameter	Meaning
dwDesiredAccess	A value indicating the level of access we want for the semaphore. In our case we wan all access to the semaphore, so we'll pass a –1.
bInheritHandle	A boolean indicating if we want child processes to be able to inherit the semaphore. Since we won't be creating any child processes we'll set this value to False.
LpName	The name of the semaphore object. This name must be unique (including unique among semaphore objects, memory mapped file, objects, etc.). This name is used to gain access to existing semaphore objects.

And here is the `CreateSemaphore` API:

Parameter	Meaning
lpSemaphoreAttributes	A structure containing security attributes if we wish to restrict who can use the semaphore. If we don't wish to restrict usage, we can just pass a zero.
lInitialCount	Sets the initial count of the semaphore to any value between zero and the maximum count. We'll set it to the maximum count to start with.
lMaximumCount	Sets the maximum count for the semaphore. This indicates the maximum number of processes that can hold the semaphore at any given time.
lpName	The name of the semaphore object. This name must be unique (including unique among semaphore objects, memory mapped file, objects, etc.). This name is used to gain access to existing semaphore objects.

```
mlngSemaphoreHandle = OpenSemaphore(-1, False, ShareName & ".sem")
If mlngSemaphoreHandle = 0 Then
  mlngSemaphoreHandle = CreateSemaphore(0, 100, 100, ShareName & ".sem")
  If mlngSemaphoreHandle = 0 Then
    UnmapViewOfFile mlngMappingAddress
    CloseHandle mlngMappingHandle
    CloseHandle mlngMutexHandle
    Exit Sub
  End If
End If
```

As with the mutex, if this fails to open or create the semaphore then we unmap and close the memory mapped file and mutex and just quit.

When this routine completes we'll have a memory mapped file and the synchronization objects (mutex and semaphore) needed to control reading and writing.

Class_Terminate

One thing to remember with Win32 API calls is that you have to clean up after yourself or bad things happen. In this case, we *must* unmap the memory mapped file and close all our handles or we'll leave things dangling around in memory. This would be bad because it can lead to memory leaks and potential system instability over time.

```
Private Sub Class_Terminate()
  UnmapViewOfFile mlngMappingAddress
  CloseHandle mlngMappingHandle
  CloseHandle mlngMutexHandle
  CloseHandle mlngSemaphoreHandle
End Sub
```

When our client releases the reference to our `MemoryMap` object we know we're done so we can close everything down safely.

All that remains now is to implement routines to read and write data from the shared memory.

SetData Method

The `SetData` method is used to write data into the shared memory. Visual Basic can't directly use raw memory. Instead we must use the `CopyMemory` API to copy the data from within our Visual Basic variables into the shared memory.

This implementation of `SetData` is relatively simple because it accepts a `PropertyBag` object as a parameter. The `PropertyBag` object has a `Contents` property that returns an array of bytes – a form ideal for copying into a chunk of memory, which is after all a bunch of bytes.

Before we can write to the shared memory however, we need to make sure no readers can use it and that none are currently in the process of using it.

```
Public Sub SetData(PB As PropertyBag)
  Dim arContents() As Byte
  Dim lngLen As Long
  Dim retval As Long
  Dim lngSemCount as Long

  ' put the contents of the propertybag into a byte array
  arContents = PB.Contents
  ' determine the number of bytes in the array (the length of our data)
  lngLen = UBound(arContents) + 1

  ' wait for the mutex and keep it once we've got it
  Do
    retval = WaitForSingleObject(mlngMutexHandle, 5000)
  Loop Until retval = WAIT_OBJECT_0

  Do
    ' wait until the semaphore is totally unused, meaning no current readers
    Do
    Loop Until WaitForSingleObject(mlngSemaphoreHandle, SYNC_WAIT) = _
      WAIT_OBJECT_0
    ReleaseSemaphore mlngSemaphoreHandle, 1, lngSemCount
  Loop Until lngSemCount = 99

  ' copy the length of our data into the first four bytes of memory
  CopyMemory ByVal mlngMappingAddress, lngLen, 4

  ' copy the data itself into the memory (starting with byte 5)
  CopyMemory ByVal (mlngMappingAddress + 4), arContents(0), lngLen

  ' release the mutex, allowing readers to enter the memory space
  ReleaseMutex mlngMutexHandle
End Sub
```

First we get hold of the mutex, keeping the mutex until we're done.

```
Do
  retval = WaitForSingleObject(mlngMutexHandle, 5000)
Loop Until retval = WAIT_OBJECT_0
```

No other thread or process can get this mutex until it is released. As we'll see in the GetData method, all readers need to get hold of this mutex before proceeding into the read process, so all new readers are blocked by this action.

Then, we must wait until all readers are done reading. We can tell this by watching the semaphore. Each reader gets a hold on the semaphore before reading, releasing it when done. If the semaphore count returns to its initial value then we know that all the readers are done.

```
Do
  Do
  Loop Until WaitForSingleObject(mlngSemaphoreHandle, SYNC_WAIT) = _
    WAIT_OBJECT_0
  ReleaseSemaphore mlngSemaphoreHandle, 1, lngSemCount
Loop Until lngSemCount = 99
```

Interestingly, the only way to get the semaphore count is to get the semaphore and release it. Upon releasing it we can find out what the value was prior to our release. This means that the highest value will be one less than the maximum value of the semaphore when it was created.

Once we know that there are no readers in the shared memory, we can copy data into the memory block.

```
CopyMemory ByVal mlngMappingAddress, lngLen, 4
CopyMemory ByVal (mlngMappingAddress + 4), arContents(0), lngLen
```

First we copy the number of bytes in our array into the first four bytes. This acts as the length of our data. Then the data itself is stored starting with the fifth byte in the block.

Once we're done, we must release the mutex so any waiting readers can get to work reading data from the shared memory.

```
ReleaseMutex mlngMutexHandle
```

Though it may look complex, this routine is really quite straightforward. The GetData method is similar.

GetData Method

Now that we can initialize, shutdown and write data into the memory mapped file, we just need a way to retrieve data from it and we're all set. This routine is very similar to the SetData method, in that it also interacts with the mutex and semaphore before using the shared memory.

```
Public Function GetData() As PropertyBag
  Dim objPB As PropertyBag
  Dim lngLen As Long
  Dim arContents() As Byte
  Dim lngSemCount As Long
  Dim retval As Long

  ' get the mutex. If a writer is using the memory we won't get the mutex
  ' until it is done and released the mutex
```

```
 Do
    retval = WaitForSingleObject(mlngMutexHandle, SYNC_WAIT)
    If retval <> WAIT_OBJECT_0 Then DoEvents
 Loop Until retval = WAIT_OBJECT_0

 ' get the semaphore and keep it until we are done. This way the writer can
 ' see how many readers are currently reading because they will all have
 ' ownership of the semaphore
 Do
 Loop Until WaitForSingleObject(mlngSemaphoreHandle, _
    SYNC_WAIT) = WAIT_OBJECT_0

 ' release the mutex to let the next reader (or the writer) get into the memory
 ReleaseMutex mlngMutexHandle

 ' create a new propertybag object
 Set objPB = New PropertyBag

 ' copy the first four bytes of memory into a Long - this is the
 ' length of our data
 CopyMemory lngLen, ByVal mlngMappingAddress, 4
 If lngLen = 0 Then GoTo leave

 ' set a byte array to the proper length
 ReDim arContents(lngLen - 1)

 ' copy the data from the shared memory into our byte array
 CopyMemory arContents(0), ByVal (mlngMappingAddress + 4), lngLen

 ' copy the byte array into the propertybag - causing it to become
 ' fully populated
 objPB.Contents = arContents

 ' return the propertybag object as a result
 Set GetData = objPB

leave:
    ' release the semaphore - thus incrementing its count
    ReleaseSemaphore mlngSemaphoreHandle, 1, lngSemCount
End Function
```

First we must get through the gateway by accessing the mutex. If the writer is holding the mutex we'll be stopped here, otherwise we'll get in, decrement the semaphore and release the mutex.

Essentially we're using the mutex here to protect a critical section of code.

```
 Do
    retval = WaitForSingleObject(mlngMutexHandle, SYNC_WAIT)
    If retval <> WAIT_OBJECT_0 Then DoEvents
 Loop Until retval = WAIT_OBJECT_0

 Do
 Loop Until WaitForSingleObject(mlngSemaphoreHandle, SYNC_WAIT) = WAIT_OBJECT_0

 ReleaseMutex mlngMutexHandle
```

The quicker we can release the mutex the better, as there may be other readers waiting to gain access to the shared memory and we don't want to block them.

Once we're in, we can create a new `PropertyBag` object to hold the incoming data. Then we retrieve the number of bytes of data stored in the shared memory and `ReDim` an array to hold that many bytes.

```
CopyMemory lngLen, ByVal mlngMappingAddress, 4
If lngLen = 0 Then GoTo leave
ReDim arContents(lngLen - 1)
```

Now that we have the right sized buffer we can copy the data from the memory mapped file into the array and use the array to set the `Contents` property of the `PropertyBag` object.

```
CopyMemory arContents(0), ByVal (mlngMappingAddress + 4), lngLen
objPB.Contents = arContents
```

At this point we have a `PropertyBag` object that is identical to the one written to the memory mapped file by the writer – even if the writer is in another thread or another process. This newly populated object is returned as the result of the function.

The last thing we need to do is release the semaphore.

```
ReleaseSemaphore mlngSemaphoreHandle, 1, lngSemCount
```

This causes the semaphore count to increment, indicating that one less reader is using the shared memory.

Upon completion of the `MemoryMap` class our `ClusterMonitor` is complete. It will now attach to all the worker servers, starting the process by which they continually keep us updated with their ratings. All the worker server ratings are written to a memory mapped file so they are available to any number of clients via the Cluster Server component we're about to create.

At this point we should save and compile the `ClusterMonitor` project. Since it is an ActiveX EXE, make sure to create a copy of the EXE and then set the project's **Binary Compatibility** option so it remains compatible with that copy.

Installing the Component

The ClusterMonitor application will need to be installed on each machine that will act as a cluster server. Don't forget to also add the appropriate registry values on that machine under the `HKEY_LOCAL_MACHINE\Software\Wrox\Cluster` key as we discussed earlier in this section.

The Cluster Server

The last server-side component we need to create is the one that directly interacts with the client workstations.

When a client wants to create an object on a worker server it first needs to know the name of the worker server to use. To get this name, each client will ask a cluster server for rating information about the worker servers – thus determining the worker server on which it should create the application's server-side object.

The `ClusterMonitor` application we just created will run on each cluster server machine to keep all the data about the worker servers current. Now we just need a way for the clients to get at that data. We'll do this by creating a new component – the cluster server.

Since the cluster server component will be accessed via DCOM from client workstations, it needs to be an ActiveX EXE (using `dcomcnfg` to make it available) or an ActiveX DLL running in MTS. A DLL in MTS is much easier to manage, so that's what we'll create.

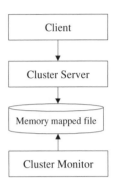

The diagram opposite illustrates the components involved in the process of determining the right worker server to use. It shows the client interacting with the cluster server component we're about to build. The cluster server component gets its data from the memory mapped file – the same one written to by the `ClusterMonitor` component we built earlier.

The cluster server component will simply retrieve the data from the shared memory, and then it will choose a worker server based on the server ratings in that data.

Choosing the worker server may seem easy. We have server ratings, so we should just be able to choose the highest rated server and be done. Except that it isn't that easy...

We can't just always choose the highest rated server. To start with, our worker server ratings are static, so we'd always end up choosing the same server – not resulting in any load balancing at all.

However, even if the ratings were dynamic, perhaps representing response time or CPU utilization, we still can't always select the highest rated server. The ratings are only updated every so often – about each half second as we've written it so far – and there may be a lot of client requests in that time frame. We don't want to direct all of them to the same server.

This is especially true if we consider that each server request is likely to be serviced in well under a second. Most database reads or writes are sub-second operations.

If we always return the highest rated server, we'll end up simply flatlining one server, then flatlining the next and the next and so on. All work for each half second would get funneled to one place.

Instead, we can treat the ratings as a suggestion. Rather than using the rating as an absolute number, we can use it as the basis for a more random server selection. The higher rated servers will tend to get more work sent their way, but even low rated servers will get some work. This is the technique we'll use in this chapter.

Setting up the Project

In Visual Basic, create a new ActiveX DLL project and change its name to `ClusterServer`. Don't confuse this with the `ClusterSvr` object we created earlier – this is a whole new Visual Basic project that will contain its own objects.

This project will be composed of just two classes:

❑ The Cluster class will be publically creatable, created and used by the client workstations.

❑ The MemoryMap class is the same as the one we created for the ClusterMonitor class – providing access to the shared memory.

Creating the Cluster Class

Select the Class1 module and change its name to Cluster.

This class is living proof that MTS can support non-transactional, non-atomic objects. There's a lot of debate and misinformation out there. All the data-centric objects we've created call SetComplete and SetAbort – taking advantage of transactional support, but also being stateless with atomic methods. If an object never calls SetComplete or SetAbort it can still run in MTS – and it can maintain state just like an object outside of MTS.

This class will have just one public method – GetServerName. It is in this method that we'll retrieve the data from the shared memory and select the appropriate worker server for the client's use.

Managing the Shared Memory

Since this object will need to interact with the memory mapped file, we'll declare a variable to hold a reference to the MemoryMap object.

```
Option Explicit

Private mobjMM As MemoryMap
```

Then in the Class_Initialize event handler we can initialize the MemoryMap object.

```
Private Sub Class_Initialize()
  Randomize
  Set mobjMM = New MemoryMap
  mobjMM.Initialize "WroxCluster", 32768
End Sub
```

Note that this is the same initialization as is done in the ClusterMonitor application. If the memory mapped file already exists we'll just use the one that's there, but if it is not then this line will create it. We want to make sure it is created the same here as in the ClusterMonitor program.

When this object terminates we need to make sure the MemoryMap object is released as well.

```
Private Sub Class_Terminate()
  Set mobjMM = Nothing
End Sub
```

While this is taken care of automatically by Visual Basic, it is always better to be thorough in coding and clean up our own object references – especially when dealing with Win32 API calls.

GetServerName Method

The real work occurs in the GetServerName method. It is here that the actual worker server is chosen and returned to the client for use.

This routine retrieves the PropertyBag object from the shared memory, then walks through the data for each worker server stored inside.

```
Public Function GetServerName() As String
  Dim lngMaxValue As Long
  Dim lngMaxIndex As Long
  Dim lngIndex As Long
  Dim lngStatus As Long
  Dim objPB As PropertyBag

  ' retrieve the propertybag object containing the data from
  ' memory mapped file
  Set objPB = mobjMM.GetData
  lngMaxValue = 0

  ' now loop through the worker servers
  For lngIndex = 1 To objPB.ReadProperty("ServerCount")
    ' retrieve the worker server's rating
    lngStatus = objPB.ReadProperty("ServerStatus" & CStr(lngIndex))
    ' if the rating is greater than zero, the server is available for use
    If lngStatus > 0 Then
      ' generate a random value based on the server rating
      lngStatus = Rnd * lngStatus + 1
      ' if the random number is the largest so far, store this server's index
      If lngStatus > lngMaxValue Then
        lngMaxValue = lngStatus
        lngMaxIndex = lngIndex
      End If
    End If
  Next

  If lngMaxValue = 0 Then
    ' we didn't find a valid server - don't return a server name
    GetServerName = ""
  Else
    ' return the selected server
    GetServerName = objPB.ReadProperty("ServerName" & CStr(lngMaxIndex))
  End If
End Function
```

Basically the algorithm simply chooses the server with the highest score. The 'score' in this case is a random number generated using the server's rating as a maximum value. This means that higher rated servers will tend to generate higher random numbers than lower rated ones – thus winning more often.

In the end, the sever server with the highest score is returned as the result of the method.

Adding the MemoryMap Class

We've already created the MemoryMap class module. Use the Project | Add File menu option to add that module into this project as well.

At this point the project is complete, so save and compile it. Since this is a COM component, make sure to take a copy of the DLL and set the project's Binary Compatibility to that copy. Now we can install the component on the cluster server machines.

Installing the Component

As this component is designed with the idea of running in MTS, simply drag and drop the DLL into an MTS package named `WroxCluster` and we're ready to go.

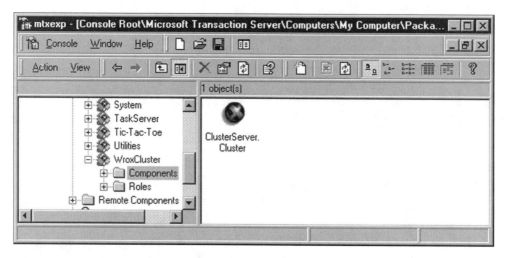

Obviously the `ClusterServer` component will only operate on a machine where the `ClusterMonitor` application is installed and running, since it relies on data placed into the shared memory by that application.

While `ClusterServer` itself doesn't rely on any registry entries, remember that `ClusterMonitor` does require them. Make sure the appropriate registry entries have been added on each machine where these two components are installed.

With this done, we can now write software to run on client workstations that can ask this component for the name of a worker server best suited to handle work.

Implementing Client Software

While we could have any client program wishing to use our load balancing interact directly with the `ClusterServer` component, it would be much better to encapsulate that functionality to make it easier.

This can easily be done by creating an ActiveX DLL with an object marked with an Instancing property of 6-GlobalMultiUse. With this setting, any project that adds a reference to the DLL will automatically gain access to the methods on this object – with no need to create any object references or that sort of thing.

Setting up the Project

Add a new ActiveX DLL project in Visual Basic and change its name to Cluster. It is the COM server name which is used in client code when accessing the object's methods, so Cluster seems like a natural.

> *Don't confuse this* Cluster *project name with the* Cluster *class name we used earlier. This component will be running on the client workstation, not on a server.*

By using the GlobalMultiUse setting for the Instancing property, we can have a CreateObject method that is called like this:

```
Set objPersist = Cluster.CreateObject("MyServer.ObjectPersist")
```

Pretty seamless overall – since the original code would have probably used the regular CreateObject statement so we've just added eight characters to make it use our load balancing cluster.

This component will need to access the registry, since that's where we'll store the name of the server machine running the ClusterServer component.

To this end, add a reference to the Windows Scripting Host Object Model (Ver 1.0) by using the Project | References menu option. We will also need to add a reference to the ClusterServer component, since we'll be using that to retrieve the worker server name on which to create each object.

Creating the ClusterClient Class

Select the Class1 module and change its name to ClusterClient. Change its Instancing property to 6-GlobalMultiUse. With this set, there'll never be a reason for a client program to explicitly create an instance of this object, as one will automatically be created when this DLL is referenced by the client application.

There are a couple of issues that we'll deal with in this component to increase our overall capabilities.

First off, this component needs to figure out the machine that is running the ClusterServer component. This will come from the registry – but not just one machine name. Instead, we'll read several so that if one is not available we can fail over to another. This will help mitigate the single point of failure otherwise implied by the ClusterServer machine.

Additionally, a client may request a number of objects to be created in quick succession. Rather than hitting the ClusterServer each time, we can get a server name and keep it for a short time. This will help increase overall performance in the case that a client creates a lot of objects in a short time.

Finally, we can also add a bit of fault tolerance to the object creation process. If we attempt to create an object and that creation fails, it may be because the worker server crashed but we got the name of that server before the load balancing mechanism noticed it was gone – even if there is only a half second window of time.

If object creation fails, it will have taken some time for DCOM to time out and return an error. We can then get another worker server name and try once more – probably succeeding on the second attempt. The user just sees a several second delay, but in the end they get their work done.

Declarations

We'll need to declare some module level variables and constants for use in the object.

```
Option Explicit

Private mobjCluster As Object
Private mstrServerName As String
Private mdtLast As Date
Private mcolServers As Collection

Private Const ERR_NO_SERVERS = vbObjectError + 1001
Private Const ERR_CANT_FIND_SERVER = 462
Private Const ERR_CANT_CREATE_OBJECT = 429
```

We'll see how these are used as we implement the rest of the code.

Class_Initialize Routine

As the object is initialized it needs to get a list of the cluster servers from the registry. This list will be used later when we need to establish a connection to the cluster server to get the name of a worker server to use.

```
Private Sub Class_Initialize()
  Dim objShell As IWshShell_Class
  Dim lngCount As Long
  Dim lngIndex As Long

  Set mcolServers = New Collection

  On Error Resume Next
  Set objShell = New IWshShell_Class
  With objShell
    lngCount = .RegRead("HKEY_LOCAL_MACHINE\Software\Wrox\Cluster\ClusterCount")
    For lngIndex = 1 To lngCount
      mcolServers.Add _
        objShell.RegRead("HKEY_LOCAL_MACHINE\Software\Wrox\Cluster\" & _
          "ClusterServer" & CStr(lngIndex))
    Next
  End With
  Set objShell = Nothing
End Sub
```

This means that each client workstation will need appropriate entries made under the HKEY_LOCAL_MACHINE\Software\Wrox\Cluster key in the registry. At the very least the ClusterCount value must indicate how many cluster servers are available, and one or more ClusterServer# (where # = 1...number of cluster servers) entries must store the server names.

GetServerName Method

This method returns the name of the worker server to use. While this method could be Private, in this case it is Public. By being publicly available we add flexibility for the client. Rather than calling our CreateObject method, a client can choose to simply request a server name for use however it sees fit.

```
Public Function GetServerName() As String
  If DateDiff("s", mdtLast, Now) > 3 Then

    If mobjCluster Is Nothing Then _
      GetClusterReference

    If Not mobjCluster Is Nothing Then
      mstrServerName = mobjCluster.GetServerName
      mdtLast = Now
    End If

  End If
  GetServerName = mstrServerName
End Function
```

Of course we'll use this method within the CreateObject method as well.

Notice that this method only retrieves a new worker server name if at least 3 seconds have elapsed since the last time it retrieved a name. This way, if a client is creating a lot of objects in short order we can avoid a lot of overhead by simply reusing the same worker server.

Also, the code checks to see if mobjCluster is Nothing. If it is, then we don't have a reference to a ClusterServer object so we need to establish one. The GetClusterReference method is used to get that reference.

GetClusterReference Method

The GetServerName method uses this method in the case that we don't have a reference to the ClusterServer component.

This routine simply creates a reference to the Cluster object on a server. If it fails on the first attempt, it will continue to walk through the list of servers we read from the registry until it either succeeds or runs out of server names.

```
Private Sub GetClusterReference(Optional Index As Long)
  If Index + 1 > mcolServers.Count Then Exit Sub

  On Error Resume Next
  Set mobjCluster = VBA.CreateObject("ClusterServer.Cluster", _
    mcolServers(Index + 1))

  If Err = ERR_CANT_FIND_SERVER Or Err = ERR_CANT_CREATE_OBJECT Then _
    GetClusterReference (Index + 1)

End Sub
```

The method uses recursion to walk through the list. If an attempt to create the server object fails, GetClusterReference just calls itself with the next index value in line. The hope is that, if the first server is offline, then a subsequent server will be online and will work.

Once we get a reference we keep it for the duration of the client application. We don't want the performance hit of creating this object each time we need a server name.

CreateObject Method

The `CreateObject` method simply builds on the methods we've just created. It uses the
`GetServerName` method to get the name of a server where the requested object should be created
and attempts to create it there.

```
Public Function CreateObject(ProgID As String) As Object
  Dim strName As String

  strName = GetServerName
  If Len(strName) > 0 Then

    On Error Resume Next
    Set CreateObject = VBA.CreateObject(ProgID, strName)

    If Err = ERR_CANT_FIND_SERVER Then
      On Error GoTo 0

      strName = GetServerName
      If Len(strName) > 0 Then
        On Error Resume Next
        Set CreateObject = VBA.CreateObject(ProgID, strName)
      End If

    Else
      On Error GoTo 0
      If Err <> 0 Then Err.Raise Err.Number, Err.Source, Err.Description
    End If

  Else
    Err.Raise ERR_NO_SERVERS, "Cluster", "No servers available"
  End If
End Function
```

If the creation fails then we try a second time – assuming that the second worker server name will be
valid. If that fails as well then we just give up – things must be really bad on the servers in such a
case.

Class_Terminate Routine

The last routine to code is the `Class_Terminate`. All we need to do here is release the reference to
the `ClusterServer` component.

```
Private Sub Class_Terminate()
  Set mobjCluster = Nothing
End Sub
```

And that's it. Save and compile. Make sure to add the required registry entries on each client
workstation and we're ready to roll.

Any client application that adds a reference to this DLL will be able to easily use the load balancing
we've implemented in this cluster software.

To illustrate this, let's update the Task Manager application to make use of the cluster.

Updating the Task Manager Application

Changing the Task Manager application to use the clustering capability is really quite simple. Since the `TaskProxyServer` objects handle all our interaction with the server-side objects, we only have one place to make a change.

If you made the changes to the `TaskProxyServer` project in Chapter 7, the code is set up to make server calls via RDS. In this section we'll convert this code to make the calls via DCOM, but using the load balancing implemented via the `Cluster` component.

Updating TaskProxyServer

Open the `TaskProxyServer` project in Visual Basic.

The first thing we need to do is change some references in the project. We no longer need references to RDS so that can be removed. However, we now will need a reference to the `Cluster` project.

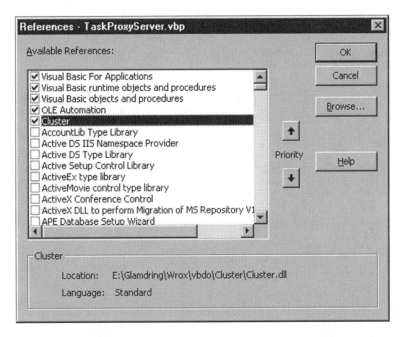

By adding this reference, we automatically gain access to the functionality provided by the `ClusterClient` object.

Updating the ClientProxy Class

The `ClientProxy` class, as it stands, is written to use RDS to communicate with the server components. To create a `ClientPersist` object we use a line like this.

```
Set objPersist = objDS.CreateObject("TaskServer.ClientPersist")
```

Before doing this however, we had to create a `DataSpace` object. Our new changes will simplify the code. We won't need to create a `ClusterClient` object because it is created automatically due to the way we designed the component. In the end, we'll be creating `ClientPersist` objects like this.

```
Set objPersist = Cluster.CreateObject("TaskServer.ClientPersist")
```

So, let's go through and update the methods.

Fetch Method

The `Fetch` method ends up looking like this.

```
Public Function Fetch(ID As Long) As String
   Dim objPersist As Object

   Set objPersist = Cluster.CreateObject("TaskServer.ClientPersist")
   Fetch = objPersist.Fetch(ID)
   Set objPersist = Nothing
End Function
```

Notice that not only did the line containing the `CreateObject` method call change, but we've removed the code that deals with the RDS object.

Save Method

Likewise, the `Save` method is updated as follows.

```
Public Function Save(Buffer As String) As String
   Dim objPersist As Object

   Set objPersist = Cluster.CreateObject("TaskServer.ClientPersist")
   Save = objPersist.Save(Buffer)
   Set objPersist = Nothing
End Function
```

DeleteObject Method

Finally, the `DeleteObject` method gets the same changes.

```
Public Sub DeleteObject(ID As Long)
   Dim objPersist As Object

   Set objPersist = Cluster.CreateObject("TaskServer.ClientPersist")
   objPersist.DeleteObject ID
   Set objPersist = Nothing
End Sub
```

And that's it. Our Task Manager application will now take full advantage of our load balanced cluster. As we use the application we'll see that various requests to retrieve or update data will be handled by the different worker servers that are part of our cluster.

Summary

While perhaps a bit esoteric, this chapter illustrates many of the issues we face in a load balanced application. There are a number of currently available technologies that provide load balancing, and COM+ will give us another option. Alternately, in this chapter we've implemented an alternative, a COM-based load balancing cluster of our very own.

To create this load balancing cluster, we built a number of key server-side components, including a component to monitor the status of each worker server, a component to monitor the status of the cluster overall and a component to provide client workstations with the name of a worker server to be used. We also created a client-side component to encapsulate the process of talking to the cluster, allowing us to keep our client application code virtually unchanged, while still taking advantage of the cluster services.

Load balancing is an important technology for highly scalable applications or situations where we need increased fault-tolerance. As Visual Basic and COM become used more and more for large, enterprise application development this type of technology will become quite commonplace.

Throughout this book I've tried to address many of the more common, but complex, issues we face when implementing applications based on distributed objects. In most cases we've built on the concepts and techniques introduced in *Visual Basic 6 Business Objects*, though there's certainly been a couple of totally new ideas tossed in as well.

Applications based on distributed objects are very powerful – taking advantage of object-oriented design as well as transactional client/server scalability. The CSLA provides a pragmatic model by which we can implement applications based on distributed objects.

By adding the concepts of state stacking and superstates to the original CSLA model we've addressed two of the most common and most complex issues that show up in typical applications. Most applications end up dealing with grandchild level objects and these techniques make those objects easy to deal with.

In Chapter 5 we implemented an OLE DB simple provider that allows us to use data binding against COM objects. This addresses one of the most limiting factors when using distributed object design – the inability to use RAD development through data binding. With this OLE DB provider we can create our application using objects, but also utilize data binding when developing the user interface.

Chapters 6 and 7 showed us new ways to pass object state across a network. We can now send state via asynchronous queues or across the network using HTTP – bypassing firewall security. Such capabilities truly broaden our ability to build flexible and robust applications using distributed objects.

Also in Chapter 7 we saw how we can build powerful browser-based applications using distributed objects. For browser independence the objects can be distributed to the web server. Better still, if the browser is Internet Explorer we can distribute our UI-centric business objects all the way out to the client itself.

Finally we've wrapped up the book by building a load balanced cluster.

To sum up, we can now build object-oriented client/server applications in a wide variety of scenarios. These may include conventional client/server environments or browser-based user interfaces. Through the use of queuing and load balancing we can build our application to scale so it can handle many, many users very effectively.

Supporting Code

Buffer Object

This object allows an application to efficiently store any number of fixed-length string values, then retrieve them all as a single byte stream. Conversely, the byte stream can be placed into a new `Buffer` object and the individual elements then retrieved.

```
Option Explicit

Private Type BufferProps
  Length As Integer
  EstCount As Long
  MaxCount As Long
  Count As Long
End Type

Private Type BufferData
  Buffer As String * 8
End Type

Private Const BUFFER_START = 9

Private strBuffer As String
Private udtProps As BufferProps
Private lngPos As Long

Public Sub Initialize(Length As Integer, EstimatedCount As Long)
  With udtProps
    .Length = Length
    .EstCount = EstimatedCount
    .MaxCount = EstimatedCount
```

```
      .Count = 0
      strBuffer = Space$(BUFFER_START + .MaxCount * .Length)
      lngPos = BUFFER_START
   End With
End Sub

Public Sub Add(Data As String)
   With udtProps
      If .Count = .MaxCount Then
        strBuffer = strBuffer & _
          Space$(udtProps.EstCount / 2 * udtProps.Length)
        .MaxCount = .MaxCount + udtProps.EstCount / 2
      End If
      Mid$(strBuffer, lngPos, .Length) = Data
      lngPos = lngPos + .Length
      .Count = .Count + 1
   End With
End Sub

Public Property Get Item(Index As Long) As String
   Item = Mid$(strBuffer, BUFFER_START + (Index - 1) * _
     udtProps.Length, udtProps.Length)
End Property

Public Property Let Item(Index As Long, Buffer As String)
   Mid$(strBuffer, BUFFER_START + (Index - 1) * _
     udtProps.Length, udtProps.Length) = Buffer
End Property

Public Function Count() As Long
   Count = udtProps.Count
End Function

Public Function Length() As Long
   Length = udtProps.Length
End Function

Public Function GetState() As String
   Dim udtData As BufferData

   LSet udtData = udtProps
   Mid$(strBuffer, 1, Len(udtData.Buffer)) = udtData.Buffer
   GetState = Left$(strBuffer, lngPos)
End Function

Public Sub SetState(Buffer As String)
   Dim udtData As BufferData

   udtData.Buffer = Mid$(Buffer, 1, Len(udtData.Buffer))
   LSet udtProps = udtData
   strBuffer = Buffer
End Sub
```

BrokenRules Object

This object implements a collection of rules that are broken. It is used by the UI-centric business objects to keep track of which business rules are broken at any given point in time.

```
Option Explicit

Event BrokenRule()
Event NoBrokenRules()

Private colBroken As Collection


Private Sub Class_Initialize()
  Set colBroken = New Collection
End Sub

Public Sub RuleBroken(Rule As String, IsBroken As Boolean)
  On Error GoTo HandleError
  If IsBroken Then
    colBroken.Add True, Rule
    RaiseEvent BrokenRule
  Else
    colBroken.Remove Rule
    If colBroken.Count = 0 Then RaiseEvent NoBrokenRules
  End If

HandleError:
End Sub

Public Property Get Count() As Integer
  Count = colBroken.Count
End Property
```

Package & Deployment Wizard

Installing Components

Visual Basic components and applications require various support files in order to run. These files include the Visual Basic runtime library along with other files referenced by a specific project and any files required by those files.

All of these files need to be installed and properly registered on the target machine before our application or component will be able to operate. To assist in this task, Visual Basic ships with the **Package & Deployment Wizard**. This wizard will analyze a Visual Basic project, detecting the required files and creating an installation package we can use to set up the component on a target machine.

This appendix will provide a high-level overview of the wizard – nothing in-depth, but enough information to create basic installation packages for Visual Basic applications.

Using the Package and Deployment Wizard

In previous versions of Visual Basic, the Setup Wizard has been pretty inflexible and undependable. The new Package and Deployment Wizard is much more powerful and provides us with the capabilities we need to deploy our application. Let's walk through the general steps needed to create a setup package for a Visual Basic project.

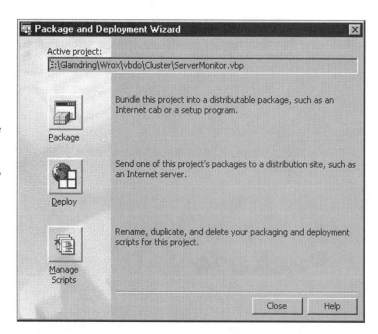

Open a Visual Basic project and start the **Package and Deployment Wizard** from the **Add-Ins** menu. You may have to select is as **Loaded** from the **Add-Ins | Add In Manager** menu before you do this. You should see a window looking something like the one shown in the figure opposite:

Select the **Package** option. This will cause the wizard to run through the process of creating a setup program.

Package Type

The wizard allows us to create more than one type of setup application. On the next panel in the wizard we get the opportunity to choose The Package Type:

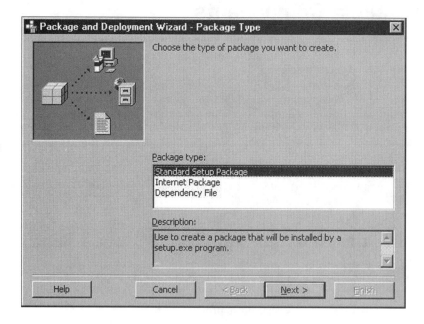

The options are:

Option	Description
Standard Setup Package	This option will create an installation package based on a conventional `setup.exe` program.
Internet Package	This option creates an installation package designed for download from within a browser. An installation package created with this option will not include a `setup.exe` program – instead depending on Internet Explorer to download the CAB file and install the components as needed.
Dependency File	This option creates a dependency file for an ActiveX component. This option is usually used against ActiveX DLL projects to create a list of all the files needed for that DLL to operate. The DLL is often later included in the setup package for an actual application – and this dependency file will be used at that point to ensure that all required files are installed.

For a typical install, choose the Standard Setup Package option.

Package Folder

The wizard will proceed to ask where the setup package should be created.

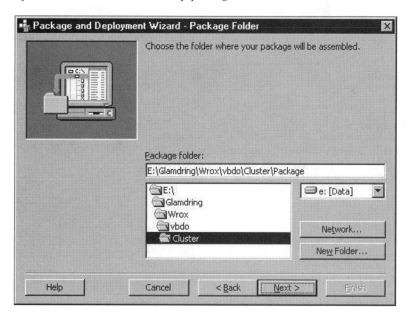

Choose the directory where you wish the package to be created.

Missing Dependency Information

In some cases the wizard may indicate that a component is missing dependency information.

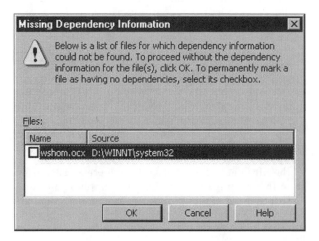

This means that a component referenced by our project is lacking the information required by the wizard to ensure that all related files are included in the installation package.

For components we've created, this can be overcome by using the Package & Deployment Wizard's Dependency File option to create the required dependency file.

If the component is not one we've created with Visual Basic then we are left to our own devices to determine any required files. This can be quite challenging at times – so it is important to never underestimate the amount of effort required to build a fully functional setup package.

I've worked on projects where it has taken several weeks to identify all the various files required – including figuring out which particular versions of each file are required for Windows 95, Windows 95 OSR2, Windows 98 or Windows NT 4.0. Locating all the required files, testing all the installs on all the variations of target platform operating systems (with assorted configurations of installed software) is rarely a trivial task.

Included Files

The next panel presented by the wizard allows us to review, remove or add to the list of files that will be included in the installation process.

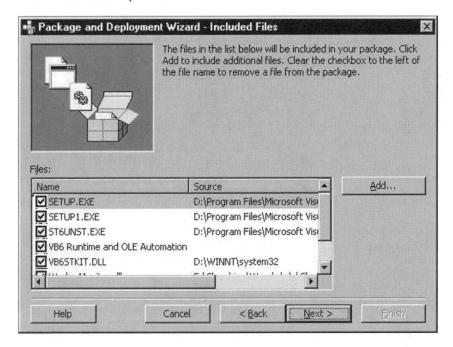

For the most part, the wizard will generate an accurate list of files. However, we may need to add to this list.

If a component was missing dependency information (in the previous step), we may need to use this panel to add any required files to the package.

Another key use for this panel is to include other files related to our application. This may include INI files, database files, informational text files or virtually anything else.

We can also add REG files using this panel. If we do add one (or more) then the next panel will allow us to tell the wizard how to treat them.

Registry Information

If we've added one or more REG files to the list of files in this package, the wizard will ask us how we want to treat those files.

REG files contain information that is to be added to the Windows registry. In Chapter 5 we created the ODSOLEDB OLE DB provider, which requires certain registry entries in order to function. Also, in Chapter 8 we created a set of COM components to implement a load balancing cluster. These components also require specific registry entries in order to operate.

We can include those required registry entries in REG files and allow the wizard to automatically install the entries on the target machine.

Alternatively, we may just want to include the REG files in the installation and *not* have them automatically run to add the registry entries. This may be useful in cases where the user will need to edit the entries to work on their particular machine or for other reasons.

The panel opposite allows us to make this choice.

We can use this panel to tell the wizard whether to copy the REG file to the target machine's hard drive or not, and also whether to run the REG file so the registry entries are added to the machine's registry.

In the panel shown here, the REG file will not be copied to the target machine's hard drive, but the registry entries will be automatically added to the Windows registry.

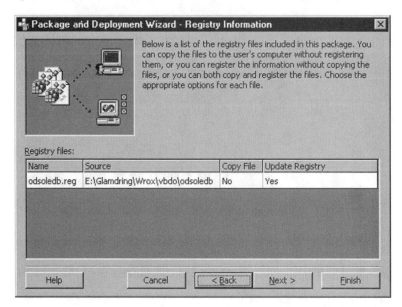

CAB Options

The next panel allows us to choose how the installation package should be created. We can have the wizard create a single, large CAB file or a series of smaller CAB files designed to fit onto floppy disks.

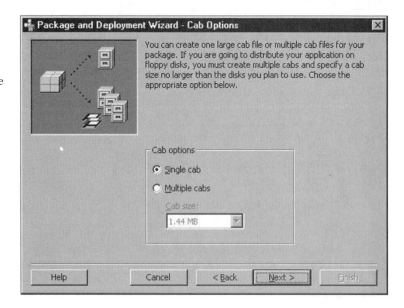

The Single cab option is most useful if we are deploying from a network drive or a CD, where the size of the CAB file won't matter. This provides the simplest install package overall, since the number of files in the package is reduced.

The Multiple cabs option is primarily used when we plan to deploy our application through the use of floppy disks.

Installation Title

As the setup program runs, a title will be displayed for the user so they know what is being installed. This title is set using the next panel.

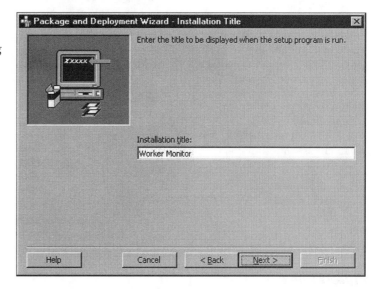

This title defaults to the project name.

Start Menu Items

The next panel allows us to control the icons that will be added to the Windows start menu.

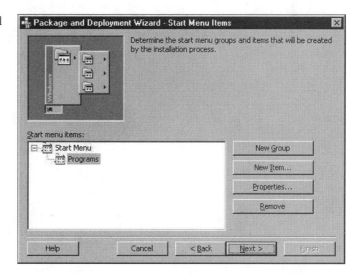

We can use this panel to add extra icons, change the location of the icons within the start menu structure and so forth.

Install Locations

We're getting toward the end now. This next panel confirms where our components will be installed. The standard components listed earlier as part of the install will automatically be placed in the appropriate locations on the target machine. However, our application's components, and those components for which dependency information doesn't exist, are flexible. We can choose to install them where we want.

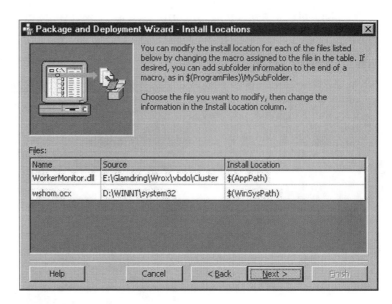

The wizard's default locations for most files are correct.

Shared Files

If our application includes COM components, the wizard will give us the option of indicating whether they should be considered to be shared.

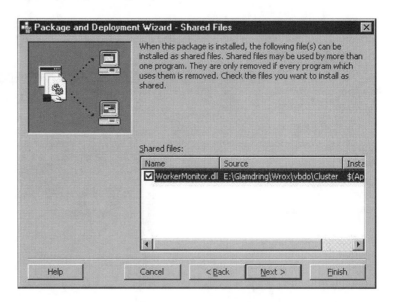

If we mark the component as shared, the uninstall procedure will act differently – not removing the file from the hard drive since the assumption is that it is being used by more than just our application.

Completing the Install

The final panel of the
wizard allows us to give
the setup script itself a
name. The wizard will
store the script –
allowing us to return
later and rerun it to
refresh our files, etc.

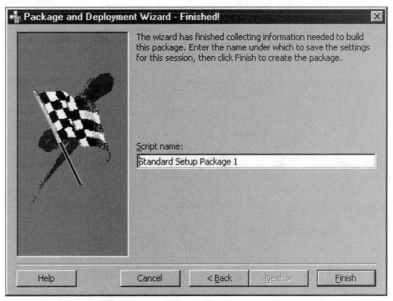

Once the wizard is complete we should have a setup program that we can run on our clients. This
setup program will install our application and any required supporting files. It will also add the
required entries in the system's registry so any COM components will be accessible.

This can include adding other registry entries required by our application or components. If we've
added a REG file to our installation package (such as we might with the ODSOLEDB provider or the
load balancing cluster components), we can use this technique to update the registry as needed.

Index

Index

B

BeginEdit method, 131, 149, 151
behaviour, 117
cascading, 71
state stacking
  implementing, 119
BrokenRules object, 57
browser
distributing objects to, 333
  data, storing across pages, 334
    frames, 334
    frameset page, 334, 335
    Session object, creating, 336
    DLL, 337
    problems, 336
browser-based architecture, 32, 35
advantages, 35
CSLA, 36
disadvantages, 35
object communication, 39
  DCOM, 39
  RDS, 39
state management
  page-based, 37
    solutions, 37, 38
technologies available, 35
business objects, 26
see also data-centric business objects
see also UI-centric business objects
business rules
  checking, 50
childless, 180
  GetSuperState method, 180
  SetSuperState method, 180
children, with, 181
  GetSuperState method, 182
  SetSuperState method, 182
CSLA, 40
  data-centric, 41, 46
    atomic methods, 47
    ByVal keyword, 48
    methods, 47
  UI-centric, 41, 42
    behaviours, common, 42
    child objects, 44
    methods that change state, 46
    methods that don't change state, 46
    methods, common, 43
    properties, common, 43
    Property Get procedures, 45
    Property Let procedures, 45

defined, 27
business tier, 18

C

CancelEdit method, 131, 149, 151
behaviour, 117
cascading, 71
state stacking
  implementing, 120
Child object, 55, 63
creating, 123
deleting, 146
Grandchild object
  managing, 123
methods, 44
methods calls
  cascading to
    Grandchild object, 124
methods calls, cascading, 124, 125
classes
abstraction, 22
class modules, 22
defined, 21
instance, 21
objects, 21
Client object, 54, 58
ApplyEdit method, 145, 193
BeginEdit method, 144
CancelEdit method, 144
CSLA methods, 59
CSLA properties, 59
declarations, 144
defined, 16
GetSuperState method, 191
instantiation, 331
Load method, 192
mcolStack object, creating, 144
mcolStack object, destroying, 144
mflgEditing flags, replacing, 146
MSMQ, 269
  dependant, 269
    advantages of, 269
    disadvantages of, 270
  independant, 269
  independent
    advantages of, 269
    disadvantages of, 269
properties, 62
recreating, 332
SetSuperState method, 192

Index

Index

Index

Index

Index

Index

Index

Index

Index

wrox
PROGRAMMER TO PROGRAMMER™

Wrox writes books for you. Any suggestions, or ideas about how you want
information given in your ideal book will be studied by our team.
Your comments are always valued at Wrox.

Free phone in USA 800-USE-WROX
Fax (312) 397 8990

UK Tel. (0121) 687 4100   Fax (0121) 687 4101

Visual Basic 6 Distributed Objects - Registration Card

Name _____

Address _____

_____

_____

City_____ State/Region _____

Country_____ Postcode/Zip _____

E-mail _____

Occupation _____

How did you hear about this book?_____

☐ Book review (name) _____

☐ Advertisement (name) _____

☐ Recommendation _____

☐ Catalog _____

☐ Other _____

Where did you buy this book? _____

☐ Bookstore (name)_____ City _____

☐ Computer Store (name)_____

☐ Mail Order_____

☐ Other_____

What influenced you in the
purchase of this book?

☐ Cover Design

☐ Contents

☐ Other (please specify) _____

How did you rate the overall
contents of this book?

☐ Excellent   ☐ Good

☐ Average   ☐ Poor

What did you find most useful about this book? _____

What did you find least useful about this book? _____

Please add any additional comments. _____

What other subjects will you buy a computer
book on soon? _____

What is the best computer book you have used this year?

_____

*Note: This information will only be used to keep you updated
about new Wrox Press titles and will not be used for any other
purpose or passed to any other third party.*

wrox
PROGRAMMER TO PROGRAMMER™

NB. If you post the bounce back card below in the UK, please send it to:

Wrox Press Ltd., Arden House, 1102 Warwick Road,
Acocks Green, Birmingham B27 6BH. UK.

—— *Computer Book Publishers* ——